MW01385325

WITHDRAWN
FROM COLLECTION
CLP

Michael Chiller-Glaus

Tackling the Intractable

Palestinian Refugees and the Search for Middle East Peace

HV640.5.P36 C46 2007
Chiller-Glaus, Michael.
Tackling the intractable :
Palestinian refugees and the
search for Middle East peace
Bern ; New York ; Oxford :
Peter Lang, 2007.

PETER LANG
Bern·Berlin·Bruxelles·Frankfurt am Main·New York·Oxford·Wien

Bibliographic information published by Die Deutsche Bibliothek
Die Deutsche Bibliothek lists this publication in the Deutsche Nationalbibliografie; detailed
bibliographic data is available on the Internet at ‹http://dnb.ddb.de›.

British Library Cataloguing in Publication Data

Chiller-Glaus, Michael
  Tackling the intractable : Palestinian refugees and the search for
  Middle East peace
  1. Refugees, Palestinian Arab 2. Arab-Israeli conflict 1993 - - Peace 3. Refugees,
  Palestinian Arab - Legal status, laws, etc.
  I. Title
  362.8'7'095694

  ISBN-13: 978-3-03911-298-2

Published with the support of the Swiss National Science Foundation, the Freiwillige Akademische
Gesellschaft Basel, the Max Geldner-Fonds, the Dissertationenfonds der Universität Basel and the Basler
Studienstiftung.

This thesis was accepted as a doctoral dissertation by the Faculty of Humanities of the University of
Basel in the summer semester 2006 on the recommendation of Professor Dr Jacques Picard (Referent)
and Professor Dr Raymond Cohen (Co-Referent).

Cover design: Thomas Jaberg, Peter Lang AG

ISBN 978-3-03911-298-2

© Peter Lang AG, International Academic Publishers, Bern 2007
Hochfeldstrasse 32, Postfach 746, CH-3000 Bern 9, Switzerland
info@peterlang.com, www.peterlang.com, www.peterlang.net

All rights reserved.
All parts of this publication are protected by copyright.
Any utilisation outside the strict limits of the copyright law, without the permission of the publisher,
is forbidden and liable to prosecution.
This applies in particular to reproductions, translations, microfilming, and storage and
processing in electronic retrieval systems.

Printed in Germany

Contents

Acknowledgments 11

Introduction 15

PART I: Historical Context and its Differing
Historiographic Narratives 29

1 THE PRE-1948 PERIOD 31

2 THE PALESTINIAN EXODUS 39

   2.1 The First Stage: December 1947 to March 1948 39

   2.2 The Second Stage: The Mass Exodus from April
       to June 1948 40

   2.3 The Atrocity Factor 43

      2.3.1 The Jewish Role in the Palestinian Exodus
           up to June 1948 44
      2.3.2 The Arab Role in the Palestinian Exodus
           up to June 1948 46
      2.3.3 Jewish Reactions to the Palestinian Exodus . . . 48
      2.3.4 Arab Reactions to the Palestinian Exodus 49

   2.4 The Third Stage: The "Ten Days" of July 1948 50

   2.5 The Fourth Stage: October and November 1948 53

   2.6 Socio-economic Factors 55

   2.7 The Exodus: A Result of Multiple Causation 56

3 AFTER 1948 59

   3.1 The Immediate Post-War Period 59

   3.2 1967: A Further Wave of Refugees 63

4   TWO DIFFERENT NARRATIVES   67

   4.1   The Israeli Narrative   67

   4.2   The Palestinian Narrative   72

5   THE SITUATION ON THE GROUND   79

   5.1   The Difficult Task of Estimating Refugee Numbers . .   79

   5.2   Definitions of a Palestinian Refugee   81

      5.2.1   Popular Definitions   82
      5.2.2   Official Definitions   82

   5.3   The Distribution of Palestinian Refugees   84

      5.3.1   Jordan   88
      5.3.2   West Bank and Gaza Strip   89
      5.3.3   Syria   90
      5.3.4   Lebanon   91
      5.3.5   Egypt   93

PART II: Contradictory Interpretations of the *Right of Return*   95

6   IS THERE A *RIGHT OF RETURN?*   97

   6.1   Israeli Views   99

      6.1.1   Regarding Palestinian Refugees   99
      6.1.2   Regarding Jewish Refugees
           from Arab Countries   102

   6.2   Palestinian Views   103

7   LEGAL PERSPECTIVES   111

   7.1   The *Right of Return* as a Treaty Obligation?   112

   7.2   The *Right of Return* and Customary
      International Law   118

   7.3   U.N. General Assembly Resolution 194   121

   7.4   The Practice of Refugee Return   126

PART III: Why and How the Issue of Refugees Has Remained
a Stumbling Block at the Peace Talks 137

8 DURING THE COLD WAR 139

   8.1 The Lausanne Conference, April–September 1949 . . . 139

   8.2 The Geneva Conference, January 1950 140

   8.3 The Paris Conference, September–November 1951 . . . 141

   8.4 The Geneva Conference, December 1973
      to January 1974 142

   8.5 Camp David, September 1978 142

9 INITIALIZING ISRAELI-PALESTINIAN
  NEGOTIATIONS 145

   9.1 The Parties Start to Talk: The Madrid Conference,
      October-November 1991 145

      9.1.1 The Multilateral Track:
           The Refugee Working Group 146
      9.1.2 The "Ottawa Process" 150

   9.2 A First Breakthrough: The 1993 Declaration
      of Principles and the Interim Agreement 151

      9.2.1 The Israeli-Jordanian Peace Treaty, 1994 152
      9.2.2 The Quadripartite Committee 153

   9.3 A Detailed yet Unsuccessful Proposal:
      The Beilin–Abu Mazen Agreement, 1995 154

      9.3.1 Within Israel: The Beilin–Eitan
           Agreement, 1997. 157

10 TACKLING FINAL STATUS NEGOTIATIONS 159

   10.1 Harpsund, May 2000: Tackling the Refugee Issue
      for the First Time 159

10.2 Camp David, July 2000: The Beginning of Oslo's End . 163
    10.2.1 Slim Chances for Success 164
    10.2.2 The Course of the Negotiations on Refugees . . 167
    10.2.3 The Collapse of Camp David:
        Reasons and Lessons 185

10.3 The Clinton Parameters: A Guiding Line
    for the Refugee Question 192

10.4 Taba, January 2001: Substantial Progress,
    yet Time Running Out 197
    10.4.1 The Talks on Refugees at Taba 199
    10.4.2 What Was Achieved at Taba? 208
    10.4.3 Lessons from Taba 214

10.5 After Oslo: The Arab League's Proposal,
    the "Roadmap", and the Bush-Letter 216

10.6 The Results of the Official Israeli-Palestinian
    Negotiations on Refugees 219

PART IV: In Search of Sustainable Solutions 223

11 PRACTICAL SOLUTIONS 227

11.1 Abu Sitta: All Palestinian Refugees
    Must and Can Return to Israel 228
    11.1.1 The Essence of the Proposal 228
    11.1.2 Analysis of the Proposal 230
    11.1.3 The Proposal's Relevance 232

11.2 The Citizenship/Residency Approach 233
    11.2.1 The Essence of the Proposal 233
    11.2.2 Analysis of the Proposal 234
    11.2.3 The Proposal's Relevance 236

11.3 The 1948 Approach 237
    11.3.1 The Essence of the Proposal 237
    11.3.2 Analysis of the Proposal 238
    11.3.3 The Proposal's Relevance 241

11.4 The Geneva Initiative 242

   11.4.1 The Essence of the Proposal 244
   11.4.2 Analysis of the Proposal 247
   11.4.3 The Proposal's Relevance 252

11.5 The Internal Approach 255

   11.5.1 The Essence of the Proposal 255
   11.5.2 Analysis of the Proposal 257
   11.5.3 The Proposal's Relevance 259

11.6 Israel's Traditional Approach 260

   11.6.1 The Essence of the Proposal 260
   11.6.2 Analysis of the Proposal 260
   11.6.3 The Proposal's Relevance 261

11.7 Agha and Malley: *Right of Return* to Swapped Areas . . 262

   11.7.1 The Essence of the Proposal 263
   11.7.2 Analysis of the Proposal 265
   11.7.3 The Proposal's Relevance 268

12 PRINCIPLED SOLUTIONS 269

12.1 Peled and Rouhana: Transitional Justice 270

   12.1.1 The Idea of Transitional Justice 271
   12.1.2 Application to the *Right of Return* 272
   12.1.3 The Relevance of Transitional Justice 274

12.2 Learning from German-Israeli Negotiations 275

   12.2.1 The Question of Formulation 276
   12.2.2 Differences and Parallels
       to the Israeli-Palestinian Case 282
   12.2.3 Lessons for the Palestinian Refugee Question . . 285

13 INTEGRATED SOLUTIONS 295

13.1 A Bi-national State 295

   13.1.1 The Essence of the Proposal 296
   13.1.2 Analysis of the Proposal 299
   13.1.3 The Proposal's Relevance 303

13.2 A Palestinian Compromise Solution 306

    13.2.1 The Essence of the Proposal 306
    13.2.2 Analysis of the Proposal 307
    13.2.3 The Proposal's Relevance 309

13.3 An Israeli Compromise Solution 310

    13.3.1 The Essence of the Proposal 310
    13.3.2 Analysis of the Proposal 312
    13.3.3 The Proposal's Relevance 313

13.4 The Gush Shalom Proposal 314

    13.4.1 The Essence of the Proposal 315
    13.4.2 Analysis of the Proposal 316
    13.4.3 The Proposal's Relevance 318

13.5 The Ayalon-Nusseibeh Proposal 319

    13.5.1 The Essence of the Proposal 320
    13.5.2 Analysis of the Proposal 320
    13.5.3 The Proposal's Relevance 323

Conclusions 327

14.1 Summary 327

    14.1.1 Historical Background 327
    14.1.2 The Legal Background of the *Right of Return* . . 329
    14.1.3 Political Background 333
    14.1.4 Proposals for Sustainable Solutions 337

14.2 Recommendations for Future Negotiations 344

Bibliography 355

Acknowledgments

As this research represents my doctoral dissertation at the University of Basel, Switzerland, my initial thanks go to my supervisor Professor Jacques Picard, who never spared time nor effort to support my ongoing work. Also my co-supervisor Professor Raymond Cohen deserves full appreciation for repeatedly providing me his precious support during the entire course of my research endeavours. I would also like to thank the *Freiwillige Akademische Gesellschaft* (FAG) in Basel for generously providing the means that allowed me to complete my research. Further thanks go to the *Paul Grüninger Stiftung*.

Several people significantly contributed during the early stage of my research by sharing their knowledge with me. Special thanks in this respect go to Ian Lustick, University of Pennsylvania, who devoted a lot of his precious time to answer my questions and to enlighten a lot of the complexities of the Israeli-Palestinian conflict for me. Also Susan Akram, Boston University, deserves my gratitude for her kind assistance whenever I contacted her; it also deserves mention that she greatly contributed to my understanding that the issue of Palestinian refugees is a crucial element of the Israeli-Palestinian peace process which requires further research.

Having undertaken a political analysis of the refugee question, I am greatly indebted to the generous professional support of two political scientists specialising on the issue of Palestinian refugees. On the one hand, I would like to thank Rex Brynen, McGill University, not only for providing his PRRN website which is a treasure for everyone researching the question of Palestinian refugees, but foremost for his repeated practical help in answering my questions before and during my research. On the other hand, my thanks also go to Yoav Peled, Tel Aviv University, who shared his available information with me and helped me in establishing some of the theoretical concepts covered in my research.

Thanks also to Joel Peters, Ben Gurion University, who with his solid experience as both an academic researching the issue of Palestinian refugees, and his involvement in the Track II talks on refugees, proved to be an important source of knowledge and inspiration. I would further like to thank Henry Siegman from the Council on Foreign Relations, who despite his busy schedule allotted time to answer my questions and provide me with a sharp analysis of both past and present aspects of Israeli-Palestinian relations. Furthermore, my thanks go to Michael Walzer from the School of Social Science, Princeton, who explained important aspects of conflict and war to me and was always willing to offer his support if needed. In this context, I would also like to thank Samer Shehata from Georgetown University for his input regarding the Arab states' perspective of the Israeli-Palestinian conflict and his helpful recommendations for further interview partners. Joseph Nye from Harvard University deserves my gratitude for his comments on the Clinton administration's approach to the Israeli-Palestinian peace process.

Further thanks go to Robert Malley, former special assistant to President Clinton, for sharing with me his precious views as an insider to the 2000 Camp David talks. Furthermore, Pierre Allan of the University of Geneva, who was personally involved in the famous initiative named after that city, deserves my gratitude for making his material on the issue available to me.

I am also indebted to both Aviv Shir-On, Israeli ambassador to Switzerland, and Anis Al-Qaq, the General Delegate of the Palestinian Authority in Switzerland, for providing me not only with their leaderships' official view on the question of Palestinian refugees, but also with their highly revealing personal views regarding possible solutions. Further informed comments and an intelligent analysis regarding the political dimension of the Palestinian refugee problem were provided to me by Jacques Pitteloud, coordinator of Switzerland's intelligence agencies, for which I am also most grateful.

Special thanks also go to my friends Fadia Saleh and Rabie Abu Latefah for showing me the concrete realities of life in a Palestinian refugee camp. Additional thanks go to Muhammad Jaradat, co-founder of the Palestinian refugee organisation BADIL, for explaining to me the demands and needs Palestinian refugees have regarding a settlement of the issue. On the Israeli side, my friend Ofer Zalzberg deserves appreciation for his continuous interest in my research and his never ending readiness to discuss various suggestions to solve the Palestinian refugee issue. Yossi Schwartz deserves thanks for his frank suggestion of unconventional proposals. Further thanks go to Rabbi Tovia Ben

Chorin, who contributed with an input of dispassionate comments, ideas, and suggestions in a manner in which only few Israelis at that point are able to tackle the emotional issue of Palestinian refugees.

Finally, the greatest vote of appreciation goes to my wife Sarah who contributed tremendously to the existence of this research. Her contribution did not only extend to countless readings of my manuscript and enriching it both in terms of content and style, but also to accompanying me on various research trips and the not always easy field work in refugee camps. Most importantly, she always offered warm support during times of intellectual solitude.

Introduction

Research Question

The Israeli-Palestinian conflict, one of the world's most eagerly debated and of seemingly unending crises, has long been considered in such deadlock that it cannot ever be resolved. Direct talks between the parties starting in the early 1990s, however, have increasingly resulted in the crystallization of solutions to most of the outstanding issues like borders and security, and even Jerusalem. The fact that Oslo as a process eventually failed has no influence on the basic formulas it brought to bear, formulas which were subsequently elaborated to great detail in the framework of the Geneva Initiative, a private proposal published in December 2003. Thus both dispassionate outside observers as no small number of Israelis and Palestinians by now know the two central building blocks of a viable solution: First, two sovereign states need to be established on the basis of the 1967 borders, with territorial modifications to be compensated by land swaps. Second, Jerusalem will be the capital of those two states and needs to be divided along ethnic lines. The one major question which still lacks a solution, and to which both politicians as well as researchers have not yet come up with a formula acceptable to both Israelis and Palestinians, is the issue of Palestinian refugees. This was illustrated by the Geneva Initiative, whose overall suggestions were met with a surprising amount of acceptance among Israelis and Palestinians. Yet the one aspect of it which generated the strongest opposition on both sides was the provision on refugees: While Israelis feared a large influx of returning Palestinian refugees, Palestinians rejected the proposal even more fervently and regarded it as a betrayal of the *right of return*. These two seemingly incompatible demands precisely describe the intractability of the matter: How can Israel's demographic concerns (the fear of a massive human inflow that might endanger Israel's Jewish character) be reconciled with the Palestinian insistence on the *right of return* and actual refugee return? This question shall precisely be the focus of this research.

Relevance of the Issue

The Israeli-Palestinian conflict has not only cost thousands of Israeli and Palestinian lives, it has also been a source of friction for regional, and at times global, stability; the benefits of settling that dispute hardly need to be explained. The Palestinian refugee problem and its consequences have shaken the Middle East and troubled the world for more than five decades. Guerrilla incursions into Israel by refugees helped trigger to some extent at least three conventional Arab-Israeli wars, in 1956, 1967, and 1982; Palestinians – among them a disproportionately high percentage of refugees – highjacking civilian airliners caused worldwide instability and fear during the 1970s and 1980s.[1] More recently, both the first and the second Palestinian intifada were largely powered by the refugee camps.

The question of Palestinian refugees is a core issue which needs to be solved in order to allow a solution of the Israeli-Palestinian conflict as a whole; in fact, a satisfactory settlement of the refugee question is absolutely indispensable in order to make an overall Israel-Palestinian agreement acceptable to the relevant constituencies. For half a century, even while the military conflict has waxed and waned, the rhetorical war between Israelis and Palestinians has gone on almost unabated: while one side insisted on "complete security" the other side demanded "absolute justice." Although there exists solid agreement that it is essential to break up this lethal vicious circle, to this point, neither politics nor academia has found the right means to do so.

In fact, and quite surprisingly considering the amount of existing research on the overall Israeli-Palestinian conflict, rather little research has been undertaken on the specific issue of Palestinian refugees. Moreover, the limited research that exists mostly focuses on either historic or legal aspects of the refugee question, yet neglects another – and

---

1   For more political and military analysis regarding the role of the refugees and the refugee issue in subsequent conflicts, see Yezid Sayigh, *Armed Struggle and the Search for State: The Palestinian National Movement, 1949–1993* (Oxford: Oxford University Press, 1997); Benny Morris, *Israel's Border Wars: 1949–1956: Arab Infiltration, Israeli Retaliation, and the Countdown to the Suez War* (Oxford: Clardendon Press, 1993); Avi Plascov, *The Palestinian Refugees in Jordan 1948–1957* (London: Frank Cass, 1981).

maybe most crucial – aspect of it, namely its political dimensions. In other words, historians make an important contribution to understanding how the problem came into being and how it developed into the present, and jurists have the essential task of evaluating the legal aspects of the Palestinian claim for a *right of return*. However, if focusing on a future-oriented solution of a problem that was created in the past, and considering that the issue of Palestinian refugees will eventually not be solved by paragraphs but by politics, the need for an additional approach becomes evident: a political analysis of the Palestinian refugee question.

Continuous years of violence and their resulting damage repeatedly demonstrated that there is no military solution to the Israeli-Palestinian conflict. It is therefore evident that the only way to solve the Palestinian refugee question is in the framework of Israeli-Palestinian negotiations. Such negotiations have already been undertaken in the past, yet have borne no concrete results to this point. While any political process between Israelis and Palestinians has lain idle for the past years, only its eventual revival can lead to a solution of the conflict. Once Israeli and Palestinian negotiators will again reach the point of tackling the issue of refugees, they will require some reference regarding reasons for the failure of past talks and some guidelines that will enable a successful agreement in the future. Ideally, this research might eventually contribute such guidelines.

The Present Stage of Research

As mentioned above, while voluminous research exists on the subject of the Israeli-Palestinian conflict as a whole, only a marginal fraction of it focuses on the question of Palestinian refugees, divided into three different sections: historic, legal, and political.

At the end of the 1980s, a group of Israeli historians ("The New Historians") has revolutionized traditional perceptions regarding the creation of the Palestinian refugee problem: These historians have come up with new archival material which brought to light the fact that, contrary to the traditional Israeli narrative, the Palestinians in 1948 did not only leave Palestine because the invading Arab armies had told them to do so to clear the way, but rather that active expulsions on the part of the Jewish forces also played a decisive role. Path breaking was the scholarly work of Simha Flapan, Benny Morris, and Yoav Gelber.[2] Yet while the historic circumstances and reasons for the creation of the Palestinian refugee problem have become increasingly known, the phenomenon still exists and lacks a solution. Further important research regarding the material dimensions of the Palestinian refugee issue was conducted by Michael Fischbach;[3] while his findings will doubtlessly be of great importance once an Israeli-Palestinian agreement on refugees has been found, they do not directly contribute to getting there.

A more present and future oriented approach was taken by several scholars of international law.[4] One of the leading experts on legal aspects of the Palestinian refugee question is Susan Akram, who has examined the legal requirements for a solution of the issue.[5] Akram, together with John Quigley,[6] is one of the primary proponents of a Palestinian *right of return*. Yet there are also jurists arguing that a legally founded *right of*

---

2 Simha Flapan, *The Birth of Israel: Myths and Realities* (New York: Pantheon, 1987); Benny Morris, *The Birth of the Palestinian Refugee Problem, 1947–1949* (Cambridge: Cambridge University Press, 1988); Yoav Gelber, *Palestine 1948: War, Escape and the Emergence of the Palestinian Refugee Problem* (Brighton: Sussex Academic Press, 2006).

3 Michael Fischbach, *The Peace Process and Palestine Refugee Claims: Addressing Claims for Property Compensation* (Washington, D.C.: United States Institute of Peace Press, 2006); and Michael Fischbach, *Records of Dispossession: Palestinian Refugee Property and the Arab-Israeli Conflict* (New York: Columbia University Press, 2003).

4 For one of the most influential studies written on legal aspects of the Palestinian refugee question, see Lex Takkenberg, *The Status of Palestinian Refugees in International Law* (New York: Oxford University Press, 1998).

5 See Susan Akram and Terry Rempel, "Temporary Protection as an Instrument for Implementing the Right of Return for Palestinian Refugees," *Boston University International Law Journal*, Vol. 22, No. 1, 2004, pp. 1–162; Susan Akram, "Palestinian Refugees and their Legal Status: Rights, Politics, and Implications for a Just Solution," *Journal of Palestine Studies*, Vol. XXXI, No. 3, Spring 2002, pp. 36–51; Susan Akram, "Reinterpreting Palestinian Refugee Rights under International Law," in Naseer Aruri, ed., *Palestinian Refugees: The Right of Return* (London: Pluto Press, 2001), pp. 165–194.

6 See, e.g., John Quigley, *The Case for Palestine: An International Law Perspective* (Duke, NC: Duke University Press, 2005).

return for Palestinian refugees does not exist: Ruth Lapidot[7] and Marc Zell[8] are the primary representatives of such an approach. Yet since the Palestinian refugee question will not be solved by lawyers but by politicians, political analysis of the issue is of crucial importance.

As to political approaches to the Palestinian refugee question, on the Israeli side, Mark Heller was one of the first to explore the refugee issue directly, first in his ground-breaking *A Palestinian State* (1983), and later in the refugee chapter of his book co-authored with the Palestinian scholar Sari Nuesseibeh, *No Trumpets, No Drums* (1991).[9] Shimon Peres devoted a chapter to the refugee issue in his 1993 book *The New Middle East*.[10] Shlomo Gazit – former Israeli military coordinator of the West Bank and Gaza, former director of military intelligence, and advisor to the Labour government on the refugee issue – authored an important study on resolution of the Palestinian refugee problem for the Jaffee Center in 1995.[11] On the Palestinian side, former negotiators Abbas Shiblak and Salim Tamari have addressed the outlines of a refugee settlement, while Rashid Khalidi has formulated some of the most influential ideas published on the topic.[12]

When delving into the search for existing political literature, one is struck with two observations. First, the bulk of the material was published before the issue of refugees was ever tackled in the Israeli-

7   See Ruth Lapidot, "Legal Aspects of the Palestinian Refugee Question," at www.jcpa.org/jl/vp485.htm.

8   Marc Zell and Sonia Shnyder, "Palestinian Right of Return or Strategic Weapon?: A Historical, Legal and Moral-Political Analysis," *Nexus*, Vol. 8, 2003, at www.nexusjournal.org.

9   Mark Heller, *A Palestinian State: The Implications for Israel* (Cambridge, MA: Harvard University Press, 1983), pp. 80–87; Mark Heller and Sari Nusseibeh, *No Trumpets, No Drums: A Two-State Settlement of the Israeli-Palestinian Conflict* (New York: Hill and Wang, 1991), pp. 86–96.

10   Shimon Peres (with Arye Naor), *The New Middle East* (New York: Henry Holt, 1993), pp. 181–194.

11   Shlomo Gazit, *The Palestinian Refugee Problem*, Final Status Issues Study No. 2 (Tel Aviv: Jaffee Center for Strategic Studies, 1995).

12   Rashid Khalidi and Itamar Rabinovich, *The Palestinian Right of Return: Two Views*, Occasional Paper No. 6 (Cambridge, MA: American Academy of Arts and Sciences, October 1990); Rashid Khalidi, "Toward a Solution," in Center for Policy Analysis on Palestine, *Palestine Refugees: Their Problem and Future* (Washington, DC: CPAP, 1994).

Palestinian peace process; at that point, therefore, such material was a mere theoretical exercise based on assumptions. While intended to be compatible to actual negotiations, any research undertaken before such talks began was forcibly of a speculative nature. Obviously, a more relevant evaluation could be made once the issue of refugees was addressed (especially in Camp David 2000 and Taba 2001), and as a result, important conclusions could be drawn regarding the feasibility of the existing literature. Indeed, a great part of what might have been considered a realistic goal for negotiations had to be revised.[13] Second, with the exception of Don Peretz's *Palestinians, Refugees, and the Middle East Peace Process*,[14] published in 1993, there exists no research extending beyond the scope of an article or single chapters within books. In other words, regarding a political solution to the refugee problem, practically no researcher has so far deemed it necessary to undertake research to the extent of a book.

There do exist some collections of separate articles. In 2001, Joseph Ginat and Edward Perkins edited a volume with the promising title *The Palestinian Refugees: Old Problems – New Solutions*.[15] Unfortunately, while indeed referring to old problems, hardly any substantial new political solutions were presented; one article dealing with supposedly new proposals, Moshe Maoz's *Traditional Positions and New*

---

13 See e.g. Peres' suggestions. Not only did he claim that Ben Gurion never gave an order to expel people during the 1948 war and that the number of Palestinian refugees resulting from that war had been "about six hundred thousand Palestinians." He rejected any responsibility for the Palestinian refugee problem and, regarding a possible solution, stated: "Israel won the war and the local inhabitants were left outside. Should Israel be held responsible for the fact that Arab countries did not absorb their Arab refugees in the same spirit of self-sacrifice and brotherhood that Israel displayed toward Jewish refugees?" See Peres, *The New Middle East*, pp. 186–187. To reduce the Palestinian refugee problem to a mere population exchange quickly proved to be futile during the actual course of negotiations.

14 In his book, Peretz mentions three practical aspects to a solution: Repatriation, Compensation, and Resettlement. Don Peretz, *Palestinians, Refugees, and the Middle East Peace Process* (Washington, DC: United States Institute of Peace Press, 1993).

15 Joseph Ginat and Edward Perkins (eds.), *The Palestinian Refugees: Old Problems – New Solutions* (Norman: University of Oklahoma Press, 2001).

Solutions,[16] was merely a reprint of Joseph Alpher's and Khalil Shikaki's *The Palestinian Refugee Problem* (1998),[17] a research in which Maoz had participated. Naseer Aruri's *Palestinian Refugees* (2001)[18] is another collection of various articles on the Palestinian refugee issue. While treating different elements of the refugee question, from historical aspects to questions of international law, it does not put any emphasis on realistic political solutions to the problem.[19]

An important contribution for the understanding of the influence and nature of Palestinian refugee mythologies, as well as their political and social underpinnings on a potential settlement with Israel, has been made by Robert Bowker's *Palestinian Refugees* (2003).[20] Finally, Ann Lesch and Ian Lustick have edited *Exile and Return* (2005),[21] which contains two precious chapters on the political dimension of the Palestinian refugee question.[22]

However, there is a striking absence of scholarly work that focuses on proposals for politically solving the question of Palestinian refugees by listing, analysing and comparing previously suggested formulas and ideas in order to find the vital guidelines and building blocks needed for solving the intractable issue of refugees; instead, the existing political research has predominantly focused on scrutinizing single ideas for

---

16   Moshe Maoz, "Traditional Positions and New Solutions," in Ginat and Perkins, *The Palestinian Refugees*, pp. 109–121.

17   Joseph Alpher and Khalil Shikaki, "The Palestinian Refugee Problem and the Right of Return," Weatherhead Center for International Affairs, Harvard University, May 1998, available at www.wcfia.harvard.edu/papers/98–07.pdf. The article contains several interesting aspects, which will be addressed in the fourth part of this paper.

18   Naseer Aruri (ed.), *Palestinian Refugees: The Right of Return* (London: Pluto Press, 2001).

19   Salman Abu Sitta's proposal for a full return of Palestinian refugees into Israel will be discussed in the fourth part of this research, where it will be explained why his suggestion cannot be regarded realistic.

20   Robert Bowker, *Palestinian Refugees: Mythology, Identity, and the Search for Peace* (Boulder: Lynne Rienner Publishers, 2003).

21   Ann Lesch and Ian Lustick (eds.), *Exile and Return: Predicaments of Palestinians and Jews* (Philadelphia: University of Philadelphia Press, 2005).

22   See Elazar Barkan, "Considerations Toward Accepting Historical Responsibility," in ibid., pp. 85–105; and Ian Lustick, "Negotiating Truth: The Holocaust, *Lehavdil*, and al-Nakba," pp. 106–130. Both articles will be referred to in the fourth part.

solving the Palestinian refugee question, yet without putting it into perspective with other proposals and without evaluating the advantages and disadvantages of each so that the weaknesses of one proposal could be compensated by the strengths of another.

It is therefore the primary purpose of this research to produce an entire volume devoted to the political aspects of Palestinian refugee issue, not only providing the historical and legal background necessary to comprehend the complexity of the issue, but above all concentrating on listing and analysing both existing and new suggestions for a political solution of the problem. The result shall provide what does not exist to date: a guideline for future Israeli-Palestinian negotiations on the issue of Palestinian refugees, offering a careful examination of the reasons for failure in the past and subsequently presenting an outline for successfully tackling the issue in the future.

Methodology

Throughout the text, the order of appearance of names (of people, countries, and nations) will generally be arranged alphabetically; for example, when speaking of "Israeli-Palestinian" relations, the former nation will appear first, while when referring to their leaders, "Arafat" will be put before "Barak." In addition, if not mentioned otherwise, the term "Israelis" exclusively refers to Jewish Israelis.

The research is divided into four parts. Part I focuses on the historical context and also relates to the differing historiographic narratives Israelis and Palestinians have. The overall aim of the first part is to provide a historic background and to examine the circumstances under which the Palestinian refugee problem was created. It is essential to understand how the problem came into being in order to be able to find a solution to it.

Part I will therefore mainly focus on the time period between 1947 and 1949, intending to shed light upon the factors that caused the Palestinian exodus. Too often these events are portrayed in an oversimplified manner, not adequately reflecting the enormous complexity involved. This research will therefore begin by reviewing the course of events that led to the Palestinian refugee problem, in order to subsequently isolate the specific factors that resulted in more than 700,000 Palestinians becoming refugees. In addition, one must not forget that not only the 1948 war created a large number of Palestinians refugees, but an additional wave was also caused – although on a smaller scale – in the 1967 war. Although the circumstances resulting in those refugees have usually attracted less attention than the 1948 wave of refugees, they doubtlessly form an integral part of the Palestinian refugee problem and shall therefore also be explored in this research.

Yet besides examining the historical events that occurred, it is also vital to comprehend how they were perceived by the two nations; not surprisingly, the same period of time is interpreted radically differently by Israelis and Palestinians respectively. For that reason, the first part shall also scrutinize the differing national narratives of Israelis and Palestinians, for these narratives play a crucial role in the search for solutions to the refugee problem.

Finally, one cannot ponder solutions to a problem without being familiar with the current situation on the ground. The concluding chapter of the first part shall therefore not only shed light on the issue of numbers and definitions of Palestinian refugees, but it will also provide an overview of the main population centres of refugees, as well as an examination of the circumstances under which they are living in those areas.

Since it is impossible to approach the issue of Palestinian refugees without being confronted with the *right of return*, this issue deserves adequate attention and shall therefore be the focus of Part II. Throughout the text, whenever applying to the specific Palestinian claim for return, the *right of return* is put in italics; this is for the reason that the *right of return* is generally not referred to as a mere right, but rather an entire concept composed of several aspects. Accordingly, while for the Israelis it is coupled with fear, associating it with a demand for a massive influx of returnees, for Palestinians, the *right of return* is an embodiment of justice and the dream of return to their places of origin. The second part of this research will therefore begin by providing a profound analysis of both Israeli and Palestinians views of the *right of return*.

Yet in addition to bearing separate connotations for Israelis and Palestinians, there is also a legal dispute as to whether a Palestinian *right of return* exits as an actual right in international law. The main focus of the second part shall therefore lie in trying to find an answer to the question whether the *right of return* does exist as a legal right; for that purpose, the legal argumentations of both proponents and opponents of the *right of return* shall be scrutinized. In addition, two other prominent examples of refugees demanding their return shall be consulted: Bosnia-Herzegovina and Cyprus. It shall be evaluated whether the manner in which both the parties involved as well as the international community have dealt with the issue can provide relevant conclusions to the case of the Palestinian refugees.

Part III will analyse past negotiations on the issue of Palestinian refugees. Such talks provide important precedents regarding Israelis and Palestinians tackling what is often referred to as the most intractable of all their outstanding issues. In fact, the issue of Palestinian refugees has long represented a major stumbling block during the peace talks and still is often referred to as the prime factor dooming any future Israeli-Palestinian negotiations regarding a permanent settlement to failure. It is therefore essential to examine the circumstances and reasons that have upheld the issue of refugees as a central bone of contention in Israeli-Palestinian negotiations.

The analysis shall first review initial Arab-Israeli negotiations on Palestinian refugees held during the Cold War. Subsequently, attention will be turned to the crucial stage when Israelis and Palestinians finally started holding direct talks and initiated the so-called Oslo Process in the 1990s. During Oslo, the issue of refugees was deemed to be one of the most difficult issues and postponed to the end, when final status issues were to be addressed. This eventually occurred in 2000 in Camp David and Taba in 2001: The course of these talks and the reasons for their failure provide a source for important conclusions regarding future Israeli-Palestinian negotiations on refugees. For that purpose, the refugee related talks in both Camp David and Taba shall be carefully traced in order to evaluate frictions and agreements between Israelis and Palestinians on the issue, as well as the reasons for these rounds of negotiations resulting in no mutually accepted settlement.

It is important to stress that the third part will solely refer to official negotiations between representatives of the respective leaderships; private proposals, such as the Geneva Initiative, will be the subject of the fourth and concluding part.

Part IV shall focus on a number of unofficial proposals and initiatives which suggest solutions to the question of Palestinian refugees. A

24

solution to this problem can only be found if all options are put on the table and consequently evaluated.[23] There is an important methodological precedent to such approach: Graham Allison's 1969 analysis of the decision-making process during the Cuban Missile Crisis,[24] where all possible options of the U.S. government to react to the installation of Soviet nuclear missiles in Cuba were first listed and subsequently analysed and evaluated. According to Allison's approach, the two extreme ends of the possible range of action were *do nothing* on the one hand and a full fledged *invasion* on the other. Yet several options are also placed in between, namely *diplomatic pressures, a secret approach to Castro*, a *surgical air strike* to destroy the missile sites, or a *blockade*.[25]

My research shall apply the same methodology to the question of Palestinian refugees: Thus the various options for solution shall be listed and subsequently evaluated regarding their implications on Israelis and Palestinians respectively, as well as to their actual relevance in terms of being a potential solution to the problem; options involving a disproportionate number of disadvantages for one or both parties certainly need to be deemed less relevant than options consisting of some balance regarding concessions required.

Moreover, the preceding part's analysis of past negotiations will have demonstrated that Israelis and Palestinians have different expectations when addressing the refugee issue: While Israelis mostly focus on practical solutions (e.g., resettlement of refugees, shutting down refugee camps, dismantling UNRWA etc.), Palestinians put at least equal emphasis on principled aspects (e.g., recognition of the *right of return*, Israeli admission of historical responsibility, etc.). Thus in order to find a solution to the Palestinian refugee question, it is essential to make a distinction between practical and principled factors – an approach which can also be essential to the solution of conflicts in general.

Consequently, the fourth part will be composed of three chapters, focusing on practical, principled, and integrated solutions. The first

---

23 This view was also confirmed by Susan Akram in an interview with the author in Boston on 9 December 2003.
24 Graham Allison, "Conceptual Models and the Cuban Missile Crisis," *The American Political Science Review*, Vol. LXIII, No. 3, September 1969, pp. 689–718.
25 Ibid., pp. 696–698.

chapter will review *practical* solutions, which are suggestions for an Israeli-Palestinian peace agreement intended to end the refugees' existence as such. The underlying idea is to solve the problem by shutting down refugee camps and providing the refugees with a permanent home. The primary tools of practical solutions are financial compensation and resettlement, either within the refugees' present host countries or in third countries. Yet another tool, the option of repatriation, which involves the return of refugees into the territory of Israel, has been and continues to be the major stumbling block preventing an Israeli-Palestinian agreement to solve the question of refugees; by contrast, a tool such as compensation merely poses the challenge of raising the necessary funds – while by no means negligible, financial issues can be overcome and are not the main factor standing in the way of an agreement. This research will therefore put strong emphasis on the main challenge, namely the aspects involving the potential return of Palestinian refugees into Israel.

The fourth part's second chapter will deal with *principled solutions*, examining formal elements such as the possible wording and formulation of an agreement, recognition of the *right of return*, as well as issues such as admitting historical responsibility and offering an apology. Practically no research concentrating on those issues has been undertaken to date in the context of finding a mutually acceptable solution to the question of Palestinian refugees.[26] The importance of these aspects became evident when in the course of past negotiations, Israel mostly focused on practical solutions to the refugee question and refused to meet Palestinian demands for the inclusion of principled aspects, such as recognizing the *right of return* and admitting some form of responsibility for the creation of the problem. Indeed, the parties have so far not been able to bridge the discrepancy between the Israeli demand for practical solutions and the Palestinian call to include principled aspects.

In order to develop schemes to overcome these contradictory positions, the concept of "Transitional Justice" will be discussed. In addition, an interesting precedent of two nations with a troubled past in search of agreement to enable future diplomatic relations is provided by

---

26 The primary exceptions being Barkan, "Considerations Toward Accepting Historical Responsibility," and Lustick, "Negotiating Truth."

German-Israeli negotiations following the Second World War. Accordingly, the manner in which Germans and Israelis managed under the heavy shadow of the Holocaust to find a formula regarding the past, satisfying both sides, will be carefully scrutinized in order to evaluate the options for applying the relevant conclusions gained to the case of Israeli-Palestinian negotiations on refugees.

The fourth part's last chapter will focus on proposals synthesising both practical and principled elements, which shall therefore be termed *integrated solutions*. All three kinds of approaches (practical, principled, and integrated) shall be analysed according to the following *methodology*: The range of solutions is determined by its two extreme ends, i.e. either allowing all refugees to return into present Israel, or allowing none to do so. Regarding the proposals falling between those two ends, they will be classified and examined in relation to the number of Palestinian refugees they imply returning to Israel. In other words, the proposal allowing all refugees to return to Israel will be followed by the proposal implying the second largest quantity of Palestinian refugees returning to Israel, then by the next smaller quantity etc., until the end of the spectrum is reached with the proposal implying that no single Palestinian refugee will return to Israel.

Each proposal will be examined by *first* presenting a summary of its underlying ideas for solving the Palestinian refugee question. *Second*, implications of such a solution for both Israelis and Palestinians respectively will be analysed. *Third*, the proposal as a whole will be evaluated in the light of previous Israeli-Palestinian negotiations as to the likelihood of it becoming a mutually accepted solution to both parties; in other words, its relevance will be assessed.

Finally, in the framework of the conclusions, a short summary of the research conducted in this volume will be presented. Subsequently, an attempt will be made to present a set of guidelines and recommendations regarding the vital components for any future Israeli-Palestinian attempts to successfully tackle the question of refugees. Obviously, there exists no one and single solution to the Palestinian refugee question, but rather a concrete solution will have to be developed by the parties involved. However, evaluating the advantages and disadvantages of a proposal for both Israelis and Palestinians shall help to find the crucial range of solutions where a compromise is feasible. Defining such area will counter claims that the Palestinian refugee issue is a zero-sum game where one side's gain is automatically the other one's loss; presenting and evaluating the available options, therefore, will provide a necessary catalogue of choice towards any future Israeli-Palestinian negotiations on the question of Palestinian refugees.

PART I

Historical Context
and its Differing Historiographic Narratives

1   THE PRE-1948 PERIOD

To trace the roots of the Palestinian refugee problem, one needs to go back to the late 19th century. At that time, the initially European idea of nationalism reached the Middle East and resulted in two peoples claiming Palestine to be theirs. The fightings from 1947 to 1948, which turned the vast majority of Palestinian Arabs[1] into refugees, was the most tragic outcome of these conflicting claims. Around two thirds of them became refugees within mandated Palestine, while one third fled into neighbouring countries.

Jewish nationalism and its claim for political sovereignty in Palestine became embodied by Zionism, a movement which began with the programmatic writings of Moses Hess, Judah Alkalai, Zvi Hirsch Kalischer and Theodor Herzl.[2] Those writings were accompanied by the immigration from Russia to Ottoman-ruled Palestine in the 1880s of Jews intending to rebuild a national home for the Jewish people on their ancient land – the Land of Israel, in Zionist terms. The immigrants were not only impelled by that positive ideal but also by the negative experience of oppression in Eastern Europe; a wave of pogroms had engulfed Russia following the assassination of Czar Alexander II in March 1881.[3]

Simultaneously, in the first years of the 20th century, with the spirit of nationalism spreading to the colonial world, Syrian, Lebanese and Palestinian Arab intellectuals began to advocate the idea of liberation

---

1   Since until 1948, all of mandated Palestine's inhabitants – whether Arab or Jewish – were "Palestinians", the term "Palestinian" on its own will be solely used for the period after 1948 and will refer to the Arab population of mandated Palestine and their descendents.

2   See e.g. Moses Hess, *Rom und Jerusalem: Die letzte Nationalitätenfrage, Briefe* (Vienna: Löwit, 1935); Theodor Herzl, *Der Judenstaat: Versuch einer modernen Lösung der Judenfrage* (Zurich: Manesse-Verlag, 1988); Leon Kellner, ed., *Theodor Herzels zionistische Schriften* (Berlin-Charlottenburg: Jüdischer Verlag, 1905); Theodor Herzl, *Gesammelte zionistische Werke: in fünf Bänden* (Berlin: Jüdischer Verlag, 1934).

3   Benny Morris, *The Birth of the Palestinian Refugee Problem Revisited* (New York: Cambridge University Press, 2004), p. 9.

from the Ottoman Empire and the establishment of an independent Arab state. At the same time, with the growing Jewish settlement in Palestine, friction developed in various localities between neighbouring Arab and Jewish communities.[4] Palestine's Arabs resented the influx of what they perceived as Russian- and Yiddish-speaking Europeans and began to fear cultural-religious subversion of their traditional lifestyle, physical encroachment and even displacement.[5]

The First World War changed the face of the Middle East. Besides disbanding the Ottoman Empire, the war also increased regional nationalist hopes and fears. The idea of national self-determination, proclaimed by the victorious Allies, continuously inspired the educated throughout the colonial world. Britain conquered Palestine in 1917–1918 and the League of Nations eventually sanctioned British mandated rule in the country; the imperial power was charged with preparing the local inhabitants for self-government. In addition, the British issued the Balfour Declaration undertaking to help establish a "National Home for the Jewish People" in Palestine while promising to safeguard "the civil and religious rights" of the existing Arab inhabitants.[6]

Post-war troubles in Eastern Europe and the attractions of good British administration prompted new waves of Jewish immigration to Palestine. The contradiction between Britain's dual commitment to fostering Jewish self-determination and safeguarding Arab rights soon became apparent, and the inevitability of the clash between Arab and Jewish national aspirations manifested itself.[7]

Palestinian Arab nationalism grew slowly but steadily. Two political camps emerged over the 1920s and 1930s. One camp assembled around the Husseini clan and the person of Haj Muhammad Amin al-Husseini, from 1921–22 the Mufti of Jerusalem and the head of the Supreme Muslim Council (SMC), as well as from 1936 chairman of the

---

4   Benny Morris, *The Birth of the Palestinian Refugee Problem, 1947–1949* (Cambridge: Cambridge University Press, 1988), p. 4.
5   Morris, *The Birth of the Palestinian Refugee Problem Revisited*, p. 9. See further Benny Morris, *Righteous Victims: A History of the Zionist-Arab Conflict, 1881–2001* (New York: Vintage Books, 2001), chapters 1 and 2.
6   See the Balfour Declaration in Walter Laqueur and Barry Rubin (eds.), *The Israeli-Arab Reader: A Documentary History of the Middle East Conflict* (New York: Penguin Books, 2001), p. 16.
7   Morris, *The Birth of the Palestinian Refugee Problem Revisited*, pp. 9–10.

Arab Higher Committee (AHC)[8]. This camp demanded the end of the Mandate, the establishment of an Arab state in all of Palestine (promising certain civil and religious rights for the Jews already in the country), and a cessation of Jewish immigration in the future. A more moderate camp, usually called the Opposition and led by the Nashashibis, was agreeable to a compromise, even one based on partition. Yet the Husseinis generally set the tone of Palestinian Arab politics and from the mid-1930s dominated the national movement.[9]

In the *Yishuv* (Palestine's Jewish population), the moderate Labour camp, led by David Ben-Gurion and his Mapai party, dominated the political arena; the right-wing Revisionists never captured more than a minority of Yishuv votes. Ben-Gurion, a pragmatist, was in general willing to accept partition and the establishment of a Jewish state in part of the country, although throughout he remained committed to a vision of Jewish sovereignty over all of Palestine as the ultimate goal of Zionism.

Anti-Jewish Arab riots in Palestine's towns in 1920–21 and 1929 were an expression of a growing animosity – triggered by religious and nationalist grievances – for the Zionist presence. Arab fears of displacement, heightened by the mass Jewish immigration from Europe of the mid-1930s (sparked by the rise of Nazism), the Jewish land purchases for new settlement, as well as a sense that violence would enhance the goal of political independence, led to the 1936 general strike and the 1936–39 Arab revolt.[10]

The strike and revolt, directed in the first instance against the British and, secondly, against what were seen as their Zionist *protégés*, spread from the towns to the countryside, during which the Husseinis and their allies gained the unchallenged leadership of the national movement. In the course of the revolt, which was eventually firmly suppressed by the British military, the Opposition, having collaborated with the

---

8   On 25 April, 1936, representatives of various Arab Palestinian factions met in Jerusalem and set up a wall-to-wall eight-man body called the Arab Higher Committee (AHC), which led the Palestinian struggle during 1936–39 and 1946–48. Amin al Husseini, elected AHC chairman, emerged as the revolt's leader. See Morris, *Righteous Victims*, p. 130.

9   Morris, *The Birth of the Palestinian Refugee Problem, 1947–1949*, p. 5.

10   Ibid.

British military in 1938–39 in crushing the revolt, expired as a major political force.[11]

The revolt persuaded London, faced by the imminent prospect of a multi-front world war against Germany, Japan and Italy, of the advisability of maintaining tranquillity in the Middle East. The British therefore dispatched the Peel Commission, which in 1937 proposed the partition of the country into two states, one Jewish and the other Arab, with a strip comprising Jerusalem and Jaffa to remain British. The Zionist movement accepted after much agonizing the principle of partition, with the commission's proposals as a basis for negotiation, while the Arab Higher Committee opposed the plan. London soon abandoned the proposal; quiet was to be achieved by appeasing Palestine's Arabs and, through them, the Arab world in general. The main step to achieve that goal was the 1939 White Paper which nearly stopped any Jewish land purchases in the country, and severely curbed Jewish immigration, blocking off a major escape route for Europe's Jews from the imminent Holocaust. Besides this measure which assured them majority in the land, Palestine's Arabs were additionally promised independence within ten years.

Yet Hitler's continuing destruction of European Jewry added urgency, momentum and political thrust to the Zionist aim of immediate Jewish statehood.[12] The fact that the most influential Palestinian leader, Haj Amin al-Husseini, made common cause with Hitler not only heightened Jewish antagonism toward Palestine's Arabs, but it cost the latter also precious British sympathies. On 28 November 1941, al-Husseini met Hitler in Berlin and promised to organize a new, pan-Arab revolt; and like the British in World War I, Hitler promised the Arabs post-war independence and the abolition of any Jewish national home.[13] In return, spelled out in the Biltmore Program of May 1942,[14]

---

11   Ibid.

12   Simha Flapan, *The Birth of Israel: Myths and Realities* (New York: Pantheon Books, 1987), p. 97.

13   Benny Morris, *Righteous Victims: A History of the Zionist-Arab Conflict, 1881–2001* (New York: Vintage Books, 2001), pp. 165–167.

14   For more details on the Biltmore Program, see Avi Shlaim, *The Iron Wall: Israel and the Arab World* (New York: Norton & Company, 2000), pp. 23–24.

the Zionist movement for the first time forthrightly declared that nothing less than full, independent Jewish statehood was its goal.

With the Arab nationalists weakened by the abortive revolt and their leaders in exile or in jail, the war years served as a pause in which both communities rested and readied for the battle which all thought imminent. The Yishuv prepared efficiently; Palestine's Arabs did not, relying on salvation by the Arab states.

The trauma of the revolt and Arab violence, the upsurge of anti-British Jewish violence by the *Irgun Zvai Leumi* (Etzel) and *Lohamei Herut Israel* (Lehi), the morally and politically costly efforts by Britain to bar illegal Jewish immigration, the moral-political pressure exercised by the Holocaust and by the growing, pro-Zionist American involvement, caused London to envisage an early withdrawal from Palestine. It therefore passed the matter on to the United Nations. The United Nations' Special Committee on Palestine (UNSCOP) recommended a solution based on partition and, on 29 November 1947, the United Nations General Assembly endorsed the recommendation to partition Palestine into two states, with Jerusalem and Bethlehem constituting a neutral international enclave.[15]

The Yishuv's overall reaction to the resolution was affirmative and the Jewish Agency (the political representation of the Yishuv and its *de facto* government) officially accepted the U.N. partition plan; most of its leaders did so out of pragmatic considerations, preferring a state on only part of the envisioned territory over no state at all. They disliked the idea of an independent Palestinian state, they were dissatisfied with the exclusion of Jerusalem, and they had grave doubts about the viability of the Jewish state within U.N. borders – a state that was to consist of roughly 500,000 Jews and 400,000 Arabs. Besides, the Yishuv's support for partition was not unanimous, with Etzel and Lechi bluntly rejecting the plan. A day after the U.N. vote, Menachem Begin, leader of the Etzel, articulated the underground fighters' rejection: "The partition of Palestine is illegal. It will never be recognized .... Jerusalem was and will forever be our capital. Eretz Israel will be restored to

---

15   See the U.N. partition resolution in Laqueur and Rubin, *The Israeli-Arab Reader*, pp. 69–77; see further Morris, *The Birth of the Palestinian Refugee Problem, 1947–1949*, p. 6.

the people of Israel. All of it. And for ever."[16] Nevertheless, the U.N. resolution represented a tremendous gain of international support for the establishment of a Jewish state; thus the Jewish Agency's decision to agree to partition.[17]

Palestine's Arabs, who had done little to prepare themselves for statehood, rejected the U.N. partition plan out of hand. The Arab Higher Committee, which represented them, rejected the whole idea of partition and denounced the plan as "absurd, impracticable, and unjust."[18] The AHC launched a three-day general strike, accompanied by violent attacks on Jewish civilians. The Arab states, loosely organized since 1945 in the Arab League, also claimed that the U.N. plan was illegal and threatened to resist its implementation by force. They subsequently began sending volunteers, arms and money to help Palestine's Arabs. Within weeks it became clear that the country was sliding into full-scale war.[19]

The British, generally adopting a neutral stand of non-interference, announced that they would terminate the Mandate and withdraw by 15 May 1948. While initially at least intending an orderly transfer of power, their actions from December 1947 to May 1948 remained primarily geared to assuring a smooth, costless withdrawal, and one which would leave their position and prestige in the Arab world intact. Inevitably, both the Jews and the Arabs accused them, in successive episodes, of partiality toward the other side.[20]

Overall, in the diplomatic struggle over the U.N. Partition Plan, it was solely the Jewish side which understook to work constructively with the U.N., and thus managed to get the best out of the termination of Britain's Palestine mandate: The recognition of the principle of a Jewish state. The Arab side, on the other hand, had its understandable reasons for rejecting the entire concept, yet was subsequently unable to bring up either a military or a diplomatic counter-weight to thwart it. Thus there was a paradox in the winter of 1947: The Jews, who accepted

---

16 Menachem Begin, *The Revolt*, rev. ed. (New York: Dell, 1977), p. 433, cited in ibid.

17 Shlaim, *The Iron Wall*, p. 25.

18 Ibid., p. 27.

19 Ibid., pp. 25–27.

20 Morris, *The Birth of the Palestinian Refugee Problem Revisited*, p. 13.

Resolution 181 were ready and well deployed to face a war should this be the outcome, and the Arabs, who rejected the Resolution out of hand and made no secret of their intention to subvert it, were not at all prepared for war.[21]

Between December 1947 and mid-May 1948 the conflict remained within Palestine's borders. During the first weeks of conflict it had been widely unclear that the two communities were indeed engaged in war; rather it seemed that they had merely embarked on a further wave of "disturbances" *à la* 1929 and 1936. Within weeks, sporadic violence snowballed into a full-scale civil war between Palestine's Arabs and Jews. The situation was additionally complicated by the fact that those two communities were highly intermingled: There were both mixed neighbourhoods and patchworks of Arab and Jewish neighbourhoods, plus an interspersing of Arab and Jewish villages in each rural district and along almost every road. From January to March 1948, Palestine's Arabs were reinforced by small contingents of volunteers from the neighbouring Arab states, while the Jews received financial and political support, and a handful of volunteers, from the Diaspora.[22]

The Yishuv's military and administrative power was vastly superior to that of Palestine's Arabs. From December 1947 to January 1948, the *Haganah* (the main Jewish militia) stayed on the defensive, wishing not to annoy the British while it re-organised and armed for war; it knew that the genuine challenge would be posed not by Palestine's Arabs but by the armies of the surrounding states. Until the end of January 1948, neither side had the upper hand. But in February and March, the Jewish forces suffered major setbacks in the battle for the roads, especially between Tel Aviv and Jerusalem. During April and May, bringing to bear its military and organizational superiority, the Haganah switched to the offensive, driven by a sense of impending logistical collapse, by the prospect of the imminent British withdrawal, and by the expected invasion of Palestine by the armies of the Arab states. Eventually, Palestine's Arab militias were defeated.[23]

---

21 Shlomo Ben-Ami, *Scars of War, Wounds of Peace: The Israeli-Arab Tragedy* (New York: Oxford University Press, 2006), p. 34.

22 Morris, *The Birth of the Palestinian Refugee Problem, 1947–1949*, pp. 6–7.

23 For more detail, see Morris, *The Birth of the Palestinian Refugee Problem Revisited*, pp. 13–14.

On 14 May 1948, the Yishuv's leaders declared the establishment of the State of Israel. On 15 May, the armies of Transjordan, Syria, Lebanon, Egypt and Iraq invaded Palestine. The war became a conventional multi-front, multi-army confrontation. After blocking the initial Arab offensives, in a series of Israeli campaigns in July and October 1948, as well as from December 1948 to January 1949, the Jewish forces managed to assure the existence of the State of Israel. In parallel, Arab Palestinian masses in each successive area conquered by the Jews fled from their towns and villages; what became one nation's independence turned out to be the other's catastrophe – or *nakba*, as it is called in Arabic.

2   THE PALESTINIAN EXODUS

The Palestinian exodus started soon after the U.N. passed the Partition Resolution in November 1947 and it unfolded in four stages, closely linked to the development of the war itself. The following paragraphs will examine each of the four stages separately in order to illustrate the complexity and multi-causality of the events that triggered the Palestinian refugee problem.

2.1 The First Stage: December 1947 to March 1948

The first stage of the exodus began with the departure of many of the country's upper and middle class families, especially from Haifa and Jaffa, towns destined to be in the future Jewish state, and from neighbourhoods of Jewish West Jerusalem. According to some, "flight proved infectious."[1] Household followed household, neighbour, neighbour, street, street and neighbourhood, neighbourhood – as later, village was to follow neighbouring village, in domino clusters. The prosperous and educated feared death or injury in the ever-spreading hostilities, the anarchy that attended the staged withdrawal of the British administration and security forces, the robberies and intimidation of the Arab militias and irregulars, plus the presumed unpleasant future that awaited them under Jewish or, potentially also under Husseini rule. Some of these considerations, as well as a variety of direct and indirect military pressures, also led during these months to the evacuation of most of the Arab rural communities in the predominantly Jewish coastal plain.[2] Most of the upper and middle class families, which moved from Jaffa, Haifa, Jerusalem, Ramle, Acre, and Tiberias to Damascus, Nablus, Amman, Beirut, Gaza and Cairo, probably thought their exile would be temporary. Besides the financial means necessary, many had wealthy

---

1   Benny Morris, *The Birth of the Palestinian Refugee Problem Revisited* (New York: Cambridge University Press, 2004), p. 590.
2   Ibid., pp. 125–130.

relatives and accommodation outside the country.[3] The urban masses and the *fellahin* (peasants), however, had nowhere to go, certainly not in comfort. For most of them, flight meant instant destitution – which obviously was not readily adopted. Yet the daily spectacle of abandonment by their members of upper classes, with its simultaneous progressive closure of businesses, shops, schools, law offices and medical clinics, and abandonment of public service posts, led to a steady erosion of morale, as well as to a cumulative loss of faith and trust in the world around them; their leaders were going or had gone, while the British were preparing to leave. As a result, the remaining urban masses and fellahin got the impression of being "left alone" to face the Zionist enemy.[4]

On a daily basis, over December 1947, January, February and March 1948, there were clashes along the fault-line between the two communities in the mixed towns, ambushes in the fields and on the roads, sniping, machine-gun fire, bomb attacks and occasional mortaring. Problems of movement and communication, unemployment and food distribution intensified, especially in the towns, as the hostilities extended. One cannot explain the mass exodus that followed without understanding the prevalence and depth of the general sense of collapse, of "falling apart" and of a centre that "cannot hold", that filled Palestine's Arabs, especially in the towns, by April 1948. In many places, it would take very little to cause the masses to pack up and flee.[5]

2.2 The Second Stage: The Mass Exodus from April to June 1948

Doubtlessly, the Haganah's adoption and implementation from December 1947 to March 1948 of a retaliatory strategy against Arab militia bases – which were mostly located in villages and urban neighbourhoods – resulted in civilian flight. However, judged from the

---

3   Simha Flapan, *The Birth of Israel: Myths and Realities* (New York: Pantheon Books, 1987), p. 89.
4   Morris, *The Birth of the Palestinian Refugee Problem Revisited*, pp. 130–33.
5   Ibid., p. 591. See also Flapan, *The Birth of Israel*, pp. 83–84.

documentation, it appears that the strategy was designed to punish, harm and deter militiamen, not to precipitate an exodus.[6] Palestinian society disintegrated under the impact of the Jewish military offensive that got under way in April 1948. Most villagers fled before or during the fighting; those who stayed put were almost invariably expelled – the exodus of the Palestinians was set in motion.

The second – and crucial – stage of the exodus stretched from April to June. During that period, the Haganah's, as well as Etzel's and Lehi's, offensives and counter-offensives of April to June 1948, the cumulative effect of the fears, deprivations, abandonment and devastation of the previous months, in both towns and villages, overcame the natural reluctance to abandon property and home in order to flee. The magnitude took many Jewish leaders by surprise.[7] As Arab military power was overwhelmingly neutralized and the Haganah demonstrated almost unchallenged superiority in successive battles, Palestinian morale collapsed, giving way to a general panic or a "psychosis of flight."[8] There was a chronological, one-to-one correspondence between the Jewish offensives and the flight of the bulk of the population from each town and district attacked.[9]

Often, the fall of villages harmed morale in neighbouring towns. Similarly, the fall of the towns and the flight of their population generated panic in the surrounding hinterlands.[10] For decades the villagers had looked to the towns for leadership; now they followed them into exile.

From April to June, Arab commanders and the Arab Higher Committee (AHC) ordered the evacuation of several dozen villages as well

---

6   This is based on a fundamental conclusion of Benny Morris, who so far did the most thorough research on the reasons for the refugees' flight. See Morris, *The Birth of the Palestinian Refugee Problem Revisited*, p. 592.

7   Flapan, *The Birth of Israel*, p. 83.

8   This wording was used in one IDF intelligence report. See Benny Morris, *The Birth of the Palestinian Refugee Problem, 1947–1949* (Cambridge: Cambridge University Press, 1988), p. 287.

9   Morris, *The Birth of the Palestinian Refugee Problem Revisited*, p. 591.

10   There are numerous examples for this phenomena: After Haifa, the flight came from Balad al Sheikh and Hawassa; after Jaffa came Salama, Kheiriya and Yazur; after Safed came Dhahiriya Tahta, Sammu'i and Meirun. See ibid., pp. 181–233.

as the removal of dependents from dozens more. The invading Arab armies also occasionally ordered whole villages to depart, in order to clear the prospective battle area.[11] In addition, Arab irregulars' commanders later in May intimidated villagers into leaving seven sites in the Galilee, apparently because they feared the villagers would acquiesce to Israeli rule.[12] Statements by the AHC announcing that "in a very short time the armies of our Arab sister countries will overrun Palestine (...) and they will settle account with the Jews"[13] were issued as a warning to the increasing number of Arabs who were willing to accept partition as irreversible and cease struggling against it. The underlying idea was than when the Arab armies came to retaliate for what the Jews did to the Arabs, such collaborators would become hostages in Jewish hands. In practice, however, the AHC statements boomeranged and further increased Arab panic and flight.[14]

However, there is also evidence that the AHC, broadcasting from Damascus, demanded that the population stay put and announced that Palestinians of military age must return from the Arab countries. All Arab officials in Palestine were also asked to remain at their posts.[15]

Yet overall such pleas had little impact, as they were outweighed by the cumulative effect of the Jewish side's tactics that ranged from economic and psychological warfare to a systematic ousting of the Arab population by the army.[16] The following analysis of the atrocity factor will provide further insight.

---

11 This included the Arab Legion order of 13 May for the temporary evacuation of villages north and east of Jerusalem for strategic reasons; villages were to remove their womenfolk and children to safer areas. See Morris, *The Birth of the Palestinian Refugee Problem, 1947–1949*, p. 288.
12 Ibid.
13 Flapan, The Birth of Israel, p. 86.
14 Ibid.
15 Ibid., p. 87.
16 Ibid.

2.3 The Atrocity Factor

From April and May[17] the "atrocity factor" played a major role in the exodus from certain areas: Arab villagers and townspeople, prompted by the fear that the Jews, if victorious, might commit savage acts, took flight.[18] The actual atrocities that were committed by Jewish forces (primarily at Deir Yassin[19]) reinforced such fears considerably, especially when magnified loudly and persistently in the Arab media, mainly by AHC spokesmen, for weeks thereafter.[20]

Apart from twenty cases of massacre, Jewish troops often randomly killed individual prisoners of war, farm workers in the fields and occasionally villagers who had stayed behind. Obviously such actions encouraged flight. There were also several dozen cases of rape, a crime viewed with particular horror in Arab societies. The fear of rape was prominent among Arabs, and this may in part account for the dispatch of women and girls out of active or potential combat zones and, in some measure, for the headlong flight of villages and urban neighbourhoods from April on.[21]

Jewish attack directly and indirectly triggered most of the exodus up to June 1948. Besides, in the case of several dozen villages, flight came as a result of direct expulsion orders and of psychological warfare ("whispering propaganda") designed to intimidate people into flight. Those villages were ordered or "advised" by the Haganah to evacuate

---

17　As well as in October and November again.

18　Flapan, The Birth of Israel, p. 89.

19　On the morning of 9 April, 1948, members of Etzel and Lehi, with help from the Haganah, attacked the Arab village Deir Yassin and subsequently committed a massacre among its population. At that time, everyone had an interest in publicizing a high Arab casualty figure: the Haganah, to tarnish the Etzel and Lehi; the Arabs and British, to blacken the Jews; the Etzel and Lehi, to provoke terror and frighten Arabs into fleeing the country. Thus in 1948 participants, observers, and journalists wrote that as many as 254 villagers were killed that day. Recent Arab and Jewish investigations, and supporting interviews, however, suggest that these numbers were an exaggeration and that the real number of Arab dead was 100–110. See Benny Morris, *Righteous Victims: A History of the Zionist-Arab Conflict, 1881–2001* (New York: Vintage Books, 2001), pp. 207–209; Flapan, The Birth of Israel, p. 94.

20　Morris, *The Birth of the Palestinian Refugee Problem, 1947–1949*, p. 288.

21　Morris, *The Birth of the Palestinian Refugee Problem Revisited*, p. 592.

during April to June. The expulsions were usually from areas considered strategically vital and in conformity with Plan D, which called for clear main lines of communications and border areas (see 2.3.1). However, in general, Haganah and IDF commanders were not forced to confront the moral dilemma posed by expulsion, since most Arabs fled before and during battle, before the Israeli troops reached their homes.[22]

2.3.1 The Jewish Role in the Palestinian Exodus up to June 1948

The so-called "Plan D" is central to analysing the Jewish role in the Arab exodus. Prepared by the Haganah chiefs in early March 1948, it was created to be an answer to both several defeats at the hand of Palestinian irregulars,[23] as well as the prospect of pan-Arab invasion, and constituted a switch from defence to offence. The aim of Plan D was to secure all the areas allocated to the Jewish state under the U.N. partition resolution as well as Jewish settlements outside these areas and corridors leading to them, so as to provide a solid and continuous basis for Jewish sovereignty. The novelty of the plan lay in the orders to capture Arab villages and cities – something the Haganah had never attempted before. Many villages served as bases for bands of irregulars; most had militias that periodically assisted the irregulars in attacks on settlements and convoys. Although the wording of Plan D was vague, its objective was to clear the interior of the country of a hostile or potentially hostile Arab population; in this sense it provided a warrant for expelling civilians. Thus by implementing Plan D in April and May, the Jewish forces – primarily the Haganah – directly and decisively contributed to the birth of the Palestinian refugee problem.[24]

---

22 Ibid., pp. 591–92; Flapan, *The Birth of Israel*, p. 96.
23 In February, the Palestinian irregulars under the leadership of Abdel Qader al-Husseini had cut the main road between Tel Aviv and Jerusalem, and had started to gain the upper hand in the fighting with the Haganah.
24 Avi Shlaim, *The Iron Wall: Israel and the Arab World* (New York: Norton & Company, 2000), p. 31.

There is a debate among researchers whether or not Plan D was a political blueprint/master-plan for the expulsion of Palestine's Arabs.[25] This amounts to the question whether it was a purely military plan with merely military and territorial objectives, or whether it also had a political component, namely assuring only a minimal Arab minority in the future Israeli state.[26] There is consensus, however, that by ordering the capture of Arab cities and the destruction of villages, Plan D both permitted and justified the forcible expulsion of Arab civilians. Plan D was, therefore, a major cause for the exodus, for it was strategically driven by the notion of creating Jewish contiguity even beyond partition lines and, thus, by the desire to have a Jewish state with the smallest possible number of Arabs.[27]

To Ben Gurion the war was just about the physical survival of a small Jewish state, it was about the conquest, the possession and the settlement of the land. Plan D was about enlarging the borders of partition and creating a contiguity of Jewish populated land. Operations Yoav and Hiram were conducted in the winter of 1948 when, for all practical purposes, Israel had won the war for survival and now it needed new lands and greater strategic depth. Ben Gurion instructed that abandoned Arab villages needed to be settled by Jews even before the end of hostilities. Settling the land in a way that created Jewish contiguity and demographic superiority was not an endeavour to be undertaken after victory. Rather, it was part of war of the war itself. Villages were destroyed, their populations either fled or were evicted, and their lands were settled by immigrants or cultivated by kibbutzim

---

25 Among those who claim that Plan D was not a blueprint for expulsion are foremost Morris, *The Birth of the Palestinian Refugee Problem Revisited*, p. 164; further Shlaim, *The Iron Wall*, p. 31; Issa Khalaf, *Politics in Palestine: Arab Factionalism and Social Disintegration, 1939–1948* (Albany, N.Y.: State University of New York Press, 1991), p. 214. Arguing the opposite are Ilan Pappe, *A History of Modern Palestine: One Land, Two Peoples* (Cambridge: Cambridge University Press, 2004), pp. 129–31; Walid Khalidi, "Plan Dalet: Master Plan for the Conquest of Palestine," *Journal of Palestine Studies*, Vol. XVIII, No. 1, Autumn 1988, pp. 3–70; Nur Masalha, "The Historical Roots of the Palestinian Refugee Question," in Naseer Aruri, ed., *Palestinian Refugees: The Right of Return* (London: Pluto Press, 2001), pp. 43–45.

26 Flapan, *The Birth of Israel*, p. 103.

27 Ben-Ami, *Scars of War*, p. 44.

in the course of the war itself. In Ben Gurion's words in April 1948: "We will not be able to win the war if we do not, *during the war*, populate Upper and Lower, Eastern and Western Galilee, the Negev and the Jerusalem area."[28] He concluded that this would be facilitated by the "great change in the distribution of the Arab population", a euphemism used by Ben Gurion.[29]

Thus, on the one hand, neither the political nor military leaderships took a concrete decision to expel the Arab population. As far as the available evidence shows, the matter was never discussed in the supreme decision-making body.[30] Yet, on the other hand, it was understood at the same time by all concerned that the fewer Arab residents remained in the Jewish state, the easier would be the military struggle to secure that state whose fate still hung in the balance.

2.3.2 The Arab Role in the Palestinian Exodus up to June 1948

The Arab leadership inside and outside Palestine probably helped to catalyse the flight in the sense that, while doctrinally opposed to the exodus, it was disunited and ineffectual. From the start, it had decided on no fixed, uniform policy and gave the masses no consistent guidelines for behaviour, especially during the crucial month of April 1948. The records are incomplete, yet they do show overwhelming confusion and disparate purpose, in parallel to policies and implementation changing on a weekly basis, differing in various areas. There was neither any central control, nor an overarching policy manifest.[31]

During the months before April 1948, especially in March, the flight of the middle and upper classes from the towns had provoked condemnations from local National Committees (NCs) and the Arab Higher Committee – while simultaneously NC members and their families were themselves fleeing their homes or already living abroad. In general, little was done to prevent flight. In addition, the surround-

---

28   Cited in ibid., p. 45.
29   Ibid.
30   Morris, *The Birth of the Palestinian Refugee Problem Revisited*, p. 593.
31   Ibid.

ing Arab states did little, before late March, to block the entry of the evacuees into their territory. The rich and middle class arrived in the surrounding capitals and were not needy; it seemed to be merely a repeat of the exodus of 1936–1939. No Arab country effectively closed its borders, although at the end of March, Syria and Lebanon severely curtailed the issue of entry visas. It is reasonable to assume that the Husseinis did not dislike the departure of many Opposition-linked families. The AHC, having almost all its members already dispersed abroad, issued no forceful public condemnations of the exodus, though occasionally it requested – without enforcing – army-aged males to remain or return, and fight. At the local level, some NCs and local commanders tried to stem the exodus, even setting up people's courts to try offenders, threatening confiscation of the departees' property. Yet enforcement seems to have been weak and unsystematic, thus the measures proved largely unavailing. Plus, bribes could overwhelm any regulation: Militiamen and irregulars had an interest in encouraging the flight – they needed the houses for quarters and there was a profit to be made out of it, since money was extorted from departees to have their empty homes "protected" while abandoned houses were looted.[32]

No evidence has been found that the AHC or the Arab leaders out-side of Palestine issued blanket instructions, by radio or otherwise, to the inhabitants to flee. However, during the start of the main stage of the exodus in April and May 1948, in certain areas, women, children and old people continued to be evacuated and entire populations of specific villages were instructed by their leaders to depart. Moreover, it appears that Husseini supporters in some areas ordered or encour-aged flight out of political calculation, believing that they were doing what the AHC expected them to do: to opt for evacuation rather than surrender, since staying would be interpreted as acquiescence in Jewish rule (amounting to treachery), and by the calculation that Palestinian misery born of the exodus would increase the pressure on the Arab states to intervene.[33] The fact that local and AHC leaders believed that the evacuation was temporary and that a mass return would soon follow

---

32 Ibid., pp. 593–94.
33 Morris illustrates this conclusion with the case of Haifa. According to him, while it was unlikely that Husseini or AHC members from outside Palestine instructed the Haifa Arab leadership on 22 April to opt for evacuation, local

helps explaining the ambivalence of the national and local Palestinian leaderships toward the exodus.

The Arab states, apart from appealing to the British to halt the Haganah offensives and charging that the Haganah was expelling Arabs, apparently took weeks to fully grasp what was happening. They did not appeal to the Palestinian masses to leave, but neither, in April, did they demand that the Palestinians stay put. Possibly Husseini and other Arab politicians realized that they would need a good reason to justify armed intervention in Palestine following British departure; the mass exodus, presented as a planned Zionist expulsion, certainly did afford such a reason.[34]

2.3.3 Jewish Reactions to the Palestinian Exodus

Already in April and May 1948, on the local and national levels, the Yishuv's leadership began to contemplate the issue of a return: Should the refugees be allowed back? The Arab states had begun pressing for Israel to allow the return of the refugees. The U.N. Mediator, Bernadotte, had energetically taken up the cause.

However, there was a political and military consensus in freshly proclaimed Israel against return. Militarily, with the war being far from over, the Israelis feared that return would mean the introduction of a large, potential fifth column. Politically, the reintroduction of a large, possibly disruptive, Arab minority was seen negatively regarding the future of a democratic Jewish state. As a result, military as well as political leaders argued against a return; both were reinforced by strident anti-return lobbying by Jewish settlements around the country.[35]

Husseini supporters, led by Sheikh Murad, certainly did. See Morris, *The Birth of the Palestinian Refugee Problem Revisited*, p. 594.

34 Morris, *The Birth of the Palestinian Refugee Problem, 1947–1949*, p. 290.
35 Ibid., p. 291.

2.3.4 Arab Reactions to the Palestinian Exodus

The dimensions and burden of the problem created by the exodus, necessarily and initially falling upon the shoulders of the host countries, quickly persuaded the Arab states – primarily Jordan – that it was best to halt the flood of refugees. The same conclusion was reached by the AHC which was severely troubled by the ease and completeness of the exodus. Consequently, a spate of appeals to the Palestinians followed in early May by Jordan, the AHC and the Arab Liberation Army (ALA)[36] to remain in place or, if already in exile, to return home. Yet, given the ongoing hostilities and the expectation of a dramatic increase in warfare along the fronts, the appeals had little effect: Refugees, who had just left active combat zones, hardly intended to return to them, especially on the eve of the invasion. Besides, in most areas the Haganah physically barred a return.[37]

***

In the warfare with Palestinian and foreign Arab irregulars, the Jewish forces initially acted strictly defensive. Yet from April 1948, the Haganah increasingly turned to the offensive in order to gain strategic control over the dis-contiguous area of Jewish settlement, expecting the imminent invasion of the surrounding Arab armies. This shift to the offensive, on the other hand, coupled with the growing stream of Arab refugees, made such an invasion of the Arab states, which felt the obligation to come to the help of their distressed brethren, almost inevitable – a vicious circle had started and was to increase.

Subsequently, the Arab invasion on 15 May 1948 and the widespread fighting made any thought of a refugee return impracticable. At the same time, the invasion substantially increased the readiness of Haganah commanders to clear border areas of Arab communities – and given the narrow, elongated shape of the new state, every area was in effect a border area.[38]

---

36   The ALA was a force of foreign Arab volunteers.
37   Morris, *The Birth of the Palestinian Refugee Problem, 1947–1949*, p. 290.
38   Morris, *The Birth of the Palestinian Refugee Problem Revisited*, pp. 594–95.

In sum, from spring 1948, a series of developments on the ground increasingly precluded any possibility of a refugee return; it was a combination of both incidental, "natural" processes and steps specifically designed to assure the infeasibility of a return, including the gradual destruction of abandoned villages, the destruction or cultivation and long-term takeover of Arab fields, the establishment of new settlements on Arab lands, and the settlement of new immigrants in abandoned villages and urban neighbourhoods.[39]

2.4 The Third Stage: The "Ten Days" of July 1948

A first truce, which had lasted thirty days, ended on 8 July 1948 and the IDF shifted to the offensive on the three fronts. In the north, the IDF conquered parts of Western Galilee and the Lower Galilee. In the south, the IDF failed to secure a corridor to the besieged Negev settlements but widened its hold on the northern Negev. The main thrust was in the centre of the country, where Operation Dani was designed to fully open and secure the vital Tel Aviv-Jerusalem road and to push back the Arab Legion from the vicinity of Tel Aviv by conquering the Towns of Lydda and Ramle and, in a second phase, Latrun and Ramallah, which dominated the highway. Operation Dani attained only its first objectives, with the IDF overrunning the Lydda-Ramle plain, which included Lydda Airport.[40]

The IDF operations of 9–18 July were triggered by the Arab armies' disinterest in prolonging the 30–day truce and, in the south, by Egyptian pre-emptive attacks on 8 July. This period became to be known as the "Ten Days" and resulted in the third wave of Palestinian refugees; they primarily fled to Jordanian-held eastern Palestine, and to Upper Galilee, Lebanon and the Egyptian-held Gaza Strip.[41]

---

39 For more information on Israel's policies toward abandoned Arab property, see Michael Fischbach, *Records of Dispossession: Palestinian Refugee Property and the Arab-Israeli Conflict* (New York: Columbia University Press, 2003), pp. 1–80.

40 Morris, *The Birth of the Palestinian Refugee Problem, 1947–1949*, p. 197.

41 Morris, *The Birth of the Palestinian Refugee Problem Revisited*, p. 414.

Again, there was no cabinet or Israeli Defence Forces (IDF) general staff decision to expel. In fact, the July fighting was preceded by an explicit IDF general staff order to all units to refrain from destruction of villages and expulsions without prior authorization by the Defence Minister. The order was issued as a result of the cumulative political pressure during the summer by some of the ministers on Ben Gurion.[42] Perhaps the order was never intended to be taken seriously – in any event, it was largely ignored.[43]

During the "Ten Days", Ben Gurion and the IDF were largely left on their own to decide and execute policy toward conquered Arab communities, without interference or instruction by the Cabinet or the ministries. That policy was inconsistent, circumstantial and haphazard. The outcome – different results in different places – was determined by a combination of factors, mainly the religious and ethnic identity of the conquered populations, specific local strategic and tactical considerations and circumstances, Ben Gurion's view on the cases brought, the amount and quality of resistance offered in each area, and the character and inclinations of particular IDF commanders. As a result of the "Ten Days", the Ramle-Lydda and Tel as Safi areas were almost completely emptied of their Arab populations, while in Western and Lower Galilee the bulk of the Christian and Druse inhabitants as well as many Muslims stayed put and were allowed to remain in place.[44]

***

From July onwards, there was a growing readiness in the IDF units to expel Arab civilians. This was at least partially due to the political feeling, encouraged by the mass exodus from Jewish-held areas to date, that an almost completely Jewish state was a realistic possibility. There were also powerful vengeful urges at play: revenge for Jewish losses and punishment for having forced upon the Yishuv and its able-bodied

---

42 Pressure in favour of the order had come from the Mapam ministers and the minister for Minority Affairs Bechor Shitrit. See Morris, *The Birth of the Palestinian Refugee Problem, 1947–1949*, p. 292.

43 See Morris, *The Birth of the Palestinian Refugee Problem Revisited*, pp. 352–53.

44 Ibid., p. 415.

young men the protracted, bitter battle. This, coupled with the Arab rejection of the partition proposal, led the Yishuv's leadership from left to right to perceive the prospect of a large Arab population inside the state as fatal. Finally, causing the Arab population to flee from each successive newly-conquered area had become an easy undertaking.[45]

The tendency of IDF units to expel civilians increased, just as did the pressures on the remaining Arabs by their leaders inside and outside of Palestine to stay put, and as did the motivation of the remaining Arabs to stand fast. During the summer, the governments of the surrounding Arab states intermittently tried to bar the entry of new refugees into their territory. The Palestinians were encouraged to stay in Palestine or – those who had already left – to return to their homes. At the same time, those Palestinians still in their villages, hearing of the misery that was the lot of their exiled brethren and hardly further believing in the prospect of salvation by an Arab reconquest of Palestine, generally preferred to stay put, despite the prospect of Israeli rule. Therefore, after July, Arab resistance to flight was far greater than before, which resulted in much less "spontaneous" flight; villagers tended either to remain in place or to leave under duress.[46]

It is reasonable to assume that Ben Gurion clearly wanted as few Arabs as possible in the Jewish state. From early on he hoped that they would flee. He hinted at this in February 1948 and said so explicitly in meetings in August, September and October. Yet no expulsion policy was ever clearly formulated and Ben Gurion always refrained from issuing clear or written expulsion orders – he preferred that his generals "understand" what he wanted done. He wished to avoid going down in history as the "great expeller" and did not want his government to be blamed for a morally questionable policy. Plus he sought to preserve national unity in wartime.[47]

However, while there was no "expulsion policy", the July offensives were characterized by far more expulsions and, indeed, brutality than the first half of the war. Yet events varied from place to place. While Ben Gurion approved the largest expulsion of the war (Lydda and

---

45 See ibid., p. 596.
46 Morris, *The Birth of the Palestinian Refugee Problem, 1947–1949*, p. 292.
47 Ibid., pp. 292–93.

Ramle),[48] the IDF's northern front, with Ben Gurion's authorization, left Nazareth's population, which was mostly Christian, in place, in accordance with a general policy of treating the Christian Arabs favourably. In the centre of the country, three Arab villages (Fureidis, Jisr az Zarka and Abu Gosh), although located upon vital axes, were allowed to stay.[49]

2.5 The Fourth Stage: October and November 1948

The months between the end of the first truce, on 8 July 1948, and the signing of the Arab-Israeli armistice agreement in spring and summer 1949 had been characterised by short, sharp Israeli offensives combined with long periods of ceasefire. In these offensives, Israel defeated the Jordanian and Egyptian armies and the ALA in the Galilee, and conquered large parts of the territory allocated by the U.N. for a Palestine Arab state. During and after these battles in July, October-November and December 1948, around 300,000 more Palestinians became refugees.[50]

Just as in July, the IDF offensives in October and November 1948 were also characterized by a degree of ambivalence regarding the troops' treatment of civilian populations in conquered territories. In the south, where Yigal Allon was in command, almost no Arab civilians remained. Allon preferred rear areas without an Arab population, and he let his subordinates know what he wanted. In the north, where Moshe Carmel was in charge, the situation was different. Many Arabs in the upper Galilee did not flee, contrary to Ben Gurion's expectations. This was partly due to the fact that before October, the villagers had hardly been touched by the war or its hardships. Also the varied religious make-up of the population contributed to the mixed picture. The IDF generally related far more benignly to Christians and Druse than to

---

48 Flapan, *The Birth of Israel*, p. 100.
49 The reasons that these villages were allowed to stay were both economical and sentimental, as all three villages had longstanding commercial and personal connections with the Yishuv. Morris, *The Birth of the Palestinian Refugee Problem Revisited*, p. 597.
50 Flapan, *The Birth of Israel*, p. 101.

Muslims, resulting in most Christian and Druse villagers staying put and being allowed to do so. Many of the Muslim villagers fled – either out of their own accord or by force. However, in some places inhabited by Muslims (like Deir Hanna, Arraba, Sakhnin, Majd al Kurum), the villagers stayed put, and were allowed to stay. In general, specific local factors played a crucial role.[51]

During the following months, with the Cabinet in Tel Aviv convinced that the Israeli-Arab enmity would remain a central feature of the Middle East for many years, the Israeli army was authorized to clear Arab communities from Israel's long, winding and highly penetrable borders to a depth of five to fifteen kilometres. One of the aims was to prevent infiltration of refugees back to their homes. The Israeli army also feared sabotage and spying. Early November saw a wave of IDF expulsions and transfers inland of villagers along the northern border.

Such was the case with Bir-Am, a Christian village on the Lebanese border known for its excellent relations with their Jewish neighbours, and a number of other villages in northern Galilee, e.g. Nebi Rubin, Tarbiha, and Ikrit. The inhabitants of those villages were evacuated southward for security reasons. Originally the army had intended to evacuate them to Lebanon but a Jewish friend intervened, appealing to the military governor and to the minister for minorities, Behor Shitreet. As a result, the order was changed to a temporary evacuation of the village for two weeks, to Jish, a village situated further south. Ben Gurion noted in his diary on 16 November, 1948, that Moshe Carmel, commander in chief in the north, who executed the eviction, spread several thousand Arabs from these villages over other parts of the Galilee. Carmel justified his action on military grounds, then promised to stop it, yet added that he could not allow the villagers to return. The reason given was the necessity of imposing a curfew on the northern border, because of the war.[52]

51 Morris, *The Birth of the Palestinian Refugee Problem Revisited*, pp. 473–90.
52 See 16 November in David Ben Gurion, *War Diaries*, (Hebrew), (Tel Aviv, 1982), 3 Vols., ed. G. Rivlin and E. Orren, p. 828 cited in Simha Flapan, *The Birth of Israel: Myths and Realities* (New York: Pantheon Books, 1987), 115.

Also some other villagers to be ordered out were spared by last-minute interventions of dovish Israeli politicians, as in the case of Jish, Tarshiha, Fassuta, Mi'ilya, Hurfeish and Rihaniya. Nevertheless, in the following months and years, other border areas were cleared or partially cleared of Arab inhabitants, which precipitated the flight of roughly another 200,000 to 230,000 refugees.[53]

2.6 Socio-economic Factors

There were distinct waves of Palestinians fleeing their homes, and the refugees can be divided into socio-economic categories. The so-called "middle class refugees" from the towns and cities constituted the first wave of the refugee exodus. They fled as the fighting between Jewish and Arab military organizations began to escalate shortly after the U.N.'s Partition Resolution. Wealthier Palestinians in towns either consisting of mixed Arab-Jewish populations or immediately adjacent to Jewish communities began leaving their homes and property for the safety of surrounding Arab cities like Cairo and Beirut as early as December 1947. That month saw the first movement of urban dwellers from Haifa and Jaffa, followed by an exodus from the Qatamon district in western Jerusalem in January 1948. The sharp escalation of urban fighting in mixed towns by the spring of 1948 prompted further departures, especially after the Jewish forces gained control over Haifa on 21–22 April 1948.[54]

Many of these urban dwellers were quite wealthy. They left behind not only luxurious homes equipped with expensive furniture and other consumer goods but also shops, warehouses, factories, machinery, and other commercial property. This was in addition to financial assets like bank accounts and valuables such as securities held in safe deposit boxes in banks. None felt that their departure was anything more than a temporary move away from a war zone.[55]

---

53   Morris, *The Birth of the Palestinian Refugee Problem Revisited*, pp. 505–536.
54   Michael Fischbach, *Records of Dispossession: Palestinian Refugee Property and the Arab-Israeli Conflict* (New York: Columbia University Press, 2003), pp. 1–2.
55   Ibid., p. 2.

The other sector of the refugee population were the villagers from the countryside. In many ways the greatest impetus for the refugee flight came when Zionist forces initiated a full-scale offensive in the spring of 1948 against Palestinian villages that lay outside of the area that the U.N. partition plan had assigned to the designated Arab state. As the fighting spread, Palestinian villagers began to leave an environment characterized by mutual violence, atrocities against civilian populations, and fear.

By 1 May, 1948, 100,000 persons had fled the civil war between Jewish and Arab Palestinian fighters, the latter assisted by the Arab Liberation Army. The large-scale fighting between Israeli and Arab armies that began in mid-May 1948 and eventually lasted until armistice agreements were signed in 1949 created a wave of hundreds of thousands of refugees who fled into Lebanon, Syria, Jordan, the West Bank and Gaza, as well as Egypt, Iraq, and beyond. While middle- and upper-class Palestinian urbanites moved in with relatives or rented new accommodation, the poor were relegated to refugee camps.[56]

2.7 The Exodus: A Result of Multiple Causation

The analysis above shows that there is no single explanation of the causes leading to the Arab exodus from Palestine from 1947 to 1949. In fact, the exodus occurred in stages and its causation was multilayered. Thus, a Haifa merchant did not leave only because of the weeks or months of sniping and bombing; or because business was getting bad; or because of intimidation and extortion by Arab irregulars; or because he feared for his prospects and livelihood under Jewish rule. Rather he left because of the accumulation of all these factors. Just as the mass of Haifaites who fled in his wake, at the end of April to early May 1948, did not flee only as a result of the collapse of the Arab militia and the Haganah conquest of 21–22 April: They rather fled because of the cumulative effect of the elite's early departure, the snipings and bombings and material deprivations, unemployment and chaos during the previous months; and because of their local leaders' instructions

---

56   Ibid., pp. 2–3.

to leave, issued on 22 April 1948; and because of the follow up orders by the AHC to continue departing; and because of Etzel and Haganah activities and pressures during the days after the conquest; and because of the prospect of life under Jewish rule.[57]

The situation was somewhat more clear-cut in the countryside. Yet there, too, multiple causation often applied; such as in the case of Qaluniya, a village near Jerusalem. There were months of hostilities in the area, sporadic shortages of supplies, disconnection of communications with Jerusalem, lack of leadership or clear instructions about what to do or expect, lack of sustained help from outside, rumours of impending Jewish assault, Jewish offences on neighbouring villages and reports of Jewish atrocities, and, finally, a Jewish attack on Qaluniya itself – after most of its inhabitants had already left. Again, evacuation was the end product of a cumulative process.[58]

Even in the case of a Haganah or IDF expulsion order, the actual departure was often the result of a process rather than of that single act. This is illustrated by the case of Lydda, which had been largely untouched by battle before July 1948. During the first months of the war, Lydda suffered from unemployment and skyrocketing prices, coupled with the burden of armed irregulars. In April and May, thousands of refugees from Jaffa and its hinterland arrived in the town, camping out in the courtyards and on the town's periphery, bringing demoralization and sickness. Some wealthy families left. There were pinprick Haganah raids. There was uncertainty about Abdullah's commitment to the town's defence. In June, an atmosphere of Lydda's "fall" was imminent. Then came the Jewish attack, resulting in bombing and shelling, the Arab Legion's pullout, the collapse of resistance, sniping, massacre – and expulsion orders. Eventually, Lydda was evacuated.[59]

In sum, the Palestinian exodus cannot be separated from the broader historical and political contexts in which the two peoples operated. For the *Yishuv/Israel*, the key factor was the still-recent Holocaust and the genuine fear that the Palestinian Arabs and/or the Arab states could perpetrate a similar massacre in the Middle East. As for *Palestine's Arabs*, the principle and realistic concern was that rising Jewish immi-

---

57 Morris, *The Birth of the Palestinian Refugee Problem Revisited*, p. 598.
58 Morris, *The Birth of the Palestinian Refugee Problem, 1947–1949*, p. 294.
59 Morris, *The Birth of the Palestinian Refugee Problem Revisited*, pp. 598–99.

gration from Europe and elsewhere would rob them of their national inheritance.[60] Overall, what happened in Palestine/Israel over 1947 to 1949 was so complex and varied, the situation radically changing from date to date and place to place, that any single-cause explanation of the exodus from most sites would be flawed. At most, one can say that certain causes were dominant in certain areas at certain times, with a general shift in the spring of 1948 from a precedence of cumulative internal Arab factors – lack of leadership, economic problems, collapse of law and order – to a primacy of external, compulsive causes: Haganah/IDF attacks and expulsions, fear of Jewish attacks and atrocities, lack of help from the Arab world and the Arab Higher Committee thus resulting in a feeling of impotence and abandonment, and orders from Arab officials and commanders to leave. In general, throughout the war, the final and decisive catalyst to flight in most places were either the attacks by the Jewish militias respectively the IDF, or the inhabitants' fear of such attack being imminent.[61]

Issa Khalaf concludes that much of what happened in 1947–48 developed according to immediate circumstances. According to this view, it was doubtful that the Jews in Palestine expected that the country's Arabs could be easily pushed out or would even leave on their own. It was rather during the various phases of the war, when military fortunes accelerated in favour of the Jews, that the Yishuv's leadership increasingly did all it could do to facilitate the removal of Arabs or to resort to psychological warfare, violence, and physical expulsion.[62]

---

60 Philip Mendes, "A Historical Controversy: The Causes of the Palestinian Refugee Problem," in www.prrn.org.
61 Morris, *The Birth of the Palestinian Refugee Problem Revisited*, p. 599.
62 Issa Khalaf, *Politics in Palestine: Arab Factionalism and Social Disintegration, 1939–1948* (Albany, N.Y.: State University of New York Press, 1991), p. 214.

3   AFTER 1948

3.1 The Immediate Post-War Period

During the second half of 1948, international concern about the refugee problem mounted and eventually translated into pressure. The pressure, initiated by the U.N. mediator Bernadotte and the Arab states in the summer of 1948, increased over the following months, as the number of refugees swelled, their physical plight became more acute, and as the discomfort of their Arab hosts grew. The problem moved to the forefront of every discussion of the Middle East crisis and the Arab side made its agreement to a settlement with Israel contingent on a solution of the problem by repatriation.

From the summer of 1948, Bernadotte, and from the autumn, the United States pressed Israel to agree to a substantial measure of repatriation as part of a comprehensive solution to the refugee problem and the conflict as a whole. On 11 December 1948, the United Nations General Assembly passed *Resolution 194*. The resolution expresses appreciation for the efforts of Bernadotte who had been assassinated in September by members of Lehi. It deals with the situation in Palestine at that time, including the role of the United Nations Conciliation Commission for Palestine (UNCCP) which consisted of representatives from Turkey, the United States and France, and which was established for the primary purpose of resolving the Palestinian refugee crisis and seeking a solution for the Israeli-Palestinian problem in line with the partition recommendation.[1] The resolution consists of 15 articles, the most widely known being Article 11, which expresses support for the return of Palestinian refugees:

---

1   See Susan Akram, "Reinterpreting Palestinian Refugee Rights under International Law," in Naseer Aruri, ed., *Palestinian Refugees: The Right of Return* (London: Pluto Press, 2001), p. 169. For more information on the UNCCP, see Michael Fischbach, "The United Nations and Palestinian Refugee Property Compensation," *Journal of Palestine Studies*, Vol. XXXI, No. 2, Winter 2002, pp. 34–50.

11. Resolves that the refugees wishing to return to their homes and live at peace with their neighbours should be permitted to do so at the earliest practicable date, and that compensation should be paid for the property of those choosing not to return and for loss of or damage to property which, under principles of international law or in equity, should be made good by the Governments or authorities responsible;

Instructs the Conciliation Commission to facilitate the repatriation, resettlement and economic and social rehabilitation of the refugees and the payment of compensation, and to maintain close relations with the Director of the United Nations Relief for Palestine Refugees and, through him, with the appropriate organs and agencies of the United Nations.[2]

Other relevant Articles are 7 (protection and free access to the Holy Places), 8 (demilitarisation and U.N. control over Jerusalem) and 9 (free access to Jerusalem).[3]

Bernadotte and the United States wanted Israel to make a "gesture" along the lines of repatriation in order to get peace negotiations off the ground. In the spring of 1949, the idea of a "gesture" matured into an American demand for Israel to agree to take back 250,000, with the remaining refugees to be resettled in the neighbouring countries. The United States threatened and cajoled, yet never with sufficient determination to persuade Israel to comply.[4]

In a final major effort, the United Nations and United States, in the framework of the UNCCP, organized the Lausanne Peace Conference, which was to last, with breaks, from April to September 1949. Under pressure from the United States, and in view of Arab refusal to discuss agreed borders until the refugee issue had been resolved, the Ben Gurion government reluctantly agreed to propose absorbing 100,000 refugees (the "100,000 offer"). This number would have included some

---

2   See UNGAR 194 in Laqueur and Rubin, *The Israeli-Arab Reader*, pp. 83–86.
3   Contrary to some Security Council Resolutions, U.N. General Assembly Resolutions have only a recommendatory character, according to the U.N. Charter. Egypt, Iraq, Lebanon, Saudi Arabia, Syria and Yemen voted against UNGAR 194. Many articles in the resolution have been ignored by all parties involved: Israel abides by Article 7, but Article 11 has not been implemented. Since the late 1960s, the resolution (only Article 11, to be precise) has been increasingly quoted by the Arab side, which has interpreted it as a *right of return* of the Palestinian refugees.
4   Benny Morris, *The Birth of the Palestinian Refugee Problem Revisited* (New York: Cambridge University Press, 2004), pp. 549–61.

35,000 refugees whose return had already been negotiated and was underway. Israel's decision was made conditional upon Arab agreement to a comprehensive peace, including resettlement of the remaining refugees in Arab countries and allowing Israel to keep all the territory it had captured.[5]

Discussion within the Israeli government at the time also touched upon the possibility of absorbing a larger number of refugees, on condition that the Gaza Strip – with some of its refugee population – would be transferred from Egyptian to Israeli control; Israel would thus be considered to have fulfilled its part in refugee repatriation and additionally improve its military security situation vis-à-vis Egypt.[6] Ultimately the Arabs rejected the two Israeli offers, while also the United States had regarded them as highly insufficient, criticising it for giving too little too late. Israel subsequently retracted them, after in addition to the rejection by the other parties also public and party political opinion in Israel had hardened against even these minimal offers of return.[7] In fact, it is reasonable to assume that Israel never had any intention of implementing the "100,000 offer" which in any event was greeted by a storm of public opposition and a heated Knesset (the Israeli parliament) debate which underlined for Ben Gurion, and all successive governments, the Israeli society's fierce opposition to the *right of return*.[8]

Meanwhile, the physical possibility of substantial repatriation grew more remote, as the abandoned villages fell into decrepitude, or were bulldozed, or settled with Jewish immigrants, who were pouring into the country and were accommodated in abandoned Arab houses. Allowing back Arab refugees, Israel argued, would commensurately reduce Israel's ability to absorb Jewish refugees from Europe and the Middle East. Time worked against repatriation. On 16 June, 1948 the Israeli government decided that the refugees would not be permitted to return to their homes but that Israel would be prepared to pay compensation for their abandoned property.[9] However, two years later, by

---

5   For more information on the "100,000 offer", see ibid. pp. 570–80.
6   For more details about the "Gaza Plan", see ibid., pp. 561–70.
7   Ibid., p. 600.
8   Shelly Fried, "The Refugee Issue at the Peace Conferences, 1949–2000," *Palestine-Israel Journal*, Vol. 9, No. 2, 2002, p. 25.
9   Ibid., p. 24.

passing the Absentees' Property Law, the Israeli government cleared the way for an extensive confiscation of the refugees' property. That law nullified all rights to property, residence and citizenship in Israel for all Palestinians who were not physically within the state's borders at that time.[10]

Two more rounds of talks – at the beginning of 1950 and in the fall of 1951 – ended in failure and the UNCCP disappeared into oblivion.[11] Attempts at mediation and direct talks between Israel on the one hand, and Jordan, Egypt and Syria (separately) on the other, also proved futile.[12]

It was Israel's formal rejection of the refugees' claim for return – a position that remains valid to this day – rather than the expulsion and the dispossession, which was the actual defining moment of the conflict. Fleeing refugees, even their dispossession, has throughout history been a steady concomitant of war, and in many cases they were allowed to return once the hostilities ceased. Yet the crucial issue this time lay in the refusal to even consider their return. The new state could not reconcile its existence with a massive return of refugees. To this day, the question of return remains a central bone of contention in the conflict. For the Palestinians, it continues to be a vital belief, a defining principle of their national identity, and their unifying collective dream. For the Israelis it was and continues to be anathema, raising existential fears regarding the survival of the Jewish state.[13]

In sum, the insufficiency of the "100,000" offer coupled with Israel's general unwillingness to repatriate the Palestinian refugees, plus the Arab states' growing rejectionism, their unwillingness to concede defeat, as well as their unwillingness and inability to absorb and resettle most of the refugees if Israel agreed to repatriate the rest, paired with the United States' unwillingness or inability to apply persuasive

---

10 The Absentees' Property Law of 5710/1950 was the single most important piece of Israeli legislation dealing with refugee land and was passed by the Knesset on 14 March, 1950. For further information, see Fischbach, *Records of Dispossession*, pp. 21–25; Flapan, *The Birth of Israel*, pp. 106–07.

11 These talks will be treated in more detail in chapter 8.

12 Yoav Gelber, "The Historical Background," in Joseph Ginat and Edward Perkins, eds., *The Palestinian Refugees: Old Problems – New Solutions* (Brighton: Sussex Academic Press, 2001), p. 29.

13 Ben-Ami, *Scars of War*, pp. 46–47.

pressure on Israel and the Arab states to compromise; all those factors meant that the Arab-Israeli impasse would remain and that Palestine's displaced Arabs would remain refugees, ignored by Israel and utilized by the Arab states as political and propaganda pawns[14] – the refugees themselves obviously being the ultimate bereaved ones.

The memory of 1948, followed by decades of humiliation and deprivation in the refugee camps, upheld the hostility of following generations of Palestinians towards Israel. Meanwhile, the Israeli-Palestinian conflict has become one of the world's most intractable ones; and at the core of that problem remains the issue of refugees.

3.2 1967: A Further Wave of Refugees

During the period from 1949 to 1967, the Palestinians receded from the political scene. Those who remained in Israel, as well as those who returned legally or illegally in the first years after the war, became Israeli citizens. The indigenous Palestinians on the West Bank and the refugees on both banks were incorporated into Jordan, which granted them full citizenship. There were also "Egyptian" Palestinians in the Gaza Strip as well as "Syrian" and "Lebanese" Palestinians in refugee camps in Syria and Lebanon – all without recognized citizenship.[15] The concept "Palestinian" as such vanished from the international community's public awareness, unless it was linked to the word "refugee."[16]

Only in the wake of the Six Day War did the Palestinians re-enter the political arena under their own banner. Since Israel occupied the West Bank and Gaza Strip but did not annex them, the inhabitants of these areas ceased to be "Jordanian" and "Egyptian" but did not become "Israeli." They reappeared as simply "Palestinians" – a term that had been forgotten for eighteen years. After relations between Israel and the Arab states stabilized in the wake of the Yom Kippur war in 1973,

---

14 Regarding Palestinian refugees in Lebanon, see Ulrike Koltermann, "Who really wants them? Palestinians in Lebanon fed up with being a bargaining chip," *The Jerusalem Times*, 27 June 1997.

15 More information on the situation of Palestinian refugees in their various countries of residence will follow in the fifth chapter.

16 See Gelber, "The Historical Background," p. 29.

the entire issue of the Palestinian question returned to the centre of the Arab-Israeli conflict.[17]

In the aftermath of the Six Day War of 1967, another 300,000 Palestinians fled from the West Bank and Gaza to Jordan (200,000), Syria, Egypt and elsewhere; they are considered "displaced persons". Of these, approximately 180,000 were first-time refugees, while the remainder were 1948 refugees uprooted for the second time.[18]

While it is not unusual for a civilian population to flee from areas of armed conflict, it is known that in the Gaza Strip, refugee flight was actively encouraged by Israel in summer 1967. Moshe Goren, Major General of the reserve forces and appointed as Governor of Gaza, recalls that namely Major General Gavish gave the order to put as many Palestinians as possible on buses to Egypt.[19] Tens of thousands of people (the *Frankfurter Rundschau* estimates between 30,000 and 40,000) were subsequently put on boats in the area of the Suez Canal.[20] In Mudai's own words, he would well have been ready to transfer the Gaza Strip's entire population, yet that was a) impossible and b) such an order was never given.[21]

Israel further conducted a census in the West Bank and the Gaza Strip after the war. It was ruled that only those present on that day were entitled to receive a confirmation affirming their official residence in those areas. Any person who was outside the West Bank and Gaza Strip during the war, was not registered. In addition, those people who had never heard of a census did not understand the guide-lines and consequently were intimidated and confused. Some concealed their sons; some were analphabetic and were not able to check whether their name was registered properly. The most dominant source of confusion and chaos was the fact that in the Arab culture, there are various definitions of a family name.[22]

---

17 Ibid.
18 See www.arts.mcgill.ca/mepp/new_prrn/background/index.htm.
19 Ruvik Rosenthal, „Die Euphorie in dem langen, heissen Sommer nach dem Juni-Krieg," *Frankfurter Rundschau*, 6 June 1997, p. 18.
20 It so happened that the Egyptians opened fire on these boats filled with Palestinians refugees; in such cases the Israelis fired back. See ibid.
21 Ibid.
22 See Harald Neifeind, *Der Nahostkonflikt – historisch, politisch, literarisch* (Schwalbach: Wochenschau Verlag, 1999), pp. 174–75 citing Sumaya Farhat-

Thus, any person not registered became an "absentee", and as a result was not allowed to return. The census was part of a strategy of the occupying force to decrease the number of Palestinians entitled to reside in the West Bank and Gaza.

Naser, edited by Rosemarie Kurz und Chudi Bürgi, *Thymian und Steine* (Basel: Lenos Verlag, 1995), p. 69.

4 TWO DIFFERENT NARRATIVES

Israelis and Palestinians approach the question of the refugees and the *right of return* from radically different perspectives. It is essential to know and understand each of the two narratives if one is to explore the question of Palestinian refugees.

Palestinian and Israeli narratives of the past are, more often than not, mutually exclusive. The debate over the *right of return*[1] epitomizes these mutually exclusive narratives, and any principal position-shift on the issue is perceived by each people to have potential detrimental consequences, on both practical and symbolical levels. On the practical level this is perceived to mean flooding Israel with refugees and thus destroying it, on the one hand, or leaving unresolved the condition of millions of refugees on the other. On a symbolic level such a position-shift would strike at the core of each people's national narrative and collective identity, challenging at once well-established self-perceptions and deeply held beliefs about the "other."[2]

4.1 The Israeli Narrative

Until it was shattered by the so called "new historians" in the 1990s, the Israeli narrative went that most Palestinians in 1948 had voluntarily left their homes at the behest of the Arab leaders who wanted them out of their armies' way, despite Jewish pleas for the local Arab population to stay and demonstrate that peaceful coexistence was possible. Yet this narrative had to be revised in the wake of the work of the New Historians which had a tremendous impact on mainstream Israeli and Jewish debates. Not only has the new research been widely reported in Israeli newspapers. Several of the New Historians' books are now

---

1   For a deeper analysis of the *right of return*, see Part II of this research.
2   Adina Friedman, "Unraveling the Right of Return," p.66, at www.prrn. org.

required reading in courses at a number of Israeli universities.[3] Also the fact that there were instances in which Palestinian villages were forcibly evacuated without justification is to a considerable extent already part of Israel's high-school curriculum. In general, all current Israeli textbooks make use of the New Historians' most recent academic studies. However, they also emphasize – as does Benny Morris – that there was no Israeli master plan for expelling the Palestinians.[4]

Nevertheless, also the present "revised" Israeli narrative still stands in stark contrast to the Palestinian one. Accordingly, the Israeli narrative rejects the *right of return* of refugees to their homes in Israel; a significant current in Israeli opinion furthermore rejects the *right of return* to the West Bank as well. The Israelis argue that it did not cause the Palestinian refugee problem. Rather the Arabs did, by rejecting the U.N. decision of 1947 to create a Jewish and an Arab state in historic Palestine – which the Jews had accepted despite the painful sacrifices it entailed – and by subsequently declaring war on Israel and attacking it in 1948. That war, like most wars, created refugee problems – a Jewish as well as a Palestinian one.[5]

Notions of "refugee-ness" heightened among Jews following World War II and the Holocaust, and Israel, more than before, came to be viewed a safe haven for Jews around the world. Shortly following the establishment of the State of Israel, thousands of Jewish refugees

---

3   The primary book among them being Benny Morris' "The Birth of the Palestinian Refugee Problem." See Barbara Schäfer, „Einführung," in Barbara Schäfer, ed., *Historikerstreit in Israel: Die „Neuen" Historiker zwischen Wissenschaft und Öffentlichkeit* (Frankfurt: Campus Verlag, 2000), pp. 7–14; Avi Shlaim, "The Debate about 1948," *International Journal of Middle East Studies*, Vol. 27, 1995, pp. 287–92.

4   Elie Podeh, "The Right of Return versus the Law of Return: Contrasting Historical Narratives in Israeli and Palestinian School Textbooks," in Ann Lesch and Ian Lustick, eds., *Exile and Return: Predicaments of Palestinians and Jews* (Philadelphia: University of Philadelphia Press, 2005), pp. 45–48.

5   Supporters of the Israeli position also like to remind that the later U.N. Security Council Resolution 242 of 22 November 1967 merely speaks of a "just settlement of the refugee problem," and does not specify to which refugees it refers. See Resolution 242 in Laqueur and Rubin, *The Israeli-Arab Reader*, p. 116.

poured into Israel from various Arab countries due to hostilities and persecution.[6]

As a result, when mentioning the Jewish refugee problem, Israelis refer to the exodus of Jews from the Arab and Muslim Middle East and North Africa from 1948 to 1955. During that period the combined population of Jewish communities in the Middle East (excluding Israel) was reduced from about 900,000 in 1948 to less than 8,000 at present. Some of these communities were more than 2,500 years old. The State of Israel absorbed approximately 600,000 of these refugees, many of whom were temporarily settled in tent cities called *Maabarot*. In what is seen in Israel as a successful integration, they were eventually absorbed into Israeli society, and the last *Maabarah* was dismantled in 1958.[7] Relating to this absorption of Jewish refugees into Israeli society, Israelis expect the Arabs to deal with the Palestinian refugees the same way as Israel did with its own refugees.

Thus, in the minds of most Jewish Israelis the notion of refugees refers not only, or even mainly, to Palestinian refugees of 1948, but rather to what they see as a parallel phenomenon of Jewish refugees: first from Europe, and later from Arab lands. Since these Jewish refugees were absorbed into the Jewish state, thereby obliterating the Jewish "refugee problem," there is a refusal to understand or accept that the same was not done on the Arab side. In other words, a parallel is drawn between the Jewish and Palestinian refugee problem, following which there are parallel expectations from the Palestinians and the Arab world to have resolved the Palestinian refugee problem, and corresponding demands from the Arab states to compensate the Jewish refugees. The Palestinian refugee issue is thus linked to the larger issue of Middle East refugees, and a solution is perceived only in some larger context. The fact that the Palestinians are a different "entity" than any given Arab country from which Jewish refugees fled is irrelevant. In fact, most Israeli Jews see Palestinians and Arabs as one and the same.[8]

Jews and Jewish refugees returned to their historical homeland – and "home" is perceived as anywhere that Jewish sovereignty exists. It is difficult, therefore, to understand that "home" may mean something

---

6   Friedman, "Unraveling the Right of Return," p. 64.
7   See "Jewish Refugees" on www.wikipedia.org.
8   Friedman, "Unraveling the Right of Return," p. 64.

different (perhaps much more specific, e.g., a village or town) to most Palestinians.[9]

Another important point is that the absorption of Jewish refugees in Israeli school textbooks refers only to the boundaries of Israel, while Palestinian textbooks assert their *right of return* to the whole of Palestine or to the original places from where the Palestinians fled. From an Israeli point of view, such a narrative has threatening implications. Yet is also important to note that since Israel's boundaries have not as yet been conclusively established, the Israeli narrative may be perceived as menacing by Palestinians, just as the Palestinian narrative may be perceived as menacing by Israelis.[10]

Overall, Israelis unequivocally reject UNGAR 194 as an expression of Arab political war against Israel. Israelis further argue that the UNRWA statistics on refugees are grossly exaggerated, frequently reflecting a systematic policy at the local level of avoiding the removal of deceased persons from the lists. The true number of refugees would only become known when the bureaucratic machinery of an agreed solution is put into place.[11]

Israelis believe that agreeing to the return of Palestinian refugees is to create an existential threat to Israel. The return, by introducing a large Arab population, would undermine the Jewish character and the viability and stability of the Jewish state. "Return" to Israel would lay the foundations for a new stage of Palestinian irredentism. It would also call into question ownership of homes, villages, and other properties, and would thus be profoundly disruptive. Virtually all the villages left behind by the refugees in 1948 were destroyed; homes and properties have long been occupied by Israelis. In this regard, the Israeli narrative maintains that Israel will continue to exercise complete control and sovereignty over its territory and its population – Jewish, Arab, and other – regardless of the solution adopted for the refugee issue.[12]

---

9   Ibid., p.65.
10 Podeh, "The Right of Return versus the Law of Return," pp.50–51.
11 Alpher and Shikaki, "The Palestinian Refugee Problem." For a good analysis of the Israeli perception of the refugee problem, see Akiva Eldar, "The Israeli Media and the Refugee Problem," in www.prrn.org under "Research Papers."
12 Alpher and Shikaki, "The Palestinian Refugee Problem."

Israelis also fear the abuse, whether deliberate or unanticipated, of any mass "return" to a neighbouring Palestinian state, in the sense that this could create a geopolitical threat to Israel itself. The indiscriminate massing of hundreds of thousands of refugees inside a Palestinian state, without regard for socio-economic considerations of absorption, could take place due to popular Palestinian pressure, regardless of the position of a Palestinian government. It could present Israelis with the spectre of a "Green March" threat, whereby masses of Palestinian refugees would gather inside the Palestinian state, along its border with Israel, and attempt to cross and return to "their" homes and properties long since destroyed or transferred to Jewish ownership. Alternatively, it could create pressures on the Palestinian economy and the regional ecobalance that might prove highly destabilizing.[13]

A psychological study on the present attitude of Jewish-Israelis on the *right of return* portrays a multifold picture. First, the term "right of return" evokes deeply negative emotions in the Jewish-Israeli public such as "destruction", "disaster" and even "holocaust", while implementing this demand would be perceived as leading to the end of the Jewish nature of the state of Israel, and by some to dire consequences such as death and exile. Second, there seems to be a greater understanding now that this is a major Palestinian demand, and that without resolving it in a manner acceptable to both sides, no permanent agreement is possible. Third, about half of the Jewish-Israeli public somewhat accepts the morality of the claim for return, however, this has only a limited effect on the range of acceptable solutions endorsed by respondents.[14]

As for potential solutions, the same study has found that most accepted was the return of the refugees to the Palestinian state. A decreasing portion of the sample was ready for the payment of reparations, or acceptance of responsibility and apology (yet without actual return). The most frequently cited figures of the number of refugees the Israelis would be willing to absorb ranged from 20,000 to 50,000.[15]

---

13 Ibid.
14 See Dan Zakay, Yechiel Klar and Keren Sharvit, "Jewish Israelis on the 'Right of Return': Growing Awareness of the Issue's Importance" in *Palestine-Israel Journal*, Vol. 9, No. 2, 2002, pp. 58–66.
15 Ibid.

4.2 The Palestinian Narrative

The Palestinian narrative maintains that in 1948, the Arab refugees were forcibly expelled by Jewish forces or fled in panic to escape carnage and that they were helped on their way by occasional massacres, committed by Jewish forces, to keep them running. Palestinians insist on the right of the refugees to return to their homes and properties or – for those who chose not to do so – to accept compensation, a demand anchored in United Nations General Assembly Resolution (UNGAR) 194. Furthermore, they demand that Israel unilaterally acknowledge its complete moral responsibility for the injustice of the refugees' expulsion and their later fate. The resettlement and absorption of Palestinian refugees in a Palestinian state in the West Bank and Gaza Strip is seen by Palestinians not as an exercise of the *right of return* but as an option, provided for by Resolution 194, which must be accompanied by compensation.[16]

Memories of destroyed villages and towns play a central role in Palestinian consciousness. The Deir Yassin massacre, committed by Irgun forces in 1948, was crucial in heightening Palestinian fears at the time and in heightening the flow of refugees. It has been, ever since, a central theme in the narration of Palestinian history, and has had a great impact on how Palestinians saw – and continue to see – their enemies. Palestinian identity has, ever since 1948, been in many ways constructed of the experience of dispossession, homelessness, insecurity, and uprootedness.[17]

No one embodies these feelings more than the refugees themselves. Indeed, the concept of *Ghurba*, or exile, is a major component of Palestinian identity. In addition, a distinct identity and character developed in the refugee camps themselves, and in those outside the mandated borders of Palestine the situation was different than that in the West Bank and Gaza Strip camps. A major agent in instilling Palestinian consciousness among the camp refugees was the educational system

---

16   Joseph Alpher, "Concept Paper: the Palestinian refugee problem and the right of return," *Middle East Policy* (Refereed), Vol. 6, No. 3, 1 February 1999, p. 167 (1). (webposted)

17   Adina Friedman, "Unraveling the Right of Return," p. 66, at www.prrn. org.

established by UNRWA. For many Palestinians, the core of the conflict, from which all else flows, is the refugee issue. They see their dispossession by Israel in 1948 as the defining element not only in the modern history of their people, but also in the entire Arab-Israeli conflict.[18]

The term "refugee" does not, in the Palestinian mind, refer only to those defined by UNRWA as refugees, living in and around camps. The concept is a central theme in the personal and collective identity of many Palestinians, and applies to anyone who fled or was forced out of their home, regardless of their official "status" today. Thus, there are in fact many more Palestinians who would identify themselves as refugees than any U.N. or other figure might show, "refugee" being more a matter of identity than an operational definition.[19]

The Palestinians view the refugee issue as basically political and national and not just humanitarian. Therefore, any solution to it must confront the question of their displacement and statelessness. That solution must also be just and fair and should be based on existing U.N. resolutions. Indeed, Security Council Resolution 242 mentions a just solution to the refugee problem as a basis to make peace between Israel and its Arab neighbours. Insistence on UNGAR 194 is a matter of justice to Palestinians. Based on these two resolutions, in the Palestinian view, the *right of return* has achieved international consensus in U.N. resolutions, setting the moral and legal standards accepted by the international community, with Israel being the only state rejecting them.[20]

In order to understand the Palestinian narrative, it is particularly helpful to review the relevant textbooks of Palestinian schools. From 1967 and until the founding of the Palestinian Ministry of Education in 1994, the educational system in the West Bank and Gaza Strip operated according to Jordanian and Egyptian curricula and textbooks respectively. Obviously, these texts were carefully scrutinized by the Israeli Civil Administration, and all parts considered offensive to Israel,

---

18 Rashid Khalidi, "Attainable Justice: Elements of a Solution to the Palestinian Refugee Issue," *International Journal*, Vol. 53, No. 2, Spring 1998, pp. 232–52, cited in ibid.

19 Ibid.

20 Alpher, "Concept Paper: the Palestinian refugee problem and the right of return."

Zionism, and Judaism were systematically deleted. Predictably, these textbooks accentuated Arab – and specifically Jordanian and Egyptian – national identity while marginalizing or completely ignoring any Palestinian national identity.[21]

With the transfer of authority in the sphere of education to the Palestinians, new Palestinian textbooks started to be published. The first Palestinian textbooks referred only briefly to the refugee problem, surprisingly ignoring the issue of the *right of return*. Post-1948 history was presented in a factual manner, as shown by the example of a textbook for fifth graders, which the period after 1948 as characterized by: "1) flight [*tasharud*] of many of the Palestinians who found refuge in Arab countries such as Syria, Lebanon, Jordan, and Egypt. 2) Many Palestinians lost their lands and as a result were compelled to learn new vocations. 3) The Palestinians were concerned to preserve their cultural existence [*kiyyanhum al-hidari*] through building Palestinian national, popular, and social institutions."[22] It is reasonable to assume that the need to produce several Palestinian textbooks as quickly as possible led to this rather cursory manner in which the historical narrative was presented to students.[23]

The Palestinian textbooks produced after 2000, on the other hand, treated the subject in a more comprehensive way. In contrast to Israeli textbooks, which refer to the cause only in their history textbooks, the Palestinian ones discuss the refugee problem in the context of several subjects: national education, language, demography, and Islamic education. When referring to Jewish immigration to Palestine, Palestinian textbooks present the issue as illegal or illegitimate. With regard to the Palestinian refugee problem and the *right of return*, a careful examination of the texts leads to the following conclusions:

---

21 Fouad Moughrabi, "The Politics of Palestinian Textbooks," *Journal of Palestine Studies*, Vol. 31, No. 1, Autumn 2001, p. 6.

22 See *Palestinian National Education*, fifth grade (1998), p. 36, cited in Elie Podeh, "The Right of Return versus the Law of Return: Contrasting Historical Narratives in Israeli and Palestinian School Textbooks," in Ann Lesch and Ian Lustick, eds., *Exile and Return: Predicaments of Palestinians and Jews* (Philadelphia: University of Philadelphia Press, 2005), pp. 48–49.

23 Ibid., p. 49.

1. The texts emphasize the victimization of the Palestinians during and after the 1948 war. 479 villages out of 807 are said to have come under Israeli occupation, while more than 370 were destroyed between 1948 and 1950. In some cases, Jewish settlements were established on the sites of demolished Palestinian villages. Often, the student is given several assignments in this connection, such as recounting the names of and collecting information on the destroyed villages. The cited number of refugees is "more than three-quarters of a million," a figure close to U.N. estimates.[24]

2. Most texts emphasize that "Jewish throngs" or "Zionist terrorist organizations" deliberately expelled the Palestinians from their land and that they faced repeated massacres, such as Deir Yassin, and other atrocities. This narrative pervades not only national education textbooks but also geography, literature, and Islamic texts.[25]

3. There exist also several textbooks, mainly in geography, which refer to "the war" as a primary reason for Palestinian flight.[26] One textbook cites five reasons for the Palestinian exodus, out of which political motivation – in other words, "compulsory emigration" – is listed only last.[27]

4. Palestinian textbooks refer to the *right of return* in three different textbooks. An Islamic education textbook asserts: "All Palestinians wait for the return of every Palestinian to his city or village from which he was made to emigrate."[28] The national education textbook for second grade students states that a refugee camp is "a place established for the Palestinian refugees who had been forced to depart

---

24 *Palestinian National Education*, seventh grade (2001), pp. 54–57; *The Palestinian Society: Demographic Education*, eleventh grade (2001), p. 34. Cited in ibid.

25 *Palestinian National Education*, seventh grade (2001), pp. 20–21, 54–57; sixth grade, 2000, p. 13, 16; *Our Beautiful Language*, seventh grade, part 1 (2001), pp. 94–95; *The Palestinian Society: Demographic Education*, eleventh grade (2000), p. 21, 34; *Geography of Palestine*, seventh grade (2001), pp. 43–44; *Islamic Culture*, twelfth grade (1998), pp. 247–48. Cited in ibid.

26 *Principles in Human Geography*, sixth grade (2000), p. 22, 33. Cited in ibid.

27 The first four reasons relate to natural, social, and economic reasons for the emigration. See *Geography in Palestine*, sixth grade (2001), p. 36. Cited in ibid.

28 *Islamic Education*, sixth grade, part 1 (2000), p. 69. Cited in ibid.

from their cities and villages in Palestine and who are determined to return to them."[29] Finally, a textbook for Arabic language and literature presents the text of a poem called "We Shall Return," which forms the basis for several questions and assignments for students.[30]

5. In contrast to Israeli textbooks, Palestinian textbooks do briefly mention the 1967 refugees. A textbook on demography states that this war led to "the second Palestinian compulsory emigration in which the number of emigrants from the West Bank exceeded 350,000."[31]

In general, the Palestinian narrative still adheres to the old Palestinian assertion that Israel's policy is solely responsible for the displacement of the Palestinians. Fouad Moughrabi claims that "objective non-Arab and non-Zionist scholars or even Israeli scholars associated with the 'new historians' revisionist interpretations of 1948" do not contest this narrative.[32] Elie Podeh rightly objects that this argument is misleading, since most of the New Historians do not claim that Israel deliberately expelled all Palestinians but instead that were certain cases of expulsion; he also further adds that apart from this selective Palestinian perception of the refugee problem, the Palestinian narrative truly and accurately reflects the sense of victimization as a result of the war.[33] Overall, an analysis of Palestinian textbook reveals that the *right of return* is a crucial theme, often discussed in written texts, maps, illustrations, and student class activities. In addition, Palestinian textbooks assert a *right of return* to the whole of Palestine or to the original places from where the Palestinians fled.

As a consequence, in Palestinian eyes, Israel can insist on its position only because it relies on brute force and coercion. Thus in such a case no lasting solution should be anticipated, and no true reconciliation with the existence of the Jewish state can be expected until it addresses

---

29 *Palestinian National Education*, second grade (2001), p. 36. Cited in ibid.
30 *Our Beautiful Language*, seventh grade, part 1 (2001), pp. 40–42. Cited in ibid.
31 *The Palestinian Society: Demographic Education*, eleventh grade (2000), p. 21, 34. Cited in ibid.
32 Moughrabi, "The Politics of Palestinian Textbooks," p. 8.
33 Podeh, "The Right of Return versus the Law of Return," p. 50.

justly the problem that has been caused by its creation. For Palestinians, indeed for the Arab world in general, this is a fundamental issue in any peace talks with Israel; in their view, Israel carries the full responsibility for the creation of the Palestinian refugee problem. Palestinians believe that the Jews used the tragedy of the Jewish displaced persons to justify mass immigration of Jews into Palestine after World War II, even if at the very same time they were deliberately causing a mass exodus of Palestinians. By denying the *right of return*, Israelis would be doing to the Palestinians what the Jews were asking the world to denounce when it was done to them.[34] In fact, the Palestinians' categorical insistence on both an Israeli acknowledgment of responsibility as well as recognition of the *right of return* originate in the feeling of being the victim of a gross injustice – an injustice for which Palestinians demand full acknowledgment.

---

34 Alpher, "Concept Paper: the Palestinian refugee problem and the right of return."

5   THE SITUATION ON THE GROUND

After having scrutinized how the Palestinian refugee problem came into being, it is now worthwhile examining the situation of the Palestinian refugees as it exists at present. This chapter shall attempt to estimate the number of refugees, analyse various definitions of a Palestinian refugee and finally give an overview as to their distribution in various countries.

5.1 The Difficult Task of Estimating Refugee Numbers

Regarding the total of Palestinian Arabs who had become refugees during and as a result of the 1947–48 war and from there onwards, numbers varied significantly – depending whether one consulted Arab, Israeli or aid organizations' sources.

While Arab officials declared a total of 900,000 or one million, Israeli spokesmen, in 1949, usually referred to "about 520,000".[1] Israel based its calculation on statistics of the British mandate-government: Before the war, 727,000 Arabs had lived within future Israel's borders, of whom 165,000 stayed put or returned by the end of 1949. According to these figures, the numbers of refugees could not surpass 562,000; taking into account fatal casualties and the departure of non-Palestinian Arabs to their home countries, Israel came up with the initial estimate of 520,000 refugees.[2] However, three years later, Israel corrected its previous aggregates and calculated the number of refugees at 630,000.[3] Third party estimates ranged between the Israeli and Arab figures. For

---

1   See www.mideastweb.org.
2   See Yoav Gelber, *Palestine 1948: War, Escape and the Emergence of the Palestinian Refugee Problem* (Brighton: Sussex Academic Press, 2001), p. 272.
3   See ibid., pp. 272–73.

example, the British government in February 1949 reckoned the number of Palestinian refugees to be 810,000.[4]

According to the United Nations Conciliation Commission, the final estimate of the number of Palestinian refugees from the 1947–48 war was 711,000.[5] However, by 1950, according to UNRWA, the number of registered refugees was 914,000.[6] The U.N. Conciliation Commission attributed this discrepancy to, among other things, "duplication of ration cards, addition of persons who have been displaced from area other than Israel-held areas and of persons who, although not displaced, are destitute."[7] UNRWA additionally attributed the high number to the fact that "all births are eagerly announced, the deaths wherever possible are passed over in silence," as well as the fact that "the birthrate is high in any case, a net addition of 30,000 names a year."[8] The UNRWA figures indeed included descendants of the Palestinian refugees born after the exodus up to June 1951. By June 1951, the UNRWA had reduced the number of registered refugees to 876,000 after "many false and duplicate registrations weeded out."[9]

The controversy over the refugees' total number remains unsolved. The gap between contradictory estimates widened with the lapse of

---

4   See "McNeil response to question by Brigadier Rayner," 16 February 1949, cited in Morris, *The Birth of the Palestinian Refugee Problem Revisited*, p. 604.

5   "General Progress Report and Supplementary Report of the United Nations Conciliation Commission for Palestine, Covering the Period from 11 December 1949 to 23 October 1950" published by the U.N. Conciliation Commission on 23 October 1950. See http://domino.un.org/unispal.nsf. Note that this is an up-dated report, replacing the widespread number of 726'000 refugees from the –despite calling itself "final"– interim estimate in the "Final Report of the United Nations Economic Survey Mission for the Middle East" published by the United Nations Conciliation Commission on 28 December 1949, available at http://domino.un.org/unispal.nsf.

6   See http://www.un.org/unrwa/refugees/whois.html.

7   "General Progress Report and Supplementary Report of the United Nations Conciliation Commission for Palestine, Covering the Period from 11 December 1949 to 23 October 1950" on http://domino.un.org/unispal.nsf.

8   See the "Report of the Director of the United Nations Relief and Works Agency for Palestine Refugees in the Near East, September 28, 1951" available at http://domino.un.org/unispal.nsf.

9   Ibid.

time owing to natural growth and migrations. In the absence of a reliable census during the war or in its wake, the contradictions cannot be resolved. It is therefore impossible to arrive at a definite, persuasive estimate. It is therefore the most reasonable conclusion to opt for the loose contemporary British formula, that of 'between 600,000 and 760,000' refugees; if needed more precisely, 700,000 is probably a fair estimate.[10]

Overall, in the absence of comprehensive census data, no definitive figures exist for either the Palestinian population or the total Palestinian refugee population.[11] As with virtually every other statistic connected to the conflict, there is considerable dispute and controversy regarding these figures. Much of the controversy is a matter of definition, and in particular whether one ought to consider as refugees the descendants of those who lost their homes in 1948 and have acquired citizenship rights in third countries. The following paragraphs will elaborate the issue of defining a Palestinian refugee.

5.2 Definitions of a Palestinian Refugee

Unfortunately, there is no single objective definition of a Palestinian refugee. Rather there are various definitions, which can be divided into two groups: popular and official. The popular definitions refer to the classifications that are widely used among the Palestinians themselves to differentiate between various types of refugees. On the other hand, there are also what shall be called official definitions, meaning the criteria of international bodies to define who qualifies for their assistance and who does not.

---

10 See also Morris, *The Birth of the Palestinian Refugee Problem Revisited*, pp. 603–04.

11 No census of the Palestinian population has been held since 1948. Those conducted in states with significant Palestinian populations often fail to indicate national origin clearly. See "Palestinian Refugees and the Politics of Peacemaking," *ICG Middle East Report*, No. 22, 5 February 2004, p. 1 on www.icg.org.

5.2.1 Popular Definitions

Palestinians displaced in 1948 are along with their descendents conventionally known as "refugees" *(laji'un)*. Those exiled during or since 1967 are with their offspring known as "displaced persons" *(nazihun)* – although a high proportion of them are 1948 refugees who after the war resided in the West Bank and Gaza Strip and thus also continue to be known as *laji'un*. Native residents of these territories who have not experienced displacement are termed citizens *(muwatinun)*. More recently, PA personnel, their families and other exiled Palestinians who acquired residency status in the West Bank and Gaza Strip as a result of the implementation of the Oslo agreements are, irrespective of their places of origin, known as "returnees" *(a'idun)*.[12]

Although widely assumed, the simple estimation that Palestinians in Israel and the occupied territories are not refugees and those elsewhere are, or that Palestinians in camps are refugees and the remainder not, is misleading. An extensive report conducted by the International Crisis Group (ICG) found anywhere between 75 to 80 percent of the population of the Gaza Strip and approximately 40 percent of West Bank Palestinians to be 1948 refugees, while simultaneously a substantial minority of Palestinians in the Arab world and beyond are not refugees and often not displaced persons either (i.e. expatriate *muwatinun*), and two-thirds of UNRWA-registered refugees do not live in camps.[13]

5.2.2 Official Definitions

While most refugees worldwide are the concern of the U.N. High Commissioner for Refugees (UNHCR), Palestinian refugees fall under the older body UNRWA, which the U.N. General Assembly Resolution 302 (IV) of 8 December 1949 established specifically to deal with the Palestinian problem.[14]

The term "Palestinian refugee" as used by UNRWA was never formally defined by the U.N. The definition used in practice evolved

---

12   Ibid.
13   Ibid., p. 2.
14   See http://domino.un.org/unispal.nsf.

independently of the UNHCR's definition, which was established by the 1951 "Convention relating to the Status of Refugees" and defined a refugee as any person who:

"owing to well-founded fear of being persecuted for reasons of race, religion, nationality, membership of a particular social group or political opinion, is outside the country of his nationality and is unable, or owing to such fear, is unwilling to avail himself of the protection of that country; or who, not having a nationality and being outside the country of his former habitual residence as a result of such events, is unable or, owing to such fear, is unwilling to return to it."[15]

In the UNHCR's definition there is no mention of descendants. Moreover, the convention ceases to apply to a person who, *inter alia*, "has acquired a new nationality, and enjoys the protection of the country of his new nationality."[16]

Under this definition, the number of Palestinians qualifying for refugee status would be well below half a million. However, an Arab veto excluded the Palestinians from that definition, by introducing the following provision into the 1951 Refugee Convention:

"This Convention shall not apply to persons who are at present receiving from organs or agencies of the United Nations other than the United Nations High Commissioner for Refugees protection or assistance."[17]

In no official document have the Palestinian refugees been defined, and UNRWA has been adopting varying definitions, such as the following operational definition: "Palestine refugees are persons whose normal place of residence was Palestine between June 1946 and May 1948, who lost both their homes and means of livelihood as a result of the 1948 Arab-Israeli conflict."[18] Not only is this is a very broad definition under which the number of refugees constantly increases; it also includes any person living in Palestine since no later than 1946 and thus also covers a range of people from outside of Palestine who came to reside there during that period, be it to support the battle against the Yishuv or merely to find employment. While appropriate for UNRWA

---

15   See www.unhchr.ch/html/menu3/b/o_c_ref.htm, Article 1A (2).
16   Ibid., Article 1C (3).
17   Ibid., 1D.
18   http://www.un.org/unrwa/refugees/whois.html.

purposes in order to decide who qualifies for assistance, its suitability for other purposes has been contested. Several researchers call for the parties to agree on a more suitable definition.[19]

UNRWA's definition of a refugee applies only to those who took refuge in one of the countries where UNRWA provides relief. The UNRWA further registers as refugees descendents in the male line of Palestinian refugees, and persons in need of support who first became refugees as a result of the 1967 conflict. UNRWA's definition in practice is thus both more restrictive and more inclusive than the 1951 definition; for example, although it excludes persons taking refuge in countries other than Jordan, Syria, Lebanon, the West Bank and the Gaza Strip, it does include the descendants of refugees.[20] Also persons receiving relief support from UNRWA are explicitly excluded from the 1951 Convention, depriving them of some of the benefits of that convention such as a certain degree of legal protection.[21] However, a 2002 decision of the UNHCR clarified that the 1951 Convention applies at least to Palestinian refugees who need support but fail to fit the UNRWA working definition.[22]

5.3 The Distribution of Palestinian Refugees

Although this chapter has shown above that it is practically impossible to determine the exact number of Palestinians who fled in 1948, one can nevertheless express the approximate proportions: In the course of the Palestinian exodus, around eighty percent of Palestine's Arabs

---

19 See Ruth Lapidoth, "Legal Aspects of the Palestinian Refugee Question," in www.prrn.org under "Research Papers."

20 Although the UNHCR also provides support for children of refugees in many cases. See "Who is a Palestinian Refugee", www.wikipedia.org.

21 For a good analysis of the legal status of Palestinian refugees, see Susan Akram, "Reinterpreting Palestinian Refugee Rights under International Law," in Naseer Aruri (ed.), *Palestinian Refugees: The Right of Return* (London: Pluto Press, 2001), pp. 165–94.

22 See "Note on the Applicability of Article 1D of the 1951 Convention relating to the Status of Refugees to Palestinian refugees" on http://domino.un.org/ unispal.nsf. This clarification specifically applies to Palestinian refugee outside the "UNRWA countries", e.g. in Egypt, as elaborated in chapter 5.3.5.

left their homes. Of this population, approximately one third fled to the West Bank, another third to the Gaza Strip, and the remainder to third countries (mostly the neighbouring Arab countries). That means that around two thirds of the refugees remained in historic Palestine. Furthermore, between 1948 and 1949, 46,000 to 48,000 Palestinian Arabs were internally displaced, i.e. within Israel. Including descendants, they number 150,000 to 200,000 at present; for the most part they have yet to recover their confiscated land.[23]

The following paragraphs shall give an overview as to the approximate number of refugees in the various areas and countries. If not mentioned otherwise, the numbers are taken from UNRWA data from June 2004. Yet one needs to keep in mind that even within the terms of UNRWA's own definition of a refugee, its statistics are not wholly accurate. They count only eligible beneficiaries and exclude Palestinians with no residency rights in its areas of operation, those who have been removed from its rolls over the years for various reasons and those who never registered with the organisation. In other instances – particularly refugees in Lebanon as examined below – UNRWA figures are significantly inflated because many refugees have for all intents and purposes permanently left Lebanon (i.e. political refugees in Europe and others prevented by the Lebanese authorities from returning) yet retain their status with UNRWA in Lebanon and have not been removed from its rolls.[24]

However, even if not completely flawless, UNRWA's figures are the only available official information to provide at least an approximate impression of the situation on the ground. In addition to their numbers,

---

23   These data are taken from the Global IDP Database of the Norwegian Refugee Council. See www.reliefweb.int. For more information on Palestinian internal refugees, see Joseph Schechla, "The Invisible People Come to Light: Israel's "Internally Displaced" and the "Unrecognized Villages," *Journal of Palestine Studies*, Vol. XXXI, No. 1, Autumn 2001, pp. 20–31;Hillel Cohen, "Land, Memory, and Identity: The Palestinian Internal Refugees in Israel," in www.prrn.org under "Research Papers," as well as Hillel Cohen, "The Internal Refugees in the State of Israel: Israeli Citizens, Palestinian Refugees," *Palestine-Israel Journal*, Vol. 9, No. 2, 2002, pp. 43–51.

24   ICG Report, "Palestinian Refugees and the Politics of Peacemaking," p. 2. We have already looked upon some problems with the UNRWA numbers in 5.1.

the refugees' situation in their present locations shall be illuminated in the following paragraphs; overall, one can preclude that the treatment of Palestinian refugees in their countries of residence has been dismal, ranging from denial of full civil rights to periodic massacres and expulsions.[25] On the basis of their status as foreigners, Arabs, Palestinians, and/or stateless persons (except in Israel and Jordan, where Palestinians have collectively acquired citizenship since 1948[26]), Palestinians, including the refugees, are subject to legal, political, and/or socio-economic discrimination by virtually every state in the Middle East.[27]

In general, estimates put the present worldwide Palestinian population at over eight millions. The population of 1967 displaced persons stands presently at approximately one million, many of them also being 1948 refugees or their descendents. In June 2004, UNRWA data showed 4,186,711 registered refugees in its "area of operation", thus West Bank, Gaza Strip, Jordan, Syria and Lebanon.[28] Palestinian sources, pointing to the categories excluded from UNRWA statistics, provide a significantly higher figure of 5.8 million refugees. Other sources, particularly Israeli ones, provide much lower figures, challenging for instance the inclusion of Palestinians who have acquired regular citizenship in Israel – thus falling under the category of internally displaced – and elsewhere. Using different definitions and lower estimates

25 See Yifat Susskind, "Background Resource: The Crisis of Palestinian Refugees and the Right of Return," 2001, at www.prrn.org; Wolfgang Köhler, "Von Integration kann in keinem Land die Rede sein," *Frankfurter Allgemeine Zeitung*, 15 May 1998, p. 8.

26 All Palestinians (including refugees) with permanent residency status in the West Bank also enjoyed regular Jordanian citizenship rights after annexation in 1948, but as a rule lost this after Jordan's July 1988 administrative disengagement (renunciation of all claims) from the West Bank.

27 Abbas Shiblak, Residency Status and Civil Rights of Palestinian Refugees in Arab Countries (Ramallah: Shaml, 2001) at www.shaml.org/publications/monos/mono1.htm#Residency Status: A Case of Uncertainty.

28 See www.arts.mcgill.ca/mepp/new_prrn/background/index.htm; and well as Khawaja, Marwan and Tiltnes, Aage A. "On the Margins: Migration and living conditions of Palestinian camp refugees in Jordan," *Fafo-report 357*, Oslo, 2002 at www.prrn.org under "Research Papers."

of Palestinians who lost their homes in 1948, some have suggested there are only two million refugees.[29]

Today about one-third of refugees live in 59 camps recognised by UNRWA;[30] camp residents have born the brunt of hardship in terms of poverty, overcrowding, lack of infrastructure, discrimination, and conflict. Most of the remaining two-thirds of refugees, as well as the camps, are situated within or in close proximity to urban areas in the respective countries and territories. There is little question that on the whole, Arab states have neglected the refugee camps, typically refusing to contribute to their improvement on the ground that the refugees are an international responsibility and seeking to exploit the refugee question – and the refugees' humanitarian plight – for their own political ends.[31] The following paragraphs shall provide an individual examination as to the numbers of Palestinian refugees and their situation in the various areas.

---

29   The ICG report lists the Anti-Defamation League as an example: "Advocating for Israel: An Activist's Guide" at www.adl.org/Israel/advocacy/glossary_print.asp. Similar discrepancies exist regarding 1967 displaced persons. Israel, using lower estimates and restricting the category to those actually displaced during the Six-Day-War and its immediate aftermath, has put forward a figure of 200,000. The Palestinians, using a higher initial estimate and adding to this descendants, as well as those deported or prevented from returning to the occupied territories since 1967, put forward a figure of 800,000. See ICG Report, "Palestinian Refugees and the Politics of Peacemaking," p.2.

30   Several neighbourhoods predominantly inhabited by Palestinian refugees and normally referred to as camps, such as Yarmouk in Damascus, Syria, are not recognised as such by UNRWA although it provides services to their inhabitants. See ICG Report, "Palestinian Refugees and the Politics of Peacemaking," p.2.

31   Until the early 1990s, Arab states generally refused to contribute either to improvement projects within the camps or to budgetary support for UNRWA. More recently, they have begun to provide both bilateral and multilateral aid. The government of the United Arab Emirates, for example, pledged to cover the reconstruction costs of homes destroyed in the Jenin refugee camp during Israeli's April 2002 incursion. In Jordan, the government rather than UNRWA pays the leases for land on which refugee camps stand. Arab host countries in general have also not obstructed inhabitants from seeking housing outside the camps. See ICG Report, "Palestinian Refugees and the Politics of Peacemaking," p.5.

5.3.1 Jordan

The largest concentration of Palestinian refugees is situated in Jordan, numbering 1,758,274 people, or about 42% of all UNRWA-registered refugees. Compared to the other countries where UNRWA operates, the situation of Jordan's refugees is the most favourable one. Out of Jordan's Palestinian refugees, 281,211 are living in refugee camps, while the vast majority of 1,477,063 lives elsewhere. In other words, fewer than one in eight Palestinian refugees in Jordan lives in a camp; besides, the term "camp" is often misleading in Jordan, since most refugee camps have effectively become urban neighbourhoods.[32] In Jordan, where the PLO and the Hashemite monarchy fought a bitter armed conflict in 1970–1971, the electoral power of citizens of Palestinian origin has been reduced through gerrymandering, and Palestinians are visibly underrepresented in the public sector bureaucracy and security forces. However, they face few restrictions in other fields of national life, have produced numerous prime and cabinet ministers (though proportionally less in recent years) and have traditionally dominated the private sector, where they are disproportionately represented in business.[33] Palestinian refugees in Jordan enjoy more political, economic and social rights than in any other host country. Most Palestinians are full citizens, having the same rights and duties, as well as enjoying a standard of living generally equivalent to that of the other Jordanians.

An exception is formed by a small number of 1967 refugees which had fled from the Gaza Strip, which was then under Egyptian occupation, and were therefore not granted any status or rights in Jordan. So to this day, this refugee group is not allowed to own property or to work and it only benefits from few social services.[34]

On the large scale, however, Jordan's Palestinian refugees are well integrated. Information from the Jordanian censuses which distinguishes between Palestinians and pre-1948 Jordanians is not publicly available. However, Jordan's Palestinian population is estimated to make

---

32 www.arts.mcgill.ca/mepp/new_prrn/background/index.htm.
33 ICG Report, "Palestinian Refugees and the Politics of Peacemaking," p. 3.
34 See Hassan Fattah, "For displaced Palestinians, a victory tinged with regret," in the *New York Times* of 18 August, 2005.

up fifty to sixty percent of the overall population, while Palestinian refugees alone make up about one-third of Jordan's population.[35]

5.3.2 West Bank and Gaza Strip

The second largest concentration of Palestinian refugees is located in the Gaza Strip, numbering 938,531 persons (about 22% of all UNRWA-registered refugees), out of which 464,075 are living in camps, while 474,456 do not live in camps. Gaza is one of the poorest, most densely populated places in the world. Within the Gaza Strip, refugees form an absolute majority of the population, yet there is resentment among them that their power within society is not commensurate with their numbers and is circumscribed by their status.[36] Since the 1950s the population of the camps has doubled, but their area has not been allowed to expand. Per capita income is $800 a year. Health problems from poor sanitation and overcrowding are exacerbated by the lack of clean drinking water. Since 1967, violence at the hands of Israeli occupation soldiers and a policy of forced economic under-development has made life for refugees in Gaza among the hardest in the region.[37]

675,000 Palestinian refugees live in the West Bank (about 16% of all UNRWA-registered refugees), out of which 177,920 are in camps, while the majority of 497,750 lives outside of them. Although the West Bank has a stronger economic base than Gaza, refugees, who comprise

---

35 See for example www.wikipedia.org. For further information on Palestinian refugees in Jordan, see Mohanna Haddad, "Palestinian Refugees in Jordan and National Identity, 1948–1999," in Joseph Ginat and Edward Perkins (eds.), *The Palestinian Refugees: Old Problems – New Solutions* (Brighton: Sussex Academic Press, 2001), pp. 150–68.

36 ICG Report, "Palestinian Refugees and the Politics of Peacemaking," p. 5.

37 Susskind, "Background Resource." See further Randa Farah, "A Report on the Psychological Effects of Overcrowding in Refugee Camps in the West Bank and Gaza Strip," April 2000, as well as Mona Marshy, "Social and Psychological Effects of Overcrowding in Palestinian Refugee Camps in the West Bank and Gaza – Literature Review and Preliminary Assessment of the Problem," August 1999, both in www.prrn.org under "Research Papers."

30 percent of the population, are among the poorest in the UNRWA's area of operation.[38]

In both the West Bank and the Gaza Strip, Palestinian refugees are stateless and live under a combination of limited Palestinian Authority administration and Israeli military occupation. The refugee camps, which since 1967 (and particularly in the course of the second intifada) have served as centres of militancy, recruitment, resistance and armed attacks against Israel, have faced harsh Israeli occupation policies.[39] As a consequence, a sharp decline in economic conditions in those territories, due to political violence and especially the mobility restrictions imposed by Israel, has brought with it a dramatic increase in unemployment and poverty rates. UNRWA has launched a series of emergency appeals to address this.[40]

5.3.3 Syria

In Syria, 417,346 Palestinian refugees were registered by UNRWA in June 2004 (about 10% of all UNRWA-registered refugees); 110,450 living in camps, 306,896 living elsewhere. Palestinian refugees in Syria are non-citizens, and subsequently are forbidden to vote, hold office, or carry Syrian passports. They are issued travel documents, yet these are not recognized by many countries.[41] However, Palestinian refugees in Syria are provided with full access to employment and social services. The fact that only about 25% of Palestinian refugees in Syria still live in camps is an indication of their social integration in that country.[42]

---

38 See Jon Pedersen, Sara Randall and Marwan Khawaja, eds., "Growing Fast: The Palestinian Population in the West Bank and Gaza Strip," *Fafo-report*, No. 353, 2001, at www.prrn.org under "Research Papers."

39 See ICG Report, "Palestinian Refugees and the Politics of Peacemaking," p. 4.

40 See www.arts.mcgill.ca/mepp/new_prrn/background/index.htm.

41 See Susskind, "Background Resource." For the impact of the peace process on Lebanon's Palestinian refugees, see Manar-al-Huda al-Husayni, "Lebanon and the Peace Process: excerpts on refugees," in www.prrn.org under "Research Papers."

42 See Hamad Said Al-Mawed, "The Palestinian Refugees in Syria: Their Past, Present and Future," 1999, at www.prrn.org under "Research Papers."

Their condition is generally similar to Syria's other inhabitants and one can assert that Palestinian refugees have been treated well in Syria.[43]

5.3.4 Lebanon

In Lebanon, UNRWA counted 396,890 refugees in June 2004 (about 10% of all UNRWA-registered refugees); 192,557 living in camps, 204,333 not living in camps. Palestinian refugees in Lebanon face the harshest living conditions: Successive governments have treated the – predominantly Sunni Muslim – Palestinians as unwelcome, destabilizing elements in the country's fragile religious and sectarian balance of forces, and have made it unmistakably clear that they object to a long-term Palestinian presence in the country.[44] Palestinian refugees in Lebanon have also frequently been used as the country's scapegoat.[45]

Apart from being stateless, Palestinians in Lebanon are barred from 73 job categories, including professions such as medicine, law, engineering and university posts. Only after Syria's withdrawal from Lebanon in 2005 and the subsequent shortage of cheap labour-forces – as Syrian labourers had left with their troops – did the Lebanese government allow Palestinian refugees born in Lebanon to legally work at manual and clerical jobs.[46] Nevertheless, they are not allowed to own property or land; even phone lines are forbidden to Palestinians in Lebanon.[47] More than 50% live below the national poverty line. Unlike other foreigners in Lebanon, they are denied access to the Lebanese healthcare system. Lebanon's ban on construction and development of infrastructure within the refugee camps, including those proposed by UNRWA in

43   See www.arts.mcgill.ca/mepp/new_prrn/background/index.htm.
44   See Simon Haddad, "Palestinians in Lebanon: Towards Integration or Conflict?," webposted on 14 May 2000, at www.prrn.org under "Research Papers."
45   See Ulrike Koltermann, "Who really wants them? Palestinians in Lebanon fed up with being a bargaining chip," *The Jerusalem Times*, 27 June 1997.
46   „Palästinenser in Libanon erhalten Arbeitsbewilligung," *Neue Zürcher Zeitung*, 30 June 2005, p. 2.
47   See Susskind, "Background Resource."

the wake of the widespread devastation caused by civil war and foreign invasion, has resulted in severe overcrowding.[48]

The number of restrictions Palestinian refugees face in Lebanon has been mounting since 1990,[49] and Lebanese authorities made it increasingly difficult for Palestinians who leave Lebanon, even temporarily, to obtain re-entry permits.

Violence against refugees is a constant threat, reinforced by the memories of the 1982 massacres at Sabra and Shatilla camps, where 2,000 refugees were slaughtered, as well as the 1985–1987 "Camps War," in which rival militias killed over 1,600 refugees.[50] In sum, Lebanon's Palestinian refugees generally live in adverse circumstances, often in poor and overcrowded refugee camps. Because of this, many have left the country, and the real number of refugees in Lebanon is likely much lower than the UNRWA figures suggest; probably less than 200,000 Palestinians are still living in Lebanon.[51]

---

48 See Ole Ugland, ed., "Difficult Past, Uncertain Future: Living Conditions Among Palestinian Refugees in Camps and Gatherings in Lebanon," *Fafo* at www.prrn.org under "Research Papers."

49 See http://english.aljazeera.net/NR/exeres/FE7BEB3D-E5C7-4CE4-8A35-8F62B8DDBB35.htm; and Julie Peteet, "From Refugees to Minority: Palestinians in Post-War Lebanon," *Middle East Report*, No. 200, July-September 1996, at www.prrn.org under "Research Papers."

50 See Susskind, "Background Resource," as well as Ellen Siegel, "After Nineteen Years: Sabra and Shatila Remembered," *Middle East Policy Council Journal*, Vol. VIII, No. 4, December 2001, in www.mepc.org/public_asp/journal_vol8/0112_siegel.asp. In addition, during the Syrian occupation, Lebanon's Palestinian refugees – like Lebanese citizens as well – had to deal with the issue of enforced disappearances, see the report from Human Rights Watch, "Syria/Lebanon: An Alliance beyond the Law – Enforced Disappearances in Lebanon," May 1997, Vol. 9, No. 3 in www.prrn.org under "Research Papers."

51 See www.arts.mcgill.ca/mepp/new_prrn/background/index.htm. In an interview with ICG, senior UNRWA officials estimated that the number of Palestinians in Lebanon almost certainly does not exceed 250'000, while a 1998 Lebanese estimate put the number at a little under 200'000. See ICG Report, "Palestinian Refugees and the Politics of Peacemaking," p. 2. Further information on Palestinian Refugees in Lebanon can be found in Kais Firro, "Palestinian Refugees in Lebanon since 1982," in Ginat and Perkins, *The Palestinian Refugees*, pp. 193–99; and Laura Drake, "The Future of Palestinian Refugees in Lebanon," in ibid., pp. 200–29. About Palestinian Emigration

5.3.5   Egypt

The first Palestinian refugees arrived in Egypt in 1948 and 1956. They were followed by those of 1967, who were prevented from returning to their homes after the war. The exact number of Palestinian refugees in Egypt is not known and the results of the census conducted by the government in 1995 are not available, yet they are said to range around 60,000. Palestinian refugees in Egypt are not protected or assisted by neither UNRWA nor the UNHCR.[52]

Upon first receiving Palestinians in 1948, Egypt refused to create refugee camps, except for several temporary facilities that were soon evacuated. In addition, Egypt did not allow UNRWA to operate on its territories (excluding Gaza). At the same time, Palestinians have been excluded from the protection of the UNHCR, based on the fact that they receive assistance from UNRWA – regardless of the fact that only those who live within its areas of operation (which do not include Egypt) are assisted. It was only in September 2002 that the UNHCR reinterpreted the relevant Article 1D of the 1951 Refugee Convention in order to emphasise that Palestinian refugees are *ipso facto* refugees and are to be protected by UNHCR if the assistance or protection of the other U.N. body ceases. In light of this, Article 1D has included those Palestinians not living in the countries of UNRWA field operations within UNHCR's protection mandate. Yet despite this, UNHCR's office in Egypt has done nothing substantial yet to put the resolution into action and Egypt's Palestinian refugees remain without assistance or legal protection.[53]

The Egyptian government has pledged "to preserve Palestinian nationality"; Palestinians living in Egypt, therefore, were not naturalized. Besides, Egypt is the only country that requires its recognized Palestinian refugees to regularly renew their visas; in addition, they

---

from Lebanon, see Mohamed Kamel Doraï, "Palestinian Emigration from Lebanon to Northern Europe: Refugees, Networks, and Transnational Practices," at www.prrn.org under "Research Papers."

52   See Oroub El-Abed, "Palestinians in Egypt," and "The invisible Palestinians of Egypt. Refugees face discrimination, poverty and no access to basic services," at www.prrn.org under "Research Papers."

53   Ibid.

have to report to a local police station every month.[54] Furthermore, Palestinians currently need to pay university fees in foreign currency, and they are no longer permitted to go to Egyptian public schools. Although having a right to employment, Egypt's Palestinians are disadvantaged and restricted as to accessing the labour market.[55] In other words, their vocational, educational and social opportunities are significantly curtailed.

54   Edward Said, "Introduction: The Right of Return at Last," in Aruri (ed.), *Palestinian Refugees*, p. 3.
55   Ibid.

PART II

Contradictory Interpretations
of the *Right of Return*

6 IS THERE A *RIGHT OF RETURN?*

The preceding analysis of the historical aspects of the Palestinian refugee question, and the so far unsuccessful attempts to solve it through political negotiations (which will be discussed in the third part of this paper), point to one key term which represents the basic bone of contention: the *right of return*. The core of the Israeli-Palestinian conflict over the question of refugees lies in the fact that one side is clamouring for their *right of return* while the other adamantly rejects it. We shall see that throughout the 2000–2001 negotiations, the Palestinians underestimated the degree to which Israelis associate even a theoretical Palestinian *right of return* with the prospect of the end of Israel as a Jewish state. On the other hand, Israelis simply cannot comprehend why Palestinian refugees, if given a chance to live in their own state, are emphasizing a right to return to what has become an alien country. Israelis fear that the Palestinians continue to harbour the desire to undermine Israel's long-term viability as a Jewish state.

In the peace negotiations, Israelis have tried to counter their anxiety by denying outright the Palestinians' *right of return*. Yet such attempts cannot be futile considering that two-thirds of the Palestinian people are still living as refugees, thus Palestinian nationalism remains, at its roots, a diaspora movement. The sense of injustice at being evicted from their land pervades Palestinians' national consciousness and has defined their struggle – even more than the desire to establish an independent state. Therefore, denying a *right of return* would not end the conflict; if would only transfer the seat of unrest to the Palestinian diaspora without eliminating the threat to Israel's security.[1]

Thus, the *right of return* cannot be ignored. Yet does it really exist as a legal "right"? This chapter is to shed light on the legal aspects of the *right of return*. The legal examination will be preceded by an analysis of the different perceptions Israelis and Palestinians have regarding the *right of return*. In addition, since U.N. General Assembly Resolution

---

1   Hussein Agha and Robert Malley, "The Last Negotiation: How to End the Middle East Peace Process," *Foreign Affairs*, Vol. 81, No. 3, May/June 2002, pp. 14–15.

(UNGAR) 194 is often cited as a legal basis for the *right of return*, this resolution will be scrutinized carefully.

UNGAR 194 was passed on 11 December 1948 by the United Nations General Assembly. As seen in the first part of this research, the resolution expressed appreciation for the efforts of Bernadotte who had been assassinated in September 1948 by members of Lehi. It dealt with the situation in Palestine at that time, including the role of the United Nations Conciliation Commission for Palestine (UNCCP) which consisted of representatives from Turkey, the United States and France, and which was established for the primary purpose of resolving the Palestinian refugee crisis and seeking a solution for the Israeli-Palestinian problem in line with the partition recommendation.[2]

The resolution consists of 15 articles, the most widely known being Article 11, which sets general criteria for the return of Palestinian refugees:

> 11. Resolves that the refugees wishing to return to their homes and live at peace with their neighbours should be permitted to do so at the earliest practicable date, and that compensation should be paid for the property of those choosing not to return and for loss of or damage to property which, under principles of international law or in equity, should be made good by the Governments or authorities responsible;
> Instructs the Conciliation Commission to facilitate the repatriation, resettlement and economic and social rehabilitation of the refugees and the payment of compensation, and to maintain close relations with the Director of the United Nations Relief for Palestine Refugees and, through him, with the appropriate organs and agencies of the United Nations.[3]

Other relevant Articles are 7 (protection and free access to the Holy Places), 8 (demilitarisation and U.N. control over Jerusalem) and 9 (free access to Jerusalem).

---

2   See Susan Akram, "Reinterpreting Palestinian Refugee Rights under International Law," in Naseer Aruri, ed., *Palestinian Refugees: The Right of Return* (London: Pluto Press, 2001), p. 169. For more information on the UNCCP, see Michael Fischbach, "The United Nations and Palestinian Refugee Property Compensation," *Journal of Palestine Studies*, Vol. XXXI, No. 2, Winter 2002, pp. 34–50.

3   See UNGAR 194 in Laqueur and Rubin, *The Israeli-Arab Reader*, pp. 83–86.

Let us proceed with an analysis of the differing manner in which Israelis and Palestinians respectively interpret not only UNGAR 194, but the *right of return* in general.

6.1   Israeli Views

6.1.1 Regarding Palestinian Refugees

Mainstream Israeli commentators are virtually unanimous in that no Israeli government can allow a substantial change of the demographic balance of the state – the very *raison d'être* of which is its Jewish character. In other words, a massive return of Palestinian refugees to Israel is out of the question for the vast majority of Israelis. Neither, for that matter, would Israel easily assume moral responsibility for the refugee issue.[4]

Shlomo Gazit formulates the Israeli position in the following manner:

> Israel denies the legality of the Palestinian claim. If it recognizes the "right" of return it would also be admitting responsibility, and perhaps even culpability for creating the problem. But Israel categorically denies any responsibility for the War of 1948. On the contrary, the guilt and responsibility are all Arab-Palestinian ... Israel would deny any responsibility even if there were no practical demands for a "return" of the refugees; even more so when recognition of such a right would deny Israel the right to control and veto the number of returnees ...
> Israel also rejects "return" for material reasons. There is no possibility of allowing the refugees to return to their original homes and lands without completely undermining the fabric of Israeli society ...[5]

---

4   Rex Brynen, "Palestinian Refugees and the Middle East Peace Process,"; Akiva Eldar, "The Israeli Media and the Refugee Problem." Both articles are available at www.prrn.org.

5   Shlomo Gazit, "The Palestinian Refugee Problem," Final *Status Issues Study No. 2* (Tel Aviv: Jaffee Center for Strategic Studies, 1995), pp. 7–8, cited in ibid.

Similarly, Shimon Peres characterizes the *right of return* as:

> ... a maximalist claim; if accepted, it would wipe out the national character of the State of Israel, making the Jewish majority into a minority. Consequently, there is no chance that it will be accepted, either now or in the future.[6]

For most Israelis, the *right of return* means nothing less than four million refugees at Israel's doorstep and has traditionally been a taboo. Prior to the second intifada, there seemed to be an Israeli readiness to accept a limited number of Palestinian refugees to be resettled within Israel proper. Yet at present, after continuous years of violence that readiness has completely disappeared. Israelis from the entire political spectrum reject the return of even a single Palestinian refugee to Israel. The Israeli Supreme Court's 2006 decision not to change the law on family reunification is the most blatant expression of the Israeli mood towards Palestinian refugees.[7]

The Palestinian demand for the full implementation of the *right of return* is the single most striking element to cause many Israelis to believe that Israeli-Palestinian peace is not possible. Israelis see a direct contradiction between the support for a "two-states for two peoples solution" and the call for the *right of return*, since they mostly do not conceptualise a right separate from its full realization. If a significant number of Palestinians were to implement the *right of return*, the State of Israel would become a bi-national state within one generation, while the State of Palestine would be a Palestinian state. Essentially, Israelis say, the *right of return* would grant the Palestinians two states in Palestine and the Israelis would become a minority in their own state.[8] Thus, the Israelis' main reasoning against a *right of return* is that it will certainly destroy Israel as a Jewish state. In other words, it has both demographic and security-related consequences. Besides, Israelis for the most part cast the blame for creating the refugee problem on the

---

6   Shimon Peres, *The New Middle East* (New York: Henry Holt and Company, 1993), p. 189, cited in ibid.
7   Gershon Baskin, "Right of Return to Palestine," 25 May 2006, at www.amin.org/eng/uncat/2006/may/may25–1.html. That decision of May 2006 by the Israeli Supreme Court stated that Palestinians without Israeli citizenship (thus Palestinians from the West Bank and Gaza) are not allowed to live in Israel even if they are married to Israeli nationals.
8   Ibid.

Palestinians and on the Arab regimes, taking little blame, if any, on themselves. At best, the events of 1948 are viewed as natural, hence excusable, wartime occurrences.[9]

Following this rationale, Israeli discourse has tended for decades to treat the refugee issue first and foremost as a *humanitarian* one, and any possible action by Israel on this issue, such as admitting a small number of refugees into Israel,[10] was framed as a humanitarian act – or rather favour – which Israel was willing to grant the Palestinians as a gesture of goodwill.

Israelis often claim that a nation's right of self-definition must include the right to maintain a democratic majority in its country. Particular relevance is attached to the case of the Jews, as they have no other state than Israel. This is regarded as distinguishing their situation from national majorities like those in Northern Ireland and Cyprus, which do have other states (Britain, Greece) where they can realize their cultural identity and speak their language. Israeli jurists claim that because of that right, international law allows states to discriminate between nationalities when it comes to immigration and acquiring citizenship.[11] That is why the various laws of return of the European countries have not been attacked in the European Court of Human Rights. Therefore,

---

9   Adina Friedman, "Unraveling the Right of Return," p.66, at www.prrn. org.

10 Notably, from the early 1950s until 1967, Israel maintained a family reunification program under which it claims that around 40,000 to 50,000 refugees returned to Israel; several additional thousands returned between 1967 and 1994. Plus, since the beginning of the Oslo process, Israel has collaborated in the *de facto* "return" to the Palestinian authority of thousands of 1948 refugees: PLO political figures and security forces, and their families. If return is defined as applying to "mandated Palestine," this may enable both Palestinians and Israelis to take satisfaction in the exercise of a return to the eventual Palestinian state alone. Yet in general, Israel, in keeping with its narrative, has preferred to avoid taking political initiatives in the refugee issue. The exception was the Israeli initiative at the Lausanne conference in the summer of 1949, as discussed in Part I. See Joseph Alpher, "Concept Paper: the Palestinian refugee problem and the right of return," *Middle East Policy* (Refereed), Vol. 6, No. 3, 1 February 1999, p. 167 (1). (webposted)

11 See e.g. Amnon Rubinstein, "There is no 'right' of return," *The Jerusalem Post*, 15 March 2005.

Israel is entitled to object to the *right of return*, as opposed to e.g. family reunifications on a humanitarian basis.[12]

Yossi Beilin, who negotiated refugees in Taba, reminds us that UNGAR 194 refers to Palestinian refugees "wishing to return," and not their right to do so. He cites that fact as the reason why the Palestinians and all the Arab states opposed the resolution when it was promulgated in December 1948. He further adds that only since the 1980s, have U.N. decisions referred to the *right of return*, a formulation the Palestinians obviously preferred.[13] He raises the question, thus, whether UNGAR 194 legally supports the claim for a "right" to return.

Overall, Israel is not willing to agree to an unrestricted influx of Palestinian refugees without having veto-power on the numbers or people flowing in. This is Israel's prerogative, and it may want to exercise it on a very limited, humanitarian basis. Second, most Israelis favour that any *right of return* should be implemented in the West Bank and Gaza, and once these territories assume independent status, Israel will have no interest nor right to prevent the Palestinians from having their own law of return.

6.1.2   Regarding Jewish Refugees from Arab Countries

Israel has long and repeatedly pointed out that some 700,000 Jews fled Arab countries in the years 1948–49. They have been successfully absorbed by Israel and now form an integral part of the fabric of Israeli society. They do not regard themselves as refugees nor are they regarded as such. Evidently there is no talk of their "right of return to Arab countries." On immigrating to Israel they were often forced to leave their property behind and in cases such as Iraq, special laws were passed depriving them of all rights to their property. It is Israel's position that when discussing issues of compensation, the property rights of the Jews who fled Arab countries be taken into account.[14]

---

12   Ibid.

13   Yossi Beilin, "What really happened at Taba," *Haaretz*, 16 July 2002.

14   See Michael Fischbach, "Palestinian and Mizrahi Jewish Property Claims in Discourse and Diplomacy," in Ann Lesch and Ian Lustick (eds.), *Exile and Return: Predicaments of Palestinians and Jews* (Philadelphia: University of Pennsylvania Press, 2005), pp. 207–224; Maurice Roumani, The *Case of the*

However, since Israel's acknowledgment in Taba 2001 that the issue of Jewish refugees from Arab countries was neither a Palestinian responsibility nor a bilateral issue (nevertheless maintaining that Jewish Refugees from Arab countries generally are entitled to compensation), this subject has lost significance in the Israeli-Palestinian context and has turned into a matter between Israel and the respective Arab countries.

6.2 Palestinian Views

As noted earlier, the *right of return* has been at the centre of the Palestinian position on the refugee issue since 1948. Nevertheless, there is no authoritative Palestinian definition of what constitutes the *right of return*.[15] Palestinian claims in this regard are rooted in the principles of neutral justice and the historical experience of Palestinian dispossession. They are also frequently buttressed by reference to UNGAR 194 (III), as well as more general principles of international refugee and humanitarian law.[16]

The Arabic term for *right of return (Haq al-'Awda)* resonates very strongly among Palestinians, not merely because of its clear political meaning. The Arabic word for "Right" *(Haq)* also means, or connotes, justice/justness, truth, and is one of God's names. Thus, the connotations the word itself evokes are of a strong, non-negotiable concept. Its connection to direct implementation is another question, yet neverthe-

Jews from Arab Countries: A Neglected Issue (Tel Aviv: World Organization of Jews from Arab Countries, 1983); and Robbie Sabel, "The Palestinian Refugees, International Law, and the Peace Process," *Refuge*, Vol.21, No.2, 2004, p.57.

15   Rashid Khalidi, "Observations on the Right of Return," *Journal of Palestine Studies*, Vol.21, No.2, Winter 1992, p.29.

16   Brynen, "Palestinian Refugees and the Middle East Peace Process"; Hani Al-Masri, "Palestinian and Arabic Media and the Issue of Refugees," at www.prrn.org. The legal aspects of the *right of return* will be discussed thoroughly in the following chapter. For a good overall discussion of the Palestinian perception, see Robert Bowker, *Palestinian Refugees: Mythology, Identity, and the Search for Peace* (Boulder: Lynne Rienner Publishers, 2003), pp.96–106.

less, it is a concept which can neither be negotiated nor compromised; it is simply a "given." The *right of return* has been a central principle in Palestinian collective identity, and it is a central element in the personal identity of many Palestinians. The refugee issue and the *right of return* are at the heart of the Palestinian national ethos and struggle and enfold memories of the nakba and the feelings of historical injustice brought upon the Palestinian people.[17]

Officially, most Palestinian public discourse on the *right of return* is unnuanced – in part to play to domestic constituencies, in part to preserve bargaining room towards Israel, and in part because the refugee issue in practical terms has not been a high priority for the Palestinian Authority to this point, since its main goal has been to reduce the impacts of Israel's occupation on the West Bank and Gaza. So the official position of the Palestinian leadership is congruent with the refugees' claim: an unrestricted right to return plus compensation based on UNGAR 194. Palestinian intellectuals are discussing the idea of a *right of return* which will be applied only on a future Palestinian state in the West Bank and Gaza (thus excluding Israel); such a concept, however, does not enjoy strong support among the majority of Palestinians.[18]

We have seen that most Israelis reduce the refugee problem to a humanitarian matter. Palestinians, on the other hand, emphasize the political nature of the problem, as well as the need for principled recognition by Israel of its responsibility for the events of 1948 and the fate that consequently befell the Palestinians. To justify their claims, Palestinians refer to various U.N. resolutions (mainly UNGAR 194) and to concepts of international law in general.

Central to Palestinian claims is the notion of *"Justice"* (also inherent in the word *Haq*), usually being absent in Israeli discourse. Strong emphasis is put on getting recognition for having gone through a grave historical wrongdoing. While Israelis highlight the notion of symmetry between Jewish and Arab refugees, Palestinians emphasize the notion of equality – or rather the lack thereof – in the relationship between

---

17 Adina Friedman, "Unraveling the Right of Return," p.66, at www.prrn. org.

18 See the results of a supporting survey published in Brynen, "Palestinian Refugees and the Middle East Peace Process."

Israelis and Palestinians. "Symmetry" as referred to by Palestinians is used in a different context, usually comparing World War II based Israeli claims from Germany to Palestinian claims from Israel.[19]

Palestinians also stress the notion of *"Choice,"* referring to the personal choice each refugee needs to have as to whether he wants to return or not. Here, it is interesting to point out that a choice not to return to one's home would not imply giving up the *right of return*, but would rather mean that while the right is a given, the mode of its exercise is a choice. The concept of choice is mostly absent in Israeli discourse, since in the concept itself lies one of Israel's greatest fears – namely that around four million refugees would in fact chose to return to their homes within Israel.[20]

Palestinians include in the concept of choice the notion that the *right of return* is primarily a *personal* right before being a *collective* one. Moreover, to most Israelis, "being home" implies living under the sovereignty of one's own state. Consequently, sovereignty is an attribute of a collective, and the return of Jews was applied to this collective, sovereign entity embodied by the State of Israel. It is therefore difficult for Israelis to conceptualise the much more salient attachment Palestinians have to their particular place (city, village, house) of origin. At the present stage, Palestinian refugees would not regard simply any place under Palestinian national sovereignty as "home."[21]

Finally, a major difference between the two parties is that Israelis aim at achieving an "end to the conflict," while Palestinians express more concern with historical justice.[22] An extensive series of interviews with refugees both in the West Bank and Gaza, as well as in Arab host countries, supports the notion that not only among non-refugee Palestinians, but also among refugees themselves there is a strong need for acknowledgment and recognition.[23] This crucial need calls for acknowledgement by Israel of responsibility for the creation of the refugee question, more often than not including acknowledgment

---

19   Friedman, "Unraveling the Right of Return," p. 67.
20   Ibid.
21   Ibid.
22   Ibid.
23   See the ICG Middle East Report No. 22, "Palestinian Refugees and the Politics of Peacemaking," at www.crisisgroup.org.

of the principle of the *right of return*. One refugee went so far as to state: "I'm prepared to accept that only one refugee will return, but on condition that this is recognised as exercising the *right of return* and not an Israeli humanitarian gesture that we have been denied for more than 50 years".[24] Such a demand could not be more contradictory to Israel's position, which is well prepared to allow some humanitarian measures, such as family reunifications – yet as long as it is not carried out in the name of the *right of return*.

Officially, the majority of Palestinians expresses the demand for a full realization of the *right of return*. In a sense, Palestinians are entrapped in their demand to recognize the *right of return*: since they have invested tremendous resources and prestige in trying to secure this right, they would lose face if a satisfactory agreement of some sort could not be achieved. Yet beyond official statements, not only Palestinian leaders and intellectuals, but a majority of Palestinians realize that Israel would not agree to the actual return of all refugees.[25] For the most part, the Palestinian leadership seeks some formal and principled recognition of a right to return and a choice-based approach which will provide the refugees with a variety of structured options. These options, which would be accompanied by a number of incentives and disincentives could be formulated in a way that only few would actually choose to return to Israel. In any event, any formulation of such an approach must satisfy, at least to some degree, the Palestinians' need for an official acceptance of responsibility on the part of the State of Israel.[26]

---

24 From an interview with a Palestinian refugee in Ramallah, 8 January 2004. See ibid.

25 Anis Al-Qaq, representative of the Palestinian Authority in Switzerland, put it bluntly: "The Palestinians are not stupid. Of course they know that Israel cannot take back four million refugees," elaborating that if a satisfactory solution on all other outstanding issues (Jerusalem, borders, settlements, etc.) was to be achieved, a majority of Palestinians would be willing to compromise on the realization of the right of return. Taken from a personal interview with the author in Bern, 14 April 2005. Also Gershon Baskin writes that in private discussions "most Palestinian leaders I have spoken with over the past years have said that they recognize, and they claim that most Palestinians realize, that the right of return will not be implemented within Israel proper." See Baskin, "Right of Return to Palestine."

26 Friedman, "Unraveling the Right of Return," p. 67.

Indeed, virtually every Palestinian interviewed insisted on recognition as a precondition for a settlement, stating, in the words of one, that "without it the problem will never disappear; the rest is details".[27] "To expect the PLO to renounce the right of return," said Wa'el Manasra, a Fatah activist, "is like asking Hamas to renounce Islam".[28] According to As'ad Abdel-Rahman, a PLO member formerly in charge of Refugee Affairs:

> Some form of recognition is absolutely crucial, for moral, political, and psychological reasons. Both in and of itself because of our history and the centrality of recognition to enabling a negotiated resolution of the refugee question, but also, specifically, because it would be coming from Israel.[29]

Another Palestinian, broadly supportive of the Geneva Initiative,[30] nonetheless lamented that it had disposed of the refugee issue as a "matter of immigration quotas. I agree with the outcome, but you need some form of acknowledgment of responsibility."[31]

Somewhat surprisingly, a report by the International Crisis Group (ICG) on Palestinian refugees found significant opposition to what they term "right of return nostalgia." The following quote not only illustrates that opposition, but also represents a view quite contradictory to the previously described Palestinian perception of the *right of return* as primarily being a personal right:

> People should understand that the homes whose keys they still have no longer exist, for the simple reason that the entire village was eradicated over half a century ago. The refugee question is a national issue about the rights of a people. If it's localised and reduced to an individual level, and your rights depend on whether your house or your village is still standing, we're finished.[32]

---

27 See the ICG interview with Bassam Salhi, leader of the Palestinian People's Party (PPP), El Bireh, 7 January 2004, at ibid.

28 ICG interview with Wa'el Manasra, Fatah activist, Ramallah, 8 January 2004, at ibid.

29 ICG interview with As'ad Abdel-Rahman, 4 January 2004 at ibid.

30 The Geneva Initiative and its relevance to the refugee question will be closely examined in the next chapter.

31 See ICG interview with a Palestinian official, January 2004, at ICG Middle East Report No. 22, "Palestinian Refugees," p. 11.

32 Ibid.

A refugee from the Jalazon Refugee Camp outside Ramallah adds: "Return to the village where your parents were born sounds beautiful and romantic, but life is complicated".[33]

In the words of Munther Dajani[34]:

> Once Israel recognizes its responsibility for the [refugee] problem, I think most of it will be solved. It would be very difficult for the refugees to go back, for example, to places like Jaffa or Haifa where Israelis are now living. It is a more reasonable solution for them to be compensated and to start a new life in Palestine.[35]

Questioning the practicality of a literal interpretation of the *right of return*, former advisor to the Palestinian negotiating team Rashid Khalidi, distinguishes between *attainable* as opposed to *absolute justice;* he, too, stresses the importance of a formal Israeli acknowledgment of wrongdoing. Khalidi further proposes reparations for those who will not be allowed to return and compensation for those who lost property.[36]

Similarly, Palestinian Legislative Council Minister Ziad Abu Zayyad distinguishes between the *right of return* to the refugees' actual former homes and the *right of return* to a Palestinian "homeland," which he argued, can be interpreted as the future Palestinian state.[37]

Salim Tamari, a key negotiator on the refugee issue, has also spoken about the *right of return* as resettlement in a future Palestinian state, coupled with a return of at least "several tens of thousands" to their original homes through family reunification.[38]

Overall, most Palestinian alternatives to an unconditional *right of return* do insist that Israel recognizes the principle of the right for return

---

33 Ibid.
34 Munther Darjani was director of research at the Palestinian Center for Regional Studies and Head of the Political Science Department at Al-Quds University.
35 Darjani made this comment in the framework of a roundtable discussion. See "Roundtable Discussion on the Right of Return: A Just Solution for the Palestinian Refugees," *Palestine-Israel Journal*, Vol. 9, No. 2, p. 68.
36 See Yifat Susskind, "Background Resource: The Crisis of Palestinian Refugees and the Right of Return," October 2000, at www.madre.org.
37 Ibid.
38 Ibid.

and compensation, yet simultaneously offer a willingness to negotiate specific modalities of a return.

A representative poll taken by the Palestinian Center for Policy and Survey Research in 2003 showed that if given the choice no more than 10% of the Palestinian refugees would actually choose to return to Israel.[39] The discrepancy between these findings on the one hand, and the Palestinians' absolute demand for recognition of the *right of return* on the other, shows that for Palestinian refugees, actual return is not the primary issue at stake – behind the sentiments expressed above by refugees and non-refugees alike lies rather first and foremost a powerful need for recognition that the Palestinians have suffered an historic injustice. At the same time, virtually all Palestinians interviewed in the ICG report recognize that a two-state settlement and full implementation of the *right of return* are fundamentally incompatible. For some, this significantly contributed to their opposition to such a settlement; for most, it led to acceptance of the necessity of a negotiated compromise on the refugee question.[40]

---

39 See Palestinian Center for Policy and Survey Research's "Refugees Polls in the West Bank/Gaza Strip, Jordan and Lebanon on Refugees' Preferences and Behavior in a Palestinian-Israeli Permanent Refugee Agreement," January-June 2003, at www.pcpsr.org/survey/polls/2003/refugeesjune03.html#findings.
40 ICG Middle East Report No. 22, p. 11.

7 LEGAL PERSPECTIVES

The existence of a *right of return* under international law in the case of the Palestinian refugees is in dispute and legal opinions on the issue come up with differing conclusions. We shall examine the arguments of both supporters and critics of the *right of return* in order to evaluate its legal relevance.

Those who claim that a "right" to return does not exist according to international law argue that Palestinian demands for a *right of return* are coupled with the call for self-determination. Dividing historical Palestine into two states, Israel and the future State of Palestine, would be incompatible with then granting an "inalienable" right to the same Palestinians to move to Israel, since "international practice …does not support the claim that the right of return following mass relocation of population is recognized under international law. This observation of state practice is enhanced by the lack of support in legal literature for the right of refugees to return to the country they have fled."[1]

State experience shows that states have indeed often allowed the return of their citizens who fled during wars. However, where there has been a division of a territory into two states on an ethnic or religious basis, there has been no such *right of return*. The Muslims who fled India for Pakistan have no *right of return* to India, the same being true for Hindus who fled from what is now Pakistan to India. The Sudeten Germans have no *right of return* to the Czech Republic. Julius Stone points out:

> Resettlement …has been the effective solution for the far greater and more complex refugee problems in Europe after World War II. It is a melancholy fact that this more humane course came to so little in the Middle East over so

1   E. Benvenisti and E. Zamir, "Private Claims to Property Rights in the Future Israeli-Palestinian Settlement," (1995), quoted in Robbie Sabel, "The Palestinian Refugees, International Law, and the Peace Process," *Refuge*, Vol. 21, No. 2, 2004, p. 54.

long a time that, for the Arab States concerned, the refugee problem was more useful than its solution.[2]

The argument further goes that if such a *right of return* were to exist, it would need to be based on one of the two accepted sources of international law, namely, an *international treaty* to which Israel is a party or a rule of *customary international law*.[3] We must therefore examine those two categories more closely.

7.1 The *Right of Return* as a Treaty Obligation?

The U.N. treaties dealing specifically with refugees carry no reference to a *right of return*. Israel is a party, however, to two general human rights treaties which do refer to a right of return: The "Convention on the Elimination of All Forms of Racial Discrimination," in which Article 5–(d) (ii) refers to "the right to leave any country, including one's own, and to return to one's country,"[4] as well as the 1966 "International Covenant on Civil and Political Rights," in which Article 12(4) states: "No one shall be arbitrarily deprived of the right to enter his own country."[5]

The question arises as to the meaning of the phrases "one's country" and "his own country," respectively. Does "his own country" refer to the country of which one is a citizen or national only; to any country in which one has been granted the right of permanent residence; or to the country which one considers 'home' and to which one is connected through history, tradition, race, religion, residence, family or other ties?[6]

---

2   Julius Stone, *Israel and Palestine, Assault on the Law of Nations* (Baltimore and London: The John Hopkins University Press, 1981), p. 68, quoted in Sabel, "The Palestinian Refugees," p. 55–56.

3   These sources of international law, together with "the general principles of law recognized by civilized nations," to be applied by the ICJ, are set out in Article 38 (1) of the Statute of the International Court of Justice. See ibid.

4   Ibid.

5   Ibid.

6   Sander Agterhuis, "The Right to Return and its Practical Application," p. 7, at www.prrn.org.

Solid ground exists for rejecting the argument that return only applies to nationals or citizens. In particular, Article 12 of the "International Covenant on Civil and Political Rights" also refers to a right of free movement within a 'State'. Given this, if would appear peculiar to interpret the Covenant as using 'country' in the context of the right to return to mean 'state'.[7]

In terms of the right to return, the Human Rights Committee, a body of experts which monitors the implementation of the Covenant, has given authoritative interpretation to the meaning of the phrase "own country." The Committee stated that the right applies even in relation to disputed territories, or territories that have changed hands. In paragraph 20 of General Comment 27, the Human Rights Committee determined that:

> The scope of "his own country" is broader than the concept "country of his nationality". It is not limited to nationality in a formal sense, that is, nationality acquired at birth or by conferral; it embraces, at the very least, an individual who, because of his or her special ties to or claims in relation to a given country, cannot be considered a mere alien. This would be the case, for example, of nationals of a country who have been stripped of their nationality in violation of international law, and of individuals whose country of nationality has been incorporated in or transferred to another national entity, whose nationality is being denied them. [8]

According to the Human Rights Committee, the scope of "own country" is clearly not limited to nationality in a formal sense; therefore, the fact that the Palestinians do not have Israeli citizenship does not prevent them from claiming a right to return. It can be stated generally that all Palestinians who involuntarily left their country of origin or were forced to leave had, as all refugees do at the time of their departure, a genuine connection with that country.[9]

International law provides a standard for measuring the existence of a "close and enduring connection" between a person and his or her "own

---

7   Ibid., p. 8.

8   See the Comment at http://hei.unige.ch/~clapham/hrdoc/docs/ccprgencom27. html.

9   Kathleen Lawand, "The Right to Return of Palestinians in International Law," in *International Journal of Refugee Law*, Vol. 8, No. 4, October 1996, p. 558, cited in Agterhuis, "The Right to Return and its Practical Application," p. 25.

country" through a set of criteria established by the International Court of Justice in 1955. In the landmark "Nottebohm Case", which focused on the determination of nationality, the Court held that "genuine" and "effective" links between an individual and a state were based on "…a social fact of attachment, a genuine connection of existence, interests and sentiments …".[10] The Court further noted that:

> Different factors are taken into consideration, and their importance will vary from one case to the next: there is the habitual residence of the individual concerned but also the center of his interests, his family ties, his participation in public life, attachment shown by him for a given country and inculcated in his children, etc.[11]

Other criteria suggested by the Court include cultural traditions, way of life, activities and intentions for the near future. The criteria established by the Court are likewise appropriate when determining a person's "own country" in that they are regarded as a standard measure of the effective existence of ties between the individual and the State.[12]

Thus, there exists the legal opinion that "one' country" and "his own country" should be understood as applying, in addition to nationals, to permanent residents and other persons with ties to the country. State interpretation of a right to re-entry, however, appears overwhelmingly to be applied only to nationals of the State. The 1969 "American Convention on Human Rights," Article 22(5) states: "No one can be expelled from the territory of the state of which he is a national or be deprived of the right to enter it." The word "national" is also used in the 1950 "European Human Rights Convention," Protocol No. 4, Article 3(2): "No one shall be deprived of the right to enter the territory of the State of which he is a national." Overall, no government interprets the Convention as meaning that the right applies to persons other than nationals or persons who were nationals. Accordingly, the *right of return* could be interpreted as a normal incident of nationality.[13]

---

10 See the Nottebohm Case (Liechtenstein v. Guatemala), Second Phase, Judgement of 6 April 1955 on www.icj-cij.org/icjwww/idecisions/isummaries/ilg-summary550406.htm.
11 Ibid.
12 Agterhuis, "The Right to Return and its Practical Application," p. 9.
13 Ibid.

Most Palestinian refugees were never granted Israeli citizenship. Thus, does the fact that they are not being Israeli nationals exempt Israel from admitting their return? John Quigley strongly rejects such proposition. He reasons that when a state experiences a change in sovereignty, the state is still obliged to allow admission to nationals who would have been entitled to admission had there been no change in sovereignty. Nationals of the former state acquire nationality of the successor state, or in other words, "the population follows the change of sovereignty in matters of nationality."[14] The U.N. General Assembly affirmed this position in 2000, when it asked states to adhere to propositions of law drafted by the International Law Commission regarding obligations of a successor state.[15] According to the Commission, a person with habitual residence in territory affected by succession of states is presumed to acquire the nationality of the successor state. Consequently, changes in state sovereignty do not eliminate a national's right to return to that state.[16]

Another argument in favour of the proposition that a national acquires the nationality of the successor state is found in international law where there has been an effort to avoid the status of statelessness.[17] To do so, the "Convention on the Reduction of Statelessness" requires that states transfer territory by treaty to incorporate "provisions designed to secure that no person shall become stateless as a result of the transfer."[18]

---

14 See Ian Brownlie, "The Relations of Nationality in Public International Law," 1963, quoted in John Quigley, "Repatriation of Displaced Palestinians as a Legal Right," *Nexus*, Vol. 8, 2003, p. 19, at www.nexusjournal.org.

15 *Nationality of Natural Persons in Relation to the Succession of States*, G.A. Res. 55/153. See www.unhcr.org/cgi-bin/texis/vtx/excom/opendoc. pdf?tbl=EXCOM&id=42bc068d2.

16 Quigley, "Repatriation of Displaced Palestinians as a Legal Right," p. 19.

17 For an individual, statelessness means no right of entry into the territory of any state. Statelessness is also a burden on other states. For humanitarian reasons, they are pressured to allow stateless persons entry and sometimes to provide other assistance. See ibid.

18 Convention on the Reduction of Statelessness, Art. 10, 30 Aug., 1961. See http://193.194.138.190/html/menu3/b/o_reduce.htm. (Israel ratified on 30 Aug., 1961). Ibid.

Quigley therefore concludes that in terms of customary international law on nationality, change of sovereignty and statelessness, Israel is obligated to recognize the nationality of displaced Palestinians and to grant them the right to return (treating the situation in Palestine as either a succession of sovereign states or as the formation of a sovereign state in a territory that previously was included under international governance such as the League of Nations mandate but did not enjoy sovereign status).[19]

Critics of Quigley point out that Israel, upon its acquisition of sovereignty, legislatively granted nationality to all those resident in its territory from the time of its creation until the adoption of the law of nationality in 1952 and to those who lawfully returned to Israel thereafter.[20] In fact, the proposition that, apart from granting nationality to residents in the territory, a state should grant nationality, on a mass basis, to those residing abroad and to their family members and descendents, including those who subsequently acquired nationality or protection of another state, finds little reflection in international law or practice. Any recommendations on granting nationality upon change of sovereignty, to the extent proposed in international law opinions, contemplate the granting of nationality to the population resident at the time of the succession or returning soon thereafter; in other words, to those who continue their habitual residence in the territory.[21] And those Palestinians indeed were granted Israeli citizenship.

It is also significant that at no point did Palestinian refugees outside Israel petition the Jewish State for Israeli nationality. That is not surprising, considering that nationality and allegiance to the respective state

---

19 Marc Zell and Sonia Shnyder, "Palestinian Right of Return or Strategic Weapon?: A Historical, Legal and Moral-Political Analysis," *Nexus*, Vol. 8, 2003, p. 100, at www.nexusjournal.org.

20 In 1952, the Israeli Knesset adopted a Nationality Law which identified those persons qualifying for Israeli citizenship. Any Jew coming to Israel automatically qualified. Persons other than Jews qualified if they had been a citizen of Palestine and had resided continuously from 1948 to 1952 or, if having left during that period, they had returned legally. See www.mfa.gov.il/MFA/MFAArchive/2000_2009/2001/8/Acquisition%20of%20Israeli%20Nationality.

21 Zell and Shnyder, "Palestinian Right of Return or Strategic Weapon?," p. 102.

are interlocking concepts. Allegiance to a Jewish State, however, was and largely remains anathema. What is being demanded is the right to return physically to their former residences without reference to nationality. Here lies the major weakness of Quigley's claim that Israel was required to grant the Palestinians Israeli citizenship: Palestinians were neither interested in Israeli nationality nor in allegiance to the Jewish State – their exclusive interest was to return to their homes.[22]

Another question is the scope of the right. The right to return of the individual refugee is usually not contested; however, it is contested in the case of large groups. Several scholars have argued in recent years that the right to return is also applicable when claimed by mass groups of people – especially in the context of Palestinian refugees.[23] According to this view, the *right of return* applies equally to masses of people as it does to the individual.

The older view maintains that, rather than falling under international human rights law, the issue of masses of dislocated people – such as in the Israeli-Palestinian conflict – is either a political problem or of self-determination. According to Stig Jagerskiold, the scope of the right of return or the right to enter one's country in the 1966 International Covenant is intended to apply to individuals asserting an individual right:

This Right is intended to apply to individuals asserting an individual right. There was no intention here to address the claims of masses of people who have been displaced as a by-product of war or by political transfers of territory or population, such as the relocation of ethnic Germans from Eastern Europe during and after the Second World War, the flight of the Palestinians from what became Israel, or the movement of Jews from Arab countries. The Covenant does not deal with those issues and cannot be invoked to support

---

22 Ibid., p. 104.
23 See Lawand, "The Right to Return of Palestinians in International Law," p. 538; Manfred Nowak, *UN Covenant on Civil and Political Rights: CCPR Commentary* (Kehl: NP Engel Publishers, 1993), p. 219–221; John Quigley, "Displaced Palestinians and a Right of Return," *Harvard International Law Journal*, Vol. 39, No. 1, 1998, p. 212; Eric Rosand, "The Right to Return under International Law following Mass Dislocation: The Bosnia Precedent?," *Michigan Journal of International Law*, Vol. 19, 1998, p. 1129. Cited in Agterhuis, "The Right to Return and its Practical Application," p. 10.

a right to 'return.' These claims will require international political solutions on a large scale.[24]

Thus according to the above view, the *right of return* applies only to individual persons, or small groups, but when ethnic conflict leads to significant population displacement, the issue must be resolved as a matter of group rather than individual rights. There is, however, no textual support for this position. Nothing in the *travaux préparatoires* implies that the drafters intended suspension of the principle in cases of mass exodus.[25]

7.2 The *Right of Return* and Customary International Law

While U.N. General Assembly Resolutions do not have the legal force to create binding international law, some claim that paragraph 11 of Resolution 194 reflected customary international law at the time. If a *right of return* were a rule of customary international law then it would, of course, be binding on Israel, irrespective of Israeli agreement or recognition of the rule.[26]

The existence of a rule of customary international law requires both State practice and *opinio juris*, namely, that State practice was part of a general recognition that a legal obligation is involved. It has been claimed that such a customary rule can be ascertained from the 1948 Universal Declaration of Human Rights, which states in Article 13(2): "Everyone has the right to leave any country, including his own, and to return to his country."[27]

---

24 See Stig Jagerskiold, "The Freedom of Movement," in L. Henkin, ed., *The International Bill of Rights* (New York: Columbia University Press, 1981), p. 180.

25 Susan Akram and Terry Rempel, "Temporary Protection as an Instrument for Implementing the Right of Return for Palestinian Refugees," *Boston University International Law Journal*, Vol. 22, No. 1, 2004, p. 79.

26 Akram and Rempel, "Temporary Protection," p. 55.

27 See the Universal Declaration of Human Rights at www.un.org/Overview/rights.html.

This provision recognizes the inherent relationship between a person and his country and is termed in unconditional wording. The exercise of the right, like others in the Universal Declaration, according to Article 29 is only subject to "such limitations as are determined by law solely for the purpose of seeking due recognition and respect for the right of others and of meeting the just requirements of morality, public order and the general welfare in a democratic society."[28] As examined in the previous section, some have argued that the *right of return* under this and other provisions does not apply to persons who are non-nationals of the expelling state. Not surprisingly, Israeli supporters have advanced this argument with some vehemence. Proponents of the *right of return*, on the other hand, claim that the view most consistent with other convention provisions, as well as with general principles of international law, is that "everyone" means all persons, nationals or non-nationals, and "his country" must be interpreted as place of origin.[29]

However, the initial problem with Universal Declaration as a source of international law is its doubtful binding character. As Ambassador Eleanor Roosevelt, the United States representative to the United Nations, explained at the time the Declaration was adopted:

> In giving our approval to the Universal Declaration today, it is of primary importance that we keep clearly in mind the basic nature of the document. It is not a treaty; it is not an international agreement. It is not and does not purport to be a statement of law or of legal obligation.[30]

The Universal Declaration is certainly a universally respected statement of ideals and has inspired much human rights legislation, including legislation in Israel. It is not, however, binding law, but rather a solemn declaration of the U.N. General Assembly which was approved by resolution of that body and which may contribute to the development of customary international law.[31] Elements of the declaration have indeed been set out in various human rights treaties, and they are binding on

---

28   Sander Agterhuis, "The Right to Return and its Practical Application," p. 5, on www.prrn.org.

29   See Akram and Rempel, "Temporary Protection," p. 78.

30   See the statement of Eleanor Roosevelt, Chairman of the Commission on Human Rights (1948), quoted in Zell and Shnyder, "Palestinian Right of Return or Strategic Weapon?," p. 99.

31   Ibid.

the parties to those treaties. Elements of the Universal Declaration that have not been incorporated into international treaties are meant to be respected by the States – without being binding international law, however.[32]

Article 13(2) of the Universal Declaration refers to "his country." Article 21 of the Universal Declaration uses the same phrase and refers to the fact that "everyone has the right to take part in the government of *his country*." (emphasis added). Since "his country", in legal terms, is usually defined as the country of one's citizenship (a definition which is supported by Article 21), it can be deduced that also Article 13(2) refers to citizens.[33]

We have already discussed the claim of the *right of return* being an individual right not applying to displaced masses of people. Accordingly, the *right of return* as stated in human rights law would not apply to displaced Palestinians because the right would not protect persons who were part of a mass relocation.[34] However, such argumentation does not consider the obligation Israel bears toward individuals under international customary law. One scholar reasons, therefore, that if the argument against a *right of return* for persons displaced *en masse* were allowed to succeed, then an argument in favour of the *right of return* for the individual displaced persons would have to fail.[35] The result would be no *right of return* at all. Such reasoning is contested by the claim that a large group of persons displaced nevertheless remains simply a collection of individuals who have been displaced. Neither the Universal Declaration nor the International Covenant on Civil and Political Rights (ICCPR) says or implies anything that would limit the *right of return* when the number of persons claiming it is large.[36] Therefore, one commentator on the ICCPR concluded that Article 12 applies, "even if masses of people are claiming this right."[37] If this was

32   Sabel, "The Palestinian Refugees," p. 55.
33   Ibid.
34   Quigley, "Repatriation of Displaced Palestinians as a Legal Right," p. 20.
35   See John Quigley, ibid., p. 21.
36   Ibid.
37   See Manfred Nowak, *U.N. Covenant on Civil and Political Rights: CCPR Commentary 220* (1993), quoted in ibid.

the case, Germans expelled from Czechoslovakia and Poland after World War II would be equally entitled to return.

Proponents of the *right of return* overwhelmingly cite UNGAR 194 as the primary source of international law to support their claim. It is thus vital to scrutinize UNGAR 194 as to its relevance and status in international law.

7.3 U.N. General Assembly Resolution 194

Israelis and Palestinians profoundly disagree about the meaning of U.N. General Assembly Resolution 194. On its face, the resolution asks Israel to repatriate the displaced Palestinians. Israel views UNGAR 194 as a call conditioned on circumstances that have not come to exist. In addition, Israel sees the resolution's call as a request only, since the General Assembly does not have the authority, under the U.N. Charter, to require member states to take a particular course of action. Palestinians, on the other hand, read UNGAR 194 as a demand, not a request; a demand that is not conditioned on any particular circumstance. Palestinians view the General Assembly's call for repatriation as a reflection of customary international law and legal norms requiring repatriation for wartime displacement and as governing how international law applies to the situation.[38]

Ruth Lapidoth, one of Israel's leading jurists dealing with the issue of Palestinian refugees, reminds us that although the Arab States originally rejected UNGAR 194, they later relied on it heavily and have considered it as a recognition of a wholesale right of repatriation. According to Lapidoth, however, this interpretation does not seem warranted:

> The paragraph [11 of UNGAR 194] does not recognize any "right", but recommends that the refugees "should" be "permitted" to return. Moreover, that permission is subject to two conditions – that the refugee wishes to return, and that he wishes to live at peace with his neighbours. The violence that erupted in September 2000 forecloses any hope for a peaceful co-existence between Israelis and masses of returning refugees. The return should take place only

---

38 Quigley, "Repatriation of Displaced Palestinians as a Legal Right," p. 17.

"at the earliest practicable date." The use of the term "should" with regard to the permission to return underlines that this is only a recommendation.[39]

Lapidoth further calls to bear in mind that the provision concerning refugees is but one element of Resolution 194 that foresaw "a final settlement of all questions outstanding between" the parties, whereas the Arab States have always insisted on its implementation, in accordance with the interpretation favourable to them, independently of all other matters.[40] As to selective interpretation: Few actually remember that the clause on refugees is but one small section of UNGAR 194. It is worthwhile recalling that UNGAR 194 also calls for an internationalisation of Jerusalem,[41] a fact which the Arab parties calling for the implementation of the resolution chose to neglect.

On the Israeli side, there is unanimous rejection of the applicability of Resolution 194 (III). The argument frequently rests on the notion that the *right of return* in international law is reserved for individuals who are or have been members of a nation state. Since the Palestinian refugees now (and before they became refugees) are not and have not been citizens of the state of Israel, the *right of return* has no legal force. Equally important according to this point of view is the claim that international law does not sanction the application of law when it is seen to be prejudicial to the interests of the state. Here again, it is argued that the application of UNGAR 194 implies the return of millions of refugees, a step which would terminate the state's Jewish character.[42]

Claims in favour of a Palestinian *right of return* are mostly backed with paragraph 11 of UNGAR 194, emphasizing that it "recognizes that under international law the Palestinian people were entitled to return to their homeland and receive economic compensation."[43] In addition,

---

39 Ruth Lapidoth, "Do Palestinian Refugees Have a Right to Return to Israel?," at www.us-israel.org.

40 Ibid.

41 See paragraphs 7, 8, and 9 of UNGAR 194.

42 Elia Zureik, "Palestinian Refugees and the Middle East Peace Process," at www.prrn.org.

43 See e.g. M. Bassiouni and E. Fisher, "The Arab-Israeli Conflict – Real and Apparent Issues: An Insight into its Future from the Lessons of the Past," in John Moore, ed., *The Arab-Israeli Conflict, Vol. I: Readings*, sponsored by the American Society of International Law (Princeton: Princeton University Press, 1974), p. 645, quoted in ibid.

further General Assembly Resolutions have repeatedly referred to Resolution 194 and described Palestinian refugee return as a right. In one resolution, the General Assembly *"reaffirms* also the inalienable right of the Palestinians to return to their homes and property from which they have been displaced and uprooted, and calls for their return."[44]

U.N. General Assembly Resolutions cannot, however, create international law. With the exception of resolutions dealing with budget and internal U.N. affairs, States are not obliged to comply with resolutions of the U.N. General Assembly. The U.N. General Assembly is not a law-making body and neither the U.N. Charter nor any other legal instrument has empowered it with a law-making capacity. The fact that the U.N. may repeat or reaffirm a resolution does not empower it with legal force.

Binding resolutions can solely be issued by the Security Council. Notably, the only resolution of the Security Council that addresses the Palestinian refugee problem is Resolution 242 of 22 November 1967, which merely calls for "achieving a just settlement of the refugee problem,"[45] without prescribing the elements of the aspired solution and without mention of repatriation. Thus, there is no basis for a right to return in the resolutions of the Security Council.[46]

Also the precise wording of UNGAR 194 deserves careful examination. The word "right" is not used at all. In addition, the Resolution uses the word "should" and not "shall". In U.N. documents the word "should" is regarded as recommendatory language and is not used where an obligation is set out. The term "should" is clearly hortatory, not obligatory. Consequently, a "right" to return – unlike the clause on compensation – cannot be specifically derived from UNGAR 194.[47]

Israel has therefore always taken the position that it is not legally obliged to repatriate the displaced Palestinians, since UNGAR 194 neither spoke of return as a matter of right for the Palestinians nor did

44 See G.A. Res 3236 (1974), at http://domino.un.org/UNISPAL.NSF/9a798adbf322aff38525617b006d88d7/025974039acfb171852560de00548bbe?OpenDocument&Highlight=2,3236.
45 See Resolution 242 at www.un.org/documents/sc/res/1967/scres67.htm.
46 Zell and Shnyder, "Palestinian Right of Return or Strategic Weapon?," p. 113.
47 Sabel, "The Palestinian Refugees," p. 55.

General Assembly resolutions normally constitute binding authority over sovereign States. Finally, Israel pointed to the use of "should" in the resolution as implying less than legal obligation.

Besides, Israeli voices argue, UNGAR 194 was adopted before Israel became a member of the United Nations. Israel was therefore unable to participate in the General Assembly vote. However, all Arab nations, including those where UNRWA had established refugee camps, were able to vote on the resolution, and all of them voted unanimously against it. The reason was not only that Arab acceptance of UNGAR 194 would have represented an indirect recognition of Israel, but also the fact that not all of the resolution's 15 different paragraphs fitted Arab interests. As mentioned above, UNGAR 194 among other issues calls for an internationalisation of Jerusalem. As a consequence, voting in favour of UNGAR 194 ultimately would also mean to object to Jerusalem being under Arab sovereignty.

Yet apart from the eventually formulated plain text, it is also essential to take a closer look at the process, under which UNGAR 194 came into being. During the debates in the General Assembly towards formulating UNGAR 194, the delegate of the United Kingdom, who drafted the resolution, however, called the provision on displaced persons a "precise directive," a characterization which makes sense only if it is a call for repatriation.[48] The U.S. delegate stated that the draft resolution "aimed at facilitating the repatriation and resettlement of refugees."[49] In the First Committee debate, no State other than Israel questioned repatriation as a right. Delegates who addressed the issue were consistent in either stating or assuming that Israel was required to repatriate the refugees.[50]

Furthermore, Israel argued that since the Assembly called for repatriation only "at the earliest practicable date," repatriation was not legally required. This argument is countered by the interpretation that the General Assembly was concerned that Israel would not implement

---

48 See U.N. GAOR, 3rd Sess. 184th mtg, 1948, (Mr. McNeill, U.K.), cited in Agterhuis, "The Right to Return and its Practical Application," p. 24.
49 See Mr. Dulles, U.S.A., in ibid.
50 The Israeli delegate, Moshe Shertok, expressed on occasion that Israel "believed that serious thought should be given to the resettling of the Arab refugees in neighbouring territories." See ibid.

repatriation promptly. The Assembly contemplated that return would be effectuated by diplomatic means through the U.N. Conciliation Commission for Palestine and assumed that the logistics of a return would require a period of time. The U.K. draft resolution had used the phrase "earliest possible date," yet after debate it was changed to "practicable" in order to clarify the intention of the proposal and as a partial response to concerns expressed by the Israeli delegation that a return prior to a peace agreement would create security problems. This amendment took place only in the English text.[51]

UNGAR 194 was drafted in both French and English. The United Kingdom drafted the French text to read *"le plus tôt possible,"* as an equivalent of the English "as soon as possible." While the English phrase was changed to "at the earliest practicable date," the French phrase was not. As a result, the repatriation clause reads "as soon as practicable" in English, and "as soon as possible" in French. One scholar, therefore, concluded that UNGAR 194 intended that the displaced Palestinians be allowed to return "as soon as practically possible."[52]

Israel further maintained that since it was being asked to repatriate only those Palestinians "wishing to …live at peace with their neighbours," it was not being asked to repatriate them all, and that the Assembly had thus not viewed their return as obligatory. The phrase "live at peace" was not explained in the debates leading to the adoption of UNGAR 194. One commentator argued that the phrase "wishing to live at peace" was meant to refer to those who were inclined to live under Israeli sovereignty. Refugees not wishing to live in peace with their neighbours were the ones who chose to live abroad.[53] Be that as it may, subsequent U.N. resolutions at any rate omitted the phrase "wishing to live at peace".[54]

Overall, UNGAR 194 (III) has been reaffirmed more than 110 times by the U.N. General Assembly and constitutes the primary authority for proponents of a Palestinian *right of return*. Such reaffirmations are significant "because of their role in the codification and progressive

---

51 Ibid.
52 Such conclusion was formulated by John Quigley in "Repatriation of Displaced Palestinians as a Legal Right," p. 25.
53 Quigley, "Displaced Palestinians and a Right of Return," p. 187.
54 Agterhuis, "The Right to Return and its Practical Application," p. 24.

development of international law."[55] When a resolution restates already existing law, as in the case of UNGAR 194, it becomes binding on member States not necessarily *via* that resolution, but through the declared law.[56] Although UNGAR 194 does not specifically mention a "right" of return, many commentators reason that such right is still implied by the resolution. Be that it as it may, the abovementioned arguments demonstrate the complexity of the question and the difficulty in determining whether there exists a *right of return* as a generally recognized right.

7.4   The Practice of Refugee Return

When examining state practice in the context of population transfers, one must differentiate between two questions. The first question relates to the *ex ante* decision to create such transfers, while the second question relates to the *ex post factum* decision to react to such transfers after their occurrence. Previous state practice, especially in the wake of the two World Wars suggested that population transfer was considered to be legal and moral, and indeed the preferred option to deal with inter-ethnic strife. This opinion has since changed. Population transfer is deemed illegal and even highly immoral. The more crucial question nowadays is the second question, related to the consequences of the transfer. The cases of Bosnia-Herzegovina and Cyprus will serve to examine that question.

a) The Legality of Population Transfer: Then and Now

At the time of the creation of the Palestinian refugee problem, the policy of what is now termed "ethnic cleansing" was viewed rather favourably. The 20th century was sometimes coined "the century of the displaced persons."[57] Millions of people became victim of resettlement

---

55   Luke Lee, "The Preventive Approach to the Refugee Problem," *Williamette Law Review*, Vol. 28, 1992, p. 829, quoted in ibid.

56   Ibid.

57   „Das Jahrhundert der Vertriebenen," as used by Nora Refaeil in her article „Das Recht auf Rückkehr zwischen Traum und Wirklichkeit: Der gordische

and expulsion. Forced resettlement and exchange of ethnically or religiously defined populations served at the beginning of the 20th century as a solution to ethnic conflicts and were considered a legal measure to promote peace and stability.[58]

The first population-exchange agreements involved Bulgaria, Greece and Turkey: The Bulgaria-Greece Treaty of Nueilly of 27 November 1919 provided for the relocation of 46,000 Greeks from Bulgaria, and 96,000 Bulgarians from Greece. This agreement inspired the Greek and Turkish governments to implement a similar policy but on a greater scale. The Greek-Turkish War which followed World War I ended in 1922 with the defeat of the Greek army in Asia Minor. This defeat, and the subsequent harsh Turkish measures against Greek communities in Turkey, precipitated a large wave of Greek refugees who fled their homes in Turkey. In light of these developments, the two enemy countries provided in their peace treaty for a mutual exchange of populations. Under the treaty, about two million Greeks, who had formerly been Turkish citizens, and about half a million Turks, who had formerly been Greek citizens, left or were forced to leave for the other side. This solution to potential inter-ethnic violence was later praised as the optimal solution, despite the plight of those individuals who had to bear the burden of relocation.[59]

The architects of the post-World War II world order were impressed by that solution,[60] and decided to repeat it with respect to about 15 million Germans living in Eastern Europe. The Potsdam Declaration, issued by the Allied Powers at the end of World War II, provided for the transfer to Germany of German populations remaining in Poland, Czechoslovakia, Hungary and Austria "in an orderly and humane manner."[61] (That the following mass transfer evidently was going to

Knoten im israelisch-palästinensischen Konflikt," *Neue Zürcher Zeitung*, 1 March 2005, p. 9.

58 Ibid.

59 See Eyal Benvenisti, "The Right of Return in International Law: An Israeli Perspective," at www.prrn.org.

60 The British Prime Minister, Winston Churchill, commented favourably on this proposed solution in his speech before the House of Commons. He relied on the positive experience of the Turkish-Greek population exchange, which he viewed as a success. See ibid.

61 See the Potsdam Conference Protocol, 2 August 1945, Section XII, at www.yale.edu/lawweb/avalon/decade/decade17.htm.

produce grave human suffering and indeed caused the death of more than two million of those expelled shall not be elaborated here.) Other transfer agreements, on a smaller scale, were implemented in certain parts of Central and Eastern Europe, following the redrawing of borders.[62] An additional policy of population transfer was adopted in 1947 to settle the dispute between Hindus and Muslims in British India and resulted in the mass relocation of millions.[63]

Thus, in the first half of the 20th century, the states' interest in having a homogenously structured ethnical composition of their populations was put above the right of individuals to live in their native country. As a result, human rights in a present sense – which, however, had not yet been formulated at that time – were grossly violated.[64]

State practice has changed since then. The mass transfer of populations that took place during the Turkish invasion of Cyprus in 1974 was condemned by the international community. In the wake of the atrocities committed in former Yugoslavia, such – although late – condemnation led to the creation of the term "ethnic cleansing" and its definition as a war crime. Thus, whatever was deemed acceptable if not legal in the in the first half of the 20th century (expulsion and ethnic cleansing) is now rejected as illegal.

b) Return as a Remedy

Obviously, not all wrongs can be remedied by reinstating the *status quo ante*. Third parties' expectations and other considerations merit respect. This equally applies to the context of mass transfer of populations. Here we can distinguish between two different approaches: one dealing with immediate response, while the other focuses on late responses to refugee problems.

Immediate response: The first and most striking precedent which supports the claim of a remedy of the nature of a legal right to individual return can be found in the Dayton agreement of 1995 regarding Bosnia and Herzegovina.[65] Its Annex 7 stipulates in Article 1:

---

62   Benvenisti, "The Right of Return in International Law," p. 8.

63   Ibid.

64   Refaeil, „Das Recht auf Rückkehr".

65   The General Framework Agreement for Peace, otherwise known as the Dayton Peace Agreement (DPA), was signed in Paris on 14 December 1995

All refugees and displaced persons have the right freely to return to their homes of origin. They shall have the right to have restored to them property of which they were deprived in the course of hostilities since 1991 and to be compensated for any property that cannot be restored to them. The early return of refugees and displaced persons is an important objective of the settlement of the conflict in Bosnia and Herzegovina. The Parties confirm that they will accept the return of such persons who have left their territory, including those who have been accorded temporary protection by third countries.[66]

This formulation was the resolution of the international community to undo the ethnic cleansing policy implemented in Bosnia-Herzegovina between 1991 and 1995, which had caused more than two million refugees and displaced persons.[67] It is backed by an elaborate institutional apparatus that oversees the implementation of this policy.[68] Thanks to the heavy involvement of this apparatus, refugees began a slow process of return to their homes;[69] however, Bosnia's overall division along

---

and ended the Bosnian civil war by establishing The Republic of Bosnia and Herzegovina, consisting of two entities, the Federation of Bosnia and Herzegovina and the Republika Srpska. See Benvenisti, "The Right of Return in International Law," p. 8.

66 Chapter 1, Article I(1) of Annex 7, General Framework Agreement for Peace in Bosnia Herzegovina, Dec. 14, 1995, available at www.ohr.int/dpa/default. asp?content_id=380. The U.N. Security Council welcomed the Dayton Accord on 15 December 1995. See www.nato.int/ifor/un/u951215a.htm.

67 "Refugees" are those who have left their homes and fled to a country outside of Bosnia, whereas "displaced persons" are those who fled their homes but remained in Bosnia.

68 The DPA created the Office of the High Representative (OHR) to oversee the civilian implementation of the agreement. Along with the OHR, other international organizations – The U.N. High Commissioner for Refugees (UNHCR), the U.N. Mission in Bosnia Herzegovina (UNMIBH), and the Organization for Security and Cooperation in Europe (OSCE), and eventually the Commission for Real Property Claims (CRPC) – played a significant operational role in the return of refugees and displaced persons to their pre-war property. For a review of the role of the international organizations in the implementation of Property Laws, see Lynn Hastings, "Implementation of the Property Legislation in Bosnia Herzegovina," *Stanford Journal of International Law*, Vol. 37, 2001, p. 221, cited in Benvenisti, "The Right of Return in International Law," p. 9.

69 According to UNHCR, since the signing of the agreement more than 428,000 refugees and 515,000 displaced persons have returned to their pre-war homes, from which 401,000 are minority returns (i.e. return of those who now belong

ethnic lines has largely remained in place and therefore the practical results of the ethnic cleansing appear to be of a permanent nature.[70] Nevertheless, regarding legal aspects, Paddy Ashdown, the High Representative in charge of implementing the Dayton-Agreement, stated: "We've invented a new human right here, the right to return after a war."[71]

---

to an ethnic minority to their pre-war places of residence which are now being dominated by a majority ethnic group). For further information on refugee returns, see the UNHCR mission to BiH at www.unhcr.ba. There is great difficulty in determining accurate numbers as there are refugees and displaced persons who returned to their pre-war homes, but chose not to report to the local authorities, or the opposite, those who have claimed their pre-war property, but de facto continue to live and work where they left to during war. See ibid.

70 Although according to UNHCR figures, more than a million refugees have returned to their pre-war homes, Bosnia has not regained its pre-war ethnic heterogeneity. This is explained by the fact that around 80 percent of the refugees who have been returned their property immediately sold or bartered it in order to live in a region of Bosnia where they now belong to the ethnic majority. Besides, studies regarding refugee return in Bosnia (such as the one conducted by the NADEL-Institute of Zurich's ETH, see www.nadel. ethz.ch) tend to focus on "durable return" and not "sustainable return" – the difference lying in the fact that regarding durable return, where returnees are asked whether they intend to remain in their places of origin, usually only those refugees are interviewed who did choose to return, while all others are not sampled. Solid numbers regarding the sustainability of Bosnia's refugee return would only be provided by a general census – yet conducting a census is vehemently resisted by most of Bosnia's political leaders whose position rests on the current formula where ethnical factors regulate the distribution of power. See „Vollendete ethnische Säuberung in Bosnien?: Kontroverse Einschätzung der Rückkehrer-Problematik," *Neue Zürcher Zeitung*, 20 October 2006, p. 7; „Der Fluch von Dayton," *Der Spiegel*, Nr. 45, 6 November 2006, pp. 134–136.

71 See "King Paddy" in *The Guardian*, 11 October 2002. The process of refugee return in Bosnia faces many obstacles put up by the ethnic majorities in control of the local governmental institutions, which included local legislation that confiscated the property left behind by those who fled the region. Such measures legalized the allocation of property along ethnic lines, which consolidated ethnic cleansing and presented a major obstacle to the repossession of property following the conflict. The result was that at the end of the conflict, Bosnia was composed of three mostly mono-ethnic areas. For a review of the various Abandoned Property Laws that were enacted during

Late Responses: The Dayton precedent has one major difference when compared to Palestinian refugees: Time. While refugees in Bosnia were able to return in the immediate years following their displacement, the time frame of the Palestinian refugees stretches over more than half a century. Thus the issue of time heightens the problem, in addition to other considerations which complicate the decision on the choice of remedies. The efforts to resolve the conflict in Cyprus – the most recent case of forced mass transfer which still lacks a solution – form a precedent and serve as a more related case of state practice.

Both in Cyprus and in Israel, people have settled in the past 30 and 50 years respectively in the areas of those expelled, and in the meantime they are claiming for themselves the right to live there. Besides, in the case of Israel, the character of the state, territory and population has changed so fundamentally that the question arises whether it still can be considered the home of the Palestinian refugees. Precisely this, however, would be a condition for giving a case to the right for individual return.[72]

In the case of Cyprus, it was the Turkish invasion, not a prior agreement, which prompted the mass relocation of populations. The conflict arose from the inability of the Greek-Cypriots and the Turkish-Cypriots to share power under a unitary system of government. In 1974, after eleven years of civil strife, Turkey invaded Cyprus and occupied its northern part. In the course of a few weeks, more than 200,000 Cypriots fled or were transferred across the "Attila Line,"

---

the war see Paul Prettitore, "The Right to Housing and Property Restitution in Bosnia and Herzegovina: A Case Study," BADIL Resource Center for Palestinian Residency and Refugee Rights – Working Paper 1, 2003; Rosand, "The Right to Return Under International Law Following Mass Dislocation: The Bosnia Precedent?," cited in Benvenisti, "The Right of Return in International Law," p. 9.

Only after extensive external pressure did the parties agree to adopt legislation that repealed the confiscations and facilitated the return of property to the original owners. This legislation was bolstered in 1999 with strong institutional mechanisms, involving local and foreign commissioners, to overcome strong local resistance to the return. While return and repossession of property is still underway, the real test still awaits the communities of Bosnia: The challenge of reintegrating hostile communities into one society, overcoming discrimination and strong separatist sentiments. See ibid.

72 Refaeil, „Das Recht auf Rückkehr".

established by Turkish forces. Greek-Cypriots evacuated the Turkish-occupied zone, while Turkish-Cypriots moved northwards and settled in the houses left by their Greek-Cypriot owners. The Greek-Cypriot refugees have since been resettled in the southern part of the island, some of them on Turkish-Cypriot property. The right to property and the right to return have since become the two major stumbling blocks on Cyprus' road to conciliation.[73]

In 1992, U.N. Secretary-General Boutros-Ghali formulated a "Set of Ideas on an Overall Framework Agreement on Cyprus," with the aim of providing a basis for negotiations between the leaders of the two communities.[74] This set of ideas, which was subsequently endorsed by the Security Council,[75] strove to strike a balance between the interests of the displaced persons and the goal of creating homogenous communities. It proposed territorial separation between the communities following ethnic lines. Two zones would have been created, each "administered by one community which will be guaranteed a clear majority of the population and of the land ownership in its area."[76] It also provided for a limited return of refugees, and for a compensation scheme to those who would not return.[77]

On 1 April 2003, U.N. Secretary-General Kofi Annan issued another plan, outlined in his report on the mission of good offices in Cyprus.[78] The report details Annan's efforts to find a compromise between the two warring communities. Annan makes a clear distinction in his report between "the positions adopted recently by the United Nations and the international community in the former Yugoslavia," and the Cyprus conflict. He emphasizes the time factor:

> In recent years the European Court of Human Rights has taken decisions recognizing the property rights of Greek-Cypriots in the northern part of the island and allocating damages at the expense of Turkey. (…) I took into account these developments and the positions adopted recently by the United Nations

---

73 Benvenisti, "The Right of Return in International Law," p. 10.
74 Annex to the Report of the U.N. Secretary-General to the Security Council S/24472 of 21 August 1992.
75 Resolution 744 (1992) of 25 August 1992.
76 Benvenisti, "The Right of Return in International Law," p. 11.
77 Ibid.
78 See the Report of the U.N. Secretary-General on his mission of good services in Cyprus, 1 April 2003, at www.un.org/Docs/sc/sgrep03.html.

and the international community in the former Yugoslavia, *but also the fact that the events in Cyprus happened 30 to 40 years ago* and that the displaced people (roughly half of the Turkish-Cypriots and a third of the Greek-Cypriots) have had to rebuild their lives and their economies during this time.[79]

The U.N. Secretary-General further acknowledges the "legitimate claims" of both the refugees and those who currently reside in their property. His compromise envisions a limited and gradual return. Each municipality or village will not absorb more than 20% of its population. Overall, each of the two political entities will re-admit refugees consisting of not more than 10% of its population. Significant economic incentives will be offered to those who choose compensation in lieu of return.[80] Interestingly, the Annan-Plan does not speak of a right of return, but of a right of residency. The decision whether to grant this right or not is taken by the respective government that is to absorb returnees.[81]

The fact that the Turkish side ultimately rejected the plan is of no relevance for an examination of the Palestinian case. The crucial point of the above suggestion to solve the question of refugees in Cyprus is the position of the United Nations, which reflects the U.N.'s reading of international law and is significantly strengthened by the endorsement of the Annan-Plan by the Security Council.[82] The U.N. position is based on two premises. The first premise is that governments have the authority under international law to negotiate away individual rights in the context of a peace agreement. The second premise is that the lapse of time, as well as demography, are relevant considerations for the negotiating governments. This position clearly rejects the reading

---

79 Ibid., Paragraph 108, pp. 23–24, emphasis added.

80 See Paragraphs 109 and 110 of ibid.

81 See Paragraphs 98–101 of ibid.

82 See the Security Council Resolution 1475 (2003), 14 April 2003, Sec. 4: "*Gives its full support* to the Secretary-General's carefully balanced plan of 26 February 2003 as a unique basis for further negotiations, and calls on all concerned to negotiate within the framework of the Secretary-General's Good Offices, using the plan to reach a comprehensive settlement as set forth in paragraphs 144–151 of the Secretary-General's report." See http://daccessdds.un.org/doc/UNDOC/GEN/N03/323/10/PDF/N0332310.pdf?OpenElement.

of international law as a system which provides each individual refugee with an unconditional right to return.[83]

In addition, unlike in the case of Bosnia and Cyprus, the goal in the Israeli-Palestinian context is not to establish a heterogeneous society under the umbrella of one state, but rather to create two sovereign homes for two peoples on the territory of the former British mandated Palestine; any other solution contradicts the aspired formula of a two-state solution.

On such grounds, the demand for an unconditional Palestinian *right of return* are put into perspective by the time lapse, the collision with the rights of those living in the expellees' areas for more than fifty years, and the inherent contradiction to a two-state solution.

***

Examining the legal aspects of the *right of return* demonstrated that it is difficult to prove that such a clear-cut right exists – it is equally problematical, however, to state that international law does not grant Palestinian refugees a *right of return*. As to this paper, which is a political analysis of the Palestinian refugee question, Marco Sassòli from the University of Geneva has probably formulated the most proper approach:

> As a professor of International Law I can make it short: The right for return exists. It is not completely undisputed, and an attorney might say that it is not sufficiently corroborated in International Law. Still this question never comes before a judge, since in International Law there usually is no judge. Accordingly, justice is not enforced by a *force majeure*, but by the parties themselves. Ultimately, they need to reach an agreement, even if one party is right and the other one is not.[84]

Sassòli is right in that the question of Palestinian refugees will not be decided in court in front of a judge, but in direct negotiations between

---

83 Benvenisti, "The Right of Return in International Law," p. 12.
84 Marco Sassòli made this remark in his presentation at the Conference „Das Ende der Reise erkennen: Palästinaflüchtlinge – Realitäten und Perspektiven," organised by the *Fachstelle OeME Bern, Forum für Menschenrechte in Israel und Palästina, OeME-Herbsttagung*, Bern, 20 November 2004.

the two parties. Or put differently, the debate over the *right of return* will be determined by politicians – not by lawyers.

Before exploring various political options for how the conflict might be solved in the future, it is vital to analyse the – unsuccessful – attempts undertaken to date. This shall be done in the next part of this paper, which will review the negotiations between the Israeli and the Palestinian leadership on the question of refugees.

PART III

Why and How the Issue of Refugees
Has Remained a Stumbling Block
at the Peace Talks

8 DURING THE COLD WAR

Conferences aimed at resolving the refugee issue have taken place sporadically from the creation of the problem until recent years. The first conference was convened by the United Nations Conciliation Commission for Palestine (UNCCP) in 1949 (as seen in the first part of this work), with the most recent taking place at Taba in 2001. Although Taba, and already Camp David in the year before, led to a significant lessening of the gaps, no mutually accepted solution to the refugee issue could be found to this point. The following chapters shall focus on how and why the issue of refugees remained unresolved by the parties. It is the main objective of this part to demonstrate that the refugee problem was the basis of disagreement between Israel and the Arab world at Lausanne in 1949 and that it was this issue which remained one of the dominant stumbling blocks both at Camp David and Taba a little more than fifty years later. The following examination will only include official negotiations between delegations representing their governments; unofficial proposals and negotiations, such as the Geneva Initiative, will be discussed in the fourth part.

8.1 The Lausanne Conference, April–September 1949

Three decisive events in the history of the Israeli-Palestinian conflict led up to the Lausanne Conference (discussed in chapter 3). The first was the 1947–49 war in which some 700,000 Palestinians became refugees. The second was the Israeli government's decision on 16 June 1948 that the refugees would not be permitted to return to their homes but that Israel would be prepared to pay compensation for their abandoned property. The third was U.N. General Assembly Resolution (UNGAR) 194, which established the UNCCP.[1]

---

1 Shelly Fried, "The Refugee Issue at the Peace Conferences, 1949–2000," *Palestine-Israel Journal*, Vol. 9, No. 2, 2002, p. 24.

Although a number of refugee delegations were present at Lausanne, they did not become major players in the negotiations. As the Arab delegations refused to talk directly with Israel, the UNCCP sat separately with each party. In order to break the ice, Israel was requested to make a good will gesture towards the refugees. Israel therefore publicly announced its readiness to promote the payment of compensation to the Palestinian refugees for their abandoned property. Yet pressure was also exerted on Israel to accept the return of a number of refugees. Israel staunchly opposed any such move and the Lausanne talks came to a dead end. But in July 1949, to the surprise of the Arab states, Israel put forward an unexpected proposal: To accept the return of 100,000 refugees to Israel. Yet Israel's decision was made conditional upon Arab agreement to a comprehensive peace, including the resettlement of the remaining refugees in Arab countries. Discussion within the Israeli government at the time also touched upon the possibility of absorbing a larger number of refugees, on condition that the Gaza Strip (with some of its refugee population) would be transferred from Egyptian to Israeli control, thereby improving Israel's military situation vis-à-vis Egypt. Ultimately, the Arab parties rejected the Israeli offer, after which Israel retracted it.[2]

Besides, it remains doubtful whether Israel ever had the intention of implementing such a proposal.[3] In fact, it was received in Israel by a storm of public opposition and a heated Knesset debate which underlined to Ben Gurion, and all successive governments, the fierce opposition of the Israeli society to Palestinian refugee return. At the end of September 1949 the UNCCP, following several futile attempts to renew negotiations, saw itself compelled to disband the conference.[4]

2 Joseph Alpher, "Concept Paper: the Palestinian refugee problem and the right of return," *Middle East Policy* (Refereed), Vol. 6, No. 3, 1 February 1999, p. 167 (1). (webposted)
3 Fried, "The Refugee Issue at the Peace Conferences," p. 25.
4 Ibid.

8.2 The Geneva Conference, January 1950

The 1950 Geneva Conference aimed to resolve practical questions, primarily the future of refugee money frozen in Israeli banks. Also on the table was the issue of family reunifications. The negotiators managed to make progress on the latter – until Israel demanded that in order to continue the discussions, the Arab states had to commit themselves to a peace-treaty with Israel. The Arab states in turn insisted that Israel first had to accept UNGAR 194. Israel, however, rejected this and refused to return to the conference.[5]

8.3 The Paris Conference, September–November 1951

In autumn 1951, the UNCCP made its final attempt to hold a peace conference. Moshe Sharett, who represented Israel in Paris, had been authorized by his government to reject the UNCCP as a mediating body, to work for direct negotiations between Israel and the Arab states, and to explore the possibility of discussing compensation without demanding an overall peace agreement like the Israeli government had done in the previous year.

Israel was surprised to find that the UNCCP proposed an Israeli gesture of allowing a part of the refugees to return. This was interpreted by Ben Gurion as imposing responsibility for the refugee problem on Israel, something he vehemently rejected. Israel thus retreated from its original intention to promote compensation payments and dismissed the UNCCP's proposals. As at Lausanne, the Arab states increased pressure by demanding the return of all refugees and Israel's recognition of this right, prior to signing a peace agreement. As a result of the mutual inability to compromise, the Paris Conference reached a stalemate. This bitter experience brought the work of the UNCCP to an end and in the following two decades no further committee-based effort was made to mediate between the Arab states and Israel.[6]

---

5   Ibid.
6   Ibid., pp. 25–26.

8.4 The Geneva Conference, December 1973 to January 1974

In the wake of the 1973 Yom Kippur War, U.S. Secretary of State Henry Kissinger initiated a new conference, again in Geneva, and tried to persuade Egypt, Israel, and Syria to obtain partial achievements by avoiding discussions of an overall solution. While Kissinger managed to make some advances, the conference itself was a failure. Opening on 21 December, 1973, it was viewed as rather ceremonial than practical and was not reconvened after 2 January, 1974. In Kissinger's protracted effort to bring states – which did not recognize each other – together at the negotiating table, the Palestinians were not invited to the conference due to Israel's incontrovertible opposition to their presence. On the one hand, this was the only time during the Cold War that the major powers were able to coerce the Arab states and Israel to attend a common conference. Yet on the other hand, that conference also demonstrated that nothing substantial could be achieved without a Palestinian delegation present and indeed, without discussing the refugee problem.[7]

8.5 Camp David, September 1978

After Menachem Begin was elected Israeli Prime Minister in 1977, Israel worked out a plan to remove Egypt from the circle of combatants by signing a separate agreement with it. The Egyptian leader of that time, Anwar Sadat, was willing to accept such a deal which offered the prospect of regaining the Sinai peninsula occupied by Israel since 1967.

Sadat's visit to Israel in 1977 compelled the Americans to accept his separatist outreach to the Israelis that was unapproved by the rest of the Arab world. As a result, a breakthrough in the Egyptian-Israeli channel was achieved. This, however, caused Egypt to be seen as having broken the united Arab opposition to Israel, and Sadat was subsequently accused of betrayal by the Arab world. In general, no

---

7   Ibid., p. 26; Yair Hirschfeld, *Oslo: A Formula for Peace: From Negotiations to Implementation* (Hebrew), (Tel Aviv: Am Oved Publishers, 2000), pp. 29–31.

Arab country at that time could allow itself a separate peace agreement with the Jewish State before the Palestinian problem was solved. Hence Sadat was compelled to win concessions from Israel on the Palestinian question. Besides, as the Palestinians were adamant that they would not participate in the talks, Egypt had to play the part of an uninvited stand-in for them. Consequently, in a meeting between Begin and Sadat in December 1977 in Ismaliya, Egypt, Begin realized how determined Sadat was to include the Palestinian cause: while Begin saw autonomy for the West Bank and Gaza as a final settlement, Sadat viewed it as a first step toward a Palestinian state. These contradictory views resulted in a deadlock, which persisted until summer 1978 when the U.S. invited Begin and Sadat to the Camp David conference.[8]

The conference opened on 5 September, 1978. Israeli Foreign Minister Moshe Dayan and Begin intended to focus on the Sinai. Yet the peace plan Sadat presented at the first meeting of the three politicians included a solution to the Palestinian problem along with a provision determining that the Palestinian refugees would be entitled to exercise their right, under the terms of UNGAR 194, to either choose between return or compensation. However, the proposal was rejected by the Israeli side. U.S. President Carter sided with the Israelis on that issue, arguing that the Egyptian offer would complicate an agreement.[9]

Already by 7 September talks were near to stalemate. Egypt and the U.S. not only asked Begin to give up the Israeli settlements in Sinai; Egypt's Under Secretary of Foreign Affairs Osama el-Baz strongly supported the right of the 1948 refugees to return to Israel based on relevant U.N. resolutions, and he also insisted on the establishment of an independent Palestinian state.[10] Dayan, on the other hand, proposed a plan which would allow Israel to expand settlements in the West Bank and Gaza Strip, while allowing some 150,000 of the 1967–refugees to return to their homes. Begin, however, did not accept connecting the issue of settlements to any other subject.

---

8   See Yaacov Bar-Siman-Tov, *Peace Policy as Domestic and as Foreign Policy: the Israeli Case* (Jerusalem: Hebrew University of Jerusalem, Leonard Davis Institute for International Relations, 1998), p. 15.

9   See the accounts of Moshe Dayan and Ezer Weizman cited in Fried, "The Refugee Issue at the Peace Conferences," pp. 27–28.

10   Ibid., p. 28.

Nevertheless, by the end of the summit, Begin eventually agreed to withdraw from Sinai and to evacuate the Israeli settlements there, as well as to grant a limited form of autonomy to the Palestinians in the West Bank and Gaza Strip in running their daily lives for a five-year transition period, during which the parties would discuss a permanent solution.[11] Carter's proposed "self-governing authority," together with Egypt, Israel and Jordan, was to be empowered to decide on the modalities for admission of persons displaced from the West Bank and Gaza Strip in 1967. As for the 1948 refugees, the Camp David plan merely called for a "just solution," with no mention of what that might entail.[12] Since the Palestinians were not even consulted, let alone involved, by the framers of the Camp David agreement, they had no intention of adapting the resulting provisions relevant to them – and the less did Israel.

In sum, the 1978 Camp David summit represented the last attempt to solve the Palestinian question during the Cold War years. Yet the Palestinian issue was treated secondary at best – subordinate to the greater goal of an Egyptian-Israeli agreement. Moreover, with emphasis being laid on the question of autonomy and the PLO being excluded from the talks, the refugee problem remained outside the realms of negotiation and was destined to persist for decades to come.

---

11 A crucial part of the Camp David agreement were the security provisions. During a transition in West Bank and Gaza for a period of five years, responsibility for external security in those territories was assigned to Israel and Jordan (although the latter was not even consulted): "Israeli and Jordanian forces will participate in joint patrols and in the manning of control posts to assure the security of the borders." See the Framework for Peace in the Middle East Agreed at Camp David in Ruth Lapidoth and Moshe Hirsch, eds., *The Arab-Israeli Conflict and its Resolution: Selected Documents* (Dordrecht: Martinus Nijhoff Publishers, 1992), pp. 196–198.
12 Naseer Aruri, "The Marginalization of the Basic Rights of the Palestinian Refugees: Geopolitics Over International Law," *Nexus*, Vol. 8, 2003, p. 65.

9 INITIALIZING ISRAELI-PALESTINIAN NEGOTIATIONS

After the signing of the Egyptian-Israeli peace treaty in 1979, there were no further peace negotiations between Israel and an Arab partner during the entire 1980s. After the end of the Cold War, however, matters changed rapidly. As the international geo-political constellation was no longer paralysed by the super powers' separate interests, the U.S. was able to organize a catalysing peace conference between Israel and its Arab neighbours, which opened in Madrid in 1991. That watershed event was to become the hotbed for any future Israeli-Palestinian negotiation. It is therefore essential – before we proceed to the Oslo process, which dominated Israeli-Palestinian negotiations during most of the 1990s – to first examine the Madrid Conference and its relevance to the refugee issue.

9.1 The Parties Start to Talk: The Madrid Conference, October–November 1991

In early 1991, after the end of the Gulf War and in line with President Bush's idea of a "new world order," U.S. Secretary of State James Baker tried to bring Israel and its Arab neighbours together at an international conference. The fiercest opposition came from Israel's Prime Minister at that time, Yitzhak Shamir, who was not willing to accept a separate Palestinian delegation, but insisted on applying the restrictive rules of Camp David, according to which the Palestinian representation was to take place only as a part of a Palestinian-Jordanian delegation. In addition, Israel demanded that the Palestinian representatives come only from the West Bank (excluding East-Jerusalem) and the Gaza Strip, and that no PLO representatives would be present – one of Israel's intentions was to leave the PLO outside and with it the refugee problem.[1] After Baker managed to persuade the Arab states and the

---

1 Shelly Fried, "The Refugee Issue at the Peace Conferences, 1949–2000," *Palestine-Israel Journal*, Vol. 9, No. 2, 2002, p. 28.

Palestinians to accept Israel's demands, the Madrid Conference opened on 30 October, 1991.[2]

Bilateral and multilateral channels of discourse were planned on subjects including the economy, water, disarmament, and refugees. When Israel met the Palestinian-Jordanian delegation for the first time, its leader, Haidar Abed el-Shafi, demanded in his opening statement no less than the full return of Palestinian refugees under the terms of UNGAR 194:

> As we speak, the eyes of thousands of Palestinian refugees, deportees, and displaced persons since 1967 are haunting us, for exile is a cruel fate. Bring them home. They have the right to return. (...) The international will had ensured their return in United Nations Resolution 194 – a fact willfully ignored and unenacted.[3]

Israel immediately opposed those demands. The following discussions were therefore brief, and for the following two years, Israel refused to conduct bilateral negotiations with the Palestinians.[4] Yet this apparent dead-end led to behind-the-scenes negotiations, which in turn led to the Oslo agreement. However, before we turn to the Oslo process, we first need to turn our attention to an important, yet often forgotten forum, which came out of the Madrid Conference: The Middle East Multilaterals.

9.1.1   The Multilateral Track: The Refugee Working Group

Since the onset of the Arab-Israeli peace process in 1991, the refugee issue was discussed in a number of different fora: the multilateral Refugee Working Group (RWG), the "quadripartite committee" (in the

---

2   For more information on Baker's diplomacy towards Madrid, see Kathleen Christison, "Splitting the Difference: The Palestinian-Israeli Policy of James Baker," *Journal of Palestine Studies*, Vol. XXIV, No. 1, Autumn 1994, pp. 39–50.

3   For the full text of Abed el-Shafi's opening statement in Madrid, see http://mondediplo.com/focus/mideast/a2299.

4   William Quandt, *Peace Process: American Diplomacy and the Arab-Israeli Conflict since 1967* (Washington, DC: Brookings Institution, 2001), pp. 310–313.

context of the Israeli-Jordanian peace treaty),[5] and in the proposed "final status" talks.[6] The variety of fora reflected not only the inherent dynamics of the issues, but also the interplay of compromises and agreements that have shaped the architecture of negotiation. Arab participants in the conflict long demanded comprehensive and international peace negotiations which would involve a multilateral negotiating framework (thus enabling Arab parties to pool their collective negotiating resources), and external participants (notably the United Nations, Europeans and the former Soviet Union, who were seen as more sympathetic to Arab aspirations than the United States). Israel, unsurprisingly, had long preferred a bilateral negotiating dynamic (which would enable it to take best advantage of its greater power) and had opposed all external involvement other than that of the U.S.

The structure that was adopted for the negotiations in 1991–92 reflected a compromise: the Arab participants (including the Palestinians) agreed to a series of bilateral negotiations with Israel (where it would not face a united Arab front), yet only under the condition that the bilateral talks were also complemented by a series of multilateral "working groups" on issues of regional significance: arms control and regional security, environment, water, regional economic development – and refugees.[7] In turn, the RWG rewarded the Palestinians with a framework that allowed them to negotiate with Israel with the simultaneous involvement of other parties – a constellation from which the Palestinians expected support for their positions.

The RWG was largely intended to reward the Palestinians for their participation in the broader peace process, and for their acceptance of several constraints on their participation. These constraints –

---

5   The "quadripartite committee" was established after the Israeli-Jordanian peace treaty in 1994, and also included Egypt and the Palestinians. It will be discussed in the section on the Israeli-Jordanian peace treaty.

6   In the framework of the Oslo agreements, difficult issues, such as refugees, Jerusalem, borders, and settlements, were to be discussed only at the end, towards negotiating the final status between Israelis and Palestinians.

7   For more information, see Dalia Dassa Kaye, "Madrid's Forgotten Forum: The Middle East Multilaterals," *The Washington Quarterly*, Vol.20, No.1, Winter 1997, pp.167–86; Robert Bookmiller and Kirsten Nakjavani Bookmiller, "Behind the Headlines: The Multilateral Middle East Talks," *Current History*, January 1996, pp.33–37.

demanded by Israel as a precondition for its participation – included a formal Palestinian representation within the framework of a joint Jordanian-Palestinian delegation, rather than independently; restriction of Palestinian representation to persons from the West Bank and Gaza, rather than the diaspora; and a prohibition on the participation of PLO officials.

It was understood that the multilaterals would generally operate by consensus, and that the chairs of the working groups would act as facilitators rather than exerting any procedural power or direction – an aspect that was underscored by terming them as "gavel holders". Canada was selected as gavel-holder for the RWG, and an overall steering committee was established for the multilaterals. Of the working groups, the RWG was clearly the most contentious one, touching as it did on sensitive – even existential – issues for many of the parties. It was for this reason that Canada was assigned RWG gavel, since it was seen by Washington as cautious and reliable while being acceptable to Israel and the other regional parties.[8]

The first two plenary meetings were held in Ottawa in May and November 1992, to be followed in the coming years by further sessions held in Oslo, Cairo, Antalya, and Geneva. In these meetings the RWG identified a number of key imperatives in its work. The first of these was *defining the problem;* that is, a need for a common understanding of the scope of the refugee problem and how to deal with it. A second priority was *promoting dialogue:* the Canadian gavel saw the RWG as a forum for regional parties to state positions, develop and test options and generally build confidence among the members. Finally, the RWG worked to *mobilize resources* for refugees. The Working Group cooperated with UNRWA to raise funds for the refugees.[9]

The RWG focused on seven main themes, each with a lead country or "shepherd". The themes were Databases (the shepherd for which is Norway), Family Reunification (France), Human Resources Development (U.S.), Job Creation and Vocational Training (U.S.), Public Health

---

8   See Rex Brynen, "Palestinian Refugees and the Middle East Peace Process," as well as Rex Brynen and Jill Tansley, "The Refugee Working Group of the Middle East Mulitlateral Peace Negotiations." Both articles are available under "research papers" at www.prrn.org.

9   Ibid.

(Italy), Child Welfare (Sweden) and Economic and Social Infrastructure (the European Union). In cooperation with the regional parties, the shepherds were responsible for defining needs, developing responses and mobilizing required resources.[10]

The experience of the RWG was described as one of "quasi-negotiation," in which discussion among the parties was complicated by differing views as to the role of the working group, and indeed whether it represented a forum for negotiations. Overall, the RWG faced a number of serious problems, which were:

a) Financial: A shortage of funds
b) Structural: The RWG did not operate as a cohesive group, but rather assembled periodically for plenary meetings or inter-sessional activities. Syrian and Lebanese non-participation in the RWG hampered the working group's efforts to target resources at refugee communities in those countries
c) Political: There remained a large gap between the publicly-articulated positions of Israel and the Palestinians on the refugee issue, with the former insisting on the "resettlement" and "rehabilitation" of refugees, while the latter emphasized the Palestinians' right to "compensation" and "return". These sorts of differences manifested themselves in discussions on family reunification, which were highly controversial and were met with stark resistance from Israel. The Israeli delegations were willing to consider family reunification as a discretionary humanitarian issue, but not as a political right for Palestinians.[11]

The most important problem was perhaps that the RWG – like other multilateral track activities – was hostage to the tone of the bilateral peace process; when the latter suffered, so did the former. This was particularly evident after Benjamin Netanyahu became Israeli Prime Minister in 1996, with the Israeli-Palestinian negotiations subsequently deteriorating. Faced with this, and especially with stepped-up Israeli

---

10   "Refugees in the Middle East Process," at www.prrn.org.
11   Ibid.

settlement activity in the occupied territories, the Arab League voted in March 1997 to suspend Arab participation in the multilaterals.[12]

9.1.2 The "Ottawa Process"

While the RWG won a quiet exemption to continue with small-scale activities, there were clear limits to what the official track would achieve. Therefore, a small group of Canadian officials and academics met in the spring of 1997 to discuss next steps. With the formal process slowed, Track II initiatives (multilateral contacts between Israelis and Palestinians in addition to the official, governmental negotiations) were proposed. Little hope was expressed that an effective dialogue could be held with hard-line members of Israel's right wing parties. However, Labour party supporters – by then out of power and freed from the constraints of representing an official Israeli position, were hoped to be more amenable to dialogue with moderate and well-connected Palestinians on the refugee issue.

While back-channel negotiations consist of secret official negotiations between representatives of contesting parties, Track II diplomacy is not official. Its structure and mode of operation have many variations. It can be run by ex-establishment persons, organizers of people-to-people activities, self-appointed advisors and academic experts. Yet it is vital that they have access to decision-makers.[13] In May 1997, it was decided to undertake such a dialogue, which resulted in the "Ottawa Process".

A so called "core group" subsequently began meeting regularly, discussing various aspects of the refugee issue and ways to resolve it. The "Ottawa Process" was a helpful forum and an additional track for Israelis and Palestinians to meet and to sound out the other side's expectations for the final status talks on refugees. It lost importance when official negotiations on a final-status started in Camp David in

---

12 Rex Brynen, "Much Ado about Nothing? The Refugee Working Group and the Perils of Multilateral Quasi-negotiation," *International Negotiations*, Nov. 1997, at http://www.arts.mcgill.ca/MEPP/PRRN/papers/ado.html.

13 Menachem Klein, "Track II Plans," in Shimon Shamir and Bruce Maddy-Weitzmann (eds.), *The Camp David Summit – What Went Wrong?* (Brighton: Sussex Academic Press, 2005), p. 178.

2000 and were continued in Taba in 2001, since Taba went far beyond documents prepared by the core group, both in its detail and vision. Some echoes of ideas raised in the Ottawa Process, however, could be seen in the negotiating texts. In general, while not being a venue for quiet pre-negotiation on the refugee issue, the core group and related Ottawa process activities generated some ideas and approaches that policymakers could call upon.[14]

9.2 A First Breakthrough: The 1993 Declaration of Principles and the Interim Agreement

A series of secret meetings between Israelis and Palestinians resulted in 1993 with the signing of the Declaration of Principles on interim self-government arrangements – later known as the Oslo Accords – between Israel and the PLO.[15] The Declaration of Principles opened

---

14 E.g., one Israeli-proposed clause in the 2001 Taba talks, to be discussed later in the next chapter, ("Although the issue of compensation to former Jewish refugees from Arab countries is not part of the bilateral Israeli-Palestinian agreement, in recognition of their suffering and losses, the Parties pledge to cooperate in pursuing an equitable and just resolution to the issue.") seemed to derive from a similar clause in the core group document ("The issue of compensation to Jewish refugees from Arab countries is not part of the bilateral Palestinian-Israeli agreement on the refugee issue. However, the parties pledge to work together to secure appropriate compensation for all those displaced by the Arab-Israeli conflict.") See the quoted passages in the Moratinos Document under www.mideastweb.org/moratinos.htm. In addition, many aspects of the approaches to refugee compensation that the parties discussed in Taba seemed to follow on from ideas that emerged from other, more public parts of the Ottawa process. See Rex Brynen, Eileen Alma, Joel Peters, Roula el-Rifai and Jill Tansley, "The 'Ottawa Process': An Examination of Canada's Track Two Involvement in the Palestinian Refugee Issue," *IDRC Stocktaking II Conference on Palestinian Refugee Research*, Ottawa, 17–20 June 2003, at www.prrn.org.

15 See the document "Israel and PLO: Declaration of Principles on Interim Self-Government Arrangements ['Oslo Agreement'] (September 1993)," in Walter Laqueur and Barry Rubin (eds.), *The Israeli-Arab Reader: A Documentary History of the Middle East Conflict* (New York: Penguin Books, 2001), pp. 413–422.

up important new avenues in the peace process, paving the way for the Gaza-Jericho Agreement of May 1994, the subsequent establishment of Palestinian administrative authority in parts of the West Bank and Gaza Strip, and the expansion of that authority under the Israeli-Palestinian Interim Agreement of September 1995 (also known as "Oslo II"). The parties also agreed to begin negotiations on the core "final status" issues (refugees, Jerusalem, borders and settlements) by the start of the third year of a five year interim period.[16] In the course of negotiations, both Israelis and Palestinians increasingly realized the following: asking the Palestinian side to give up the demand for refugees to be allowed to return into Israel proper was interlinked with the Palestinian demand for Israel to withdraw to the borders of 1967. Such linkage would be the only reasonable starting point for the planned negotiations on a permanent status agreement.[17]

These agreements further had an impact on the environment for dealing with the refugee issue: With the subsequent establishment of interim self-government in the Gaza Strip and portions of the West Bank, many Palestinian refugees came under the limited jurisdiction of the Palestinian Authority (PA). The PA was empowered to issue travel documents/passports to West Bank and Gaza residents, as well as to register previously unregistered Palestinians in those territories as residents.

9.2.1   The Israeli-Jordanian Peace Treaty, 1994

The issue of Palestinian refugees was also addressed in the text of the Israeli-Jordanian peace treaty of October 1994. In Article VIII/2, the parties agreed to seek to resolve the refugee problem:

---

16   Article V, paragraph three of the Declaration of Principles laid down that the following five subjects would be negotiated only in the final agreement: Jerusalem, security, borders, foreign relations, and refugees. The period of discussions was to last five years, during which mutual confidence between the parties was to be built. No form of a permanent agreement was determined at that point. See ibid., p. 414.

17   See the Israeli-Palestinian roundtable discussion, available at Shamir and Maddy-Weitzmann, *The Camp David Summit*, p. 237.

a. In the case of displaced persons, in the quadripartite committee[18] together with Egypt and the Palestinians;
b. In the case of refugees,
   I) In the framework of the Multilateral Group on Refugees,
   II) In negotiations, in a framework to be agreed, bilateral or otherwise, in conjunction with and at the same time as the permanent status negotiations pertaining to the territories referred to in Article 3 of this treaty [i.e. the territories "that came under Israeli government control in 1967"][19]

This formula essentially endorsed the frameworks already established under the Madrid process (the RWG), and the Oslo agreement, while leaving open the possibility that the architecture of the latter might be open to consensual modification or elaboration.[20] In addition, the Israeli-Jordanian peace agreement led to the creation of an additional forum: The Quadripartite Committee.

9.2.2 The Quadripartite Committee

The Israeli-Jordanian peace agreement established an additional means for addressing the refugee issue: The Palestinian-Israeli-Jordanian-Egyptian Continuing (or "quadripartite") Committee, formed in compliance with Article XII of the Oslo agreement to "decide by agreement on the modalities of admission of persons displaced from the West Bank and Gaza Strip in 1967, together with the necessary measures to prevent disruption and disorder."[21]

The Quadripartite Committee first met in Amman in May 1995, subsequent meetings were held in Beersheba, Cairo, Gaza, Amman,

---

18 See the following section.
19 See the text of the agreement in Laqueur and Rubin, *The Israeli-Arab Reader*, p. 483.
20 Brynen, "Palestinian Refugees and the Middle East Peace Process."
21 According to the terminology of the Oslo agreements, "refugees" are Palestinians who fled Israel proper in 1948, while "displaced persons" are those who fled the West Bank and Gaza when these areas were occupied by Israel in 1967. Complicating things further is the fact that many displaced persons are also refugees. See Brynen, "Palestinian Refugees and the Middle East Peace Process."

and Haifa. Work and progress within the committee was slow, with major differences over the definition of a 'displaced person' and hence the number of potential returnees. Israel was not eager to permit the return to the West Bank and Gaza Strip of Palestinians displaced in 1967. Instead, debates largely centred on definitions. Israel insisted on a minimalist definition of a "displaced person" (namely those actually displaced by the fighting in 1967), totalling around 200,000 persons. The Arab parties held to a broader definition (including those trapped outside the territories by the outbreak of war, those who had left the territories after 1967 but who had later been refused readmission by Israel, deportees and their descendents), totalling around 1.1 million.[22] The deterioration of the peace process in 1997 caused an end to the committee's work.

9.3 A Detailed yet Unsuccessful Proposal: The Beilin–Abu Mazen Agreement, 1995

While the official Oslo Accords related to the refugee question a final-status issue and therefore delayed discussions on it, another document – the Beilin–Abu Mazen Agreement – dealt fundamentally with this issue.[23] In order to prepare the way for eventual final-status talks, scheduled to begin in May 1996, Shimon Peres, then Israeli Foreign Minister, designated one of his aides, Yossi Beilin, to meet with Arafat's deputy, Mahmoud Abbas (Abu Mazen). Subsequently, four academics participated in a series of secret meetings in Stockholm, two Israelis and two Palestinians. The Israeli academics were Dr. Yair Hirschfeld and Dr. Ron Pundak, the trailblazers for Oslo; the Palestinian academics were Dr. Hussein Agha and Dr. Ahmed Khalidi. The Israeli academics reported to Beilin; the Palestinian academics, to Abu Mazen. On 31 October 1995, Beilin and Abu Mazen met in Tel Aviv with their advisers and put the final touches on the broad outline of an eventual

---

22   Ibid.

23   See the Beilin–Abu Mazen agreement at www.mideastweb.org/beilinabu-mazen1.htm.

"permanent status" agreement.[24] These were not formal negotiations, and consequently, the outcome was not binding. Nevertheless, these talks went further than any others of an official nature in bridging some of the most difficult differences between the two sides.

Item VII of the discussions included a mutual understanding between the parties to recognize each other's difficulties with the subject of the *right of return*, with neither side giving up its principled stand on the issue:

1. Whereas the Palestinian side considers that the right of the Palestinian refugees to return to their homes is enshrined in international law and natural justice, it recognizes that the prerequisites of the new era of peace and coexistence, as well as the realities that have been created on the ground since 1948, have rendered the implementation of this right impracticable. The Palestinian side, thus, declares its readiness to accept and implement policies and measures that will ensure, insofar as this is possible, the welfare and well-being of these refugees.

2. Whereas the Israeli side acknowledges the moral and material suffering caused to the Palestinian people as a result of the war of 1947–1949, it further acknowledges the Palestinian refugees' right of return to the Palestinian state and their right to compensation and rehabilitation for moral and material losses.[25]

Most of the following paragraphs dealt with a compensation and rehabilitation mechanism, intended to ensure that in practice the *right of return* would be less worthwhile and attractive to the refugees than absorption either in their present home, or in a third country.[26] While no refugee would return to Israeli territory, there would be no limitation on immigration to a Palestinian state, resulting in the final provision:

7. The PLO considers the implementation of the above a full and final settlement of the refugees issue in all its dimensions. It further undertakes that no additional claims or demands arising from this issue will be made upon the full implementation of this Framework Agreement.[27]

24 Avi Shlaim, *The Iron Wall: Israel and the Arab World* (New York: Norton&Company, 2000), pp. 554–55.

25 See www.mideastweb.org/beilinabumazen1.htm.

26 Yossi Beilin, *Manual for a Wounded Dove* (Hebrew), (Tel Aviv: Miskal, 2001), pp. 137–39.

27 See www.mideastweb.org/beilinabumazen1.htm.

The document's ideas and formulations demonstrate rather impressively how prosperous Israeli-Palestinian negotiations can be if held in a sprit of trust and with a willingness to compromise. Yet neither Beilin nor Abu Mazen, nor any of their representatives, signed this agreement, nor has it ever been officially released. Besides, Yasser Arafat did not fully agree with it and hence withheld his support, as did the three Israeli prime ministers who had to deal with it: Rabin was assassinated before the draft was presented to him; Shimon Peres rejected it for several reasons;[28] and the director general of the Foreign Office under Benjamin Netanyahu, Eitan Bentsur, heard of its contents from Beilin but it is unclear how he related to it.[29] Ehud Barak did not accept its concept and also rejected a similar document, including a mechanism for solving the refugee problem, which Beilin was going to present him on the eve of the Camp David Conference to take place in 2000 (see the following chapter).[30]

Finally, on 16 September, 2000, less than a month after the Camp David Conference had finished, the agreement was published in the Israeli media. Barak was embarrassed when asked about why he had not brought it up in Camp David, yet the publication also embarrassed Abu Mazen, who was accused of giving up the *right of return*.[31] Neither Israeli nor Palestinian delegates have ever since referred to the Beilin–Abu Mazen Agreement.

Yet before Israelis and Palestinians were going to tackle final status issues, a number of Israelis from various political factions hammered

---

28 Beilin presented the plan to Peres a week after Rabin's murder. Beilin recommended adoption of the plan both as the basis for the permanent status negotiations that were to start on 4 May 1996 and as the Labour platform for the elections scheduled for 29 October 1996. But Peres could not be persuaded to endorse the plan, for three main reasons: he wanted future relations between Palestine and Jordan spelled out, he regarded the ideas on Jerusalem as inadequate, and he wanted to retain the Jordan Valley as Israel's strategic border. In addition, having been demonized by Israel's right as an appeaser of the Arabs, as an unelected Prime Minister, Peres did not dare proceed immediately to sign such an agreement. See Quandt, *Peace Process*, pp. 555–56; and Yossi Beilin, *Touching Peace* (Hebrew), (Tel Aviv: Miskal, 1997), pp. 209–212.
29 Beilin, *Manual for a Wounded Dove*, p. 68.
30 Ibid., pp. 126–27.
31 Ibid., pp. 153–54.

out an agreement that was to establish a united Israeli position on crucial issues outstanding in the negotiations with the Palestinians; there was no corresponding occurrence on the Palestinian side. Since it also referred to the issue of refugees, we shall next examine the inner-Israeli document which became known by the names of its main drafters, Beilin and Eitan.

9.3.1   Within Israel: The Beilin–Eitan Agreement, 1997

Beilin not only pursued negotiations with the Palestinians but also an Israeli internal dialogue with a group of Likud MPs led by Michael Eitan, in a similar effort to find common ground. Their agreement, reached in January 1997, noted with regard to refugees:

3. The right of the State of Israel to prevent the entry of Palestinian refugees into its sovereign territory will be recognized.
4. The administration of the entrance of refugees into the Palestinian entity and the limits to that entry will be decided upon during the negotiations of the permanent settlement, within the larger discussion of Israel's security issues.
5. An international organization will be founded, in which Israel will play an important role, with the goal of financing and carrying out projects for compensation and rehabilitation of the refugees in their places. The organization will also address Israeli claims for reparations for Jewish refugees from Arab countries.
6. Israel and the Palestinian entity, each within its own boundaries, will rehabilitate the refugees on the basis of the disengagement of the UNRWA, the repealing of the refugee status and the arrangement of housing and employment with international aid. (For Israel this refers to the Shoafat and Kalandia refugee camps in Jerusalem.)
7. Israel will continue its policy of family reunification on the basis of existing criteria.[32]

Although the Beilin–Eitan agreement was clearly a rather more restrictive vision than the one reached between Beilin and Abu Mazen, both papers, as well as various academic studies,[33] identified three major aspects of a final status settlement of the refugee issue:

---

32   See the text of the Beilin–Eitan agreement at www.knesset.gov.il/process/docs/bei-eit_eng.htm.
33   Brynen, "Palestinian Refugees and the Middle East Peace Process."

- the debate over the Palestinian claimed *right of return;*
- the question of compensation and reparations;
- the resettlement of Palestinian refugees, either in their current countries of exile or elsewhere.[34]

The above points were to be discussed directly between Israelis and Palestinians once they would address final status issues – which occurred in the year 2000. Those negotiations were going to be the first time that the two parties would approach the refugee question in order to find a mutually accepted solution; to this point, the only agreement had been to postpone the entire issue to the end of the negotiations, thereby momentarily neutralizing its explosive potential. The course of events once Israelis and Palestinians did officially (as opposed to the unofficial talks held by Beilin and Abu Mazen) tackle the question of refugees shall be reviewed in the following chapter.

---

34 Ibid.

10 TACKLING FINAL STATUS NEGOTIATIONS

After Ehud Barak was elected Israeli Prime Minister in May 1999 – replacing Benjamin Nethanyahu under whom the political process had been totally deadlocked – he initially put negotiations with the Palestinians on the back-burner, concentrating on Syria instead. After the attempts at reaching a peace agreement with Syria failed, Barak turned his attention to the Palestinians – who had not been particularly flattered by Barak's strategy in giving them second-class priority. Nevertheless, Israeli and Palestinian delegates at that point re-established contact to conduct serious peace-negotiations for the first time in three years. This time, the most intractable issues – like Palestinian refugees – were finally to be officially addressed.

10.1 Harpsund, May 2000: Tackling the Refugee Issue for the First Time

Preliminary Israel-Palestinian contacts were held on a highly secret level. After several preparatory sessions in Jerusalem, Abu Ala (and his younger son), Hassan Asfur, Shlomo Ben Ami, and Gilead Sher were invited in May 2000 to the Swedish prime minister's official residence in Harpsund, Sweden.

Harpsund provided excellent conditions for the planned talks. Apart from a majestic landscape, the extreme northern latitude facilitated an atmosphere of nonstop negotiations: day and night became blurred, as the sun would set at one in the morning and rise again just one hour later. Moreover, the Swedes would prove to be excellent hosts; they did not seek to insert themselves in the talks and merely offered a venue.[1]

---

1   See Clayton Swisher, *The Truth about Camp David: The Untold Story about the Collapse of the Middle East Peace Process* (New York: Nation Books, 2004), pp. 205–06.

For both sides, the refugee issue was equally difficult, as discussions over the fate of refugees touched at the core of the conflict for Israelis and Palestinians alike. For Israelis, any demand for compensation was considered an attack on the state's legitimacy. For Palestinians, a refusal to acknowledge the injustice of the 1948 expulsion, and thus the *right of return*, was considered a rejection of their very identity. Furthermore, this would entail an abrogation of UNGAR 194.

Although Barak had given an extremely limited mandate to Ben Ami and Sher (insisting that only the issues of territory, borders, security, and refugees be addressed; Jerusalem was to be left out), refugees were among the early issues the negotiations addressed on the first weekend meetings, on 12–15 May. After more than a half-century of deadlock, Palestinian delegates listened in Harpsund as – for the first time under an officially held dialogue – Ben Ami and Sher offered Israel's proposed solution: Refugees would be given the option of resettlement in either Arab countries, the proposed Palestinian state, or third countries outside the Arab world, such as the U.S. and Canada. The figures to be allowed for "family reunification" to Israel proper were extremely low (according to Ben Ami, 10,000 to 15,000), and would only be absorbed over a period of many years, subject to Israel's sovereign discretion.[2]

Israel's ideas on both territory and refugees were rejected outright by Abu Ala and Asfur as inadequate. Yet nevertheless, through all the exhaustive debates that emerged, after months of delays since Barak had taken office, important taboos were at least being discussed directly by high-level negotiators. Sher, making use of his legal skills, brought important organization to the talks, and began to draft "non-papers" as the discussions progressed.[3]

On 20 May, the sixth version of a "non-paper" was written, entitled "Framework Agreement on Permanent Status" (FAPS).[4] Article 7 discussed the refugee question for the first time (the notations I or P mark Israeli and Palestinian positions):

49. Taking into consideration the suffering caused to [P: Palestinian refugees] [I: individuals and communities] as a result of the 1948 [I: Arab-Israeli] War and recognizing that a just, humane, political, and realistic solution to their

---

2   Ari Shavit, "End of a Journey," *Haaretz*, 15 July, 2002 cited in ibid., p. 208.
3   Ibid.
4   See www.brookings.edu/press/appendix/peaceprocessappen_z.htm.

right. The Parties are determined to put an end to their suffering based on UNSCR 242 [P: and leading the implementation of UNGAR 194] [which] is essential to put an end to the Israeli-Palestinian conflict.

50. The Parties [I: together with the Arab States and the international community,] share a historical commitment for final resolution of Palestinian Refugeeism in all its legal and practical aspects and alleviating the moral and material suffering due to the 1948 War.

51. Israel further acknowledges that the Palestinian refugees [P: were a victim of this war] [I: suffered as a result of the Arab-Israeli conflict];

52. The Parties agree to call for the establishment of an International Commission (Commission). The Commission shall consist of Israel, the PLO/Palestine, Egypt, the Host Countries - Jordan, Syria, Lebanon, the United Nations, the United States, the European Union, Japan, the Russian Federation and Norway.

53. The Commission shall prepare a special Form that will be filled by all Palestinian refugees. The [P: Commission] [I: Parties] shall determine the format and content of the Form aiming to provide the Commission with the refugees' answer to whether he or she wishes to:

a. [P: return to their homes in Israel with compensation];
b. return to Palestine with compensation;
c. remain in his current place of residence with compensation; or
d. move to a third country with compensation.

54. Every Palestinian [household] defined as refugee in 1948 may attach its entire property claim due to the 1948 War to one Form to be submitted to the Commission. [I: No further individual claims may be filed. The completion of the property compensation shall resolve the entire collective and individual Palestinian claim for Property due to the 1948 War.]

55. [I: As a matter of Israeli sovereign discretion, Israel may facilitate phased and particular family reunification of [XX] Palestinian Refugees with their families in their present place of residence in Israel. Family reunification shall be carried on based on humanitarian grounds and conditions by acceptance of Israeli citizenship and waiver of refugee status.]

56. A Fund for Palestinian Refugees (Fund) shall be established [I: and managed by an internationally recognized financial institution] [and the World Bank] and directed by the Commission. It will collect, manage and disburse the resources pertaining to the resolution of the Palestinian refugee problem, and verify and evaluate all claims based on criteria, timeline, and procedures to be agreed in the CAPS.

57. The transfer of compensation to a claimer shall be conditioned on his/her waiver of all further refugee-related proprietary claims against Israel.] [sic]

58. The Commission will call the international community to support and contribute to the Fund. [P: The nucleus of the Fund shall be financed by a [I: finite] allocation [I: of XX USD] by the Custodian of the Absentee Property in Israel]

59. [I: The Funds for rehabilitation of the refugees shall be allocated with the aim of eliminating the formal and practical aspects of the Palestinian refugee problem and enabling the refugees to rebuild their lives, hence, settling the claim of the Host Countries.

60. [I: Upon the establishment of Palestine, the negotiations aimed at solving the Palestinian Refugee [sic] shall continue with the legitimate representative of the Palestinian people, which will succeed the PLO.]

61. [I: The mandate of the Fund and the Commission shall be concluded between the Parties in the FAPS and the CAPS based on this Article.] The commission shall complete its work within [...] of the date of signing this agreement [P: and no later than [...]. The work of the Commission shall form an integral part of the permanent Status Agreement.

62. [I: This article shall apply to all persons defined as "Palestinian Refugees" by UNRWA.]

63. The full implementation of this Article and the completion of the Commission's work as described in paragraph (X) shall resolve the Palestinian refugee's problem in a final and permanent way [I: thus amounting to the implementation of the UNGAR 194].

Yet the discussions at Harpsund were hampered by a leak to the press which primarily put the Palestinians delegates in a most uncomfortable position:[5] The secret negotiations became known at a time when Palestinian prisoners were on a hunger strike and violent demonstrations to commemorate the Palestinian nakba-day (on 15 May, the day Israel was established) caused casualties on both sides. A firestorm of controversy followed among the Palestinians, since other Palestinian negotiators in the front channel felt blindsided. Yasser Abed Rabbo, head of the official Palestinian negotiating team, went as far as publicly condemning this external dialogue and announcing his resignation as the lead FAPS negotiator. Criticisms in the Palestinian press began to emerge that these negotiators were selling out on core issues – just as they

---

5   The source of the leak was probably to be found with Abu Mazen, who had felt betrayed by not being involved. See Swisher, *The Truth about Camp David*, p. 209.

were accused of having done with the original Oslo Accords – drawing the considerable concern of both Abu Ala and Asfur. Sher recalls the severe impact this had on Abu Ala, who as a result practically stopped negotiating.[6] Nevertheless, an official summit addressing final status was going to be held a couple of months later.

10.2 Camp David, July 2000: The Beginning of Oslo's End

The first time Israel and the Palestinian Authority tackled the refugee issue (as well as the other items for final-status negotiations) publicly and in a major summit was in July 2000 in Camp David. It was also the highest-level Israeli-Palestinian conference ever: Israeli Prime Minister Ehud Barak was to negotiate directly with Palestinian Authority Chairman Yasser Arafat, with U.S. President Bill Clinton acting as mediator.

Barak, after having failed to reach an Israeli-Syrian peace agreement, succeeded in persuading Clinton to support the Prime Minister's initiative for an Israeli-Palestinian high-level summit that was to solve all outstanding issues. The Palestinians had serious reservations, as they felt that the necessary groundwork needed for carrying out the ultimate round of negotiations to end the Israeli-Palestinian conflict had not yet been sufficiently laid out. They therefore called for additional preparatory work. Since that request was not granted and heavy pressure to come to Camp David was applied on them by both Barak and Clinton, the Palestinians were reluctant and perceived Camp David to be a trap set for them by Israel and the U.S. to force them into concessions. Such consternation was certainly a far from ideal start to a summit. The following section will elaborate on why chances for success were accordingly slim.

---

6   Sher accounts that Abu Ala appeared to him during the last hours in Harpsund "like a balloon whose air had been let out". See Gilead Sher, *Just Beyond Reach: The Israeli-Palestinian Peace Negotiations*, 1999–2001(Hebrew), (Tel Aviv: Miskal, 2001), pp. 94–95.

10.2.1 Slim Chances for Success

Scrutinizing the actual talks on refugees obviously cannot be done in a vacuum, and we therefore first need to shed light on the actual situation that laid the groundwork for the Camp David summit. After highlighting the political constellations on both the Israeli and the Palestinian side on the eve of the summit, as well as the manner in which matters were addressed during the actual summit, one is left with little surprise as to why no breakthrough was to be achieved.

On 5 July 2000, with an eye on the clock regarding his ending term, President Clinton announced that Arafat and Barak would meet at Camp David, starting on 11 July, for the "make or break" summit. Arafat was reluctant to agree, maintaining that more preparation was needed if a full agreement was to be negotiated.[7] Barak, by contrast, seemed eager to plunge into the last round of peacemaking, even though his coalition government was crumbling around him. By all accounts, this was not a summit that was guaranteed to succeed. But a looming outbreak of renewed violence – episodes of violence in the preceding May had given a foretaste to what might occur if political progress continued to be absent[8] – plus Arafat's announcement that in the absence of a final status agreement he would unilaterally declare statehood (and presumably, the state's borders) on 13 September, 2000,[9] convinced the U.S. administration to take the risk.

---

7   See Akram Hanieh, "The Camp David Papers," *Journal of Palestine Studies*, Vol. XXX, No. 2 (Winter 2001), p. 76; Bill Clinton, *My Life* (New York: Alfred A. Knopf, 2004), pp. 911–12.

8   15 May 2000 marked the worst West Bank and Gaza Strip violence in nearly four years. Palestinian policemen joined civilian protesters and, on several different occasions, opened fire at IDF troops, severely wounding several of them. These protests marked the Naqba Day, the Palestinian commemoration of the 1948 Arab failure to prevent the establishment of Israel. According to a Palestinian security officer, the riots were called for by Arafat's Fatah organization. A senior IDF intelligence official characterized these events as "controlled violence" encouraged by the PA leadership. See Haaretz, "Clashes in Territories Rage as Negotiators Meet," May 16, 2000; Jerusalem Post, "Four Palestinians Killed in Clashes," May 16, 2000; Haaretz, "Not by Force," May 26, 2000.

9   Arafat picked that date since the Declaration of Principles had been signed on 13 September, 1993. It stated that final status talks were to begin no later than

Camp David II, as the new round of diplomacy was soon labeled, bore many resemblances to the original of 1978. Once again, the negotiating teams would be impounded at the presidential retreat; there would be a near total news blackout; the U.S. president would be deeply involved in trying to forge compromises; and the promise of substantial American aid might help to pry loose compromise positions.

Yet the two summits also had significant differences. First, each of the regional leaders was considerably weaker than Begin and Sadat had been in 1978. In fact, Barak arrived at Camp David in the worst possible circumstances for him. In Israel, his popularity rating was at an all-time low and he no longer had a majority in the Knesset; in other words, Barak's coalition government was unraveling as he traveled to Camp David.[10] Barak intended to circumvent his parliamentary opposition by submitting a possible accord to a referendum. So whereas Begin could count on support from opposition parties for the concessions he would have to make to win peace with Egypt, Barak could expect to face fierce opposition if he were to come close to meeting the minimum demands of the Palestinians. Similarly, Arafat was suspected by his constituents of being too eager to become the first president of a Palestinian state. If the price were major territorial concessions to Israel or a relinquishment of rights in Jerusalem or concerning refugees, many Palestinians would oppose the deal. For most Palestinians, the acceptance of Israel within the 1967 lines was already a huge concession and should not be

---

May 1996, with May 1999 as the envisaged end of the transitional period. Yet it was an ambiguity of the Oslo II Accord that it did not explicitly address the question of what would happen if no agreement on final status were reached by the end of the interim period. This became a contentious issue in early 1999, as Palestinians stated that they had the right to declare statehood after May 4, 1999, while the Israeli government countered that such an action would be a violation of the agreement and would open the way for Israel to respond by annexing territory in the West Bank. See Quandt, *Peace Process*, pp. 329–30.

10 This fact caused the American diplomats who greeted Gilead Sher to be baffled: "When your prime minister came to Shepardstown for the negotiations with the Syrians, he surprised us by announcing that he couldn't make any concessions because he was 'tied up politically by his coalition.' And now he's coming to Camp David at the head of a minority government, but that isn't preventing him from discussing much further-reaching ideas." See Sher, *Just Beyond Reach*, p. 65.

the starting point for further concessions. In 1978, by contrast, Sadat was assured of domestic support if he could recover Egyptian territory, although many in the Arab world condemn him for short-changing Palestinian rights.[11]

Despite other claims, Clinton's own role at Camp David was astonishingly strong. Although he was approaching the end of his tenure in office,[12] both negotiating parties seemed to have a degree of confidence in him and were unsure about his successor. Some thought this might give him unusual leverage for a lame-duck president.[13] Clinton also remained surprisingly popular within the U.S. and could count on bipartisan support for his Middle East efforts, at least up to the point where he might feel it necessary to press the Israelis on sensitive issues or ask Congress for a very large aid package.[14]

Clinton had a remarkable ability to persuade both Israelis and Palestinians that he sympathised with them. He had avoided taking stands on many of the most controversial issues, urging the parties to reach compromises, but hesitating to put forward an American plan. If Camp David II were to follow the pattern of the original, this posture would come under pressure as each side tried to win American support for its own stance. Based on his previous record, Clinton could be expected to side with Barak more than with Arafat. Carter, by comparison, had been much more willing to take stands on substance, often to the irritation of both his guests. He sided with Begin on the issue of full peace and with Sadat on the question of full withdrawal from Sinai. He did not hesitate to use fairly blunt pressure to get them to withdraw from positions that he judged to be unreasonable. On one occasion he told Begin that he would have to denounce his intransigence in public if the talks failed, just as he had bluntly told Sadat that the U.S.-Egyptian relationship would be finished if Sadat walked away from the negotiating table. Clinton seemed unlikely to use such harsh tactics, but it was unclear if his more conciliatory manner would be enough to budge the parties from their positions.[15]

---

11 Quandt, *Peace Process*, pp. 362–63.
12 Clinton's second and last term as President would end by the end of 2000.
13 Quandt, *Peace Process*, pp. 363.
14 Ibid.
15 Ibid.

Already on the opening of the conference on 11 July, 2000, the known positions of Israelis and Palestinians on the key issues were quite far apart – with the issue of refugees being a central bone of contention right from the beginning. While Barak maintained that there would be no recognition of a *right of return* for Palestinian refugees, Arafat insisted on a recognition of the refugees' right to return to their homes or to compensation. The only issue on which the two sides seemed likely to agree was that a Palestinian state of some sort would be part of the final agreement.

Many observers expected the talks at Camp David to fail because of the incompatibility of these stances.[16] The opinion was raised that another interim agreement, leaving some issues for later resolution, was the best that could be hoped for.[17] Yet both Barak and Arafat showed little interest in another interim agreement. For the Palestinians, such a deal would simply postpone the time when they might expect a normalcy and political independence within their own state. For the Israelis, an agreement that failed to resolve the conflict once and for all would leave them having made concessions with little in the way of a *quid pro quo*. Oslo's incrementalist approach with the logic of small, confidence-building steps as the way to reach peace seemed to have exhausted itself. Clinton, using a term from American Football, saw the urgent need for a "Hail Mary pass" – one dramatic effort to score a touchdown.[18]

10.2.2 The Course of the Negotiations on Refugees

From 11 to 26 July, Barak and Arafat, with the Americans playing a crucial mediating role, tackled the major issues dividing Israel and the Palestinians: besides the refugees also Jerusalem, the borders between a future Palestinian state and Israel, the Israeli settlements, and the problem of water supplies and pollution. Over the summit hung the state of pressure both Barak and Clinton were in, due to their political time

---

16   John F. Harris, "Going for Broke, Coming Up Short," *Washington Post*, 26 July, 2000, p. A22.
17   Ibid.
18   Ibid.

running out, in addition to Arafat's deadline to unilaterally declare statehood on 13 September in the absence of a final status agreement.[19]

The refugee question was already addressed on 11 July, the conference's first day. At 7 pm, in a private meeting between Clinton and Arafat,[20] the president tackled the issue. Yet it was not the first time that the two leaders conversed on that matter. In a preparatory meeting in Washington on 15 June, 2000, Arafat had told Clinton: "On the refugee issue, yes, there's Resolution 194, but we have to find a happy medium between the Israelis' demographic worries and our own concerns."[21] On 11 July, Arafat opened by revealing to Clinton what was close to the latter's own bottom-line position on refugees:

> We want the principle of the right of return to be laid down, and afterward we can talk about the practical details of its implementation. It's impossible for all the refugees to come back, since some of them are settled in the countries they live in.[22]

In other words, Arafat presented Clinton a pragmatic approach which merely insisted on *recognizing the right of return in principle*, while being open to negotiate its practical implementation. Yet Arafat's position also entailed that the Palestinians would not agree to discuss practical solutions as long as the Israelis did not start by recognizing the principle of the *right of return* – the foundation for a vicious circle was laid.

Israel was strictly opposed to recognizing a Palestinian *right of return*. In fact, in its opening position, the Israelis set down the following condition: "Palestinian refugees would not be granted the right of return to places under Israeli sovereignty, under any circumstances, nor would Israel accept any ethical or legal responsibility for the fact that

---

19 Benny Morris, *Righteous Victims: A History of the Zionist-Arab Conflict, 1881–2001* (New York: Vintage Books, 2001), p. 659.

20 Four members of the American team were also present at the meeting: Madeleine Albright, Sandy Berger, Dennis Ross, and Robert Malley. Arafat was accompanied by Abu Mazen and Nabil Aburdeineh. See Charles Enderlin, *Shattered Dreams: The Failure of the Peace Process in the Middle East, 1995–2002* (New York: Other Press, 2003), p. 181.

21 Ibid., p. 164.

22 Ibid., p. 181.

a refugee problem exists."[23] Barak later said: "Neither I nor any other Israeli prime minister would be ready to take in a single refugee based on the political principle of the right of return, because that would undermine Israel's *raison d'être*."[24] Thus, as seen in the second part of this paper, Israelis and Palestinians had – and continue to have – a fundamentally different approach to the term *right of return*.

Despite the obvious difficulty, Madeleine Albright – U.S. Secretary of State at that time – imagined a deal on the issue of Palestinian refugees to be possible

> because some Palestinian negotiators were willing to discuss privately the idea of a limit on the number of refugees who would be allowed to return to Israel, while the Israelis had agreed that an international system could be set up to compensate refugees and the governments that had hosted them.[25]

In addition, she also indicated the main bones of contention at Camp David: "The border and refugee issues, although almost impossible to resolve, were easy compared to the problem of Jerusalem."[26] In fact, had the parties succeeded in finding a solution to the Jerusalem question, the refugee issue would have probably been solved too. Yet as long the Jerusalem question remained unresolved, no substantial progress could be achieved on the refugee question.

The Israeli representatives to the Working Committee on Refugees included former Minister of Justice Dan Meridor and senior negotiator Elyakim Rubinstein;[27] both were known for their hawkish views regarding the *right of return*. As to the Palestinian delegates at the refugee talks, they were all refugees themselves or sons of refugees, among them Abu Mazen and Akram Hanieh, both known for their fervent opposition to giving up the *right of return*. While the Israelis wanted

---

23 Danny Yatom, "Background, Process and Failure," in Shimon Shamir and Bruce Maddy-Weitzmann (eds.), *The Camp David Summit – What Went Wrong?* (Brighton: Sussex Academic Press, 2005), p. 37.

24 Ehud Barak, "The Myths Spread About Camp David Are Baseless," in ibid., p. 145.

25 See Madeleine Albright, *Madame Secretary: A Memoir* (New York: Miramax, 2003), p. 486.

26 Ibid., p. 487.

27 Rubinstein is a representative and influential voice in Israel, a fact that was further underlined when he was appointed as Supreme Court Justice in May 2004.

to focus on compensation mechanisms, the Palestinians demanded an Israeli principled recognition of the *right of return* based on UNGAR 194.[28] Israel rejected the existence of such a *right* and the massive return of refugees, though it agreed to absorb "several thousand" refugees over ten years as a part of a "family reunion scheme."[29]

A major part of the Camp David discussions on refugees revolved around the past, not the present and future. Issues were further complicated by the fact that Israeli and Palestinian visions regarding the Palestinian exodus were diametrically opposed. Accordingly, the Israelis denied any responsibility for the Palestinian exodus. The Israelis at Camp David rather argued that there had neither been any massacres committed by Jews in 1948 nor any expulsions or wholesale destruction of villages. According to the Israeli delegates, the Arab countries were to blame for the exodus because they supposedly urged the Palestinians to leave their homes and wait for liberation.[30]

The refugee committee hardly progressed. Israel was not willing to take any moral or legal responsibility for the creation of the refugee problem, but at most to express sorrow over what befell the Palestinians as a result of the Arab-Israeli war of 1948. Since any discussion on the *right of return* was taboo for Israel – in its eyes tantamount to declaring a war of destruction on the Israeli state by flooding it with millions of Palestinian refugees – it was impossible to hold talks on a timetable for an implementation of return. Israel was merely ready to discuss compensation for the Palestinian refugees – with parts of the planned international fund being used to compensate Jews who fled from Arab countries. The only commitment Israel was ready to give was allowing several thousand Palestinians to return over a ten-year period through "family reunification" and "humanitarian cases."[31]

On 13 July, the U.S. presented a "discussion draft" to both delegations which was to serve plainly as a basis for negotiations.[32] This non-

---

28   Sher, *Just Beyond Reach*, pp. 213–17.
29   Ibid. p. 659.
30   See Hanieh, "The Camp David Papers," p. 82.
31   Ibid.
32   See the paper on www.brookings.edu/press/appendix/peaceprocessappen_ aa.htm This is one of the few documents written during the Camp David summit. The Palestinians did not present written proposals at Camp David. Neither did the Israelis submit a document; their proposals were made orally

paper was declared as not representing an U.S. position but rather an "U.S. estimation based on discussion with the parties." The alternative possible solutions ("ALT:") provided were intended to facilitate discussions and not to reflect the position of any of the parties. Similar to the non-paper worked out in Sweden, "I" referred to the assumed Israeli position, while "P" did accordingly to the Palestinian one. Article V focused on Palestinian refugees:

1. The two sides agree on the necessity of a just settlement of the refugee problem which is a human tragedy caused by the 1947–1949 war. [P: the Palestinian refugees have the right of return in accordance with international law and natural justice to be exercised in a way that is consistent with promoting peace and implementing UNGA 194] [I: There is a need to find a comprehensive and lasting solution to the refugee problem through a concerted international effort.]

> ALT 1: The Palestinian side reiterates its insistence on the refugees' right of return in accordance with international law and natural justice. The Israeli side acknowledges the moral and material suffering caused to the Palestinian people as a result of the 1948 war and will take part in a comprehensive international effort to resolve the Palestinian refugee problem.
> ALT 2: In order to implement the provisions of relevant UN resolutions, including paragraph 11 of UNGA resolution 194, the parties agree to the programs and measures described below.

2. Given the magnitude of the refugee problem, the Parties will request the international community to establish a program to facilitate the settlement of refugees and to provide them with compensation and rehabilitation assistance directly or indirectly through the governments of their host countries. The United States and other countries have indicated their readiness to assist in these international efforts to resolve the refugee problem.

3. As part of the international effort Israel will [I: as a matter of its sovereign discretion] facilitate phased entry of _____ refugees to its territory [P: per year on the basis of the refugees' exercise of their right of return] [I: on humanitarian grounds provided they join their families in their present place of residence in Israel, accept Israeli citizenship and waive their legal status as refugees.] In addition, in the context of pledges made by the international community, Israel will make an annual financial and/or in-kind contribution [of $_____] to the international program and/or to Palestinian efforts to deal with the refugee problem.

---

to the Palestinians and were generally presented as "American ideas." See Enderlin, *Shattered Dreams*, p. 187.

4. The programs and measures described in this Article will bring an end to plight of the Palestinian refugees and will fulfil the provisions of relevant UN resolutions.

5. [I: The Parties agree that a just settlement of the Israeli-Arab conflict should settle the property claims by Jewish individuals and communities due to the 1948 conflict. An international mechanism should be established to deal with these claims.]

6. The Refugee Annex to this Agreement sets forth further details concerning the agreed arrangements for addressing the refugee problem.

Yet a discussion on the refugee issue was overshadowed by heated discussions on the status of Jerusalem, as proposed in Article VI. Finally, both Israelis and Palestinians rejected the non-paper as unacceptable.[33] While for the Israelis it was too far-reaching on Jerusalem, the Palestinians suspected this paper to be the result of an American-Israeli alliance. Eventually, both Israelis and Palestinians disliked the "I" and "P" approach.[34]

On 14 July at 8 p.m., Clinton received the negotiators from the work group on the refugees,[35] who presented their report:

Nabil Shaat: We've examined the problem. If we're going to achieve peace and an agreement to cancel all claims, it's essential that we find a just solution. We can't live under the threat of new demands for compensation. Resolution 194 of the U.N. General Assembly, which stipulates a return and reparations for the refugees, constitutes the basis of a just solution. We have to discuss the right of return.

Reparations must involve:

> (1). items registered by the Israeli department of abandoned property (we have a copy of their list);
> (2). compensation to be paid to individuals; and
> (3). public property abandoned by the Palestinian community.

We have other claims to present, in connection with the suffering inflicted on the refugees, their relocation, and the like.

---

33 See Enderlin, *Shattered Dreams*, pp. 187–93.

34 See Albright, *Madame Secretary*, pp. 485–86; and Dennis Ross, *The Missing Peace: The Inside Story of the Fight for Middle East Peace* (New York: Farrar, Straus and Giroux, 2004), p. 662.

35 Abu Mazen and Nabil Shaath for the Palestinians, Elyakim Rubinstein and Gidi Grinstein for the Israelis. Also present were Madeleine Albright, Sandy Berger, Aaron Miller, and Robert Malley. See Enderlin, *Shattered Dreams*, p. 196.

Our first two claims, on the matter of abandoned property and individual damages, will be addressed solely to Israel. In accordance with the solution to the refugee problem, UNRWA will gradually cease to exist.

Although we are aware of the demands for compensation made by Jewish refugees who left Arab countries, it is our opinion that these claims can in no case be equated with Palestinian claims or cancel them out. (...)

We have a moral and legal responsibility. For us, this is a historic moment. Just as the Jews suffered horrible crimes during the Second World War and have presented claims for reparations, even in Switzerland, we likewise think that the Palestinian claims must be taken into consideration. (...) Israel's recognition of its responsibilities in the refugee problem would be a historic gesture.

Elyakim Rubinstein: Can the problem be resolved? We agree [with the Palestinians] that it has to be. We've had a good conversation, but very important discrepancies remain between us on our concept of history and the concrete aspects of the problem. Our [the Israeli] vision is a humanitarian one. On the historical level, we can't agree to be held responsible for the refugee problem. What happened in 1948 is a subject of controversy, and the peace process shouldn't be the arena in which historical truth is pronounced. We want to do our part toward a solution that will put an end to the refugees' suffering, but we're not going to get there by imposing the right of return.

The discrepancies can be overcome. (...)

Concretely, with regard to the entry of refugees into Israel [sic] territory, we're prepared to specify an agreement that would allow a small number of them to move to Israel in the framework of family reunification. The compensation of refugees should not be a punishment imposed on Israel. We don't have the wherewithal, and we don't consider ourselves to blame. But we will most certainly participate in financing the international fund for the compensation of refugees.

Bill Clinton: Are you in agreement on the four possibilities [of individual solution] offered to the refugees?

Rubinstein: We have to be cautious. The problem is to know what's feasible, concretely.

Clinton: I asked this question because, if you participate in the international fund, and if we reach an agreement that the fund will finance all the reparations, I'll get together the necessary amount.[36] But will *you* make a commitment to do what you have to do to settle all the claims?

---

36   One needs to recall that Clinton was about to leave for the G8 summit in Japan in the coming days, where – should the parties reach an agreement on refugees – he would have called for financial contribution from the industrialized countries to be used for the integration and compensation of the Palestinian refugees, and any other financial claim that might arise. See Sher, *Just Beyond Reach*, p. 216.

Rubinstein: Yes but with caution.

Clinton: (…) If the Palestinians accept the principle that all claims for compensation will be examined by the international fund, and the Israelis agree to contribute to it, that will lighten a part of the burden that could be imposed on Israel. The budget of an international fund should reach ten billion dollars, maybe more. Israel obviously can't underwrite that large a sum. But I don't think Israel will find it in its interest to refuse to make a minimum contribution. An agreement on this issue should cover all the demands for compensation.

Rubinstein: I understand why the Palestinians are comparing their claims to those of the Jews in Europe, but, when you get right down to it, the problem is totally different.

Clinton: Of course there's no comparison. If an agreement is reached on the specification of a maximum amount in view of these reparations, will you make the archives available?[37]

Rubinstein: (…) We're committed to having Jordan take part in resolving this problem. Palestinian refugees are forty percent of the Jordanian population. (…) An agreement would imply the disappearance of refugee status in Palestine, Israel, and everywhere else. The international fund, or a similar organization, should make it possible to settle the problem of Jewish refugees from Arab countries.

Clinton: There we have a basis for going ahead on a solution. I'm asking you to make progress in two directions: (1) find a common language that will enable you to overcome your philosophical differences; (2) on the concrete level, reduce your secondary differences.

The final agreement will be judged by what it brings individuals. [It should be] explicit on this. Try to move forward on the concrete aspects.

Shaat: You clearly see what's involved in the problem of compensation, but, for us, the concept of return is very important. Only 10 to 20 percent of the refugees would want to have their right of return acknowledged. (…)

Rubinstein: Ten to 20 percent of the refugees amounts to between 400,000 and 800,000 people!

Abu Mazen (tugging on Nabil Shaat's sleeve): No, no! That's not the case. We have to agree on the number of refugees (…)!

Rubinstein: There should not be very many of them. We have to reach an agreement on compensation without moving away from the principle of family reunification.

Sandy Berger: We have four days to reach a compromise.[38]

---

37   This is the register of all property abandoned by the Palestinian refugees in 1948.

38   This excerpt from the Camp David negotiations on refugees (including the text in brackets) can be found in Enderlin, *Shattered Dreams*, pp. 196–200.

Thus in the above report, the *Israelis* summarized problems that had come up in the working group on refugees, especially regarding responsibility and the *right of return*. The Israelis refused to be held responsible for the refugee problem. Therefore, their approach to the Palestinians did not derive from responsibility but rather was of a humanitarian nature. Israel signaled readiness to participate in an international fund to compensate refugees. As to practical return, Israelis signaled that no large numbers of refugees could return to Israel proper and that such limited return could only be implemented under the framework of "family reunifications", not the *right of return*. The *Palestinians*, on the other hand, did demand the *right of return;* however, distinguishing between the actual right and mechanisms for implementing it. They further demanded compensation for property lost. *Clinton* committed to raise the necessary financial means in the event of an agreement. Besides, Clinton seemed to accept the principle of a "ceiling" regarding compensation, meaning that the maximum overall sum necessary to solve the refugee question in all its financial aspects (compensation, integration in third countries, etc) would be defined in the framework agreement.[39]

There exists no evidence on how this meeting was perceived by the Palestinians. As to the Israelis, it is known that they left the encounter with a good feeling, as Clinton had demonstrated solid mastery of the complex matter of refugees and they agreed to his conclusion about the range of possible agreement. However, the Israelis also expressed hope that the Americans (obviously first and foremost Clinton) would check on the progress made in the refugee group on a daily basis in order to assure advancement in the negotiations. That did not occur; until the end of the summit, the Americans did not hold one single follow-up meeting, which, according to Sher, resulted in the working group on refugees wasting its time with fruitless discussions.[40]

---

39 Sher, *Just Beyond Reach*, p. 216.
40 Ibid.

No Agreement on the Right of Return

On 16 July, the Israelis submitted a proposal,[41] far-reaching on the subject of compensation (however, only for lost property, as Israel refused to pay compensations for personal suffering), yet which did not recognize the *right of return* or accept Israeli responsibility for the refugee problem. The Palestinians demanded compensation also for their past suffering, a claim that Israel rejected.[42] There was no progress in the discussions. In the Israeli delegation, the hawks opposed a suggestion, which enjoyed some support from Barak, to totally reject the *right of return* while simultaneously considering the problem from a Palestinian point of view and to address claims of Israeli responsibility. Rubinstein saw this as damaging to "the ethos" of the State of Israel.[43] Although not mentioned in any written proposal, it was clear to the Israeli delegation that priority should be given to the Palestinian refugees in Lebanon, due to harsh conditions they were living in.[44]

After the Camp David summit, several Palestinian negotiators would disclose that they could not have afforded to make concessions on the refugee question before the other key issues were resolved.[45] When Clinton returned on 23 July from his trip to the G8 summit in Japan and heard that the parties had discussed the *right of return* for ten straight days without a result, he decided to henceforth concentrate on Jerusalem.

In a meeting with Clinton on the 23 July, the Palestinians asserted their central issues regarding the refugee question:

1. The right of every Palestinian refugee to return to his home in accordance with UNRWA 194.
2. The need for a mechanism to implement that right, starting with the return of refugees in Lebanon, who would be given priority. A

---

41 See the proposal in ibid., pp. 419–44. Article 6 refers to Palestinian refugees.
42 Israel proposed to grant each refugee a "personal rehabilitation package" independent from property claims the refugee might submit. The Palestinians rejected the Israeli proposal to declare that package as a compensation for the refugee's ongoing suffering. See ibid., p. 217.
43 Sher, *Just Beyond Reach*, p. 164.
44 Ibid., p. 216.
45 Ibid.

timetable, including numbers of refugees, would then be established for the return of all those who wished to do so.

3. After the recognition of the *right of return* and the establishment of an implementation mechanism, a compensation regime could be instituted.

4. The issue of Jews who had left Arab countries and the compensation of these people was not the responsibility of the Palestinian side and would not be discussed.[46]

These points were countered with an Israeli rejection both to accept responsibility for creating the refugee problem and to recognize a *right of return*. The Israelis were prepared to allow the return of several thousands of people over a number of years under a "family reunification" program and for "humanitarian reasons." They were equally willing to discuss an international compensation fund which would also allocate compensation for Jewish refugees from Arab countries.[47]

According to Hanieh, during that meeting, Clinton undoubtedly realized that the refugee issue was far more difficult than he had been made believe by his advisers, who had maintained that progress could be achieved solely on the basis of compensation, resettlement in the host countries, and a liberal immigration policy to some Western countries.[48]

Although it was not recognized at the time by the delegations, some of the committee meetings were making significant first steps in discussing refugees. At various points these talks were held between Israelis most ardently opposed to the *right of return*, including Dan Meridor and Elyakim Rubinstein, and Palestinians who were perceived by Americans and Israelis as being the most rigidly principled, including Nabil Shaat and Abu Mazen, although some of their colleagues privately said the exact opposite was true.[49] The fact that the Israelis regressed at Camp David from some of their earlier ideas at Sweden derived from the Israeli assumption that if they offered flexibility on the territorial issue, the eventual peace agreement would not stand or

46   Hanieh, "The Camp David Papers," p. 94.
47   Ibid.
48   Ibid., p. 95.
49   Swisher, *The Truth about Camp David*, p. 279.

fall on the refugee issue.[50] Besides, none of these four negotiators had been involved in Sweden. Yet it is interesting to note that, to a certain extent, both delegations represented the range of Israelis and Palestinians who would ultimately have to endorse any compromise.

The talks on Palestinian refugees were over fifty years in the making, and though some, like Meridor and Abu Mazen, had debated the topic with each other privately as early as 1997,[51] Camp David was the first time they had negotiated the issue in the context of a U.S.-mediated effort to reach a workable solution. Meridor knew that any refugee compromise would take a long time to condition both publics, definitely more time than the eight days set aside at Camp David. Sharing the sentiment of most Israelis, Meridor related how the refugee issue was perceived in Israel:

> ... I say to [the Palestinians]: "You ...say to your people, 'All the land is ours – Haifa, Tel Aviv, all is ours.' But there are Jews. Five million Jews, and we need to live with them." This is reality. So we should have all of it but the cantons. So we retain power, we have a part of it since the first time. And all our aspirations will be realized in that as safe. You Arabs who lost your home or were expelled or ran away or whatever, you want to return to the land you will be in the land – in the part that is called Palestine. Not in the part that is called Israel, because you can't go to your home anyway because your home is now not in existence anymore – inhabited by Jews for sixty years or something.[52]

Another Israeli delegate at Camp David, Amnon Lipkin-Shahak, presented an additional perception of the Israeli team:

> Arafat's difficulties with all the critical issues were clear. Everyone, possibly including Arafat, realized that no agreement could be reached unless the Palestinians gave up the Right of Return. Had he gone along with the American and Israeli offers at Camp David, he would have had to explain to his people that he, who throughout the years had repeatedly promised to return the refugees to the places they had left, was abandoning the Right of Return. (...) These reversals would not have been easy for the Palestinians to swallow, especially

---

50 As expressed by Shlomo Ben Ami in ibid.
51 This was disclosed by Meridor in an interview with Swisher in 2003. See Ibid.
52 Ibid., p. 281.

since they had not been prepared for them. Arafat believed that he did not have the backing of a public that was capable of endorsing such changes.[53]

However, after Camp David some Palestinians[54] conceded, off the record, that Arafat had been indeed willing to accept a limited *right of return*, in all likelihood within the framework of "family reunification" raised at Harpsund, so long as the Palestinians received recognition of that right and a viable state with Palestinian sovereignty over East Jerusalem and the Haram al-Sharif/Temple Mount. They further pointed out that with those compromises in hand, Arafat would be in a strengthened position to go to the Al Aqsa Mosque and address the entire Palestinian diaspora: "There is no reason to go live in Israel now. Come home and help us build the state we have!"[55] Also Robert Malley stated that the Palestinians had agreed to negotiate a solution to the refugee issue that would not end up threatening Israel's Jewish majority.[56]

Malley, who attended most of the refugee talks, noted that Palestinians were not asking for a full *right of return*. What they expected was *recognition of the right of return in principle*, after which they would agree "to take into account Israel's interest."[57] For the Palestinian negotiators, this was a massive concession – indeed, it was one that they knew was considered totally unacceptable to a great many of their own people.

In contrast to the issue of Jerusalem, there was no Palestinian position on how the refugee question should be dealt with as a practical matter. Rather, the Palestinians presented a set of principles. First, they insisted on the need to recognize the refugees' *right of return*, lest the agreement lose all legitimacy with the vast refugee constituency – roughly half the entire Palestinian population. Second, they acknowledged that Israel's demographic interests had to be recognized

---

53 Amnon Lipkin-Shahak, "The Roles of Barak, Arafat and Clinton," in Shamir and Maddy-Weitzmann, *The Camp David Summit*, p. 48.

54 This was told to Charles Enderlin in the strictest confidence by several Palestinian negotiators on the condition of anonymity. See Swisher, *The Truth about Camp David*, p. 282.

55 Ibid.

56 See Deborah Sontag, "Quest for Middle East Peace: How and Why it Failed," *New York Times*, 26 July 2001, reprinted in the *Journal of Palestine Studies*, Vol. XXXI, No. 1 (Autumn 2001), p. 82.

57 Ibid.

and taken into account. Thus the Palestinians were trying to reconcile these two competing imperatives – the demographic imperative and the *right of return*. In fact, in one of his last pre-Camp David meetings with Clinton, Arafat had asked Clinton to "give [Arafat] a reasonable deal [on the refugee question] and then see how to present it as not betraying the right of return."[58]

Some of the Palestinian negotiators proposed annual caps on the number of returnees (though at numbers far higher than their Israeli counterparts could accept); others wanted to create incentives for refugees to settle elsewhere and disincentives for them to return to Israel proper. Yet all acknowledged that there could not be an unlimited, "massive" return of Palestinian refugees to Israel. The Palestinians did insist, however, that Israel recognize that it bore responsibility for creating the problem of the refugees.[59]

As to the Israelis, the Palestinian demands on the *right of return* were unreassuringly, vague, and indeed threatening. Besides, in the eyes of the Israeli delegates, Palestinian proposals at Camp David constituted a dangerous legal loophole, since once a *right of return* in any form was granted to the Palestinians, it would be highly problematical to reasonably formulate why they should be barred from exercising that right. In an important remark, Malley accurately described the difficulty:

> It's hard, because [once the principle of return is recognized,] why should it be 10,000, 20,000, 30,000, 40,000, 50,000? There is no logical break point, unless you're prepared to say – which the Israelis said – no right of return to Israel at all, and let Israelis do family reunification, which is where we headed. But it is very hard for the Palestinians to basically agree we're giving [the Israelis] one principle completely, whereas on all the other ones, there's some flexibility, some nuance, some compromise.[60]

In any event, the Palestinian negotiators at Camp David never – despite the claims of a number of Jewish organizations – demanded the return to Israel of millions of refugees. The figures discussed in the course of the talks varied from several hundred to several thousand Palestinians to

58 See Robert Malley and Hussein Agha, "A Reply to Barak," *The New York Review of Books*, Vol. XLIX, No. 10, June 13, 2002, p. 46.

59 Ibid.

60 From an interview with Malley on 30 July, 2002. See Swisher, *The Truth about Camp David*, pp. 281–82.

be allowed to return with Israel's authorization.[61] Unfortunately, much as they tried, the Palestinians proved utterly unable to make their case at Camp David, and they were therefore depicted as uncompromising and incapable of responding to Barak's supreme effort. The Palestinians, however, considered that they were the ones who had come up with creative ideas to address Israeli concerns. Consequently, while insisting on the Palestinian refugees' right to return to homes lost in 1948, they were prepared to tie this right to a mechanism of implementation providing alternative choices for the refugees while limiting the numbers returning to Israel proper.[62]

Unfortunately, Barak did not come to Camp David seeking the necessary tradeoff, namely the Palestinian renunciation of a factual *right of return* in exchange for a full Israeli restoration, or even close to a full restoration, of the 4 June, 1967, line; much less was Barak willing to grant Palestinian sovereignty over the Haram al-Sharif/Temple Mount. As negotiations approached the second week, these issues were far too underdeveloped.[63]

The Last Days of Camp David

Towards the end of the Camp David negotiations, Clinton organized the teams into marathon sessions on each of the core issues. In the morning of 24 July, the Palestinians again proposed that Israel accept the *right of return* in principle and then engage in discussions over how that right would be implemented. There were a number of logistical and financial burdens presented to the Palestinians, such as how Israel would feed, clothe, and employ the refugees they would absorb from the diaspora. Israel suggested allowing an unlimited number of refugees in Lebanon to leave their miserable camps and make a symbolic trip home, via the Fatima Gate along the Israeli-Lebanese border – to their ultimate destination in the Palestinian state.[64]

With knowledge that the *right of return* to Israel proper would be severely constrained because of Israel's "demographic concerns," the

61   Enderlin, *Shattered Dreams*, p. 324.
62   Robert Malley and Hussein Agha, "Camp David: The Tragedy of Errors," *New York Review of Books*, Vol. XLVIII, No. 13, August 9, 2001, p. 62.
63   Swisher, *The Truth about Camp David*, p. 282.
64   Ibid., 323.

Palestinians looked for practical ways to shift emphasis to other aspects of UNGAR 194, such as the creation of a compensation fund, from which remuneration could be given to refugees in lieu of physical return to Israel.[65] Most of the Israeli negotiators, foremost Rubinstein, were unyielding on the question and refused to entertain this notion, which they believed would be an implicit Israeli acknowledgment of culpability for the refugee problem, thus making Israel legally vulnerable.[66]

The Israelis countered Palestinian claims by raising counterclaims, seeking compensation for the estimated 600,000 Jews who fled or were expelled from Arab states following the 1948 war. Yet the Palestinians had sound defenses to these arguments, as both sides understood that the Palestinians were not responsible for those expulsions, nor had they materially benefited in any sense from what other Arab governments had done; rather the opposite was the case, as the influx of Jewish immigrants in the new Israeli state after 1948 displaced the Palestinians even further from their homes.[67]

For the Palestinians, to accept the Israeli proposals in the hope that Barak would then move further risked diluting the Palestinian position in a fundamental way, namely by shifting the terms of debate from the international legitimacy of U.N. resolutions on Israeli territorial withdrawal and on refugee return to imprecise ideas suggested by the U.S. and Israel. Without the guarantee of a deal, this was tantamount to gambling with what the Palestinians considered their most valuable currency: international legality. The Palestinians' reluctance to do anything that might undercut the role of U.N. resolutions that applied to them was reinforced by Israel's decision to fully implement those that applied to Lebanon and unilaterally withdraw from that country in the months preceding Camp David.[68]

Gilead Sher recorded that, on the concrete aspects, a broad understanding had been reached, especially on the creation of the international

---

65 Recall that according to UNGAR 194, "compensation should be paid for the property of those choosing not to return and for loss of or damage to property which, under principles of international law or in equity, should be made good by the Governments or authorities responsible."

66 Swisher, *The Truth about Camp David*, pp. 323–24.

67 Ibid., p. 324.

68 Malley, "Camp David," p. 63.

fund. He recalled how Muhammad Rashid, Arafat's financial adviser, had told him in the course of an informal discussion that any solution to the refugee problem had to include three elements: prompt attention to the Palestinian refugees in Lebanon, timely and effective compensation, and the housing of the refugees returning to evacuated Jewish settlements in the Palestinian state.[69] As to Arafat, he was not ready to be more specific beyond repeating that, in the case of an agreement, he would make sure Israel would not have to confront a demographic problem.[70]

There were other factors involved throughout the entire Camp David refugee talks that bothered Palestinians. As mentioned before, Barak assigned the refugee-portfolio to Rubinstein, the most cautious and extremely hesitant Israeli negotiator, to work with Abu Mazen, himself a Palestinian refugee from Safed, now inside Israel. Abu Mazen saw the appointment of Rubinstein as a clear signal that Barak did not plan to take the refugee issue seriously. Meanwhile, the Americans and Israelis pursued the young-guard Palestinians to work around Abu Mazen's demand that first the *right of return* be recognized in principle. They took the matter up with Mohammed Dahlan, Mohammed Rashid, and Hassan Asfur, the latter of whom triggered Abu Mazen's deeply rooted animus. For the old-guard negotiators, the perceived disrespect of being passed over made them all the more rigid in their demands.[71]

In fact, the Palestinians believed that they were being manipulated by the Americans. They said American officials had made a crucial mistake in trying to nurture special relationships with two younger-generation Palestinian officials whom they thought were pragmatic: Muhammad Rashid, Arafat's Kurdish economic adviser, and Muhammad Dahlan, the Gaza preventive security chief. That angered the veteran Palestinian negotiators, who felt that the Americans were seeking to divide and weaken them.[72]

One of those senior members was Abu Mazen. He had arrived at Camp David being convinced that the Americans intended to promote Muhammad Dahlan at his expense. As a result, Abu Mazen, whose

69   Sher, *Just Beyond Reach*, p. 227.
70   Enderlin, *Shattered Dreams*, p. 252.
71   Swisher, *The Truth about Camp David*, pp. 324–25.
72   See Sontag, "Quest for Middle East Peace," p. 81.

influence on Arafat was second to none, came to Camp David believing that the attempt to reach out to the younger Palestinian negotiators was directed against him; he reacted accordingly, taking himself out of the game (At one point in the middle of the summit he was even absent physically, having flown back to the Middle East for his son's wedding). Throughout, his behaviour at Camp David was entirely passive.[73] Hence, chances for progress on the refugee issue, of which he was in charge on the Palestinian side, were gravely impeded; being furious about the American tactics, Abu Mazen pledged that Camp David would never succeed if such games continued and that he would use the refugees issue to foil it, if need be.[74]

Stagnation on Jerusalem Blocks Progress on Refugees

At the later stage of the conference, the issue of Jerusalem increasingly became a sticking point. A highly placed Palestinian explained that, in the absence of progress on Jerusalem, Arafat at some point forbade Nabil Shaat to further discuss the functioning of the international compensation fund for the refugees. This, however, had been the subject on which the talks seemed to make the most progress. According to several Israeli delegates, the question of the refugees' *right of return* to Israel was the Palestinians' final card in the negotiations. They were not going to give in on this point until agreements were concluded on all the other pending issues: Jerusalem, borders and security.[75]

The central bone of contention in the Israeli-Palestinian negotiations on Jerusalem was the rule over the Temple Mount/Haram al-Sharif. Arafat reiterated that follow-on negotiations should begin, as the gaps were beginning to narrow. Yet such an answer could not satisfy the

---

73 Martin Indyk, "Sins of Omission, Sins of Commission," in Shamir and Maddy-Weitzmann, *The Camp David Summit*, p. 102.

74 Sontag, "Quest for Middle East Peace," p. 81. Not only Abu Mazen was angered by the Americans: angered by the unwillingness of the Palestinians to put forward any position regarding territory, Clinton attacked Abu Ala, actually screaming at him, in the presence of the Israeli delegation. This humiliation of Abu Ala took him out of the process as well, and he turned passive and negative. As a result, the two people who were in a position to influence Arafat at Camp David were simply not willing to cooperate. See Indyk, "Sins of Omission," p. 102.

75 Enderlin, *Shattered Dreams*, p. 252.

political needs of either Barak or Clinton, who after almost a year of pursuing negotiations exclusively with Syria were now trying to rush the Palestinians to an agreement on their terms, according to their own political timetables. Eventually the conference ended on 25 July without an agreement. Thus, Camp David essentially failed because of disagreement regarding sovereignty over the Temple Mount/Haram Al-Sharif – and without an agreement on Jerusalem, it was impossible to reach an agreement on refugees.

The general failure of Camp David because of one central issue – Jerusalem – leads to the conclusion that the other crucial issues – primarily refugees, but also borders and settlements – cannot be addressed detached from one another, but rather must those issues be considered as a whole. Thus a solution can only be achieved in the framework of a "package deal."

10.2.3   The Collapse of Camp David: Reasons and Lessons

It would have been unrealistic to expect that a conflict of more than half a century could be resolved in one single two-week long summit. Therefore, the failure needs to be put into perspective. Above all, it was the first time that Israeli and Palestinian negotiators seriously tackled the issue of refugees. While no breakthrough was achieved, neither could progress be denied. In addition, Camp David served as a bridge for a further round of negotiations, which again would produce a substantial step forward regarding a solution to the refugee issue: Taba. Therefore the following paragraphs shall examine the period between the collapse of Camp David and the next – and to this point, last – round of official Israeli-Palestinian negotiations on the refugee issue which were to take place in January 2001 in Taba.

Upon his return from Camp David to Gaza, Arafat received a hero's welcome by Palestinians who cheered him for not having compromised the *right of return*. According to Nabil Shaat, Arafat "rode home on a white horse" because he had showed Palestinians that he "still cared about Jerusalem and the refugees."[76] A totally different reception awaited Barak, who was met by demonstrators angered by what

---

76   See Sontag, "Quest for Middle East Peace," p. 83.

they viewed as his far-reaching concessions to the Palestinians. They were not an isolated few. In an opinion poll conducted among Israeli Jews during the week following the failure at Camp David, it became evident that Barak's tentative movement on the refugee question met with the greatest resistance of all of the Camp David compromises. Some 76 percent of Israeli Jews rejected a permanent settlement with the Palestinians if it included Israel's acceptance of 100,000 Palestinians within its borders (Israel's press had circulated that number as the number of Palestinian refugees that Barak had been willing to accept into Israel's borders; however, there was no factual basis for such a proposition of Barak's). There would have been greater readiness to transfer East Jerusalem to Palestinian sovereignty and to turn over 90 percent of the West Bank and Gaza Strip than to accept tens of thousands of Palestinian refugees.[77]

While the Americans had helped move both sides closer, the piecemeal ideas collected during the various committee meetings bore no resemblance to a coherent "offer", as far as the Palestinians were concerned. From their review of the notes on all the collective positions described at Camp David, the makings of an enduring peace for generations of Palestinians to come were nowhere to be found. As to refugees, there had yet to be Israel's historic acknowledgment of its role in creating the refugee problem, even amid the alternative remedies the Palestinians were coming closer to accepting.

After the summit had collapsed on 25 July 2000 and ended with no agreement, both Israelis and Palestinians let fly with recriminations. In private, Barak and to a degree also Clinton expressed astonishment and anger at the Palestinian rejection of the most far reaching Israeli concessions ever offered. Arafat, for his part, regarded the Israeli proposals as inadequate – in his view, they awarded the Palestinians the trappings rather than the reality of sovereignty and, besides, Israel would continue to rule large chunks of the West Bank, such as the Jordan Valley and the area around East Jerusalem. The Americans – breaking a pre-

---

77 *Haaretz*, 7 August, 2000, cited in Jacob Tovy, "Negotiating the Palestinian Refugees," *Middle East Quarterly*, Spring 2003, at www.meforum. org/article/543.

Camp David promise not to blame Arafat if talks failed[78] – did blame Arafat for the collapse of the talks, charging that, unlike Barak, he had failed to offer any concessions on the important issues.[79] However, the American critique was not univocal. Malley, for instance, announced his *mea culpa* a few months later by announcing that Barak's offers were "greeted by the U.S. team too often with unwarranted enthusiasm," based on the distance Israel had gone, rather than "the distance that remained … to reach an acceptable compromise."[80]

Reasons for the Failure

Why did Camp David II fail? The easy answer is to blame one party or the other for intransigence, and there is doubtlessly some blame to be apportioned. Yet the negotiators were dealing with extraordinarily difficult issues that required a great deal of nuanced discussion and compromise. One of the problems with the Oslo approach was that it put off the negotiations of the most difficult issues (first and foremost refugees) in the belief that a gradual process of partial agreements would help to build confidence between the two sides. It is vital to point out that adopting such an approach was not entirely wrong. Some issues did seem to become easier with the passage of time, such as the eventual establishment of a Palestinian state. However, one could not realistically have expected that after being avoided for more than five decades, the entire Israeli-Palestinian conflict in general – one of the world's most complex disputes – and the explosive issue of refugees in particular would be resolved in a fortnight.

Insufficient preparation and amateur conduct on both sides were major reasons for the failure of the summit. The Israelis arrived at the summit without being prepared on the complex and sensitive issue of Jerusalem. This mistake was exacerbated when Barak directed

---

78 See Charles Smith, "Book Review: The Truth about Camp David: The Untold Story about the Collapse of the Middle East Peace Process," *Middle East Policy Council Journal*, Vol. XII, No. 1, Spring 2005.

79 Morris, *Righteous Victims*, p. 659

80 The above text is based on remarks delivered on 7 March 2001 by Malley in a report from a Palestine Center briefing: "Former Peace Team Member Discusses U.S. Failures under Clinton Administration." See www.thejerusalemfund.org/carryover/pubs/20010314ftr.html.

the summit discussions to an exaggerated focus on Jerusalem and, specifically, on the most sensitive issue there: the Temple Mount/ Haram Al-Sharif. The logic of the negotiations required the opposite approach: the Palestinians were prepared to reach an agreement on all the other issues, and to leave the two most sensitive issues (the Temple Mount and the Palestinian refugees) for the end of the negotiations. This set-up would have provided both sides with a clear balance of the gains and losses involved, and also would have provided an incentive to reach an agreement on these most sensitive issues. Instead, Barak added fuel to the fire in the form of an Israeli demand to change the religious status quo in the area of the Haram Al-Sharif by – in addition to demanding Israeli sovereignty over the compound – installing a Jewish prayer-area there.[81]

Barak had a clear strategy and set strict boundaries for the upcoming negotiations. However, both Barak's tactics and his behaviour at the summit were highly problematic. It started with Barak's maximalist approach to the negotiations, namely that nothing must be concluded as long as there remained even one point of difference. In addition, to avoid having the Palestinians transform Israeli positions into a firm commitment, his proposals were submitted to the Palestinians through American mediation. Barak himself did not have any face-to-face meetings with Arafat, who might seize on some minor verbal discrepancy and have it influence the talks. On several occasions, at critical moments of the summit, Barak's advisers suggested that he spoke directly with Arafat – Barak refused. At meals he regularly and openly ignored him, an attitude that the Palestinians took as an insult and unwillingness to negotiate.[82] This lack of a trusting relationship between the two leaders caused one of Clinton's Camp David advisers to exclaim, with a touch of regret in his voice: "Too bad Shimon Peres isn't here! At least *he* would have spent all day and all night talking to Arafat and wouldn't have let him go to bed without getting an accord out of him!"[83]

---

81   Ron Pundak, "From Oslo to Taba: What Went Wrong?," *Survival*, Vol.43, No.3, Autumn 2001, p.42.
82   Charles Enderlin, *Shattered Dreams: The Failure of the Peace Process in the Middle East, 1995–2002* (New York: Other Press, 2003), p.178.
83   Ibid., p.268.

The Palestinians made a crucial mistake when they expressed doubts about the importance and holiness of the Temple Mount for the Jewish people. The legitimate Palestinian claim for sovereignty over the Haram al-Sharif was not strengthened by the inconsiderate attempt to ignore the historic Jewish connection to the site. As a result, the Israeli public was rendered suspicious of the Palestinians' strategic aims and the erosion of support for Barak was further accelerated. In combination with un-nuanced public declarations by the Palestinian negotiating team regarding the *right of return* of every refugee to the State of Israel, such statements created a suspicion among the vast majority of the Israeli public, from left to right, that it was still the Palestinian intention to eradicate the Jewish state. How the vast majority of Israelis – including famous members of the so-called "peace camp" – misinterpreted (and keep doing so to this day) Palestinian claims becomes evident in the words of Amos Oz, a celebrated Israeli writer and fervent peace activist: "They [the Palestinians] insist on their 'right of return,' when we all very well know that around here 'right of return' is an Arab euphemism for the liquidation of Israel."[84] In fact, Palestinian insistence on the *right of return* appeared like an attempt to destroy the foundation on which Oslo was based: the principle of two states for two peoples, the legitimacy of a national home for the Jewish people and the mutual recognition of the right to self-determination of the Palestinian people. In other words, the Israeli fear was that Palestinians had not given up the PLO's original plan to destroy Israel and were now pursuing this plan with a strategy to flood Israel with millions of Palestinian refugees.

Thus to Israelis, some official Palestinian statements created the impression that the Palestinian position regarding refugees and the *right of return* were maximal and uncompromising. Yet in practice, the real Palestinian position on the issue during the negotiations was far more moderate and pragmatic. However, the Palestinians had touched upon two highly sensitive Israeli nerves: the religious and the national. It was a major blow to negotiations.[85] Not surprisingly, to this day, if asked for

---

84   See Amos Oz's op-ed after the failure of Camp David: *New York Times*, 28 July, 2000.

85   Pundak, "From Oslo to Taba," pp. 42–43.

the reason why Camp David failed, most Israelis – incorrectly – would point to the *right of return* as the primary reason.[86]

Yet it needs to be stressed that despite the conclusion of some that Camp David broke down because of the issue of Palestinian refugees that was not the case. In fact, looking at the big picture, i.e. the overall summit, with simultaneous talks regarding Jerusalem, territory and security arrangements being held, the issue of refugees was hardly discussed at Camp David and Clinton's ideas mentioned it only in passing.[87] The issue of Jerusalem was the one on which the negotiations broke down twice: before Clinton left for Japan, and after he came back, at the end of the summit. The parties simply could not reconcile competing Israeli and Palestinian claims of sovereignty over the Haram al-Sharif/Temple Mount. Various formulas were put forward, but no agreement could be found.[88]

Lessons to Be Learned

There is certainly no lack of conclusions to be drawn regarding further negotiations on refugees after the failure of Camp David. One crucial lesson which needs to be internalised was described correctly by one of the negotiators:

> Attention must be paid to the other side's perceptions, not just their objective requirements. On the issue of the Right of Return of the refugees, for example, it was image that held sway over substance. Here was an ethos that had been built up and nurtured over decades as one of the cornerstones of the Palestinian national struggle. The Palestinian negotiators considered it their duty to show, even if only verbally, that they were bringing an end to the tragedy of the refugees and that their dream of Return was about to be realized. As a result, for many of our Palestinian counterparts, the wording of this section [on refugees] in the draft agreement was perhaps more important than the

---

86 Yossi Ginossar, "Factors that Impeded the Negotiations," in Shamir and Maddy-Weitzmann, *The Camp David Summit*, p. 51.

87 See Indyk, "Sins of Omission," p. 103. The fact that refugees were certainly not at the center of discussions, but rather barely discussed was also confirmed by Robert Malley in a phone interview with the author on 19 October, 2004. Besides, Malley further mentions this point in his article with Hussein Agha, "A Reply to Ehud Barak," *The New York Review of Books*, 13 June, 2002, p. 46.

88 Indyk, "Sins of Omission," pp. 103–04.

practical mechanisms to be set up to help rehabilitate the refugees and mobilize the international community to aid them. I believed, and continue to do so, that some flexibility on our part over the wording would have satisfied such an emotional need and devotion to an image on the part of the Palestinians. They might have been quite content to have left it at that, and would not have demanded the actual Right of Return into Israel itself for all the refugees, which in my eyes is not part of their core interests and is, of course, inconceivable in Israeli eyes.[89]

He further concluded that the core elements of the permanent settlement – refugees, Jerusalem, borders and security – could not be resolved in isolation, but rather that all these issues must be resolved together.[90] The experience of Camp David has clearly shown that without progress on a crucial issue such as Jerusalem, there could not be progress regarding the issue of Palestinian refugees.

As Quandt points out, it is striking that the participants at Camp David could say with a straight face that Jerusalem had not really been discussed until the last day or so.[91] Under such circumstances, it is no surprise that compromise positions could not be agreed upon. Indeed, much of what took place at Camp David had a rather informal, improvised quality about it. Nothing was put on paper, for fear that it might leak and embarrass one party or the other. Verbal understandings, however, had a way of dissolving when the Americans tried to translate them into concrete terms for a deal. The technique used at Camp David I – of a "single negotiating text" that was regularly revised in light of the reactions of each side – was not used at Camp David II, and as a result it was hard to know at the end of the talks what, if anything, had actually been agreed upon. Since nothing was final until everything was agreed, especially Jerusalem, it was technically accurate to say that no agreement had been reached on anything.

Following the failure at Camp David, further quiet contacts continued. The eruption of widespread violence – the second intifada – in late September 2000, however, made negotiations more difficult, and hastened the slow collapse of the Barak government. The rapidly approaching end of the Clinton Administration further created an

---

89 Gilead Sher, "Lessons from the Camp David Experience," in ibid., p. 62.
90 Ibid., p. 66.
91 Quandt, *Peace Process*, pp. 367–68.

additional source of pressure, as the overall feeling was that time was running out.

Nevertheless, the conditional compromise positions considered at Camp David would not be so easily swept from the table and would provide a benchmark of sorts for continued negotiations at a later stage.[92] Indeed, Camp David did serve as a basis for the next round of negotiations – the Taba Talks.

10.3   The Clinton Parameters: A Guiding Line for the Refugee Question

Before the parties met again, trying to achieve what they had not achieved in Camp David, Clinton presented a series of guidelines that were to serve as a point of reference for future negotiations. The Clinton Parameters, as they soon were called, were based both on Clinton's conclusion why negotiations up to that point had remained fruitless and on Clinton's ideas on how to overcome these difficulties in the future.

Clinton managed to persuade both sides to make another effort in late December 2000. He met with Israeli and Palestinian negotiators at the White House on 23 December, to present his own suggestions for a compromise.[93] Clinton's parameters were not the terms of a final deal, but guidelines for final accelerated negotiations he hoped could be concluded in the coming weeks. He said that his terms were not binding on his successor when he would leave office in January 2001.[94]

---

92   Ibid.

93   Present were Madeleine Albright, John Podesta, Samuel (Sandy) Berger, Steven Richetti, Bruce Reidel, Dennis Ross, Aaron Miller, Robert Malley, Gamal Hillal, Saeb Erekat, Mohammad Dahlan, Samih-el Abed, Gaith el-Omari, Shlomo Ben Ami, Gilead Sher, Pini Medan, Shlomo Yanai, and Gidi Grinstein. See Enderlin, *Shattered Dreams*, p. 333.

94   A version of the Clinton proposals can be found at Walter Laqueur and Barry Rubin (eds.), *The Israeli-Arab Reader: A Documentary History of the Middle East Conflict* (New York: Penguin Books, 2001), pp. 562–64. The Palestinian response can be found in "Remarks and Questions from the Palestinian Negotiating Team Regarding the United States Proposal," Negotiating Affairs Department, Palestine Liberation Organization, www.nad-plo.org/

Regarding the issue of refugees, reading his parameters straight out to the Israelis and Palestinians present, Clinton stated the following:

> The issue of Palestinian refugees is no less sensitive than Jerusalem. But here again my sense is that your differences are focused mostly on how to formulate your solutions, not on what will happen on the practical level. I believe Israel is prepared to acknowledge the moral and material suffering caused to the Palestinian people as a result of the 1948 War and the need to assist the international community in addressing the problem. I also believe the Palestinian side is prepared to join in such an international solution and that we have a pretty good idea of what it would involve.
>
> The fundamental gap seems to be how to handle the concept of the right of return. I know the history and how hard it would be for the Palestinian leadership to appear to be abandoning this principle. At the same time, I know the Israeli side cannot accept any reference to a right of return that would imply a right to immigrate to Israel in defiance of Israel's sovereign policies on admission or that would threaten the Jewish character of the State.
>
> Any solution will have to address both of these needs. It will also have to be consistent with the two-state approach that both sides have accepted as the way to end the Israeli-Palestinian conflict. A new State of Palestine is about to be created as the homeland of the Palestinian people, just as Israel was established as the homeland of the Jewish people. Under this two-state solution, our guiding principle has to be that the Palestinian state will be the focal point for the Palestinians who choose to return to the area, without ruling out that Israel will accept some of these refugees.
>
> I believe you need to adopt a formulation on the right of return that will make clear there is no specific right of return to Israel, itself, but that does not negate the aspirations of Palestinian refugees to return to the area. I propose two alternatives:
>
> – Both sides recognize the right of Palestinian refugees to return to historic Palestine.
> – Both sides recognize the right of Palestinian refugees to a homeland.
>
> The agreement would define the implementation of this general right in a way that is consistent with the two-state solution. It would list the five possible homes for refugees;
>
> 1) The State of Palestine
> 2) Areas in Israel being transferred to Palestine in the land swap
> 3) Rehabilitation in host country
> 4) Resettlement in third country
> 5) Admission to Israel.

eye/new15.html. On 7 January 2001 Clinton outlined his proposals in a public speech to the Israel Policy Forum. See the text at www.brookings.edu/press/appendix/peace_process.htm.

In listing these five options, you would make clear that return to the West Bank, Gaza, or the areas acquired through the land swap would be a right for all Palestinian refugees, while rehabilitation in their host countries, resettlement in third countries, or absorption into Israel would depend upon the policies of those countries. Israel could indicate in the agreement that it intended to establish a policy so that some of the refugees could be absorbed into Israel, consistent with Israel's sovereign decision.

I believe that priority should be given to the refugee population in Lebanon. Taken together the parties would agree that these steps implement Resolution 194.[95]

Thus, in other words, on the issue of refugees, the Clinton Parameters differed little from the ideas discussed at Camp David. The refugees would have the *right of return* – but only to their homeland, understood to be the future Palestinian state. Refugees who did not move to Palestine would have the right to choose between rehabilitation in their current places of residence, relocation to another country, or return to a location within the borders of Israel subject to that country's sovereign discretion (and within the category of family reunification). A new international mechanism would be set up to look after the rehabilitation of the refugees, to which Israel would contribute as part of its compensation to the refugees.

One crucial idea of the Clinton Parameters was to effect trade-offs. Regarding refugees, this implied exchanging the *right of return* for sovereignty over the Temple Mount.[96] Not surprisingly, therefore, critics suggested that the plan offered little recognition of the Palestinian *right of return*, nor any realistic foundation for financing refugee compensation.

Eventually, Israelis and Palestinians accepted Clinton's proposals as the basis for further negotiations (however, with Arafat taking his time, waiting ten days before offering his response – a costly delay considering the fact that only thirty days remained in Clinton's presidency), yet with both having a number of reservations. While Israel's list of reservations was rather minor, mainly dealing with security arrangements, deployment areas, and control over passages, the Palestinians had far more stipulations. Regarding refugees, Arafat wrote in a letter faxed to Clinton on 28 December, 2000:

---

95 www.brookings.edu/press/appendix/peaceprocessappen_ab.htm.
96 Indyk, "Sins of Omission," p. 106–07.

I have many questions relating to the return of refugees to their homes and villages. I have a negative experience with the return of displaced Palestinians to the West Bank and Gaza during the Interim Period. Because the modalities remained tied to an Israeli veto, not one refugee was allowed to return through the mechanism of the interim agreement, which required a quadripartite committee of Egypt, Jordan, Israel, and Palestine to decide on their return. Equally, I don't see a clear approach dealing with compensation of the refugees for their land, property and funds taken by Israel under the aegis of the Israeli custodian of absentee property.[97]

In addition, on 2 January, 2001, the Palestinian negotiating team presented a detailed set of "remarks and questions" regarding Clinton's parameters.[98] It became evident that the Palestinians were most dissatisfied with the part of the U.S. proposal relating to the refugee issue, where they objected the following:

The United States proposal reflects a wholesale adoption of the Israeli position that the implementation of the right of return be subject entirely to Israel's discretion. It is important to recall that Resolution 194, long regarded as the basis for a just settlement of the refugee problem, calls for the return of Palestinian refugees to "their homes," wherever located—not to their "homeland" or to "historic Palestine."

The essence of the right of return is *choice* [emphasis added]: Palestinians should be given the option to choose where they wish to settle, including return to the homes from which they were driven. There is no historical precedent for a people abandoning their fundamental right to return to their homes whether they were forced to leave or fled in fear. We will not be the first people to do so. Recognition of the right of return and the provision of choice to refugees is a pre-requisite for the closure of the conflict.

The Palestinians are prepared to think flexibly and creatively about the mechanisms for implementing the right of return [emphasis added]. In many discussions with Israel, mechanisms for implementing this right in such a way so as to end the refugee status and refugee problem, as well as to otherwise *accommodate Israeli concerns* [emphasis added], have been identified and elaborated in some detail. The United States proposal fails to make reference to any of these advances and refers back to earlier Israeli negotiating positions.

---

97   An unofficial translation of this letter can be found at www.brookings. edu/press/appendix/peaceprocessappen_ac.htm.

98   See the Palestinian Negotiating Team's "Remarks and Questions Regarding the Clinton Plan," 2 January, 2001, in Laqueur and Rubin, *The Israeli-Arab Reader*, pp. 567–573.

In addition, the United States proposal fails to provide any assurance that refugee rights to restitution and compensation will be fulfilled.[99]

Obviously, the Palestinians put heavy emphasis on the issue of *choice*. Coupled with their readiness "to think flexibly and creatively about the mechanisms for implementing the right of return," including consideration of Israeli concerns, the above Palestinian document carried an important message: The Palestinian position on the *right of return* was not one insusceptible to compromise. In other words, Palestinians signaled readiness to settle for less than the return of all refugees and were also willing to consider Israeli fears, as long they were given a choice regarding the modalities of return.

The Palestinian conditions and reservations were further amplified as the possibility of Ariel Sharon becoming prime minister in February appeared more probable as each day passed. Such a possible scenario had an important implication for the Palestinians: As they saw it, if Sharon was elected after the Palestinians had unequivocally deposited their acceptance of Clinton's parameters, Sharon would use these Palestinian concessions – retreating from UNSCR 242 and 338, as well as UNGAR 194 – as a new baseline, which he would try to further carve out.[100]

Overall, the Palestinians were not satisfied with Clinton's parameters, which they wanted to renegotiate. They were not responding with the same sense of urgency as the Americans or as Barak, who was facing elections and knew that the fate of the peace process could decide them. Yet, unlike what had occurred at Camp David and although having their reservations, there was no outright Palestinian rejection of Clinton's parameters. This resulted in the Palestinians agreeing to the Clinton Parameters as a basis for further negotiations – including on the issue of refugees.

This left Clinton at the end of his term with both parties reluctantly accepting his general framework, yet without time to push for a full agreement. It is regrettable that Clinton had not presented his parameters earlier – a lot of bloodshed might have been prevented.[101]

---

99 Ibid., pp. 570–71.

100 Swisher, *The Truth about Camp David*, p. 402.

101 After the meeting, Israel Hasson, one of the Israeli delegates, asked the assembled peace team: "Why so late? Everything would have been different if you'd submitted this proposal in September or at Camp David!" Several

Nevertheless, the Clinton Parameters would form a frame of reference for all future Israeli-Palestinian negotiations on a final-status deal.

However, shifting the focus from politicians to the masses of people on both sides, the mood among Israelis and Palestinians was far from supportive of the Clinton Parameters; the outbreak in September 2000 of the second intifada, since then continuously taking toll of Israeli and Palestinian lives on an almost daily basis, coupled with the failure to reach a comprehensive agreement after almost a decade of negotiations caused mutual suspicion and distrust of the other side to be high. Nevertheless, the leaderships of both Israelis and Palestinians, which had engaged in secret meetings during the autumn, agreed to continue talks in Taba.

10.4 Taba, January 2001: Substantial Progress, yet Time Running Out

As polls began to show a certain victory of Sharon, there seemed little point in keeping up negotiations. Nevertheless, while the amount of violence and casualties of the second intifada kept constantly rising, Palestinian and Israeli delegations met for a last effort at Taba, during 21–27 January, 2001 (with an interruption of two days in between[102]) – this time without leaders or U.S. mediators, as Barak was unwilling to risk further political capital and the incoming Bush administration to be sworn in on 20 January opposed any U.S. participation, restricting the deputy consul general in Jerusalem to holding debriefing meetings on the development of the talks, and only with the Israelis.[103]

---

of Clinton's advisors looked at him approvingly. See Enderlin, *Shattered Dreams*, p. 339. The document containing the Clinton Parameters would have been ready to be made public in September already; in a videotaped interview with Enderlin, Dennis Ross later bitterly regretted having held back the presentation of the American document until 23 December – too late to save the peace process. See ibid., pp. 279–80.

102 After two Israelis were shot in Tulkarem on 23 January, Barak ordered the Israeli delegation to return to Jerusalem.

103 Swisher, *The Truth about Camp David*, p. 402.

Nevertheless, the Clinton parameters laid the foundation for those final negotiations in Taba.

The Taba negotiations began on 21 January, 2001. For the first time since Ehud Barak was elected, the Palestinians had the full "peace cabinet" opposite them: Shlomo Ben Ami, Amnon Lipkin-Shahak, Yossi Beilin, and Yossi Sarid, assisted by Gilead Sher, Israel Hasson, Pini Medan, and Avraham Dichter. Arafat's delegation consisted of Abu Ala, Saeb Erekat, Yassir Abed Rabbo, Nabil Shaat, Hassan Asfur, and Mohammad Dahlan.[104]

No Americans were present at these negotiations. George W. Bush, the new President, and Secretary of State Colin Powell decided not to get involved with the Middle East at that point. The European Union lent a hand and was represented by Miguel Moratinos.

Yet chances for success were slim even before the talks started. The general impression was that time had run out. Indeed, at that point no breakthrough could be expected: Clinton was practically out of office, meaning that the influence, attention, and capabilities of his administration had come to its nadir – the same essentially also applied for Barak, who was widely expected to lose the upcoming Israeli elections.[105] In a phone conversation with Clinton on 1 January, 2001, Barak stated that he had no intention of concluding any accord before the elections.[106] Therefore, it was clear to the Israeli delegation that even if – in the case of the most optimistic scenario – an agreement with the Palestinians was achieved, Israel would not sign a document before both the elections and a subsequent referendum on such an agreement were held.[107] It is therefore all the more surprising how the gaps between Israelis and Palestinians did lessen in Taba.

---

104 Yossi Beilin, *The Path to Geneva: The Quest for a Permanent Agreement, 1996–2004* (New York: RDV Books, 2004), p. 22.

105 Due to the lack of political time both Gilead Sher and Amnon Lipkin-Shahak were against going to Taba, with Lipkin-Shahak retrospectively using the least diplomatic language by claiming: "Taba was bullshit. Taba was an election exercise – don't trust nothing. Taba was not aimed to reach an agreement. Taba was aimed to convince the Israeli Arabs to vote." See Swisher, *The Truth about Camp David*, p. 403.

106 Enderlin, *Shattered Dreams*, p. 343.

107 Sher, *Just Beyond Reach*, p. 397.

10.4.1 The Talks on Refugees at Taba

A sub-committee[108] headed by Yossi Beilin on the Israeli side and Nabil Shaat on the Palestinian one, eventually succeeded in crystallizing an agreement on the refugee question. Before the start of the conference, Ben Ami, head of the Israeli delegation, had instructed Beilin to negotiate the return of a merely symbolic number of refugees, in line with the spirit of the talks in Harpsund, as well as with the Clinton Parameters, while "generosity and creativity" was to be applied to the formulation of a narrative regarding the suffering and the tragedy of the Palestinians.[109]

As to the Palestinian instructions for the upcoming negotiations: Arafat had made clear to Shaat that compensation payments would not solve the issue regarding the *right of return*. Compensation was to be demanded and accepted for property and suffering. In the words of Shaat, "Arafat was not going to sell the right of return for money."[110] The Palestinians were further going to demand that each refugee would be given one year and a half to decide his preference: whether to return to the Palestinian state or to Israel. The negotiations with Israel were to focus on the number of returnees.[111]

Palestinians started with a tough position. On 22 January, they submitted a position paper insisting that Israel not only acknowledge moral and legal responsibility for the refugee problem but also its responsibility for preventing a solution in accord with UNGAR 194. Israel, continued the Palestinian paper, should admit any refugee intent on returning to its territory and willing to live in peace there. Further, all refugees without exception should be compensated by Israel for their abandoned property and for the suffering inflicted upon them as refugees. Collective compensation should be paid to the future Palestinian state for public lands and buildings appropriated by the State of Israel.

---

108 Only two committees were formed in Taba: One would negotiate at all topics except for refugees, which were discussed by the second committee, consisting of Yossi Beilin and Nabil Shaat. This points out the centrality of the refugee question.

109 See Shlomo Ben-Ami, *A Front Without a Rearguard: A Voyage to the Boundaries of the Peace Process* (Hebrew), (Tel Aviv: Miskal, 2004), p. 433.

110 Ibid., p. 440.

111 Ibid.

Finally, Israel should pay compensation to the Arab states for their expenses as hosts for the refugees. International bodies would be set up in order to implement and supervise the repatriation and compensation operations.[112] These demands went significantly further than previous Palestinian demands for a *right of return*.[113]

Beilin replied with a "private response" to the Palestinian position paper and expressed "sorrow" for suffering and losses incurred by the Palestinian refugees. As to a practical solution, Beilin based his position on the Clinton Parameters. Israel would thus absorb a limited number of refugees (several tens of thousands) over a number of years, based on a family reunification scheme. Preference would be given to refugees in Lebanon, due to Israel's "moral commitment to the swift resolution of the plight of the refugee population of the Sabra and Shatila camps."[114]

Eventually, the parties at Taba reached a formula which permitted the Palestinians to not give up the principle of *right of return* along with an agreement that in practice the solution would be the settlement of refugees in places other than Israel. In other words, the negotiators achieved a draft determining the parameters and procedures for a solution of the delicate issue of Palestinian refugees, along with a clear emphasis that its implementation would not represent a demographic threat to Israel. Yossi Beilin offers the following synopsis of the understandings reached with Nabil Shaat:

> Since it is reasonable to assume that the refugees living on the West Bank and Gaza will be rehabilitated and move to housing within the Palestinian state; since the refugees living in Jordan have been enjoying full citizenship for a whole generation; and since in Syria the refugees have the possibility of working and earning a living, the only remaining problem is Lebanon, where the real figure is no less than 180,000 but no more than 220,000. The refugees in Lebanon must be taken away from there, but the number of refugees that countries like Canada, the United States, and certain European countries are willing to accept is much higher than the number remaining in Lebanon,

---

112 See the "Palestinian Paper on Refugees," 22 January, 2001, at http://mond-ediplo.com/focus/mideast/a3276.

113 Tovy, "Negotiating the Palestinian Refugees".

114 See ibid., as well as the "Private Response on Palestinian Refugees", Taba, 23 January, 2001, at www.monde-diplomatique.fr/cahier/proche-orient/israelrefugees-en.

and any of them wanting to be absorbed into the Palestinian state when it is established will be able to do so.

Whoever wants to settle in the sovereign area of Israel before the Six-Day War can do so in housing built for them on the land that Israel will transfer to the Palestinian state in exchange for areas it annexes on the West Bank.[115] Israel will continue to issue permits for family reunification and special humanitarian cases, and will also be able to deal with a very limited number of refugees which it will absorb in the course of the coming years. UNRWA (…) will close down within five years.

The matter of compensation to the refugees is very complex, but it can be resolved, and herein lies the key to their rehabilitation. Tens of billions of dollars will be collected from various entities worldwide, mainly, but not solely, from the U.S. and Europe, as well as from Israel. The fund will be used for universal compensation to every refugee family, personal compensation for property presently in the possession of Israel, as well as compensation to be given to countries such as Jordan, which has absorbed refugees over the last few decades. The relationship between the international organization that will replace UNRWA – and deal with the rehabilitation of refugees – and the compensation fund; the relationship between these compensation funds and the compensation due to Jews who have left the Arab countries, leaving their property behind; and the assessment of compensation for loss of property – all of this requires very detailed work toward the permanent agreement, on which we have established only guidelines in principle over long hours.[116]

Beilin favoured an agreement which would include a narrative (i.e. a concise history of events in the eyes of each party), recognition of the suffering and distress of the refugees, and that separate interpretations of UNGAR 194 would be implemented with the Clinton Parameters.[117] Yet during an internal meeting held by the Israeli team on the afternoon of 22 January, Sher told Beilin that any agreement on refugees had also to include property and compensation of Jewish refugees from Arab countries.[118] This illustrated that Israel's main focus remained on practical steps aimed at solving the refugee problem,

---

115 Gilead Sher points out that proposals for Israel to build housing for Palestinian refugees in areas to be swapped from Israel to Palestine were already exchanged in Sweden. Ben Ami also supported the idea of settling refugees in these areas. See Ben-Ami, *A Front Without a Rearguard*, p. 447; Sher, *Just Beyond Reach*, p. 402.

116 Beilin, *The Path to Geneva*, pp. 238–39.

117 Ibid., p. 239.

118 Sher, *Just Beyond Reach*, p. 402.

despite the Palestinians regarding formal aspects of the problem as equally important.

Due to the great detail, into which the negotiations went, each side had to ask itself what it really wanted – beyond the obvious fact that the Palestinian leadership wished to announce to its people and to the world that *every* refugee had the right to return to his home, while the Israeli side wanted to announce that *no* Palestinian refugee would be allowed to enter the borders of Israel. Nevertheless, working on practical solutions, Beilin came to the conclusion that "the problem was much more easily resolved than had been imagined, and that on the majority of questions it was possible, immediately or in the near future, to come to terms."[119] In addition, the Israeli delegation as a whole concluded that serious progress had taken place in both the approach and the style of negotiations which were held on the question of Palestinian refugees.[120]

Unfortunately, at this point, practically no sources exist to give more insight into the inter-Palestinian dynamics at Taba. On the Israeli side, several key actors have published relevant material in recent years.[121] Although such documents present the point of view of one side, it still allows us to get an idea about the essentials of Taba. Accordingly, it is known that in a meeting held by the Israeli delegation on 23 January, Beilin reported progress in his talks with Shaat, mainly regarding the preamble of an agreement. That preamble was to include – without recognizing the *right of return* – formulations and a narrative that were to be a "moral compensation" to the Palestinians.[122] Beilin mentioned two open issues, which had to be resolved by Arafat and Barak: first, the number of refugees Israel was ready to accept, and second, the amount which Israel would contribute to the international compensation committee. Regarding the number of refugees, Beilin was told by Shaat that Arafat was interested in the return of 300,000 refugees, while Shaat himself reasoned that since Ben Gurion had raised at the Lausanne

---

119 Beilin, *The Path to Geneva*, p. 245; Ben-Ami, *A Front Without a Rearguard*, p. 434.
120 Sher, *Just Beyond Reach*, pp. 406–07.
121 See, e.g., Beilin, Ben-Ami, Sher.
122 Ben-Ami, *A Front Without a Rearguard*, p. 439.

Conference in 1950 the idea of allowing 100,000 refugees to return, a compromise between those two numbers had to be found now.[123]

Ben Ami did not share Beilin's optimism at the Taba talks, pointing out that those two points – the number of refugees Israel was going to accept and the financial amount Israel was going to contribute to the international fund – were exactly the two bones of contention in the refugee talks since Harpsund to which no solution has been found to date. Ben Ami later pointed out that Israel could not accept between 100,000 and 300,000 refugees, even claiming that Moratinos mentioned Palestinian demands in Taba mounting to at least 250,000 refugees.[124] As an alternative to negotiating on the number of refugees Israel was going to allow into its territory, Ben Ami suggested that the Palestinians use Singapore-style modern technology in order to accommodate thousands of refugees that would return – under the framework of "family reunifications" – into the territories that the Palestinians were going to receive in a land-swap as a compensation for Palestinian territories annexed. Ben Ami's proposal rested on the logic that the Palestinian leadership could claim a significant realization of the *right of return* since the refugees would be returning into Israeli territory. This solution to the *right of return* was refused by the Palestinians who claimed that such a scenario would prevent the freedom of choice as to where in Israel to return to. Ben Ami's response to the Palestinian rejection pointed to a central contradiction between the Palestinian refusal and the logic of a two-state solution: why is a Palestinian state going to be established if the Palestinian exiles will be absorbed into the Israeli state?[125]

Progress on Practical Aspects of the Refugee Problem –
Dissension over the Right of Return

In the four days of negotiations at Taba, the two sides generally managed to accomplish a lot. As to the refugee issue (which was the only one on which drafts had been exchanged), consent was formulated on the development of events, and almost full agreement was reached

---

123 Ibid.
124 Ibid., p. 440.
125 Ibid., p. 447.

with respect to principles for resolving the problem. The financial compensation by Israel was left for the permanent agreement stage, while reference to the number of refugees that Israel would be ready to accept remained symbolically to be assessed by the leaders.[126]

In addition, there was progress regarding the formulation of a narrative which would bypass a full Israeli recognition of the *right of return*. However, the Palestinians never indicated whether that formulation would substitute their claims for Israel to recognize the *right of return*. The issues of establishing a mechanism for the resettlement of refugees and paying compensation to them had already been discussed in Sweden. Again, the same two questions remained open: the number of refugees Israel was going to absorb and the financial amount it was going to contribute to the compensation payments.[127]

Thus, while principles began to crystallize, the details still needed to be worked out. Therefore, in an update delivered to Barak on 23 January, referring to an expected summit between Arafat and Barak, Sher urged the two leaders to find an agreement on:

- A formulation of a national narrative for each of the two parties;
- The maximum number of refugees to be accepted by Israel, out of humanitarian reasons and for the purpose of family reunifications, subordinate to Israel's sovereign discretion;
- The maximum amount of the Israeli contribution to the international effort to rehabilitate the refugees[128]

On the one hand, from the discussions in Harpsund and Camp David, as well as in the subsequent Clinton Parameters, there was constant progress on finding practical solutions to end the refugees' status as such;[129] the primary means to do so were resettlement and financial compensation. On the other hand, however, just as in the aforementioned

---

126 Beilin, *The Path to Geneva*, p. 247.
127 Ibid.
128 Sher, *Just Beyond Reach*, pp. 407.
129 In fact, Gilead Sher claims that nothing new in the refugee issue was set up in Taba and that the talks there were merely a repetition of previous discussions – which Beilin had not attended. See Sher, *Just Beyond Reach*, pp. 400–01. However, Sher also writes that the Palestinians later categorically denied that Shaat had related to papers from the negotiations in Sweden and Camp David. See ibid., p. 406.

negotiations, also in Taba did the two parties not figure out how to address the *right of return* – a concept which the Palestinian wanted to be recognized while the Israelis countered that "U.N. Resolution 194 mentions the *aspiration* to return but not the right"[130] – and the question of the responsibility for creating the refugee problem. The compromise that started to crystallize was to avoid claims for full responsibility, to avoid claims for renouncing the disputed right and to equally avoid claims for recognizing that right[131] – in other words, any mention at all of the term *right of return* was to be avoided.

However, the overall failure of the Taba Conference did not allow the agreements achieved on refugees to be put to the test. After several days of negotiation, the participants realized that they would not have time to conclude an accord, and they prepared a final statement.

The Breakup of Taba as the Overall End of Israeli-Palestinian Negotiations

The talks broke up on 27 January with a joint announcement by the parties, affirming that the Taba discussions were "without precedent in the positive atmosphere in which they have proceeded" and that "significant progress had been made." The two sides affirmed that "they have never been so close to an accord." The statement concluded with the two negotiating teams' "shared belief that the remaining gaps could be bridged with the resumption of negotiations following the Israeli elections."[132]

Yet when Abu Ala was presenting to the heads of the committees his planned remarks for the beginning of the forthcoming press conference, and came to the matter of refugees, he suggested: "On the refugee issue it is better for me to state that we demanded the right of return and that you, the Israelis, refused." According to Yossi Beilin, both he and Nabil Shaat almost leaped from their seats, shouting: "Not true!" and asked him to report "the enormous progress that had taken place, including a way to present the subject that would not be detrimental

130 Beilin, *The Path to Geneva*, p. 239. Emphasis made by the author.
131 Beilin, *Manual for a Wounded Dove*, p. 208. The same concept of reaching a compromise by simply avoiding the entire term "right of return" was later also applied in the Geneva Initiative.
132 *Haaretz*, 28 January 2001 and Enderlin, *Shattered Dreams*, p. 350.

to either side [by avoiding the term *right of return*[133]]."[134] Abu Ala did not accept their position, adding further: "It is also good for you!" – a remark that was interpreted by Beilin as saying: "Why should you get embroiled right before the elections in an agreement with us on the refugee issue? It is better for each side to stick to its own position."[135]

Abu Ala could not be dissuaded and indeed made his planned statement at the following press conference on Saturday night, 27 January. The impression created, especially among the Israeli reporters, was that even here, in the best of talks, in which the parties had narrowed their gaps as never before and had resolved almost all the disputed issues, the Palestinians still claimed for themselves full implementation of the *right of return* of the Palestinian refugees into Israel, a position which Israel would not accept. Obviously, it followed that a permanent agreement would therefore be impossible, whatever the solutions to all the other issues at stake.

Thus, in Beilin's words, "the issue on which there had been the greatest consensus became a symbol of the inability to reach a solution."[136] Yet unjustly so, as he later explained:

> The Palestinians know that no Israeli government will ever allow Palestinian refugees into sovereign Israeli territory under the principle of the Right of Return. All Israeli governments, Right and Left alike, have allowed Palestinian refugees into Israel under the humanitarian umbrella of family reunification, but no government will ever agree to incorporate a Right of Return in any permanent status agreement. (...) Therefore, the Palestinians will keep the Right of Return as their last card, waiting for the right time to play it. The assumption that the Palestinians will always insist on the unrestricted Right of Return is a mistake.[137]

Also Sher, although being critical toward parts of the Moratinos-Paper (to be discussed in the next section),[138] was explicit regarding the issue of refugees:

---

133 Remark added by the author.
134 Beilin, *The Path to Geneva*, p. 248.
135 Ibid.
136 Ibid.
137 See Beilin's remarks in a roundtable discussion, available at Shamir and Maddy-Weitzmann, *The Camp David Summit*, p. 238.
138 Sher, *Just Beyond Reach*, p. 412.

It is clear to me that the problem of the refugees is completely resolvable. Prior to Camp David, all parties agreed on a mechanism dealing with refugees' claims. An international fund would be established, to which Israel would also contribute. The refugees would be rehabilitated in their present places of residence or in the Palestinian state once it is established or, alternatively, in countries outside the region, such as Canada, Australia and Norway, each of which have already stated they would accept tens of thousands of refugees. There would be no Right of Return to the State of Israel. Almost none of the Palestinian leaders – and I will take issue with anyone who says differently – truly believed that refugees would be allowed to return to Israeli territory. All the talk surrounding this issue was just empty propaganda and negotiating maneuvers. The fact is that the Right of Return was never an obstacle to reaching a permanent status agreement, neither at Camp David nor at any point thereafter.[139]

Abu Ala and Ben Ami agreed that the talks would continue in a more limited framework over the next few days, ahead of a possible meeting between Arafat and Barak in Sweden by the end of the month, both in order to adopt a number of resolutions attainable only at such a level, and in order to conclude how and when the talks would continue should Barak win the elections. Yet a series of events prevented the Arafat-Barak summit. First of all, Clinton's absence was prominent. At this critical stage, he was no longer available, be it as mediator or guarantor. The Swedes themselves became hesitant about holding the summit. Finally, on 28 January, 2001, Arafat issued a harsh speech in Davos where he accused Israel of economically strangulating the Palestinian people and of waging "a savage, barbarous war and fascist military aggression against our Palestinian people."[140] The speech's content and spirit gave the Israelis the impression that Arafat was not prepared for a reconciliatory summit meeting.

The same day, 28 January, Barak called a halt to all talks with the Palestinians and devoted the remaining week to prepare for the elections

---

139 Gilead Sher, "Lessons from the Camp David Experience," in Shamir and Maddy-Weitzmann, *The Camp David Summit*, pp. 66–67.

140 See Enderlin, *Shattered Dreams*, p. 358. According to Beilin, also members of Arafat's own entourage were surprised upon the aggressive nature of the speech. Their explanation was that Arafat's statements for the Davos conference had been prepared well in advance, while Gaza was under attack by IDF helicopters, a long time before the Clinton Parameters and the Taba talks, and that nobody had taken the trouble to update the speech. See Beilin, *The Path to Geneva*, p. 249.

to be held the following month. Serious official Israeli-Palestinian peace talks had come to an indefinite halt; nevertheless, the basis of a future accord had been set down.

10.4.2 What Was Achieved at Taba?

Compared to the Camp David summit, which produced a number of accounts from members of the Israeli, Palestinian, and American delegations, considerably less has been written about the Taba talks. In fact, Miguel Moratinos' account is the only document on the Taba talks accepted by both sides: The "Moratinos Non-Paper" was compiled by the special envoy of the European Union to the Middle East, Miguel Angel Moratinos, at the request of the two parties. It remained the most authoritative and authentic reference that gave a widely accurate assessment of the Taba talks. Moratinos, the only outsider present at Taba (though not at the meetings themselves) interviewed the negotiators after each session,[141] and prepared the document on the basis of their reports. The final document, successive drafts of which were sent to both sides for comment and correction, was completed and approved by both sides in summer 2001. It constituted a kind of minutes, a summary of the positions of each side at the time the talks ended. The document, which was not to be published, was eventually leaked and published by *Haaretz* on 14 February, 2002.[142]

Moratinos and his diplomatic adviser, Christian Jouret, had originally written a report on the negotiations, which was entitled "European Narrative of What Happened at Taba in January 2001 in the Israeli-Palestinian Negotiations on Permanent Status Issues." This non-paper became generally acknowledged by the parties as being a relatively fair description of the outcome of the negotiations.[143] Regarding refugees, the Moratinos document stated the following:

---

141 See Akiva Eldar, *Haaretz*, 14 February, 2002.

142 See also "The Taba Negotiations (January 2001)," *Journal of Palestine Studies*, Vol. XXXI, No. 3, Spring 2002, pp. 79–89.

143 The approval of the document was not univocal, however. While Enderlin called parts of it an "embellished" account of the understandings reached, Gilead Sher rejected it as unacceptable and mostly based on the Palestinian account. See Enderlin, *Shattered Dreams*, p. 351; Sher, *Just Beyond Reach*,

3. Refugees

Non-papers were exchanged, which were regarded as a good basis for the talks. Both sides stated that the issue of the Palestinian refugees is central to the Israeli-Palestinian relations and that a comprehensive and just solution is essential to creating a lasting and morally scrupulous peace. Both sides agreed to adopt the principles and references with could facilitate the adoption of an agreement.

Both sides suggested, as a basis, that the parties should agree that a just settlement of the refugee problem in accordance with the UN Security Council Resolution 242 must lead to the implementation of UN General Assembly Resolution 194.

3.1 Narrative

The Israeli side put forward a suggested joint narrative for the tragedy of the Palestinian refugees. The Palestinian side discussed the proposed narrative and there was much progress, although no agreement was reached in an attempt to develop and [sic] historical narrative in the general text.

3.2 Return, repatriation and relocation and rehabilitation

Both sides engaged in a discussion of the practicalities of resolving the refugee issue. The Palestinian side reiterated that the Palestinian refugees should have the right of return to their homes in accordance with the interpretation of UNGAR 194. The Israeli side expressed its understanding that the wish to return as per wording of UNGAR 194 shall be implemented within the framework of one of the following programs:

A. Return and repatriation

1. to Israel
2. to Israel swapped territory
3. to the Palestine state.

B. Rehabilitation and relocation

1. Rehabilitation in host country.
2. Relocation to third country.

Preference in all these programs shall be accorded to the Palestinian refugee population in Lebanon. The Palestinian side stressed that the above shall be

---

p.412. Raymond Cohen objected that "the importance of Taba has been inflated by Moratinos, and his account bore no relation to what really happened there. He wanted to put the most favorable spin on inchoate events." Quoted in Peter Carnevale, "Psychological Barriers to Negotiations," in Shamir and Maddy-Weitzmann, *The Camp David Summit*, p.211.

subject to the individual free choice of the refugees, and shall not prejudice their right to their homes in accordance with its interpretation of UNGAR 194.

The Israeli side, informally, suggested a three-track 15–year absorption program, which was discussed but not agreed upon. The first track referred to the absorption to Israel. No numbers were agreed upon, but with a non-paper referring to 25,000 in the first three years of this program (40,000 in the first five years of this program did not appear in the non-paper but was raised verbally). The second track referred to the absorption of Palestinian refugees into the Israeli territory, that shall be transferred to Palestinian sovereignty, and the third track referring to the absorption of refugees in the context of family reunification scheme.

The Palestinian side did not present a number, but stated that the negotiations could not start without an Israeli opening position. It maintained that Israel's acceptance of the return of refugees should not prejudice existing programs within Israel such as family reunification.

3.3 Compensation

Both sides agreed to the establishment of an International Commission and an International Fund as a mechanism for dealing with compensation in all its aspects. Both sides agreed that "small-sum" compensation shall be paid to the refugees in the "fast-track" procedure, claims of compensation for property losses below certain amount shall be subject to "fast-track" procedures.

There was also progress on Israeli compensation for material losses, land and assets expropriated, including agreement on a payment from an Israeli lump sum or proper amount to be agreed upon that would feed into the International Fund. According to the Israeli side the calculation of this payment would be based on a macro-economic survey to evaluate the assets in order to reach a fair value. The Palestinian side, however, said that this sum would be calculated on the records of the UNCCP, the Custodian for Absentee Property and other relevant data with a multiplier to reach a fair value.

3.4 UNRWA

Both sides agreed that UNRWA should be phased out in accordance with an agreed timetable of five years, as a targeted period. The Palestinian side added a possible adjustment of that period to make sure that this will be subject to the implementation of the other aspects of the agreement dealing with refugees, and with termination of Palestinian refugee status in the various locations.

3.5 Former Jewish refugees

The Israeli side requested that the issue of compensation to former Jewish refugees from Arab countries be recognized, while accepting that it was not a Palestinian responsibility or a bilateral issue. The Palestinian side maintained that this is not a subject for a bilateral Palestinian-Israeli agreement.

3.6 Restitution

The Palestinian side raised the issue of restitution of refugee property. The Israeli side rejected this.

3.7 End of claims

The issue of the end of claims was discussed, and it was suggested that the implementation of the agreement shall constitute a complete and final implementation of UNGAR 194 and therefore ends all claims.[144]

Some complementary information was provided by a fairly accurate account in Haaretz on 29 May 2001:

- The five options for resettlement will be shaped in a manner that will channel immigration as much as possible to options other than a return to Israel. This will include a series of incentives, an accelerated rehabilitation program and generous economic aid, which will be offered to Palestinians who forgo the option of immigration to Israel.
- The immigration quotas will also be geared to induce refugees to opt for the alternatives to living in Israel. It was agreed that the immigration quotas for Israel would be lower than those set for other destinations. According to an estimate by foreign sources, it will be possible, in negotiations, to reach agreement on a quota of 40,000 refugee immigrants to Israel over a period of five years. In any event, it was agreed that Israel had the sovereign right to decide who would enter its territory and who would be barred from entering.
- Dealing with the personal status of each refugee will be conditional upon his relinquishing refugee status and accepting the same rights as those in whatever place he chooses to reside. This means that the refugee agrees the place he chooses will be his final place of residence. In addition, this will mean forgoing claims to property in Israel. The Israeli side attached great importance to this point, viewing it as confirmation of the end of Israel's commitment with respect to the refugee problem.
- The new international body will replace UNRWA, which will be dismantled within five years. The new body will assume responsibility for dealing with the refugees at both the personal and the community level. This will include establishing infrastructure and making provision for education, housing, health and welfare, and professional training. Israel would like UNRWA to shut down its operations, on the grounds that the organization's existence perpetuates the Palestinian problem rather than solving it. It was agreed that refugee certificates that UNRWA issues would be cancelled. Refugee camps containing those who choose to be rehabilitated where they are

---

144 See www.jmcc.org/documents/moratinos.htm.

will be annexed to adjacent cities. Thus the refugee camps will lose their extraterritorial status.
- The international body will raise funds and give compensation for private real estate that was expropriated from the refugees. There is still an unresolved dispute concerning property of common ownership, collective compensation, and movable property, such as vehicles and the other items that the refugees left behind.
- Israel demanded that a ceiling be set for the amount of compensation to be paid and the amount of refugees absorbed; this would then become part of the permanent agreement. The Palestinians demanded that compensation be set on a case-by-case basis, with no ceiling – that is, with a separate assessment of the worth of each refugee's case. Israel argued that the adoption of that system would perpetuate the problem, because the Palestinians would quickly find themselves in a confrontation with the administration, which would attempt to reduce the assessed value of their property. One idea that was discussed was for the amount to be calculated within a designated time, using a method that would take account of macro-economic considerations and individual case-by-case calculations.[145]

A Comparison between Taba and the Beilin-Abu Mazen Proposal

Although many observers claim that Israelis and Palestinians were never closer to an agreement on refugees than at Taba, a comparison with the (unofficial) Beilin-Abu Mazen Plan drafted six years earlier shows striking similarities to the proposals of Taba; however, there were also differences between the two proposals. Let us take a closer look:

Narrative: The Palestinian position at Taba was that Israel recognized its moral and legal responsibility for the forced displacement and dispossession of the Palestinian civilian population during the 1948 war and for preventing the refugees from returning to their homes in accordance with UNGAR 194. The Beilin-Abu Mazen Plan, on the other hand, did not attribute responsibility to any of the parties.

Citizenship and Return: The Israeli proposal at Taba represented a significantly greater concession concerning refugees than set forth in the Beilin-Abu Mazen Plan, including:

- recognition of a limited return of refugees to Israel (in addition to family reunifications);

---

145 See Akiva Eldar, "How to Solve the Palestinian Refugee Problem," *Haaretz*, 29 May 2001.

- unrestricted resettlement and citizenship in the Palestinian state; and
- recognition of the right of host countries to compensation.[146]

Compensation: Regarding compensation, the Israeli and Palestinian positions at Taba clearly differed from the Beilin-Abu Mazen Plan. According to the latter, compensation was to be paid following the establishment of the "International Commission for Palestinian Refugees" (ICPR). However, the Beilin-Abu Mazen Plan was not clear about what the basis for assessment of refugee claims would be, namely whether the approach was to be a lump-sum, or an individual one. It was not clear who would contribute and how contributions would be determined. At Taba, the Israeli position envisaged a lump-sum payment. In addition, at Taba the Israelis requested that the issue of compensation to former Jewish refugees from Arab countries be recognized. The Palestinian side, however, maintained that this was not a subject for a bilateral Palestinian-Israeli agreement.[147]

Ultimately, however, time ran out for the Taba negotiations to produce a comprehensive agreement on refugees and other permanent status issues. Against the backdrop of escalating violence, negotiations were extremely difficult, and in addition, neither Israeli nor Palestinian public opinion was inclined to compromise. The negotiations at Taba were interrupted by Barak after two Israelis were killed in the West Bank. The talks resumed and then halted again with the agreement to pick up after the elections – yet they never did. In February 2001, facilitated by continued Palestinian violence, Barak suffered a humiliating electoral defeat at the hands of hardline Likud leader Ariel Sharon. With Sharon's accession to the position of prime minister, the prospects for meaningful permanent status negotiations quickly faded.

---

146 Tanja Salem, "Palestinian Refugees: How Can a Durable Solution Be Achieved?," Centre for European Policy Studies, Working Paper No. 6, July 2003, p. 11. Available under "Research Papers" at www.prrn.org.
147 Ibid., pp. 11–12.

10.4.3 Lessons from Taba

Taba ended without a formal agreement. Does it therefore need to be regarded as failure? Absolutely not. As Ian Lustick points out, one needs to realize that both in Camp David II and in Taba, for the first time, Israelis and Palestinians failed to achieve an accord because, in talking more or less directly to each other, they could not reach *full* agreement on a few issues – Jerusalem and refugees – that were so highly fraught that they had hardly ever been formally discussed before Camp David II. But peace negotiations between Israelis and Palestinians finally had penetrated through procedural and representation questions, technical issues, and many if not most of the large substantive issues; the Camp David negotiations failed largely due to the tactics and highly inflammatory issues that all parties have recognized as requiring the kind of negotiation which took place at Taba. However, the realization for the need for negotiations as they took place in Taba only became apparent after the attempt of Camp David II had failed.[148]

Many Israelis continued to believe that throughout the final status talks, the Palestinians were inflexible in their demand that all refugees be given the *right of return* to their former homes; that belief raised existential fears in Israel. Yet Beilin, the Israeli who headed negotiations on refugees at Taba, emphasized that the two sides were exploring an agreed narrative that would defuse the explosive nature of this issue and protect the Jewish identity of Israel. He added that about 200,000 Palestinians living in East Jerusalem would drop off the Israeli demographic rolls, and a mechanism was to be devised giving refugees more financial incentive to settle outside Israel.[149]

In the words of one of the senior Palestinian negotiators, Abu Ala: "When other issues move, this [i.e., the Palestinian refugee issue] will move. It's not a deal breaker."[150] Nabil Shaat, who had negotiated refugees on the Palestinian side in Taba, added: "If Camp David was too little, Taba was too late,"[151] as there was a lack of time in view of

---

148 Ian Lustick, "Through Blood and Fire Shall Peace Arise," *Tikkun*, May/June 2002.
149 Sontag, "Quest for Middle East Peace," p. 84.
150 Ibid.
151 Ibid.

the impending Israeli elections. Also Arafat gave clear signals of being in favour of a pragmatic and realistic solution. Already in 1990 he had affirmed: "The right of return is sacred. However, we are ready to discuss the conditions of its application."[152] In an interview with Haaretz in 2004, Arafat even went as far as to emphasize that it was "clear and obvious" that the refugee problem needed to be solved in a way that would not change the Jewish character of the State of Israel.[153] In an op-ed piece in the New York Times on 3 February 2002, Arafat called for "creative solutions to the plight of the refugees while respecting Israel's demographic concerns." He further stated: "We understand Israel's demographic concerns and understand that the right of return of Palestinian refugees, a right guaranteed under international law and UN Resolution 194, must be implemented in a way that takes into account such concerns." However, there remains the crucial question how to reconcile those two claims, namely Israel's demographic concerns and the Palestinian emphasis on the *right of return*.

One clearly recognizes one common denominator in all the conferences from Lausanne to Taba: the refugee problem was mostly one of the major difficulties, if not *the* main hurdle to reaching an agreement. Taba provided a basis to which future Israeli-Palestinian negotiations on refugees can refer. Such negotiations have not occurred to date on a governmental level. The peace process as laid out in the Oslo agreements factually ended with Taba. The contact between Israelis and Palestinians has since come primarily in the form of violence. Yet, several non-governmental and private initiatives regarding the Israeli-Palestinian conflict, including the question of refugees, were presented; they shall be discussed in the concluding part of this paper. This chapter shall end with an overview of the three governmental documents and peace initiatives that also address the issue of Palestinian refugees: the Arab League's Proposal, the "Roadmap", and the Bush-Letter.

---

152 Quoted from the *Mideast Mirror*, 26 February 1990, cited in Robert Bowker, *Palestinian Refugees: Mythology, Identity, and the Search for Peace* (Boulder: Lynne Rienner, 2003), p. 155. Yitzhak Shamir, Israeli prime minister at that time, dismissed the statement.

153 See David Landau and Akiva Eldar, "A Jewish state? 'Definitely'" in *Haaretz*, 18 June 2004.

10.5 After Oslo: The Arab League's Proposal, the "Roadmap", and the Bush-Letter

The Arab League's Proposal: The first international initiative after Taba mentioning the Palestinian refugee question was adopted by the Beirut Arab Summit Declaration of 28 March 2002. The Summit Declaration's section on refugees called for an "achievement of a just solution to the Palestinian refugee problem to be agreed upon in accordance with U.N. General Assembly Resolution 194." This formulation has been seen as significant by some in that it failed to explicitly mention the *right of return*, but instead echoed the sort of ambiguous focus on UNGAR 194 that Palestinian and Israeli (Labour Party) negotiators adopted in the last round of final status negotiations in Taba in January 2001.[154] Israel saw the inclusion of UNGAR 194 unfavourably, yet adding the phrase "to be agreed upon" was not only the most open formulation ever offered by the Arab League but also one that could, and indeed has been, interpreted by many as providing Israel with a veto in the matter of the return of refugees.[155]

Unfortunately, the release of the Arab League's Beirut Proposal came at an extraordinarily unfavourable moment: On the previous day, on 27 March 2002, a Palestinian terrorist had blown up a hotel in Netanya which was packed with Israelis celebrating the Jewish Passover. The magnitude of the attack triggered an escalation of the second intifada and resulted in an Israeli reconquest of the West Bank in what was termed by Israel "Operation Defensive Shield." The Arab Leagues proposal went down in a continuously spinning circle of Israel-Palestinian violence and has not received proper attention.

The Roadmap: Although it equally bore no results, unlike the Arab League's Beirut Proposal, the so-called "Roadmap" did not go unnoticed: in April 2003, the diplomatic Quartet (comprised of the U.S., E.U., Russia, and the U.N.), in an effort to bring to an end the escalating violence between Israelis and Palestinians, released its "Performance-Based

---

154   Ibid.; Wolfgang Köhler, „Balanceakt zwischen zwei Extremen," *Frankfurter Allgemeine Zeitung,* 27 March 2002, p. 2.
155   Galia Golan, "Plans for Israeli-Palestinian Peace: From Beirut to Geneva," *Middle East Policy,* Vol. XI, No. 1, Spring 2004, p. 40.

Roadmap to a Permanent Two-State Solution to the Israeli-Palestinian Conflict". Phase II of the Roadmap focused on "the option of creating an independent Palestinian state with provisional borders and attributes of sovereignty, based on the new constitution, as a way station to a permanent status settlement." Phase III called for "Israeli-Palestinian negotiations aimed at a permanent status agreement in 2005."[156] However, the 2005 deadline has passed with no Israeli-Palestinian negotiations toward final status taking place.

The Roadmap only marginally mentioned the refugee issue, which was reserved for permanent status negotiations. Using the model of the Arab League's Proposal, the Roadmap demanded "an agreed, just, fair, and realistic solution to the refugee issue." The inclusion of "realistic" can be seen as suggesting that the quartet did not believe that maximalist solutions are likely to form part of an eventual peace agreement. That could particularly apply to a large-scale refugee return to former homes in Israel. Yet the term is elastic enough as to include almost any possible outcome of negotiations.[157]

The Roadmap based itself on U.N. Security Council Resolution 242 of 1967, which with regard to refugees merely called for "a just settlement of the refugee problem". The Roadmap also established as one of its foundations the Beirut Arab Summit Declaration of March 2002. The Summit Declaration's section on refugees called for an "achievement of a just solution to the Palestinian refugee problem to be agreed upon in accordance with U.N. General Assembly Resolution 194." This formulation has been seen as significant by some in that it failed to explicitly mention the *right of return*, but instead echoed the sort of ambiguous focus on UNGAR 194 that Palestinian and Israeli (Labor Party) negotiators adopted in the last round of final status negotiations in Taba in January 2001.[158]

When the Israeli cabinet voted to accept the steps included in the Roadmap it explicitly emphasized that "both during and subsequent to the political process, the resolution of the issue of the refugees will not include their entry or settlement within the State of Israel." The Israeli

---

156 For the full text of the Roadmap, see www.mideastweb.org/quartetrm3.htm.
157 Rex Brynen, "The Roadmap and the Refugees," at www.prrn.org.
158 Ibid.; Wolfgang Köhler, „Balanceakt zwischen zwei Extremen," *Frankfurter Allgemeine Zeitung*, 27 March 2002, p. 2.

government also included, in a list of fourteen reservations to the U.S., a request that "in connection to both the introductory statements and the final settlement, declared references must be made to Israel's right to exist as a Jewish state and to the waiver of any right of return for Palestinian refugees to the State of Israel."[159]

The Bush-Letter: With the Roadmap officially still being on the table, U.S. President Bush went some considerable way to accepting the Israeli position in an April 2004 exchange of letters with Prime Minister Sharon regarding Israel's announced disengagement from Gaza. Specifically, Bush stated that "It seems clear that an agreed, just, fair and realistic framework for a solution to the Palestinian refugee issue as part of any final status agreement will need to be found through the establishment of a Palestinian state, and the settling of Palestinian refugees there, rather than in Israel." The Bush formulation was considerably less nuanced than the Clinton Parameters, and not surprisingly received substantial Arab and Palestinian criticism.[160] In fact, U.S. stated policy had hitherto been that the Palestinian refugee issue would be addressed in the context of the final status negotiations.[161] This was the first time that the U.S. had explicitly rejected *a priori* a right for Palestinian refugees to return to Israel.[162]

After Bush's letter, no further governmental initiatives or documents referring to the Palestinian refugee question were published. Before we turn to the various private and non-governmental initiatives in the next part of this paper, let us briefly summarize the results of the official Israeli-Palestinian negotiations on refugees which have taken place to this point.

---

159 "Statement from the Prime Minister's Bureau," Israeli Government Press Office, 25 May 2003, available at www.mideastweb.org/roadmapreservations. htm.

160 Ibid. For the exchange of letters, see www.bitterlemons.org/docs/bushletter. html.

161 Brian Knowlton, "Bush Shifts Views on the West Bank," *International Herald Tribune*, 15th April 2004, p. 1.

162 Sander Agterhuis, "The Right to Return and its Practical Application," at www.prrn.org.

10.6 The Results of the Official Israeli-Palestinian Negotiations on Refugees

After the outbreak of the second intifada on 29 September 2000, the peace process has been in a state of collapse. That intifada left both populations deeply shaken, precipitating Barak's downfall and the breakdown of permanent-status negotiations. This tragic deterioration was the result of a double miscalculation. The Palestinian side reached the mistaken conclusion that the Israeli public and Barak were not prepared to pay the price necessary for a genuine peace. Both the Israeli public and the prime minister were in fact willing to go the necessary distance, on the condition that the Palestinians expressed publicly the conciliatory positions which they had stated privately, and that they demonstrated determination in combating terrorism. The Israeli side, for its part, reached the mistaken conclusion that the Palestinians were bent on destroying the Israeli state both from within (i.e. by a vast influx of Palestinian refugees) and without (by terrorism and violence). In reality, the Palestinians had not altered the basic position they had held since 1993: a two-state solution, with a non-militarised Palestinian state along 1967 borders, and a pragmatic solution to the refugee problem.[163]

In sum, during the intensive permanent status negotiations that took place from the summer of 2000 until January 2001, some progress was made between Palestinian and Israeli negotiators in identifying a common middle ground. On the Israeli side, there appeared to be recognition that Israel would have to accept some refugee return, admit some responsibility or regret for the refugee issue, and accept primary responsibility for financing refugee compensation. On the Palestinian side, there was recognition that Israel would not permit practical implementation of the *right of return* to fundamentally change the demographic face of the Jewish state. As a consequence, voluntary refugee repatriation (primarily to the future Palestinian state) and resettlement (in either present host countries or, to a much lesser extent, other countries) would also be important elements of an eventual agreement.

---

163 Ron Pundak, "From Oslo to Taba: What Went Wrong?," *Survival*, Vol. 43, No. 3, Autumn 2001, p. 44.

However, these understandings were rendered moot – temporarily perhaps – by the election of Ariel Sharon as Israeli prime minister in February 2001; an event which practically signified the end of Oslo, as Sharon had no intention of continuing that process.

More generally, the upsurge in violence that began in the autumn of 2000 hardened public opinion on both sides. Among Palestinians, popular support for the *right of return* remained strong, and the violence and increasing harshness of Israeli occupation, coupled with ever increasing Israeli settlement construction, deterred many from considering compromise. Within Israel, partially violent protests by Palestinian citizens of Israel as to their second-class treatment led many Israeli Jews to fear any future return of even token numbers of 1948 refugees, while the second intifada severely weakened both sides' support for the Oslo peace process overall.[164] Nevertheless, the Taba talks indicated that the Palestinian leadership recognized the vital Israeli sticking point, namely that any "return of refugees" should a) not prejudice the Jewish nature of the state and b) would be subject to Israel's sovereign decision. Without these qualifications, the Palestinians' proclaimed allegiance to the two-state solution would indeed seem disingenuous. In fact, Palestinians would appear as aspiring to a one and one-half state solution, with a Palestinian state existing alongside a bi-national state.[165] A major challenge facing the entire mainstream Palestinian leadership has been how to get the message across convincingly to the Israeli people that the Palestinians do accept these qualifications, without simultaneously alienating large segments of the Palestinian people.[166]

Reviewing the entire – official – peace talks between Israelis and Palestinians, one can say that Taba was the most fruitful discussion on the issue of refugees. Taba will certainly stand as a model for serious future negotiations. That is demonstrated by the Geneva Initiative, a kind of virtual – and non-official – peace agreement hammered out by Yossi Beilin, Yasser Abed Rabbo, Robert Malley, Ghaith al-Omari and

---

164 See "Palestinian Refugees and Final Status: Key Issues," at www.prrn.org.
165 The term "one and one-half state solution" has been used by Malley in his article "American Mistakes and Israeli Misconceptions," in Shamir and Maddy-Weitzmann, *The Camp David Summit*, p. 109.
166 Tony Klug, "The Infernal Scapegoat," *Palestine-Israel Journal*, Vol. VIII, No. 3, p. 13.

others, which was in fact developed from what had been discussed at Taba; Geneva stands as the closest that Israeli and Palestinian negotiators have come to a reasonable two-state solution.

Having reviewed the official Israeli-Palestinian negotiations on refugees to date, the next part of this paper shall focus on the main focus of this research: The synopsis of various private, non-official proposals for a political solution of the issue of Palestinian refugees.

PART IV

In Search of Sustainable Solutions

After having reviewed the official peace process, i.e. the negotiations between the Israeli and the Palestinian leaderships, we shall now turn to the known unofficial proposals and initiatives suggesting solutions to the question of Palestinian refugees. While most of these proposals have been published in the form presented (yet with its title in some cases chosen by the author), two of them – the Citizenship/Residency Approach and the Internal Approach – were formulated by the author, inspired by both existing proposals and interviews with experts regarding the Palestinian refugee question.

The following chapter will review *practical solutions;* thus ideas for an Israeli-Palestinian peace agreement intended to end the refugees' existence as such. The underlying idea is to give refugees a permanent home (as opposed to their lives in refugee camps); primarily via financial compensation and resettlement, be it within their present countries of residence or to third countries. This chapter will not deal with *principled aspects*, such as whether to recognize the *right of return* or not, which shall be scrutinized in the next chapter. Finally, proposals considering both practical and principled solutions shall be examined; this will form the concluding chapter, focusing on *integrated solutions.*

11 PRACTICAL SOLUTIONS

According to Susan Akram, any successful and durable solution to a refugee problem is an overall combination of three factors: voluntary repatriation, host country absorption, and third country resettlement,[1] to be complemented by the right to claim restitution of property, and/or compensation for losses caused by the refugee-producing state.[2] We shall primarily focus on the most intractable one of these elements: *repatriation*, i.e. the return of refugees into the State of Israel, an issue which has been and continues to be the major stumbling block preventing an Israeli-Palestinian agreement to solve the question of refugees. With the involvement of the international community – which indeed has repeatedly offered its assistance – the issues of compensation, host country absorption, and third country resettlement can doubtlessly be overcome. However, Israelis and Palestinians still need to find a formula which, on the one hand, satisfies the Palestinian demand for refugee return while, on the other hand, does not contravene Israeli demographic concerns. Finding the essentials to such formula shall be the goal of the following three chapters, which will analyse various private proposals to solve the Israeli-Palestinian quarrel over the question of Palestinian refugees.[3]

---

1   Those three points – along with an Israeli recognition of its responsibility for the Palestinian refugee problem and an Israeli apology for the suffering caused – were also indicated by Muhammad Jaradat (Co-founder of the Palestinian refugee organisation BADIL) to be the Palestinian basis for any refugee agreement with Israel. Interview with the author in Bethlehem, September 2004.

2   Susan Akram, "Reinterpreting Palestinian Refugee Rights under International Law," in Naseer Aruri (ed.), *Palestinian Refugees: The Right of Return* (London: Pluto Press, 2001), p. 175.

3   The criteria of human quantity was chosen because the previous chapter's analysis of the political negotiations demonstrated that other factors, such as the amount of compensations paid, were secondary. During the Camp David negotiations, Clinton had agreed to raise the necessary financial means in the event of an agreement. Doubtlessly, the U.S., along with the rest of the international community, would be willing to contribute to the solution of the Israeli-Palestinian conflict once merely financial issues remain outstanding.

The following *methodology* shall be used: The range of solutions will be determined by its two extreme ends, i.e. either allowing all refugees to return into what is now Israel, or to allow none to do so. As to the proposals falling between those two ends, they will be examined according to the number of Palestinian refugees they imply returning to Israel. In other words, the proposal allowing all refugees to return to Israel will be followed by the proposal implying the second largest number of Palestinian refugees returning to Israel, then by the next smaller number etc, until we reach the end of the spectrum represented by the proposal implying that no single Palestinian refugee will return to Israel.

Each of the following proposals will be examined by *first* presenting a summary of its underlying idea for solving the Palestinian refugee question. *Second*, implications of such a solution for both Israelis and Palestinians respectively will be analysed. *Third*, the proposal as a whole will be evaluated in the light of previous Israeli-Palestinian negotiations as to the probability of it becoming a mutually accepted solution for both parties; or in other words, its relevance will be assessed.

11.1 Abu Sitta: All Palestinian Refugees Must and Can Return to Israel

11.1.1 The Essence of the Proposal

Salman Abu Sitta represents the far end of the Palestinian political spectrum. His solution to the Palestinian refugee question is nothing less than a total return of all refugees into the territory of what has become Israel. For that purpose, he has devised a concrete plan, emphasizing that such a solution is entirely feasible.[4]

The crucial issue is thus not compensation, but the issue of the physical return of the Palestinian refugees. Therefore, the main hurdle which needs to be overcome is satisfying the Palestinian demand for the *right of return* while taking into account Israeli demographic concerns.

4   See Salman Abu-Sitta, *From Refugees to Citizens at Home: The End of the Palestinian-Israeli Conflict* (London: Palestine Land Society and Palestinian Return Centre, 2001).

Abu Sitta vehemently rejects the claim that there was not sufficient space within Israel to absorb millions of Palestinian refugees. He further dismisses assertions of Israel not being able to absorb a large influx of people by pointing to Israel's successful absorption of more than one million persons mostly from the former Soviet Union who immigrated to Israel throughout the 1990s.

According to Abu Sitta's studies, nearly 80% of Jewish Israelis live on only 15% of Israel's territory, mostly in urban areas. The other 85% of the land, which is where most of the refugees originate, remains sparsely populated (by only about 154,000 out of more than five million Jewish Israelis). Meanwhile, the land left by the Palestinian refugees is inhabited by only 1.5% of the Israeli population. Abu Sitta concludes, therefore, that there are sufficient land resources for the refugees to return to their places of origin and to live in co-existence with the Jewish Israelis living there at present.[5]

Abu Sitta has formulated his ideas in a proposal termed "The Return Plan," which divides Israel into 41 "natural regions" and determines for each region the number of urban and rural Jewish-Israelis, the Arab-Israelis and the refugees whose homes were in that region.[6] The regions are further divided into three groups: A, B and C (similar to the West Bank under the Oslo agreements).

Area A of the Return Plan consists of the first eight natural regions and has an area of 1683 sq.km (8% of Israel). Counting more than three millions, or about 70% of Israel's Jewish population, this is where the majority of Jewish-Israelis live. Abu Sitta points out that this space is similar in size, yet not in location, to where Jews lived in pre-1948 Palestine. The next five natural regions form Area B and spread over 1,318 sq.km (7% of Israel) in which 419,000 Jewish-Israelis (10% of Israel's population). The size of this area is close to the land of the Palestinians who remained in Israel. Accordingly, 80% of Jewish Israelis live in 15% of the land. This leaves Area C (17,325 sq.km, or 85% of Israel), an area which is attributed to being similar to the land inhabited by Palestinians who have become refugees. Currently, about 800,000 urban Jewish-Israelis, 154,000 rural Jewish-Israelis and 465,000 Arab Israelis live

5   From an interview with al-Jazeera, 28 May 2005, at www.alJazeera.net.
6   See Salman Abu-Sitta, "The Feasibility of the Right of Return," June 1997, at www.prrn.org.

in Area C. Abu Sitta concludes therefore that 154,000 Jewish-Israelis are cultivating the land of more than four million refugees who are prevented from returning to it.[7]

The proposed plan emphasizes that it is possible to allow the return of the refugees to their original homes in the majority of places, and closeby in others. With the return of the refugees, Israel overall density would be 482 persons/sq.km, instead of the present 261 persons/sq.km.
In the Return Plan, Area A will remain largely Jewish (76% Jews), Area B will be mixed and Area C will be largely Arab (81% Arabs). Abu Sitta recommends "some adjustments" which would "be desirable from a practical point of view"[8]: In densely populated Area A, it would be preferable to relocate rural Palestinians (about 900,000) to Areas B and C. Conversely, "only 154,000 rural Jewish-Israelis may have to relocate from Area C to Area A, after the end of their lease, to allow Palestinian farmers to recover their land. That is if they do not wish to mix with Palestinian farmers. This disparity in the numbers of relocated population (…) appears to be advisable to enhance the homogeneity of population."[9] Finally, the return of the Palestinian refugees "shall not cause dislocation of Jews and only minor voluntary relocation."[10]

11.1.2   Analysis of the Proposal

Implications for the Israelis

Abu Sitta's concrete plan for the return of all Palestinian refugees claims that such a solution was entirely feasible and that it did not pose any threat to Israel, or that such a threat, if it exists, was irrelevant. Yet such proposal, while perhaps technically convincing, is unacceptable to the overwhelming majority of Israelis. Just as Israelis tend to underestimate or completely ignore the meaning Palestinians attribute to the *right of return*, so does such a plan disregard, or deem unimportant, Israeli demographic and security-related fears. The issue of "physical

---

7   Ibid.
8   Ibid.
9   Ibid.
10   Ibid.

space" to absorb the refugees is hardly the most central concern of most Israelis.[11]

It is inconceivable that any state would allow an unrestricted influx of non-nationals to its territory, as this contradicts any state's sovereign right to determine who's allowed to enter its territory.

The question also raises the legal status of the masses of Palestinian refugees returning to Israel. Israel could not absorb hundreds of thousands of new residents without granting them some legal status. Thus, would they receive Israeli citizenship? This would entitle them to live but also to vote in Israel. Given their high rate of natural growth, they would soon – if not immediately – become a dominant factor in Israeli politics. This would mean the end of Israel's identity as a Jewish state. The issue of voting rights could be circumvented in the short run by not granting the refugees citizenship but merely permanent residency (similar to the U.S. Green Card, enabling residence and employment in the country indefinitely). However, in the long run, it is hard to imagine keeping the following generations born in Israel deprived of citizenship.

In addition, a solution comprising the return of all refugees to Israelis contradicts the logic of a two-state solution: Why establish a Palestinian state if the Palestinian refugees will be absorbed in the Israeli state?

Abu Sitta's plan emphasizes that (almost) no Jewish-Israelis would have to be relocated within Israel in order to realize his proposal. Yet as most of the houses and villages from where the refugees originated no longer physically exist or have been inhabited by other people for over half a century, it remains unclear to where exactly the refugees should return. If it will not be to their place of origin (which, besides, is not easy to define for the second and third generation of refugees born abroad, who have never been to these places) but kilometres away from it, the question arises why a resettlement to the Palestinian state to be established nearby should not be envisaged in the first place.

In sum, the Return Plan is detrimental to anything Israel would be ready to accept to solve the question of Palestinian refugees.

---

11   Adina Friedman, "Unraveling the Right of Return," p. 67, at www.prrn.
      org.

Implications for the Palestinians

For the Palestinians, the plan presented by Abu Sitta represents the full embodiment of their claims regarding the *right of return*, as it consists of a full acknowledgment and realization of that right. Certainly, extremely few Palestinians would object such a plan.

However, Palestinians also realize that a plan like the one proposed by Abu Sitta is of a maximalist nature and has no chance of ever being accepted by the Israelis. As shown in Part II's discussion on the *right of return* (particularly the ICG-interviews mentioned there), most Palestinians are more willing to compromise on the issue than Abu Sitta's Return Plan does. Among Palestinians, Abu Sitta's demands are regarded as the far end of the claims regarding the *right of return*.[12]

11.1.3 The Proposal's Relevance

Abu Sitta's Return Plan is unacceptable to the Israeli side, as it completely ignores Israel's demographic, security-related, and societal concerns. Besides, it stands in total contradiction to the idea of a two-state solution. The Palestinian side certainly would not object to Abu Sitta's Return Plan, while knowing, however, that it would be unrealistic to expect Israel to endorse it. Thus, since it does not stand a chance of being accepted by *both* parties, the Return Plan, while being an interesting intellectual exercise, lacks relevance in the context of an envisaged mutually accepted solution of the Palestinian refugee question.

---

12 Conversely, Abu Sitta shows little respect for more moderate Palestinians or Western critics. For his attacks on Sari Nusseibeh and Khalil Shikaki, see Salman Abu Sitta, "Who Undermines the Right of Return?," 18 August 2003 at www.electronicintifada.net; for a tirade on "the Russian American Jewish lawyer, Donna Arzt", despite her being an outspoken supporter of the cause of Palestinian refugees, see Salman Abu Sitta, "The Return of Refugees; the Key to Peace," November/December 2000, at www.prrn.org.

11.2 The Citizenship/Residency Approach

Right after Abu Sitta's Return Plan follows a proposal which also potentially allows the return of a large number of refugees into Israel – however, while simultaneously aiming to reduce a demographic threat to Israel. This is to be achieved by not granting Israeli citizenship, but merely residency, to the returning refugees, who subsequently would not be allowed to vote in national Israeli elections. By not awarding the returning refugees any electoral power, Israel's Jewish character is to be preserved.

11.2.1 The Essence of the Proposal

In the framework of a two-state solution, it would be agreed that there will be a differentiation between residency and citizenship. Refugees returning to Israel would become citizens of Palestine but residents of Israel. Accordingly, Jewish Israelis living in Palestine (mostly settlers) would be citizens of Israel yet residents of Palestine. Just as Green Card-holders in the U.S., the local residents would be able to vote for local issues, police, education, utilities, etc., but only citizens would be allowed to vote in national elections of the respective state.[13]

The citizenship/residency proposal suggests developing a formula which would allow Palestinian refugees to return to the State of Israel without affecting Israel's solid Jewish majority. The goal would be to defuse Israel's major concern regarding security, i.e. the worry that demographics would inexorably destroy the State of Israel. Although physically present in the State of Israel, the Palestinian refugees would not be able to vote; since they would not have any electoral power, they

---

13 While the Citizenship/Residency Approach outlined here has been formulated and named by the author, others have also raised the idea of resolving the refugee question by operating with citizenship and residency. See, e.g., Michael Sanders, "Solving the Israel-Palestine Conflict," 11 December 2001, at www.worldnetdaily.com; Israel Harel proposed to "take the Arabs on both sides of the green line as one body and the Jews on both sides as one body, and give the Arabs Jordanian citizenship and the Jews Israeli citizenship." See Israel Harel in Leslie Susser, "Israel: Preventing the Unthinkable," *Jerusalem Report*, 15 December 2003.

could not alter the Jewish character of the state. Conversely, the plan suggests that Israeli Jews remaining in the West Bank after a Palestinian state is established there should also keep their Israeli citizenship while receiving Palestinian residency rights.

11.2.2 Analysis of the Proposal

Implications for the Israelis

Although the citizenship/residency proposal would be slightly easier to accept for Israelis than Abu Sitta's Return Plan, it still includes a number of points problematic to them. First and foremost, the number of refugees to be accepted would be of crucial importance. Should that number be unlimited, Israel would hardly agree to such proposal which might lead to the return of hundreds of thousands of Palestinian refugees.

The fact that those refugees would not be entitled to vote certainly diffuses some of the problem, since the repatriated refugees could not influence parliamentary elections. Political and legislative decisions would continue to be taken by the Jewish-Israeli majority. The Arab-Israeli minority, however, might find itself under pressure to relinquish their Israeli citizenship and to adopt Palestinian citizenship instead. Also the question of dual citizenship would have to be regulated if the citizenship/residency proposal was to be put into practice.

However, the question arises how long such a situation could be upheld. It is hard to imagine numerous generations of descendents of the repatriated Palestinian refugees being born in Israel, subsequently going through Israel's educational system and growing up learning fluent Hebrew, to be denied Israeli citizenship indefinitely. Thus, Israel's demographic concern would only be neutralized in the short run.

In addition, Israel's demographic concerns do not solely stem from the refugees' potential electoral power. The absorption of a large population of a different ethnic group, whose culture, religion, language, and ethnic bonds are different from the majority in that state, would be considered worrisome by any state. Although Israel has proven its capacity of absorbing a large number of immigrants, the difference between Jewish immigration to Israel and the return of Palestinian refugees is obvious: the former have come to Israel not only with the intention of blending into the culture and language of the majority, but also willing to serve in the military. The interest of returning Palestinian refugees, on the other hand, would primarily be to recover their land and houses, and not to find a new identity as Israeli citizens.

Therefore, if an agreed number of Palestinian refugees were to return to Israel, the citizenship/residency proposal would certainly reduce Israeli concerns to some extent. However, an unrestricted and massive repatriation of Palestinian refugees into Israel, without granting the latter a sovereign veto power, would face similar – although slightly less – Israeli opposition than Abu Sitta's Return Plan.

Implications for the Palestinians

As opposed to the Israelis, the citizenship/residency proposal would be highly satisfactory to Palestinians, since it would – at least implicitly – recognize the *right of return* and enable its implementation. The Palestinian key demands are centred on the recognition of the *right of return* along with the option of exercising that right; depending on the precise wording of a negotiated agreement based on the citizenship/residency proposal, both conditions could be fulfilled to a large extent. Attaining Israeli citizenship, on the other hand, was never part of the refugees' agenda.

Being Palestinian nationals would vest the repatriated Palestinian refugees with a citizenship of their own and would also award them an international legal status. In addition to a formal national identity, refugees returning to Israel would have the Palestinian state to represent and defend their interests. Having Israeli residency, they would be allowed to live and work in Israel indefinitely, eventually being able to vote in local elections. Besides, their status as non-Israeli citizens would also bar them from the theoretical possibility of being drafted to the Israeli army. On the other hand, they probably would have to pay taxes to the Israeli authorities. Yet besides fiscal burdens and the absence of electoral powers, the citizenship/residence proposal would offer Palestinian refugees the realization of their aspirations for return, plus awarding them most of the same rights Israeli citizens have without specific burdens such as military service.

A different situation would arise if not all but only a specific number of Palestinian refugees were allowed to return to Israel and to receive residency there. This would be a compromise between the Palestinian demand for refugee return and Israel's demographic concerns. Such restricted version of the citizenship/residency proposal would only be acceptable to Palestinians if presented within a generally satisfactory framework, that is an overall peace agreement offering them a satisfactory solution on all other issues (primarily territory and Jerusalem).

11.2.3 The Proposal's Relevance

The citizenship/residency proposal offers a solution as to the scenario of allowing refugee return, while simultaneously reducing Israeli demographic concerns. The crucial point lies in the extent of the proposal. If any refugee desiring to return to the territory of today's Israel were allowed to do so, even if that person would not receive Israeli citizenship but merely residency, Israel would not accept such proposal. Just as any other sovereign state, Israel would want to have some control over the influx of people to its territory.

However, if the citizenship/residency proposal was applied to the return of an agreed number of refugees whose total would not be exceeded, then it could serve as an acceptable compromise to the Israelis. After all, Israel has repeatedly allowed the return of Palestinians in the framework of family unifications. In addition, in past negotiations with the Palestinians, Israel has signalled its readiness to allow the return of a limited number of refugees. There, the question arose under which name the refugees would be allowed to return: Israel preferred to call it a humanitarian gesture while the Palestinians insisted that return to their former homes was their right.

Just as Israeli acceptance of the citizenship/residency proposal would increase if the number of refugees to which it would apply decreased, the exact opposite would be the case on the Palestinian side: the smaller the number of refugees allowed to return, the more Palestinians would see it as an infringement of the *right of return*. Yet again, the Palestinians have already signalled in the past that if all other outstanding issues were solved to their content, they would be ready to compromise on the number of Palestinian refugees actually returning. Nevertheless, Palestinians would still insist on a formal acknowledgment of the right of refugees to return. Such acknowledgment might be implicit to the citizenship/residency proposal, yet it lacks an explicit and mutually agreed stand on the *right of return*.

Therefore, should the citizenship/residency proposal be formulated to apply to an unrestricted number of Palestinian refugees, it would be rejected by the Israeli side. Palestinians, on the other hand, could only accept it with an appropriate and explicit reference to the *right of return*. Thus, for a mutual Israeli-Palestinian acceptance of the citizenship/residency proposal, agreement needs to be found on the number of Palestinian refugees it would apply to, as well as its reference to the *right of return*.

11.3   The 1948 Approach

Some have proposed to solve the Palestinian refugee question by letting those Palestinians who were actually born in the territory of what has become the State of Israel to return.[14] There are about 200,000 who would qualify for such a proposal, all of them over the age of 58, most of whom will not be having more children, and, therefore, they would have virtually no long-term effect on Israel's demographics.

11.3.1 The Essence of the Proposal

According to the 1948 approach, Israelis and Palestinians would agree that there will be a full return of those Palestinian refugees who were born in the territory of what subsequently became Israel; at present, it is estimated that there are around 200,000 people fitting that category. In addition, it would have to be defined who would be eligible to accompany those refugees: the narrowest definition would include the return of any Palestinian who left in 1948 along with his or her spouse, yet not their progeny born after 1948. In the framework of negotiations, this narrow definition could be expanded to also include minor children (under 18 years).

---

14   See Rami Khouri describing such proposal by Thomas Pickering in the *Daily Star*, 22 April 2006; Evelyn Gordon, "Why not say yes to the 'right of return'," *The Jerusalem Post*, 25 May 2005; Danny Rabinowitz, "Return of the Native," *Haaretz*, 8 August 2003; Yossi Alpher, "Refugees forever?" 14 January 2002, at www.prrn.org.

Thus, if only those born on Israeli territory were allowed to return – and provided that all of them actually would return – they would number at most 200,000 people. Along with one spouse, a maximum of 400,000 Palestinian refugees would return to Israel; yet since Islam allows a man to marry up to four women, the total number of returnees might be above 400,000. If each such returning couple had two or three minor children, the total of returning refugees might total around one million people.

Yet the maximum number of one million needs to be put into perspective. First, it is most unlikely that all refugees eligible for return would actually chose to do so. Second, it is questionable whether Israel would accept more than one spouse per person. After 1948, Israel neither tolerated upholding polygamy among Israel's Arab citizens, nor among Jews from Arab countries who maintained such tradition (as was frequently the case with Yemenite Jews). Third, since most of these returning refugees would be past child-bearing age, they would not represent any long term demographic concern for Israel. Fourth, since the youngest of the original 1948 refugees would at least be 58 years old, most of their children will be over 18. Thus, the 1948 Approach would allow all those who left their homes in present Israel to return, however, without having a long-term impact on Israel's demographic composition.

11.3.2 Analysis of the Proposal

Implications for the Israelis

The 1948 Approach offers a number of advantages for the Israelis. First, it could allow the return of all those who had fled what later became Israeli territory. Due to the limited number of those refugees and their present age, they would pose no demographic threat to Israel. Second, Israel could claim to have satisfied the core of the Palestinian demand for a *right of return*, namely the return of all refugees who had personally gone through the circumstances making them refugees, as they were still born on the territory which has become Israel.

We have seen in the first part of this research that the international body responsible for all refugees is the U.N. High Commissioner for Refugees (UNHCR).[15] Since an Arab veto prevented Palestinian

---

15   See 5.2.2.

refugees from coming under the UNHCR's sphere of responsibility, a special U.N. body in charge of them was established: UNRWA. We have further seen that according to the UNHCR's definition of a refugee, the status of refugee is not passed on to one's children. Under UNRWA's definition, on the other hand, the status of a Palestinian refugee can be passed on indefinitely. Thus, in the framework of the 1948 Approach, Israel could declare that it offers Palestinian refugees the right to return – yet according to the UNHCR's definition of a refugee rather than UNRWA's definition.

If Israel publicly announced that under a final-status agreement, it is prepared to accept all Palestinian refugees (including their spouses and minor children), yet according to the UNHCR's definition of refugees rather than UNRWA's, the ball would be in the Palestinians' court. If they further insisted on a full *right of return*, including for the descendents of the 1948 refugees, then the Palestinians would have to explain why Palestinian refugees merit a concession granted to no other refugees in history: the right to pass their refugee status on to their descendents. Moreover, offering the return of all 1948 refugees would give the Israelis important leverage to demand reciprocal concessions from the Palestinians on issues such as Jerusalem and borders.[16]

The most critical point for the Israelis regarding the 1948 Approach lies in the uncertainty regarding how many Palestinian refugees actually would choose to return. We have seen above that in the – albeit unrealistic yet theoretically possible – scenario of a full return of all those eligible, Israel might have to accept up to one million people. It is therefore quite possible that Israel would demand some ceiling regarding the maximum number of refugees it would be able to absorb; this could be done by limiting the number of accompanying spouses to strictly one, as well as by barring the entry of further children once a certain number of refugees has already returned to Israel.

Since most of the 1948 refugees are of an advanced age, the vast majority of those returnees could probably not be integrated into Israel's labour market. Consequently, they would mostly be living from Israeli welfare.[17] Yet, due to their age, the returnees' dependence on

---

16   See Gordon, "Why not say yes to the right of return."
17   However, this would not pose a significant strain to Israel's welfare system, since Israel's current welfare system is practically non-existing: After Netanyahu

welfare in any event would be temporary. In sum, the 1948 Approach's overall advantages to Israelis outweigh its disadvantages to them.

Implications for the Palestinians

For Palestinians, the biggest advantage of the 1948 Approach would be the fact that all those who fled from the territory of what later became Israel would be allowed to return. Depending on the precise wording of the agreement, return might be undertaken along with their minor children. This could theoretically lead to the actual return of several hundreds of thousands of Palestinian refugees. Nevertheless, because of the partial exclusion of immediate family and the total exclusion of extended family, the 1948 Approach does not embody the full realization of Palestinian demands regarding Palestinian refugees.

In fact, although without any formal reference to the *right of return*, the idea of Israeli acceptance of the return of the first generation of 1948 refugees (only) was put forward by Israel at Taba in January 2001.[18] However, it was rejected on the Palestinian side in the view as being impractical and inhumane, considering the age of potential returnees, and the difficulties of tearing them away from their immediate and extended families. While the idea proposed at Taba did not include any of the refugees' children, the 1948 Approach might be extended to include minor children, an addition which would lessen the extent of the returnees' separation from immediate family.

Yet even if extended to include minor children, given the age of the potential returnees, it appears unlikely that such approach would represent a practical solution acceptable to Palestinians: very few elderly people would be willing to start a new existence in a place they had not been to for decades, all the more if that implies their being cut off from a large part of their families.

Thus, a Palestinian acceptance of the 1948 Approach would hardly be motivated by practical considerations as to improving the refugees' situation on the ground, since only a small percentage of the refugee population would be affected. At most, the 1948 Approach could be

---

(in the role of Minister of Finance between 2003 and 2005) undertook a major economic reform, budgetary means for the Israeli welfare system were radically reduced to a bare minimum.

18   Rex Brynen, *FOFOGNET*, 21 April 2006.

some form of compromise if negotiations reach a stage where the other outstanding crucial issues are basically solved and all that remains is a solution of some sort to the question of refugees. Yet Palestinians could only accept the 1948 Approach if it included some form of Israeli recognition of the *right of return*, at least for the first generation of Palestinian refugees.

11.3.3 The Proposal's Relevance

For Israelis, the 1948 Approach would be an attractive solution to the question of Palestinian refugees, as it would probably involve no major return of Palestinian refugees, while those actually returning would – due to their age – pose no demographic threat to Israel. Since the uncertainty regarding the precise number of people who would want to return is hardly acceptable for a sovereign state, Israel might insist on a ceiling limiting the maximum number of 1948 refugees allowed to return. Possibly, such ceiling would only apply to those refugees returning along with their minor children; once an agreed quota is exhausted, further 1948 refugees could only return without their children.

For Palestinians, on the other hand, the 1948 Approach is less attractive, as it would compromise their half-century long demand for all Palestinian refugees along with their descendents to be allowed to return. Under the 1948 Approach, however, only a handful of the overall population could return. In addition, due to their advanced age and the resulting separation from immediate and extended family, it is unlikely that a substantial number of refugees would opt for such return. In practical terms, therefore, the 1948 Approach would change little as to the situation of most Palestinian refugees.

The 1948 Approach is morally problematic, as it requires the separation of families. This was an important reason for the Palestinians rejection of a similar proposal in Taba. However, Taba was operating under an enormous time pressure and none of the participants expected a breakthrough. Thus, if Israeli-Palestinian negotiations were to resume under more favourable circumstances, the 1948 Approach would not necessarily be doomed to failure. Yet for Palestinian acceptance, it would certainly need to compensate the proposed separation of families by e.g. some form of extended family reunifications.

Overall, if all other political issues between Israelis and Palestinians were solved and if it was to include some form of Israeli recognition of the *right of return* (at least for the first generation of Palestinian refugees), the 1948 Approach might well provide the compromise necessary to put an end to the conflict regarding Palestinian refugees. It would at least offer some psychological satisfaction to the Palestinian demand for having the *right of return* acknowledged, while simultaneously properly respecting Israel's demographic concerns. The fact that the UNHCR does not extend refugee status to the descendents of refugees might be a helpful diplomatic bridge for a mutually aspired compromise.

11.4   The Geneva Initiative

The most detailed proposal to solve the question of Palestinian refugees is found in the Geneva Initiative. After the breakdown of the Taba talks – which also signified the breakdown of the peace process as a whole – a number of both Israelis and Palestinians involved at Taba (led by Yossi Beilin and Yasser Abed-Rabbo) decided to continue negotiations on a private level.[19] The Swiss government and private citizens offered their good offices and some of the venues. The Geneva Initiative was officially released on 1 December 2003. Besides being available on the internet,[20] it was also widely published in the Israeli and Palestinian media; in addition, each Israeli household was sent a copy of the Geneva Initiative.

Basically, the Geneva Initiative is an extension of the Clinton Parameters, incorporating and further developing ideas raised at Taba. The uniqueness of the Geneva Initiative, distinguishing it from any other proposal to solve the Israeli-Palestinian conflict, is its highly detailed formulation. The Geneva Initiative devotes considerable attention to the major issues, like refugees, Jerusalem, and security. Each of these topics

---

19   For insider accounts, see Yossi Beilin, *The Path to Geneva: The Quest for a Permanent Agreement, 1996–2004* (New York: RDV Books, 2004); Menachem Klein, *The Geneva Initiative: An Inside View* (Hebrew), Jersusalem: Carmel, 2006.

20   See the text of the Geneva Initiative on www.geneva-accord.org. Article 7 refers to refugees.

receives many pages of detail, including timetables, maps, modalities and mechanisms for implementation.

Yet the presence or absence of two other constraints on the Geneva Initiative negotiators should also be noted. *First*, the unofficial and informal character of the agreement signified that the parties have been able to adopt positions which might be substantially more difficult for official representatives to take. This greater flexibility was most evident on the Israeli side, where the representatives largely represented the dovish wing of the left (Labour/Meretz/Peace Now) of the Israeli political spectrum. Even at Taba, refugee positions staked out by Beilin and the Israeli team had gone beyond the preferences of then Labour Prime Minister Ehud Barak. On the Palestinian side, some participants (holding or having held formal positions within the PA/PLO) were aware that their semi-official status might be interpreted as signalling a formal position that future Palestinian negotiators could be held to, and were inclined to caution as a result. Nonetheless, the Palestinian team generally went beyond the Palestinian public and political consensus, as evidenced by the subsequent refusal of Fatah, the PA cabinet, the Palestinian Legislative Council, or the PLO Executive Committee to endorse the contents of the Geneva Initiative.[21]

Second, the Geneva Initiative has emerged in a clearly less propitious set of circumstances than those of the Oslo era. Particularly the second intifada (and especially the active protest by Arab citizens of Israel in the early months of the unrest) which has substantially undercut whatever weak support existed in Israel for the return of any refugees to the territory of Israel. Indeed, present political discourse in Israel often focuses on the notion that Israel's Arab population is already too large and that demographic policies need to be adopted to preserve the Jewish proportion of the population. In such context, any refugee return at all is highly unpopular and therefore a hard sell. At the same time, on the Palestinian side, violence, the intensification of Israeli occupation, and hardline policies (especially of the Sharon government) have added to greater political polarization and disinclination to compromise. Indeed, a substantial portion of Palestinians in the West Bank and Gaza at present feel that peace with Israel is impossible. Both within the Pales-

---

21 See Rex Brynen, "The 'Geneva Accord' and the Palestinian Refugee Issue," 29 February 2004, at www.prrn.org.

tinian territories and in the diaspora, *right of return* advocacy groups are more vocal and active than ever, strengthened in part by effective use of new information and communication technologies.[22]

It is therefore less surprising that regarding refugees, the Geneva Initiative's negotiators only managed to complete an agreement by entirely omitting the use of the term *right of return*, and by not mentioning any concrete numbers regarding refugee return. In addition, the Israelis had refused the Palestinian negotiators' demand to mention at least the principle of the *right of return*.[23] As a result, the Geneva Initiative does not explicitly relinquish the *right of return*, yet the text of the agreement does not directly acknowledge the *right of return* either. Instead, the Geneva Initiative states that an "agreed resolution of the refugee problem is necessary for achieving a just, comprehensive and lasting peace."[24] However, the two parties did agree that any refugee return to the State of Israel shall explicitly be "at the sovereign discretion of Israel."[25] Evidently, this signifies that only a small fraction of refugees would be returning to Israel. It is for this reason that the Geneva Initiative appears last but two on our range of practical proposals to solve the refugee issue. Let us next take a more precise look at the Geneva Initiative's provisions regarding refugees.

11.4.1 The Essence of the Proposal

The starting point of the Geneva Initiative's section on refugees is the acknowledgment that, concerning "the rights of the Palestinian refugees," U.N. resolutions 194, 242 and the Arab League's 2002 peace proposal shall represent the basis for resolving the refugee issue. Presumably in response to Israeli concerns that recognizing the *right of return* for the refugees would leave a door open for future demands, the Geneva Initiative clearly states that the provisions in the agreement and their implementation would constitute the final settlement of the refugee issue and all claims connected with it. The *right of return* is not

---

22 Ibid.
23 See Uzi Benziman, "Corridors of Power: The Genie of Geneva," *Haaretz*, 7 November 2003.
24 See Article 7.1.a of the Geneva Initiative.
25 See Paragraph 4 of Article 7 of the Geneva Initiative.

mentioned at all, while the two sides further agreed to relinquish the declarative part regarding the background of the creation of the refugee problem, and thus bypassed irreconcilable differences of opinion. The Geneva Initiative rather proposes solving the Palestinian refugee question in a practical way.

The preamble to the Geneva Initiative affirms that "this agreement marks the recognition of the right of the Jewish people to statehood and the recognition of the right of the Palestinian people to statehood." In so doing, the Geneva Initiative explicitly calls for a two-state solution of the Israeli-Palestinian conflict. While not going as far as recognizing Israel as a Jewish state,[26] it nevertheless ties such statehood (including Israel's) more closely to ethnic identity. The phraseology is intended to assuage Israeli concerns that the Palestinians seek to "(re)Arabize" Israel through demographic change and refugee return.[27]

Furthermore, an International Commission is to be created with "full and exclusive responsibility" for implementing the initiative's stipulations on the refugee issue, specifically overseeing and managing the process by which permanent residence is determined and realized. This commission would consist of the two parties, who would call upon the U.N., UNRWA, the World Bank, as well as the EU, Switzerland, Canada, Norway, Japan, Russia and other (unspecified) states to join the Commission. The Commission would appoint a panel of experts to deal with compensation issues and determine amounts to be contributed to an international fund, with Israel's final contribution (from which the value of the fixed assets of the settlements to be transferred to the Palestinian state would be deducted) to be fixed. UNRWA – and along with it the status of refugees as such – would cease to exist five years after the start of the Commission's operations.

Regarding the crucial question of permanent residence, refugees will have the right to freely choose between four options: the Palestinian state, third countries, the State of Israel, or the present host country.[28]

---

26 Something then Palestinian Prime Minister Mahmud Abbas was pressed, but declined, to do at the Aqaba summit with U.S. President George Bush and Israeli Prime Minister Ariel Sharon in June 2003.

27 See Brynen, "The 'Geneva Accord'," p. 3.

28 The text of the initiative actually lists a fifth option: return to areas of Israel which would subsequently be swapped to the Palestinian state. Thus, the fifth

All these options must be in accord with the sovereign discretion of the countries involved. Each of the third countries will submit to the International Commission the number of refugees it is willing to accept. Also Israel would have to submit such number; as a basis for this number would consider the average of the total numbers submitted by the other countries. Priority in all the above shall be accorded to the Palestinian refugee population in Lebanon – the most disadvantaged community in the diaspora, and the group most likely to be rejected by the current host government.

The way in which Israeli admissions of returnees is determined plays a crucial role. At Taba, the parties had sought to agree on a capped limit to the number of refugees, which would be enshrined in the agreement. Although no number was ever agreed, the Israeli side suggested 25,000 persons over three years, or 40,000 over five, with refugee return to be resolved over a fifteen year period.[29] This seemed to suggest a minimum of 25,000 to 40,000 persons, with the possibility of 120,000 to 125,000 on a generous reading. The Palestinian side had no number in mind, but did seek "six figures" (i.e., at least 100,000) in the negotiations.[30]

By contrast, according to the Geneva Initiative, Israel would determine its own number at its "sovereign discretion," a formulation similar to that in the Clinton Parameters of December 2004.[31] Yet the actual number of refugees to return to Israel was not mentioned during the negotiations towards the Geneva Initiative. In the words of Yasser Abed-Rabbo: "The number of refugees was never discussed because we cannot rule on this matter ahead of time unless it refers to the later stage when it will be possible to implement the solution."[32] The Geneva Initiative does call upon Israel (Article 7.4.iii.) to "consider the average of

---

option in practical terms amounts to the return of refugees to the Palestinian state. A detailed proposal by Agha and Malley focusing on swapped areas will be discussed in the last section of this chapter.

29   See Brynen, "The 'Geneva Accord'," p. 4.
30   Ibid.
31   The Clinton Parameters read: "…some of the refugees would be absorbed into Israel consistent with Israel's sovereign discretion." See www.brookings. edu/press/appendix/peaceprocessappen_ab.htm.
32   This quote was taken from Al-Quds (Jerusalem), 16 October 2003, cited in MEMRI's "Palestinian Reactions to the 'Geneva Understandings'," Inquiry and Analysis Series, No. 154, 11 November 2003.

the total numbers submitted by different third countries [for Palestinian refugee resettlement]" – yet "consider" has no force of obligation and clearly places no binding requirements on Israel. Moreover, for two reasons, any such average could turn out to be strikingly low.

First, post-9/11 restrictions on immigration and asylum (especially regarding populations from the Middle East) might reduce the number of places countries are willing to offer. Indicative of this danger, UNHCR reported that refugee resettlement under its auspices dropped by 56% between 2001 and 2002 largely for this reason. A second reason might be purely mathematical: although a few countries might be relatively generous in accepting refugees, a large number of small resettlement offers by various countries would pull down the average. In 2002, for example, UNHCR resettled approximately 21,000 refugees under its auspices. While few countries took large numbers (8,142 in the U.S.; 4,744 in Canada; 2,771 in Australia), many accepted only a handful (Chile: 3). As a result, the *average* was only around 1,000 persons.[33]

We shall next see that the Geneva Initiative's Article 7 regarding refugees was the one single section of the agreement to cause – although out of distinct motivations – the largest opposition among both the Israeli and Palestinian publics.

11.4.2   Analysis of the Proposal

As previously noted, Article 7 (regarding refugees) has proven to be the Geneva Initiative's most controversial element – to both Israelis and Palestinians. When details of the agreement were first released, Israeli proponents quickly noted that the Palestinians had surrendered the *right of return* – something they saw as a major argument to convince Israelis. Yet this put Palestinian proponents on the defensive as they were accused by their own constituents of having relinquished the *right of return*. Several Palestinian negotiators of the Geneva Initiative engaged in semantic struggles in an effort to assert that they had not surrendered refugee rights. Unconvincing to Palestinian audiences, these statements were quickly seized upon mostly by the Israeli right, but

---

33   See UNHCR, "Refugees by Numbers 2003," and "Resettlement Statistics 2002," at www.unhcr.ch, cited at Brynen, "The 'Geneva Accord'," p.4.

also by critics in the centre, to demonstrate that the Geneva Initiative did not in fact deliver what Beilin and others had suggested. Ambiguous positions of Arafat, Fatah, the PA, and the PLO on the Geneva Initiative further increased Israeli suspicions; being strongly rejected by the Israeli, Sharon-led government, also the Palestinians were given the impression that the other side was not serious with its proposals. The net effect was that a majority of Palestinians rejected the refugee portion of the agreement because they saw it as giving up too much, while many Israelis rejected it because it gave up too little.[34] We shall next review these two contradictory positions in greater detail.

Implications for the Israelis

While the Geneva Initiative does not specifically mention the *right of return*, the reference to UNGAR 194 and the existence of an option for the refugees to choose a permanent place of residence in Israel is anathema to most Israelis.[35] Consequently, the Geneva Initiative's initiators have been at pains to explain that the agreement clearly limits such option, explicitly providing Israel, like any sovereign state, the right to determine which and – most important – how many refugees could actually return to Israel. Yet many Israelis fear that the promised "sovereign state's veto" might turn out to be a mirage; their concern is that the mention of UNGAR 194 and the Arab League's Peace Proposal offers a large needle's eye through which the Palestinians will be able to thread the demand for return in the future.[36]

A large proportion of Israelis oppose any refugee being allowed to return; their opposition is rooted in the fear of setting precedents or implicitly granting a *right of return* which could open floodgates in the future. Therefore, the Geneva Initiative's complicated clause regarding numbers also raises problems, including among the Israeli left, as they fear that "the average of the total" numbers accepted by other, third states might lead to Israel having to accept a large number of refugees against its will. It requires careful reading to comprehend that Israel

34   Brynen, "The 'Geneva Accord'," pp. 10–11.
35   Galia Golan, "Plans for Israeli-Palestinian Peace: From Beirut to Geneva," *Middle East Policy*, Vol. XI, No. 1, Spring 2004, p. 47.
36   Uzi Benziman, "Corridors of Power: The Genie of Geneva," *Haaretz*, 7 November 2003.

would not be bound by the average numbers accepted by other states, but rather would the latter serve as a mere basis for Israel's own calculations. The Geneva Initiative stresses clearly that Israel is sovereign in its decisions regarding the numbers of refugees it will accept.

The Geneva Initiative includes no statements of *moral regret* or *responsibility*, but proposals (in the context of Article 7 on refugees) for a series of "reconciliation programs" between the two sides; these programs would be intended to exchange historical narratives, foster educational contacts, and promote cross community programs. They could also include "appropriate ways of commemorating those villages and communities that existed prior to 1949."[37]

The Geneva Initiative emphasizes (as did the Israeli position before and at Taba) that implementation of the agreement constitutes the *end of both refugee status* (Article 7.6) *and refugee claims* (Article 7.7). One important aspect of the Geneva Initiative, embodied by a single incomplete sentence, is contained in Article 17: It calls for a U.N. Security Council or U.N. General Assembly resolution endorsing any peace agreement. While a resolution by the General Assembly would have little practical effect, a Security Council resolution would have considerable force in international law, superseding UNGAR 194 and reinforcing the agreement's claim to represent an end to the conflict.[38] In fact, a Security Council resolution affirming an Israeli-Palestinian agreement would supersede all existing U.N. resolutions, including UNGAR 194's paragraphs regarding refugee return.

The Geneva Initiative thus offers a solution to the refugee problem highly favourable to Israel. Although not realized by vast segments of the Israeli public, the Geneva Initiative would, on the one hand, exempt Israel from having to recognize a Palestinian *right of return*, while, on the other hand, actual return to Israel would most likely be low and in any event conditional upon Israeli approval.

Implications for the Palestinians

On the Palestinian side, the Geneva Initiative has reopened discussion of the *right of return*, its meaning and its implementation. It remains to

---

37 Article 7.14/d of the Geneva Initiative.
38 Brynen, "The 'Geneva Accord'," p. 10.

be seen whether as a consequence there will be greater or lesser flexibility on the issue. It has also stimulated greater countervailing activity on the part of refugee advocacy and right-of-return organizations, as they seek to mobilize against what they see as an erosion of, and assault against, refugee rights (understood in their maximalist sense).[39]

Palestinian critique largely focuses on the fact that according to the Geneva Initiative, the arrival of Palestinian refugees to live within the State of Israel is not considered and declared as "return" but rather absorption of refugees similar to that in third countries (such as Canada and Norway) towards whom there is no historical claim. In other words, the Geneva Initiative basically treats Israel like a neutral third country; accordingly, the number of refugees which Israel will accept is to be determined by Israel on the basis of "the average of the total numbers [admitted] by the different third countries."[40] Most Palestinians are not ready to accept that Israel is not only spared from recognizing the *right of return*, but that the agreement mentions no Israeli responsibility or regret for the creation of the refugee problem either.

Although a large proportion of the refugees might ultimately choose not to exercise a proposed return to the territory of Israel (choosing instead to return to a Palestinian state, a third country or to remain in their present host country), the Palestinian refugees in particular along with the majority of Palestinians are nevertheless not prepared to relinquish their *right* to return or to negotiate implementation without an official Israeli acknowledgment of responsibility to the creation of the problem. Besides, the vast majority of Palestinians regards the *right of return* as an individually held right which no negotiator is entitled to relinquish on behalf of other persons.

In addition, there has been Palestinian criticism referring to the fact that the Palestinian delegation for the Geneva negotiations did not include any representatives of the refugees. Having neither been

---

39   See, e.g., al-Awda/ Palestinian Right of Return Coalition, "Defend the Right of Return," 13 October 2003 and "Statement by Refugee Communities," November 2003, both at www.al-awda.org; BADIL, "Peace Agreements and Refugees – Lessons Learned," *Occasional Bulletin 14*, December 2003, at www.badil.org/Publications/publications.htm. See also MEMRI's "Increased Palestinian Adherence to the Right of Return Following the Geneva Initiative," Special Dispatch No. 634, 26 December 2003.

40   Article 7.4.iii of the Geneva Initiative.

consulted nor in any way involved, it is not much of a surprise that virtually all Palestinian refugee organizations oppose the Geneva Initiative's provisions regarding refugees.

Yet the Geneva Initiative's proposed option for Palestinian refugees to return to the "areas in Israel being transferred to Palestine in the land swap"[41] deserves several remarks. First, regarding the proposed border, the Geneva Initiative includes Israeli territory near the Hebron area, an area in which until 1948 the Palestinian village of Duheimeh existed. Many civilians were killed when the Israeli army took over the village in 1948, and the ruins of the deserted village have remained unsettled ever since, as Israel did not build there. Therefore, the transfer of this territory to the Palestinian state would enable the refugees of Duheimeh, unlike those of other villages, to implement a full return in the sense of rebuilding their village on its exact original spot – an option which might lead to a heavily symbolic event. Second, the Geneva Initiative's proposed extension of the Gaza Strip would provide Palestinians with lands which before 1948 belonged to persons now living in Gaza's refugee camps. Apart from the symbolism of refugee soil being returned to Palestinians, such allocation of land might be used, given the overcrowding in the refugee camps, to build entirely new cities there for the use of refugees in general. Third, the Geneva Initiative's drawing of the border in the Latrun area, while leaving in Israel's hands the whole of the main Jerusalem-Tel Aviv highway, allocates to the Palestinians most of the pre-1967 Latrun enclave in a way which would enable the restoration of three villages destroyed by Israel in 1967.[42]

Nevertheless, the Geneva Initiative's section on refugees in its present formulation is for the most part unacceptable to the vast majority of Palestinians. The reason for rejection lies less in the demand for an actual massive return of refugees, but rather in the wish for formal recognition of the refugees' right to return. Therefore, both Israel's role in absorbing refugees (which amounts to that of any third country) outlined in the Geneva Initiative, as well as the absence of some form of Israeli apology or at least recognition of partial responsibility for

---

41   See Article 7.4.b of the Geneva Initiative.
42   See Adam Keller, "A Comparison of three Drafts for an Israeli-Palestinian Peace Agreement," at http://gush-shalom.org/archives/compare_eng.html.

the creation of the refugee problem, do not meet minimum Palestinian requirements.

11.4.3 The Proposal's Relevance

While many of the Geneva Initiative's suggestions regarding a solution of the conflict found large support among the Israeli and Palestinian populations, the one element which was rejected by a majority of both Israelis and Palestinians was the provision regarding refugees. While most Israelis opposed the suggested solution to the refugee question because they interpreted it as allowing a potential large return of Palestinian refugees; also the recognition of UNGAR 194 was seen unfavourably by most Israelis. On the Palestinian side, the central reason for the Geneva Initiative's ideas regarding refugees was the lack of recognition of the *right of return*; in fact, the *right of return* was not mentioned at all. Instead, Palestinian refugees are offered various options of "resettlement," with Israel being merely one of them. Thus the arrival of Palestinian refugees to live on Israeli territory would not be considered "return" but rather absorption of refugees similar to that in third countries towards whom there are no historical claims. Accordingly, the number of refugees which Israel would accept is to be determined by Israel on the basis of "the average of the total numbers [admitted] by the different third countries."[43]

Polls have shown that the refugee section of the Geneva Initiative has less support than almost any other component, with only 35% of Israelis and 25% of Palestinians supporting this aspect of the agreement, while 61% of Israelis and 72% of Palestinians oppose it.[44] The most obvious explanation for this mutual rejection of the Geneva Initiative's proposals on refugees is the fact that the two parties are far apart on the refugee issue, especially regarding any return of refugees to Israel. In fact, the *right of return* has become something of a dangerous litmus test increasingly imposed by publics, politicians, and commentators on

---

43 See Keller, "A Comparison of three Drafts."
44 See the PSR's Press Release of the joint Palestinian-Israeli Public opinion poll, 16 December 2003, at www.prrn.org.

both sides: Israelis insist on its explicit repudiation, while Palestinians look for its reaffirmation.[45]

The effect of wide Israeli and Palestinian rejection of the Geneva Initiative's proposals on refugees is probably compounded by at least three other factors: the apparent ambiguity of the PLO/PA/Arafat on the issue (signalling some support to certain audiences, while rejecting it towards others), the relatively detailed nature of the Geneva Initiative (which offers more room to nitpick or oppose), and the association of the agreement with individuals such as Yossi Beilin and Yassir Abed-Rabbo. Whatever their considerable merits and commitment to peace, Beilin is widely decried in Israel as "delusional" (Ehud Barak) and a "failed politician" (Tommy Lapid), responsible for the "foolishness" of the Oslo accords (Silvan Shalom). On the Palestinian side, Abed-Rabbo is a non-Fatah political figure who has alienated a great number of even Fatah people with whom he is most closely associated and he mostly owed much of his influence to whatever access Arafat granted him. Nitpicking and political baggage may help to explain why support for Geneva appears to have declined over time. It would also explain why a November 2003 International Crisis Group/Baker Institute poll outlining a solution basically congruent to the Geneva Initiative – yet with neither details nor personalities attached – secured greater support, from 53% of Israelis and 56% of Palestinians.[46]

On the other hand, the amount of support the Geneva Initiative did attract also allows an important conclusion. The overall Geneva package unites between 40% to 50% of both the Israeli and the Palestinian population; a not inconsiderable achievement in the context of violence and political polarization characterizing the years since the outbreak of the second intifada. This in turn highlights the need to see an agreement on refugees as part of, and embedded in, a broader peace settlement – not an element that publics ought to assess in isolation.[47]

Critics of the Geneva Initiative who charge that it has abandoned the refugees' *right of return* are, in a practical sense, quite right: although there is no specific renunciation of the right, there is no recognition of such either, and under the terms of the agreement there is likely to be

---

45 Brynen, "The 'Geneva Accord'," p. 11.
46 See the poll on the ICG's website www.crisisgroup.org.
47 Brynen, "The 'Geneva Accord'," p. 11.

extremely little return at all to Israel. Despite the Geneva Initiative's assertion that it would represent a "permanent and complete resolution of the Palestinian refugee issue," it could be argued that the individual rights of refugees under international human rights law (notably the Universal Declaration of Human Rights) cannot be abrogated by intergovernmental agreement, and hence would continue regardless. While this might be correct in a strict legal sense, in the absence of any mechanism to adjudicate and execute such claims (and given the unlikelihood of Israeli courts ever ruling in the refugees' favour), such an individualized right has very little substance in practical terms.[48] Rex Brynen points out that the international community continuously sends conflicting signals by, on the one hand, praising the Geneva Initiative for its moderation, yet, on the other hand, routinely approving U.N. General Assembly resolutions which invoke UNGAR 194 without specifying what member states themselves understand by the refugee component of that resolution.[49]

The Geneva Initiative seeks to overcome the diametrically opposed positions of the Israeli and the Palestinian publics regarding refugees by dealing with the question practically and not symbolically. Thus, the *right of return* is simply not mentioned in the agreement. Instead a mechanism is proposed that grants Palestinian refugees the right to "Free and Informed Choice,"[50] while giving Israel the right to restrict the numbers of people entering its territory and authorizes an international committee to settle any disputes. Yet in such a constellation, it is a forgone conclusion that between the sovereign Israeli decision and the free choice of refugees, a conflict is likely to occur. Therefore, coupled with Palestinian dissatisfaction over the lack of reference to the *right of return* and/or some Israeli recognition for its part of the responsibility regarding the refugee problem, it is reasonable to assume that the solution proposed in the Geneva Initiative would not close the refugee file, but instead would rather open it to a prolonged quarrel in conditions that will not be to either side's benefit. The problem could be solved, e.g., by complementing the Geneva Initiative's suggestions, which focus almost entirely on

---

48 Ibid., p. 4.
49 See Brynen, "The 'Geneva Accord'," p. 12.
50 Article 7.5 of the Geneva Initiative.

purely practical aspects of the Palestinian refugee question, with some form of principled solution regarding the *right of return*, while also avoiding the inevitable clash between the refugees' envisioned free choice to return and Israel's sovereign veto power to block such return by finding an agreement on the maximum number of refugees Israel would be required to accept.

11.5   The Internal Approach

Not all Palestinian refugees have left the boundaries of what became the State of Israel in 1948; roughly a quarter of those Palestinians who remained within Israel became "internally displaced". They and their descendents number around 200,000 of today's Israeli Arab citizens. If they were allowed to return to some of their places of origin, the *right of return* could be implemented without in any way altering the percentage of Israel's Arab population, as those people already are residing within Israel.

11.5.1   The Essence of the Proposal

The Internal Refugees in Israel are Palestinians who were uprooted from their villages in the course of the 1948 war, but found refuge within the borders of the state and became its citizens. From 1948 until the present, they have continuously voiced their demand to return to their villages, only to be met by the refusal of all Israeli governments. For the most part, their lands were allocated to Jewish settlement.

In recent years, and most intensively since the 1990s, the subject is once again emerging on the public agenda of the Arab population in Israel. Israel's Arab parties and the Arab-Jewish party *Chadash* demanded a solution to the problem in their election platforms of 1996 and 1999. Dozens of committees were established by former inhabitants of abandoned villages and their descendents, under the umbrella of a national committee and organizing events in the villages. Finally, commemorating the *nakba* in abandoned villages has turned into a tradition among Arab citizens of Israel in recent years, demanding the return of internal refugees to their villages, which were mostly destroyed during the 1950s and 1960s.[51] Thus, in any case, the issue will eventually need to be addressed by Israel.

This could be done in combination with finding a solution to the Palestinian demand for a *right of return*. Just as Palestinian refugees outside Israel claim the right to return to their places of origin, so do the internally displaced. The overall failure of negotiations between Israel and the Palestinians at Camp David in 2000, which was explained in the official Israeli political discourse as stemming from Palestinian obstinacy over the *right of return*, only increased existing significant Israeli opposition to any concessions for the internal refugees. The reasoning for that approach varies between explanations regarding security and a declared wish to maintain the Jewish character of the state.[52]

The internal refugee committees are aware of the fears of the Jewish-Israeli public and establishment concerning their demands. They also realize that a return to the pre-1948 situation is not possible. Therefore, in general, they are not demanding the return of *all* of their land, but only those parts of it which are not worked or settled. According to their initial surveys, a substantial part of the lands in many abandoned villages is deserted; those are the lands they demand to get back.[53]

Therefore, another proposal to solve the debate around the *right of return* would be to let the internally displaced return to their places of origin – where possible. If applied to all of Israel's internally displaced people, close to 200,000 people would be implementing the *right of return*.[54] Such number would exceed any concrete suggestion made in the course of Israeli-Palestinian negotiations and therefore would enable more people to exercise the *right of return* than either of the two parties would have ever imagined. The underlying idea of the Internal Approach, as this proposal shall be called, would be to allow a large number of Palestinians refugees to return to their former homes; such

---

51 See Hillel Cohen, "Land, Memory, and Identity: The Palestinian Internal Refugees in Israel," *Refuge*, Vol. 21, No. 2, 2004, pp. 9–10.

52 Ibid., p. 12.

53 Ibid.

54 A report on Al-Jazeera even estimates about 250,000 Arab-Israelis to be internal refugees. See Jonathan Cook, "Palestinians recall day of catastrophe," 3 May 2006, at http://english.aljazeera.net.

return would in no way affect Israel's demographic balance, as those people already are residing in Israel, being citizens of the state.

11.5.2   Analysis of the Proposal

Implications for the Israelis

The Internal Approach is characterized by two striking advantages for the Israeli side: first, it could settle its dispute regarding Palestinian refugee return by satisfying Palestinian demands for a substantial return of refugees. Second, this would be done in a manner which would not affect Israel's current demographic balance. Besides, the Internal Approach would enable Israel to kill two birds with one stone: not only would it end its external conflict with the Palestinians, but also an urgent internal issue would be addressed and solved.

Yet the fact that the question of internal refugees is a domestic Israeli issue also casts doubt over whether Israel would agree to negotiate it with an external body like the Palestinian Authority or the PLO. Such potential debate over representation could be solved if both Israelis and Palestinians agreed that Israel's internally displaced would have to be included in the negotiations on Palestine refugees; in such case, representatives of the internally displaced themselves could be involved in the talks. This, of course, would trigger a debate within Israel as to its refusal to address the claims of the internally displaced already much earlier. Initiating such a debate would compel courageous decisions by the Israeli government. In addition, just as in the overall debate regarding the *right of return*, Israel would probably be expected by the internally displaced to express some form of regret and to take part of the responsibility for creating and upholding the problem – so far, no Israeli government has signalled any intention of doing so.

Allowing the internally displaced to return to their places of origin would result in quite a drastic change to Israel's current landscape. Sites, which the Israeli government intended to keep for its own settlement purposes, would have to be restored to the returning internally displaced. This would result in areas, which are currently unpopulated, becoming populated by the returnees. Thus, although the percentage of Arab citizens within Israel would remain the same, their residential distribution would change from the present large concentrations in relatively few, specific areas into covering virtually every part of the country. This, of course, would finally reduce the present state of overcrowding in practically every Arab village within Israel;[55] an issue, which Israel in any case will have to address at some point. Yet altering its current policy of allowing virtually no territorial expansion to its Arab citizens would represent a drastic change in Israel's overall relation to its Arab minority – a change which Israel has not excessively contemplated up to now.

Implications for the Palestinians

The internal approach would allow a considerable number, exceeding any realistic Palestinian expectations, of refugees to actually return to their former villages and houses. It is questionable, however, whether the majority of Palestinians would feel significantly affected by the fulfilment of the demands of the internally displaced refugees within Israel. Most Palestinians outside Israel associate the internal refugees – who are Israeli citizens and who like the rest of the Arab-Israeli population have largely been loyal to the state since its establishment – more to Israelis than to Palestinians.

The official body representing the total of refugees in the negotiations with Israel would be the Palestinian Authority. The PA, however, is mainly accountable to the Palestinian population of the West Bank and Gaza, which will form the future State of Palestine. It will be difficult for the PA to gain the support of Palestinians living in those territories for an agreement which, in the provisions regarding refugees, would solely address the internally displaced within Israel. Consequently, Palestinians in the West Bank and Gaza would need to be presented with an agreement satisfactory to them on all other issues so that they could agree that the *right of return* would only be implemented by those already living in Israel. Again, without reference to all Palestinian refugees and to the *right of return* in particular, such agreement would not receive the support of a majority of Palestinians.

---

55 At present, the Israeli authorities generally do not allow Arab-Israeli villages to build new housing outside the boundaries of those villages. In addition, since the establishment of the State of Israel – unlike in the Jewish sector – no single new Arab village or city has been built. The result is strong overcrowding within Arab-Israeli places of settlement.

On the other hand, if an agreement otherwise satisfactory to Palestinians were to be achieved, the Internal Approach could offer another diplomatic tool for a compromise on the refugee question; Palestinians, aware of Israel's demographic reservations, realize that only a limited number of Palestinians refugees, if any, will eventually be able to return to Israel.

11.5.3 The Proposal's Relevance

The Internal Approach would be beneficial to Israel: it could satisfy Palestinian claims for a substantial refugee return, while keeping its current demographic balance. Simultaneously, an urgent inter-Israeli issue would be solved. As to the Palestinians, most of them would not directly benefit from the implementation of the Internal Approach, since only those already living in Israel would be reaping the concrete fruits; yet Palestinians could still claim the prestige of having advanced the national cause of refugee return.

The Internal Approach would pose a difficult task to any Israeli government, as it would have to reverse the strategies and policies it has applied towards the Arab minority since the establishment of the state. Yet the Internal Approach would also cause the Palestinian leadership serious difficulty, namely getting popular support in the West Bank and Gaza for an agreement from which only Israel's Arab citizens would benefit.

Although the Internal Approach also offers advantages to both parties (the Palestinians could take credit for a substantial return of refugees, while the Israelis could permit such refugee return without subsequently facing an increase in the percentage of its Arab citizens), due to the above described difficulties involved, it appears unlikely that the Internal Approach would be the primary choice of either the Israeli or the Palestinian leadership. However, if negotiations were to reach a stage where each party could save face by some form of diplomatic compromise, the Internal Approach might provide such a tool.

11.6   Israel's Traditional Approach

Israel's traditional solution to the question of Palestinian refugees is – just as its Palestinian counterpart at the other end of the scale – an absolutist position and usually represented Israel's opening position in negotiations with the Palestinians.

11.6.1   The Essence of the Proposal

Israel's traditional solution advocates the resettlement of refugees inside the future Palestinian state and/or in Arab countries. It denies the *right of return* – to Israel – and the actual exercise of return to all refugees. The traditional Israeli solution calls for compensation, rehabilitation, and resettlement outside Israel – in one variation, mainly inside a future Palestinian state; in another variation, largely or entirely in other Arab states or beyond the Middle East. In either case, Israel would retain a measure of control over the inflow of refugees to the new Palestinian state. Compensation paid would not be to individual refugees but to their collective and linked to the concept of reciprocity between Palestinian refugees and Jewish refugees from Arab countries. According to its traditional proposal, Israel would make no acknowledgment of responsibility for the refugee issue, or the suffering of Palestinian refugees.[56]

11.6.2   Analysis of the Proposal

Implications for the Israelis

Since this proposal is an Israeli concept, it is no wonder that it is mainly composed to Israel's benefit. The principal advantage for Israel of this solution is that it poses no existential threat or demographic problem; moreover, it closes the file on the refugee problem. Israeli control over the inflow of refugees to the new Palestinian state would ease Israeli

---

56   The traditional Israeli Solution was outlined by Joseph Alpher and Khalil Shikaki, "The Palestinian Refugee Problem and the Right of Return," Weatherhead Center for International Affairs, Harvard University, May 1998, available at www.wcfia.harvard.edu/papers/98–07.pdf.

fears concerning a "green march" situation, whereby masses of Palestinian refugees would gather inside the Palestinian state, along its border with Israel, and attempt to cross and return to their former homes and properties long since destroyed or transferred to Israeli ownership. Such scenario could also create pressures on the Palestinian economy and the regional eco-balance that might prove destabilizing for the entire Middle East. On the other hand, Israeli non-interference in the resettlement of at least part of the refugees inside the new Palestinian state would reinforce Israeli recognition of the sovereignty of that state, and a successful resettlement program would reinforce Israeli perceptions that good peace relations are worthwhile.[57]

Implications for the Palestinians

Probably the only advantage of the proposal for Palestinians would be that the resettlement of at least some of the refugees outside of the future Palestinian state would ease the socio-economic burden of absorption on the nascent state. On the other hand, the proposal's principal disadvantage is that, insofar as it avoids extracting from Israel some acknowledgment of the injustice inflicted upon the refugees, it lacks justice from a Palestinian perspective – if not juridically, then in a psychological and historical sense. Hence it would not be considered final by Palestinians; such agreement would not be stable and might lead to the reopening of the Palestinian refugee issue in the future.

11.6.3 The Proposal's Relevance

The traditional Israeli solution calls for compensation paid by Israel to Palestinian refugees to be reciprocally linked to Jewish refugees from Arab countries. However, such concept is obsolete since both Israelis and Palestinians agreed in Taba that the issue of Jewish refugees from Arab countries is not a matter of Israeli-Palestinian negotiations, but rather a bilateral issue between Israel and the relevant Arab states.

Moreover, the linkage between Israeli compensation to Palestinian refugees and Arab compensation to Jewish refugees, coupled with the proposal's demand for resettlement of Palestinian refugees within

---

57   Ibid.

other Arab states, would give those Arab states a veto power of sorts, which would further complicate matters between Israelis and Palestinians – negotiations which by themselves are not exactly simple. One can easily conceive of a situation in which the refusal or reluctance of, for example, Egypt, Iraq, Syria, and Yemen to compensate Jews who after 1948 fled from those countries to Israel would prompt Israel to refuse compensating Palestinian refugees, thereby paralysing the entire process mainly at the expense of the Palestinian refugees.[58]

In addition, large-scale resettlement inside the future Palestinian state would constitute a heavy and potentially destabilizing absorption burden. On the other hand, settlement of significant numbers of Palestinians outside their state would risk the "de-Palestinization" of some or all of them. In any case, Palestinians would see Israeli control over the inflow of refugees as an objectionable interference in their internal affairs. At the same time, for Israel, such immigration control within another state would be extremely difficult to enforce (e.g., distinguishing tourists from immigrants, etc.), and hence would be a source of constant friction.[59]

Therefore, Israel's traditional solution to the question of Palestinian refugees can at best serve as an opening position for negotiations. It can not be deemed a realistic option not only because of its shortcomings regarding Palestinian needs, but also because of its aspects which are even disadvantageous from an Israeli point of view.

11.7 Agha and Malley: *Right of Return* to Swapped Areas

We have seen that Abu Sitta's Return Plan represents one extreme end (namely the return of *all* refugees) on the range of possible scenarios to resolve the Palestinian refugee question. Consequently, on the other far end, we find a proposal calling for *no* refugee to return, discussed in the above section. Hussein Agha and Robert Malley have taken the idea of no refugee returning to Israel even further. While their proposal also

---

58 Ibid.
59 Ibid.

results in no refugee returning to the State of Israel, the underlying idea is much more creative than a blunt rejection of refugee return to Israel: the refugees are to be given the right to return to certain border areas which will then be swapped with the Palestinian state in exchange for territory annexed from the Palestinians. Thus, unlike for example the above discussed traditional Israeli solution, the percentage of Israel's Arab population would not just remain at its present level – it would actually decrease.

11.7.1 The Essence of the Proposal

Hussein Agha and Robert Malley address the challenge of finding a stable and durable solution that accommodates both the refugees' yearning to return to the areas left in 1948 and Israel's demographic fears. According to Agha and Malley, such solution can be accomplished by relying on two basic principles. First, refugees should be given the choice of returning to the general area where they lived before 1948 (along with the choice of living in Palestine, resettle in some third country, or be absorbed by their current country of refuge if the host country agrees). Second, any such return should be consistent with the exercise of Israel's sovereign powers over entry and resettlement locations. Many of the refugees presumably want to go back to their original homes. Yet these homes, and indeed, in many cases, the entire villages where they were located, either no longer exist or are now inhabited by Jews. Thus, Agha and Malley conclude that the next best option from the refugees' own perspective would be to live among people who share their habits, language, religion, and culture; that is, among the current Arab citizens of Israel. Israel would therefore settle the refugees in its Arab-populated territory along the 1967 boundaries. Those areas would then be included in the land swap with Palestine and thereby end up as part of the new Palestinian state.[60]

---

60 The most likely solution to territorial questions between Israelis and Palestinians will be swaps: Israel would annex a minimal amount of land in the West Bank and in return provide Palestine with the equivalent amount of land from Israel proper. These swaps would be based on demographic and security criteria and be designed to preserve the viability and contiguity of both states. Israel would incorporate a large number of its West Bank settlers

The authors list a number of reasons why their proposal, coupled with generous financial compensation and other incentives to encourage refugees to resettle in third countries or in Palestine, would promote several key interests. On one side, Palestinian refugees would carry out the *right of return*. For them, returning to the general area from which they fled or were forced to flee in the 1948 war would be extremely significant because it would cross an important psychological and political threshold. Although they would not return to their original homes, the refugees would get to live in a more familiar and hospitable environment – and one that would ultimately be ruled not by Israelis, but by their own people. Through the swap, Palestine would acquire land of far better quality than the desert areas adjacent to Gaza that have been offered in the past. For Israelis, meanwhile, this solution would actually improve the demographic balance, since the number of Arab Israelis would diminish as a result of the land transfer.[61]

The authors further address a number of problems which might appear when implementing their proposal. Israelis, accordingly, might fear that it will add to the anxiety and discontent of the Israeli Arabs who remained under Israeli sovereignty. Agha and Hussein relate to such potential objection by reminding that the demographic and political problems posed today by the Israeli Arab community in any case already demand urgent action. Accordingly, resolving the broader Israeli-Palestinian conflict would be the best way to neutralize the Israeli-Arabs' potentially irredentist feelings.[62]

As to possible Palestinian objections, Agha and Hussein rightly assume that some might argue that the above plan represents nothing more than a sleight of hand, disguising resettlement in Palestine as a return to their pre-1948 lands. Here, the authors ask rhetorically whether the refugees actually want to live in Jewish areas that have become part of an alien country, and they go on questioning whether the refugees would rather live under Israeli rule than Palestinian rule;

---

and the Palestinians would achieve their goal of 100 percent territorial restitution. See Hussein Agha and Robert Malley, "The Last Negotiation: How to End the Middle East Peace Process," *Foreign Affairs*, Vol. 81, No. 3, May/June 2002, pp. 13–15.

61 Ibid., pp. 15–16.
62 Ibid., p. 16.

obviously assuming the latter being the case. Finally, the authors doubt that there is any other way of implementing the *right of return* without calling into question Israel's Jewish identity[63] – that, of course, is also a central question of this research.

11.7.2 Analysis of the Proposal

Implications for the Israelis

The idea of settling Palestinian refugees in parts of Israel which would then be swapped to the Palestinians – who could claim of having exercised the *right of return* into the State of Israel – is not new to Israelis. As described in the previous part, Ben Ami also suggested such a concept to his Palestinian negotiating partners in Taba, who rejected it, claiming that such a scenario would prevent the freedom of choice as to where in Israel to return to.[64]

The proposal of Agha and Malley goes beyond Ben Ami's Taba offer in that it not only prevents any single Palestinian refugee from returning to the State of Israel (and remaining within the state), but it would also reduce the percentage of Arab-Israelis in Israel. Thus, not only would Israel be spared from having to absorb Palestinian refugees – it would also reduce the number of its current Arab citizens. Such concept would certainly appeal to no small number of Jewish Israelis. Especially in the wake of the second intifada, ideas such as encouraging Israel's Arab citizens to emigrate or to hand over predominantly Arab populated territories within Israel to the future Palestine state, in exchange for settlement blocs, have grown increasingly popular among Israel's majority Jewish population.[65]

---

63 Ibid.

64 Shlomo Ben-Ami, *A Front Without a Rearguard: A Voyage to the Boundaries of the Peace Process* (Hebrew), (Tel Aviv: Miskal, 2004), p. 447; Gilead Sher, *Just Beyond Reach: The Israeli-Palestinian Peace Negotiations, 1999–2001* (Hebrew), (Tel Aviv: Miskal, 2001), p. 402.

65 According to a survey published in the *Jerusalem Post* on 9 May 2006, 62% of Jewish Israelis believe the government should encourage its Arab citizens to emigrate. The idea was taken up by Avigdor Liebermann, a far right member of the Israeli parliament, who proposed at the fifth Herzliya Conference in December 2004 an Israeli-Palestinian peace agreement which would trade

However, while the Agha-Malley proposal might well find wide acceptance within Israel's Jewish majority population, it would be strongly rejected by Israel's Arab citizens. Unlike within Israel's Jewish sector, proposals such as the one made by Avigdor Lieberman to transfer the so-called "Triangle" including its Arab citizens to the future Palestinian state,[66] were vehemently rejected by Israel's Arabs.[67] The vast majority of Israel's Arabs prefers its current status and standard of life in Israel to the uncertainty of a Palestinian state yet to be established and which will have to prove itself not only as to its adherence to democracy and human rights, but also the ability to create employment and economic prosperity.

If a plan such as suggested by Agha and Malley was ever to be implemented, Israel's Arabs would doubtlessly appeal to the Israeli Supreme Court, which – in the opinion of most Israeli lawyers – would never approve of such plan. In the words of Yossi Fuchs, "the state can decide that the Triangle area, populated mostly by Israeli Arabs, is no longer part of Israel. But it cannot revoke the citizenship of the people living there. The people [Israeli Arabs] who remain there will still be Israeli citizens."[68] And one of a citizen's most basic rights is to reside within the state issuing the citizenship.

Agha and Malley present their proposal as an option "to neutralize their [the Israeli Arabs] potentially irredentist feelings." Yet the question arises whether it might not trigger the precise opposite. Already often related to by Jewish Israelis as threatening elements and a potential fifth column, Israel's remaining Arabs would hardly be encouraged to

---

land based on population presence. In concrete terms, he suggested linking the Arab triangle area inside Israel – including its Arab Israelis – to the West Bank and annexing all the Israeli settlements in the West Bank to Israel. Liebermann's proposal was not met by any opposition from Israel's Jewish citizens.

66 See ibid.
67 See *The Jerusalem Times*, 24 March 2006.
68 Yossi Fuchs is an attorney and belongs to the right wing of Israel's political spectrum. He is a member of the Legal Forum for the State of Israel and a member of the Likud central committee. Although he supports reducing the number of Israel's Arab citizens, he acknowledges that taking away a person's citizenship runs counter to Israeli and international law. See Tovah Lazaroff, "Lieberman's land swap plan illegal", *The Jerusalem Post*, 26 March 2006.

continuous loyalty to the Israeli state if the latter took concrete steps to rid itself of part of its Arab citizens.

Finally, the location of the areas to be swapped might be of crucial significance. The primary region to meet both the criteria of having a large concentration of Arab citizens and to also form a border area is the Galilee's "Triangle" and its Wadi Ara valley. There, Umm el-Fahm stands out as a large Arab city being adjacent to the West Bank, and would naturally be among the first areas to be swapped. However, not only Umm el-Fahm but the Wadi Ara valley as a whole is located in an area of primary strategic importance overlooking one of Israel's major east-west traffic arteries, namely Road No. 65, which connects the cities of Hadera and Afula, and which also serves as an important connection between the Mediterranean Sea and the Sea of Galilee. Since Road No. 65 runs right through Wadi Ara, embedded by Arab population centres to its north and south, it would have to be relinquished along with Israel's Arab citizens residing there. Thus, a swap of land and population would also imply relinquishing the "Wadi Ara Road", which would be a heavy toll – a toll which Israel would not necessarily be ready to pay.

Implications for the Palestinians

As mentioned above, a similar proposal was already presented to the Palestinians in Taba. There, Ben Ami raised the idea of settling Palestinian refugees in the territories that the Palestinians were going to receive in a land-swap as a compensation for Palestinian territories annexed. Ben Ami's proposal rested on the logic that the Palestinian leadership could claim a significant realization of the *right of return* since the refugees would be returning into Israeli territory. Yet this solution to the *right of return* was refused by the Palestinians who claimed that such a scenario would prevent the freedom of choice as to where in Israel to return to.

However, the previous part has also shown that negotiators in Taba acted under a lot of constraints, primarily time, which was running out, and a rapid escalation of violence. Therefore, if negotiations were to resume under calmer circumstances and if other core issues – Jerusalem and territory – were resolved, it is entirely possible that Palestinians might accept such compromise in order to achieve an overall agreement. Yet Palestinian acceptance of such a proposal would only be possible, if the technical solution of settling refugees in swap-areas would be combined with some Israeli acknowledgment of responsibility in creating the refugee problem and eventually also a principled recognition of the *right of return* – even if only to be implemented in those parts of Israel to be swapped to the Palestinians. But in any event, a Palestinian state will be unlikely to accept Israel's Arab citizens against their will if the latter wish to remain within the boundaries of the State of Israel.

11.7.3   The Proposal's Relevance

While a majority of Israelis – its Jewish citizens – might be ready to accept a proposal such as presented by Agha and Malley, the Arab minority of Israel would strongly disapprove of being transferred to a Palestinian state. Besides morally questionable aspects, the proposal would not fulfil legal standards, neither by Israeli nor by international law. Thus while appealing to a great many Jewish Israelis and in a similar form already proposed by Israeli official negotiators, internal resistance by Israel's Arab citizens and judiciary system would thwart the implementation of Agha's and Malley's idea.

Ironically, the proposal might be implemented more easily on the Palestinian side, however, only if it is coupled with some formal Israeli acknowledgment of responsibility for its part in creating the refugee problem and some Israeli reference to the *right of return*. If the proposal simply remains a technical solution to repatriate Palestinian refugees to the State of Israel without really doing so, Palestinians will hardly accept it.

In sum, the Agha-Malley proposal is a creative intellectual exercise trying to implement the *right of return* without threatening Israel's demographic situation – on the contrary, such plan would leave Israel with a smaller percentage of Arab citizens than it currently has. Yet in its present formulation, the proposal made by Agha and Malley could neither be adopted by the Israeli nor by the Palestinian side.

12 PRINCIPLED SOLUTIONS

After having reviewed a number of purely practical solutions to the question of Palestinian refugees, we shall now turn our focus on proposals emphasising principled aspects; on which little research has been undertaken to date. Our analysis of the peace process has demonstrated that Israel primarily intended to focus on practical solutions: the problem of Palestinian refugees was to be solved primarily by means of resettlement (including some absorption to Israel under the framework of family reunifications) and financial compensation, ultimately allowing the gradual shutting down of the refugee camps and the phasing out of UNRWA. Yet the Palestinians were not ready to accept such approach, claiming that also the *right of return* needed to be recognized by Israel along with an Israeli acknowledgment of some responsibility for the refugee problem. The parties so far have not been able to bridge the divide between the Israeli demand for practical solutions and the Palestinian call to include principled aspects.[1]

Thus the need arises to also examine possible principled solutions to the question of Palestinian refugees. Principled solutions refer primarily to issues such as the recognition of the *right of return* and a possible apology for having caused the suffering of another people, as the Palestinians have repeatedly demanded from Israel. In fact, Israelis and Palestinians were not able to reach an agreement because of the inability to solve such principled aspects of the Palestinian refugee

---

1   In general, as seen in Part II's legal discussion of the *right of return*, the demand that nations act morally and acknowledge their own gross historical injustices is a novel phenomenon. Traditionally, *Realpolitik* was the stronghold of international diplomacy. National security and economic interests excluded other considerations. But beginning at the end of World War II, and quickening since the end of the cold war, questions of morality and justice have received growing attention as political issues. As such, the need for restitution to past victims has become a significant part of national politics and international diplomacy. See Elazar Barkan, "Considerations Toward Accepting Historical Responsibility," in in Ann Lesch and Ian Lustick (eds.), *Exile and Return: Predicaments of Palestinians and Jews* (Philadelphia: University of Pennsylvania Press, 2005), p. 85.

question. The analysis of those aspects shall therefore be the focus of this chapter. Unlike the other two chapters of Part IV, the following two sub-chapters shall list proposals which do not imply the return of Palestinian refugees, but rather address principled aspects that need to be considered if the Israeli-Palestinian dispute on refugees is to be solved. In other words, the following two approaches do not *per se* entail the return of refugees, yet might serve as a basis for negotiations on practical aspects of the refugee question.

First, the idea of Transitional Justice shall be presented in order to asses what options it offers for solving the question of Palestinian refugees. Second, we shall try to find out what enabled Germany and Israel to overcome their tragic past and how the conclusions drawn could be applied to the case of the Israeli-Palestinian dispute over refugees.

12.1   Peled and Rouhana: Transitional Justice

Two scholars, Yoav Peled and Nadim Rouhana, have developed a concrete model intending to allow Israelis and Palestinians to agree on the historical circumstances of the Palestinian refugee question, and which is to serve as a basis for later talks regarding actual refugee return. Peled and Rouhana address the fact that for the Palestinians, the *right of return* is an inalienable right that defines their national identity and their struggle for liberation, while for Israelis it is perceived as an existential threat to the Jewish character of their society, if not to their very existence. The resulting national consensus within each of the two societies has been built in a manner which seems to stand in complete opposition to that of the other side. However, Peled and Rouhana argue that a morally and politically sound basis could and should be established for a workable solution; such basis is to be provided by the notion of "transitional justice."[2]

---

2   Yoav Peled and Nadim Rouhana, "Transitional Justice and the Right of Return of the Palestinian Refugees," *Theoretical Inquiries in Law*, Vol. 5, No. 2, July 2004, pp. 317–332.

12.1.1 The Idea of Transitional Justice

Peled and Rouhana stress that a basis for future negotiations on the *right of return* could be established by a conception of justice that is not merely *corrective* or *compensatory*, but rather *transformative*. Such conception, which the authors call "transitional justice," does not seek to achieve a balance between violated rights and compensatory measures. It rather aims to establish the principles that should govern the transition from a morally deficient society or situation to a morally superior one. The successful transition itself is what endows the measures necessary for its achievement with their moral value. In other words, in transitional justice, the practical outcome that is being sought should itself be the basis on which the moral arguments are grounded.

While transitional justice necessarily addresses past injustices, it is future-oriented rather than past-oriented in terms of where its moral emphasis lies. It seeks to affirm and restore the dignity of those whose human rights have been violated; to hold perpetrators accountable, emphasizing the harm they have done to individual human beings; and to create social conditions in which human rights will be respected. Consequently practical aspects would not interfere with moral ones, but rather serve as their foundation. Transitional justice also takes the power balance between the parties into account. Its goal, therefore, is not to be absolute, but rather to be *attainable*. In general, transitional justice's overall goal is reconciliation rather than retribution (which would satisfy solely the victims of past injustices) and forgetfulness (which would benefit only the perpetrators).[3]

Transitional justice singles out two major steps as being necessary for reconciliation between parties involved in an historic conflict: recognition and restitution. *Recognition* entails revealing the historical truth about the injustices committed and according the victims dignity and respect as right-bearing human beings. The recognition of the narrative told by the victims of injustice is to serve as a necessary precondition for reconciliation. Thus recognizing the victims of historic injustice

---

3   Ibid., p. 320.

requires, first and foremost, that the historical truth about the injustice committed against them be revealed.[4]

The primary form of according recognition to victims of historic injustice, as well as compensating their material losses, is to be through *restitution*, which would also represent some form of recognition. The question of restitution raises the issue of responsibility: who is the actor responsible for the injustice? Can the present generation, or immigrants who arrived after the injustice had been committed, be held accountable for the actions of their predecessors? The authors stress that when considering restitution, one should not only discuss the form it should take (restoration of citizenship status and expropriated property, reparation, monetary compensation, etc.) but also its magnitude.[5]

12.1.2 Application to the *Right of Return*

Peled and Rouhana argue that the principles of transitional justice suggest separating the *right* to return, which is non-negotiable for the Palestinians, from the means and ways of *realization* of that right in practice, which would need to be regulated by negotiations between Israelis and Palestinians; those negotiations are not part of transitional justice but ideally would be enabled by it. Furthermore, the only *right of return* that can be meaningfully recognized by Israel is the right of the Palestinian refugees to return to the State of Israel within the borders of its formal sovereignty, whatever these borders may be following a future Israeli-Palestinian peace agreement. Since the recognition of a right necessarily creates an obligation and since there is no moral value in creating an obligation for someone else, Israel cannot meaningfully recognize the right of the refugees to return to a third country, not even to the future state of Palestine. In this respect, the Geneva Initiative, which gives the Palestinian refugees the *right* to return only to territories that will be under the sovereignty of the future Palestinian state and does not grant them the *right* to return to their places of origin in

---

4   Ibid., pp. 317–322.
5   Ibid., pp. 317–323.

Israel,[6] fails in the eyes of Peled and Rouhana to meet the moral challenge that must be met for reconciliation between the two peoples.[7]

Accordingly, if Israel were to recognize the *right* to return, this would satisfy an essential Palestinian demand and would enable them to negotiate the means to realize the *right of return* in a way that would take Israeli concerns and interests into account. This has been made clear already by many Palestinians, including people in positions of authority. Yasser Arafat even went further, expressing understanding for "Israel's demographic concerns."[8] So far, however, neither present nor past Israeli officials, not even those actively engaged in seeking an understanding with the Palestinians, have agreed to recognize the Palestinian *right of return*. They have maintained – erroneously, according to Peled and Rouhana – that the Palestinian demand for recognition of the refugees' *right of return* signifies a denial of the right of the State of Israel to exist with both a Jewish majority and character.[9]

If Israel was to recognize the *right of return*, many of the goals stipulated by transitional justice as necessary for ending the dispute on Palestinian refugees would be met:

1) *Truth.* The Palestinian narrative of 1948 would become legitimate in Israel, leading to recognition of the nakba and of the Palestinians' identity as its victims. This is a necessary first step towards finding a joint historical narrative, an important goal of transitional justice.

2) *Recognition* of the moral worth of the Palestinians as human beings that has been denied since 1948 (continuously expressed by Arab and Israeli military occupation and the disrespectful treatment of Palestinian refugees in some Arab countries).

3) *Responsibility*, both collective and individual, of Israel and Israelis for the nakba in general and for individual atrocities would be assumed. This would at the same time require Palestinians, as well as the involved Arab states, sharing their part of the responsibility.

---

6   See Article 7.4.i of the Geneva Initiative stating that refugee return to the Palestinian state "shall be the right of all Palestinian refugees."

7   See Peled and Rouhana, "Transitional Justice," p. 327.

8   See Yasser Arafat, "The Palestinian Vision of Peace," *New York Times*, 3 February 2002, p. A15.

9   See Peled and Rouhana, "Transitional Justice," p. 327–28.

4) Public Discussion. This has been stifled in Israel due to the fear of recognizing the *right of return.* Such fear will, obviously, no longer be necessary once the *right of return* is recognized, and this will open up the possibility of airing the history of 1948, including the opening up of still-classified material in various Israeli archives.[10]

Overall, in terms of the Israeli-Palestinian conflict regarding refugees, recognition by Israel of the *right of return* would also entail assumption of responsibility for the uprooting of the majority of Palestinian society in 1948. This would satisfy a demand that has become a fundamental element in Palestinian national identity. Recognition would subsequently enable the two parties to enter negotiations over restitution, including compensation and most importantly the implementation of the *right of return.* Peled and Rouhana stress that in these negotiations, as numerous Palestinian political leaders have indicated, Israeli demographic concerns would be taken into account.

12.1.3 The Relevance of Transitional Justice

The concept of transitional justice introduces a number of highly positive aspects. First and foremost, the underlying idea of separating recognition of the *right of return* from its implementation is a good and right approach. Also an Israeli recognition for its part of the responsibility for the creation of the refugee problem – an integral component of transitional justice – is an indispensable element for Palestinians to settle the dispute on refugees. Equally important is the fact that transitional justice recognizes Palestinian refugees as the victims of an injustice; such recognition is a central step towards reconciliation between Israelis and Palestinians.

On the other hand, transitional justice also demands that Israelis and Palestinians mutually recognize the other's respective national narrative, in order to subsequently even formulate one single common narrative. However, negotiations at Camp David and Taba have illustrated what difficult, if not impossible, endeavour the attempt to find a narrative acceptable to both Israelis and Palestinians is. Furthermore, the question arises whether a successful solution to the question of Pal-

---

10   Ibid., pp. 328–329.

estinian refugees really requires Israelis and Palestinians to recognize each other's narrative, or whether that would merely be a nice supplement. The experience of Taba has shown that the two parties could have lived with separate narratives as long as the issue of the *right of return* would be settled to their mutual satisfaction.

Transitional justice merely signifies that Israel would recognize the *right of return*, and such recognition would not be accompanied by any practical political consequences, such as refugee return; an issue which is to be solved separately. Thus transitional justice may serve as a basis for solving the question of Palestinian refugees; the idea of separating the recognition of the *right of return* from any concrete political consequences might indeed form an important platform to a subsequent agreement on refugee return. Yet in terms of solving the question of Palestinian refugees, transitional justice alone cannot be but the beginning, since in order to find a solution acceptable to both Israelis and Palestinians, practical aspects need to be addressed as well.

12.2 Learning from German-Israeli Negotiations

A highly interesting and fruitful way to tackle the principled aspects of the Palestinian refugee question is by trying to draw conclusions from what is probably the most relevant historical precedent: German-Israeli negotiations regarding reconciliation and the establishment of diplomatic relations in the aftermath of World War II. These talks were held under the heavy shadow of the Holocaust. It is important to stress that the parallel does not refer to equating the Palestinian nakba with the Jewish holocaust; the parallel rather lies in the fact that two parties with a – to say the least – troubled past, as in the case Germany and Israel, managed to overcome their historic burden and to mutually accept an agreement which enabled full and peaceful diplomatic relations for the future.

Obviously, German-Israeli negotiations were also characterized by major differences when compared to Israeli-Palestinian negotiations: in the German-Israeli case, negotiations were neither about a common border nor about claims concerning land or the repatriation of refugees. In fact, the German-Israeli negotiations intended to find a formulation regarding moral claims which needed to be solved in order to enable the establishment of diplomatic and economic contacts between the two nations. Yet precisely this is also the case in our Israeli-Palestinian case: leaving aside other outstanding issues, such as territory and borders, and merely focusing on the refugee question, one will find that Israelis and Palestinians first need to find a formula satisfying principled needs before the practical ones can be addressed.

We shall therefore scrutinize, on the one hand, how Germany and Israel succeeded in reaching such formula which satisfied the needs of both sides, and, on the other hand, an attempt will be made to apply the conclusions reached to the Israeli-Palestinian case regarding refugees.

12.2.1 The Question of Formulation

As early as 1945 Weizmann and other Zionist leaders had considered the possibility of obtaining substantial financial support for the building of the Jewish state and its economic consolidation by demanding compensation for the property of murdered European Jews. Such idea was not popular among Jews. It is known that in the late 1940s and early 1950s, the attitudes of many Israelis were extremely anti-German. The dominant view in Israel was categorical rejection of any contact with Germany or Germans.[11]

Yet despite overwhelming Jewish disgust with and hatred toward Germany and Germans, an agreement, based on direct negotiations, was reached between the Israeli and German governments over how a small measure of justice for survivors of the Holocaust and for the Jewish people as a whole might be achieved through reparations payments that would, among other goals, be explicitly devoted to the absorption of new Jewish immigrants in Israel.

A crucial element in moving Israeli leaders toward direct negotiations with Germany was the severity of Israel's economic circumstances in the years following the establishment of the state; not only had Israel to recover from the war that had accompanied its establishment, but the new state also had to absorb an enormous number of Jewish

---

11   Tom Segev, *The Seventh Million: The Israelis and the Holocaust* (New York: Hill and Wang, 1993), p. 197.

immigrants which would cause Israel's population to double and triple within the following years.[12] Yet under no circumstances did Israel's leaders want to create an impression of having sold moral absolution to Germany on the backs of millions murdered. Therefore, Israeli and non-Israeli Jewish leaders required some kind of public declaration of regret which would express the German nation's acknowledgment of responsibility and sorrow for the suffering of Jews at German hands as well as its condemnation of Nazi policies, but that would omit any explicit words of "forgiveness" on the Jewish side.[13]

In March 1951, Ben Gurion's government delivered a note to the four occupying powers of Germany, demanding $1.5 billion as a German indemnity, emphasizing "that no amount of material compensation would ever expiate the Nazi crimes against the Jews."[14] The result was a suggestion that Israel approach Germany directly. In fact, some exploratory contacts between German and Israeli representatives had already occurred. In this pre-negotiation period, Israeli emissaries pointed out the critical importance – indeed, the necessity – for a solemn and official German statement of collective responsibility for the Holocaust if practical negotiations were to begin.[15]

Although German Chancellor Adenauer claimed to have already condemned Nazi crimes on numerous occasions, he accepted the Israeli demand for a solemn expression of Germany's moral perspective on the

---

12 Other arguments, including revenge and the achievement of a vicarious sort of victory over Germany, were also important. Defending the government's efforts to gain German reparations through direct contacts with Bonn, Ben Gurion, Golda Meir and Pinchas Lavon emphasized the aspect of revenge and equity involved in forcing Germans to work for the rehabilitation of Jews and described the increased vitality of Israel that would result from the reparations as enhancing the "victory" of the Jewish people [who survived] over Hitler [who did not]. See Ian Lustick, "Negotiating Truth: The Holocaust, *Lehavdil*, and al-Nakba," in Ann Lesch and Ian Lustick (eds.), *Exile and Return: Predicaments of Palestinians and Jews* (Philadelphia: University of Pennsylvania Press, 2005), p. 109.

13 Segev, *The Seventh Million*, p. 201.

14 Nicholas Balabkins, *West German Reparations to Israel* (New Brunswick, N.J.: Rutgers University Press, 1971), p. 88, quoted in Lustick, "Negotiating Truth," pp. 109–110.

15 Ibid., p. 110.

Holocaust.[16] Negotiations then proceeded between the Adenauer government, on the one hand, and the government of Israel and the World Jewish Congress, on the other, over the wording of the declaration to be made by Adenauer on behalf of the German people; the negotiations lasted from July through September 1951. On 27 September 1951, Adenauer made the solemn speech before the *Bundestag* demanded by the Israelis and their non-Israeli Jewish associates.

Before that speech, however, in the summer of 1951, Israeli negotiators had pushed Adenauer to put in his speech references to the guilt of the German people, the existence of groups in Germany still actively anti-Semitic, the role of the German army in the Holocaust, and the innocence of the people killed by the Nazis. They further wanted an explicit reference to Israel. Adenauer did accept many adjustments in his original draft but refused to describe the German nation as "guilty of the extermination of the Jews." He refused to mention Israel by name, to include an explicit reference to the "innocence" of the victims, to acknowledge the role of the German army, or to agree that the entire German nation be said to be guilty of the crimes committed by the Nazis.[17]

Most of Adenauer's speech dealt with legal and educational principles honoured in the Federal Republic, which had the purpose of combating anti-Semitism. In the end, the speech contained one single relevant paragraph – a set of formulations drafted, redrafted, and negotiated in exquisite and painful detail.[18] Although kept secret at the time, its wording had been negotiated, edited, and approved by the government of Israel and the World Jewish Congress before it was read out by Adenauer in the German parliament.[19] The key paragraph of the text referred explicitly to the question of Germany's relationship to its Nazi past and to the Jewish people:

---

16 Segev, *The Seventh Million*, p. 201.
17 Ibid., pp. 203–204.
18 As Ian Lustick points out, it is worth noting that in some respects, it is reminiscent of another famous paragraph – the Balfour Declaration – whose text was the result of tortuous negotiations between the World Zionist Organization and the British cabinet. See Lustick, "Negotiating Truth," p. 128.
19 Ibid., p. 111.

The government of the Federal Republic and with it the great majority of the German people are aware of the immeasurable suffering that was brought upon the Jews in Germany and the occupied territories during the time of National Socialism. The overwhelming majority of the German people abominated the crimes committed against the Jews and did not participate in them. During the National Socialist time, there were many among the German people who showed their readiness to help their Jewish fellow citizens at their own peril – for religious reasons, from distress of conscience, out of shame at the disgrace of the German name. But unspeakable crimes have been committed in the name of the German people, calling for moral and material indemnity, both with regard to the individual harm done to the Jews and with regard to the Jewish property for which no legitimate individual claimants still exist.[20]

In relation to what we now know and was widely believed then about the Holocaust and the involvement, support or acquiescence of the majority of Germans in the war against the Jews, this statement would seem to offer rather little in the way of acknowledged responsibility. Moreover, the paragraph sticks firmly to the passive voice. It begins by exculpating the majority of Germans.[21] The statement does not provide an enumeration of German crimes or include any specific indication of who the perpetrators were. Contrary to the repeated demands of the Israeli negotiators, the statement did not include words which pointed clearly toward an admission of guilt or responsibility. Nor did it include the expression of sentiments of regret or repentance. Nor did it contain an apology. The most that can be said about the paragraph is that some of these sentiments may be inferred from the description of "unspeakable crimes committed in the name of the German people, calling for moral and material indemnity."[22]

In fact, the sentence containing this formulation is worthy of particularly close examination, especially the artful phrase: "in the name of the German people." It was a deft manoeuvre. Israel had demanded a declaration of guilt and acceptance of responsibility for the crimes committed by the German people under the previous regime. Instead, the German Chancellor was admitting that (unnamed) persons had

---

20   Segev, *The Seventh Million*, p. 202.
21   Indeed, two of its four sentences describe the opposition of the "overwhelming majority" of Germans to the Nazis' extermination policies and the efforts of "many" to protect Jews.
22   Lustick, "Negotiating Truth," pp. 111–112.

committed crimes that had publicly been in the name of the German people, yet not endorsed or committed by them. Implicitly, what the phrase further suggested was that it was only out of the German people's enormous sense of honour that they felt duty bound to pay "indemnity" for actions done, not by them, but in their name. Ian Lustick compares such offer to a tire manufacturer, who might agree to compensate those who purchased faulty tires with the company's brand name on the tires, even if the tires were not admitted to have been produced by the company.[23] In other words, the phrase "in the name of the German people" had the effect, and perhaps the intent as well, of distancing these acts from the Germans of the Nazi era.[24]

In retrospect, the only element as remarkable as the paucity of Adenauer's carefully scrutinized and widely heralded public statement on the Holocaust was how little critical attention it received. For most Israelis who opposed negotiations with Germany, such a declaration was irrelevant no matter what its content; Germany and Germans would remain unacceptable and no reparations agreement could be tolerated. For most others, the fact of the declaration, rather than its relative lack of content, was treated (usually implicitly) as a *sine qua non* for accepting the distasteful process of entering into a reparations agreement with Germany. Alternatively, it was taken as the beginning of the process that would enable the Federal Republic to be accepted by the world community, whether Israel accepted the reparations idea or not.[25]

The Israeli government's immediate response to Adenauer's Bundestag statement (issued the day before it was actually delivered) acknowledged that "the declaration was an attempt on the part of the Federal Government to solve the problem."[26] Thus it was accepted as satisfying Israel's demand for a public and solemn declaration of moral responsibility. Emphasizing that no German statement, "however sincere and repentant," could erase the crimes that had been committed,

23   Ibid., p. 112.
24   Jeffrey Herf, *Divided Memory: The Nazi Past in the two Germanys* (Cambridge, Mass.: Harvard University Press, 1997), p. 282.
25   Lustick, "Negotiating Truth," p. 112.
26   Quoted by ibid. from Nana Sagi, *German Reparations: A History of the Negotiations* (Jerusalem: Magnes, 1980), p. 72.

the Israeli government spokesman nevertheless commented that "it seems the German Federal Government unreservedly acknowledges that it has an obligation to make moral and material reparations."[27] Foreign Minister Sharet emphasized the same idea, stating that nothing Germany could do could fully atone for the sufferings of the victims of the Holocaust. However, he added: "The Government of Israel regards it, nevertheless, as significant that the Government and Parliament of Western Germany ... have issued an appeal to the German people to divest themselves of the accursed heritage of anti-Semitism and racial discrimination and declared their readiness to enter into negotiations with representatives of the Jewish people and the State of Israel."[28]

On 30 December 1951, the Israeli cabinet decided to present the Knesset with its proposal to conduct direct negotiations for reparations with the German government. The Israeli government's response to the Adenauer speech – formally repeating its views about full collective responsibility and guilt on part of the German people, while accepting as operative a declaration that fell far short of that – had enabled the process of negotiations to begin.

Nevertheless, there was strong opposition in Israel against the reparations negotiations, led by Menahem Begin.[29] To counter fierce criticism that no amount of money could represent adequate indemnification for millions of murdered Jews, Sharet preferred to speak of *shilumim* (payments) rather than *pitzuim* (compensation for injury) to describe the reparations. Again, semantics played a crucial role: while the Hebrew word *shilumim* was chosen to avoid the image that the payments were

---

27 Lustick, "Negotiating Truth," p. 113, quoting from the *New York Times*, 28 September 1951.

28 Ibid., quoting from the *New York Times*, 30 September 1951.

29 In fact, new evidence points to Begin having organized a plot by former members of Etzel to kill Adenauer, even offering his golden watch to finance the operation: On 27 March 1952, an unknown person handed a package addressed to Adenauer to two boys at Munich's central train station. The explosion of the package bomb eventually killed a policeman. A short while later a group of Jewish extremists sent two smaller package bombs to Wassenaar close to The Hague, where Germany and Israel were negotiating about the reparations. A few weeks later, five Israelis were arrested in France for attempting to assassinate Adenauer. See the *Frankfurter Allgemeine Zeitung* and *Haaretz*, 13 June 2006.

closing an account of guilt, the German word *Wiedergutmachung*, meaning to make something good again, was intended, for Germans, to convey the opposite.[30]

Eventually, a reparations agreement came into being – the Luxembourg treaty – signed on 10 September 1952 by representatives of Israel, the Federal Republic of Germany, and the World Jewish Congress. It has been meticulously implemented, resulting in payments of $50 billion to Israel and to individual survivors and their families.[31]

12.2.2 Differences and Parallels to the Israeli-Palestinian Case

Fundamental differences make it difficult to compare efforts of Germans and Jews, on the one hand, and Israelis and Palestinians, on the other, to achieve reconciliation based in part on expression of regret, apology, or political or economic compensation. The greater scale of horror in the German-Jewish case might easily lead to the conclusion that Jewish/Israeli-German reconciliation would be much harder to achieve than Israeli-Palestinian.

However, other factors work in the opposite direction. Compensation paid – especially its in-kind parts from Germany's industry – to Israel and to individual victims of Nazism had a largely positive, invigorating effect on the German economy and greatly improved its political and diplomatic situation. While peace with the Palestinians would certainly improve Israel's economic prospects and its international standing, satisfying Palestinian political demands and demands for the return of refugees might pose threats to Israel's demographic, political, and security interests that the German agreement with Israel did not pose for Germany.[32]

The Nazi regime was destroyed in a war of its own making. Its successor acknowledges that regime to have been German, but traces no political, moral, or ideological ancestry to it. Governments in Israel, on the other hand, arise as products of an establishment that proudly

---

30 Lustick, "Negotiating Truth," pp. 117–118.
31 Ibid., p. 118.
32 Ibid.

represents itself as responsible for the Israeli victory in 1948 and thus for the Palestinians' nakba. Most Germans drew back from denying or defending the Nazi war against the Jews, and debates over "revisionist" interpretations of the Holocaust are marginal affairs compared with the widespread conception that eventually formed among Germans and others of the Holocaust as an icon for the greatest crime that could be committed by one people against another. Even though in Israel, revisionist history has greatly increased Israeli appreciation of the suffering of Palestinians in 1948 and the injustice of acts of expulsion and of enforced exile that produced and have maintained that suffering, yet still, these findings have not achieved the emotionally reassuring status for Palestinians of official truth in Israel, although they are much more widely accepted outside of Israel.[33]

Thus, on the one hand, it is apparent how different the counterpart is that Palestinians find in contemporary Israeli governments from the Germans with whom Israeli and Jewish organizations negotiated in the early 1950s. Yet, on the other hand, the degree of those differences may be substantially exaggerated in the contemporary mind because of the tendency to forget how differently Germans of the early 1950s, including Adenauer and the officials of his government, saw Germans, Jews, and the Holocaust, from the way that it is believed most Germans came, much later, to view German-Jewish relations and the crimes of the Nazi period. It is important to remember that the Jews of the early 1950s who participated in these negotiations were dealing with Germans in the first decade after the war, when the experience of the Third Reich and the disastrous consequences of its collapse were fresh in their minds. It was with their beliefs, preferences, sensitivities, prejudices, and espoused values that those Jews had to contend, not with the "politically correct" attitudes of subsequent generations of Germans.[34]

Overall, a considerable challenge was faced by Jewish negotiators seeking to justify any contact at all with Bonn, let alone talks to arrange an agreement that would help rehabilitate Germany as an accepted member of the civilized world, the NATO alliance, and the new, emerging community of Western Europe. In this context, an Israeli delegation

---

33   Ibid., pp. 118–119.
34   Ibid., p. 119.

representing a mildly apologetic, yet still Zionist, government in Israel may not pose quite as different a challenge to Palestinian negotiators as that posed by Adenauer's government in its negotiations with the government of Ben Gurion and Sharet.[35]

Simultaneously, there were also powerful constraints under which the Adenauer government operated in its efforts to some workable agreement with Israel and with Jews in general. In fact, impressions that most Israelis would be resistant to expressing sympathy or solicitude to the suffering of Palestinians or to recognizing the extent of their own country's responsibility for that suffering may seem less decisive in judgments about agreements which may be possible between Israel and the Palestinians, if the state of mind of Germans at the time of the reparations agreement with Israel is considered. There was intense opposition inside Germany, especially on the Right, including within Adenauer's Christian Democratic Party, to an agreement involving admission of guilt or generous restitution to Jews. Indeed, German public opinion appears to have been opposed to paying much or anything to the Jews, and Adenauer's negotiations with Germans appear to have been as difficult as his negotiations with the Jews.[36]

Thus an initially negative affect on public opinion does not signify that two governments cannot develop a compromise which in the end will enable a mutually accepted agreement. The following section will

---

35 Ibid.

36 By 1949, the Allies had executed more than four hundred Nazi war criminals, while German demands for the commutation of remaining capital punishments, parole of scores of high-ranking Nazis still imprisoned, and an end to the threat of prosecution against tens of thousands of former Nazi officials were building in intensity. German public opinion was obsessed by the disappearance of hundreds of thousands of German prisoners of war and the plight of millions of German refugees and expellees from Eastern Europe. In November 1950, trying hard to reflect dominant feelings in Germany that Germans were as much the victims of Nazism as were the Jews, Adenauer continued to press demands for clemency, an end to the tribunals, and an end to de-nazification on the American authorities as one of the highest priority for his newly formed government. While it is true that according to American public opinion surveys, 68% of Germans in 1951 supported "restitution for the Jews" and only 21% were opposed, these figures were registered *after* the Americans decided to commute or reduce the sentences of the great majority of convicted war criminals. See ibid., pp. 119–120.

seek to crystallize those aspects of the German-Israeli agreement, which could be applied to Israeli-Palestinian negotiations on refugees, and explore possible option to do so.

12.2.3 Lessons for the Palestinian Refugee Question

There is much to be learned from this episode of German-Israeli negotiations for gaining a perspective on what is achievable, useful, or likely in the Israeli-Palestinian case. It bears repeating, however, that such learning in no way can be interpreted as suggesting that the Holocaust and the nakba were intrinsically similar events.[37] However, this is why the comparison may be so valuable. In other words, given that it is virtually impossible to imagine a more horrible crime committed by one nation against the other than that which Nazi Germany committed against the Jews, we may therefore infer: if at least a workable form of reconciliation has been possible between Israel and Germany, it cannot be said to be impossible with regard to Israelis and Palestinians; and if official and symbolic acts as restrained, self-serving, and watery as the formula read out by Adenauer could be adequate to the political task, it may not be necessary for a future Israeli government to explicitly and fully acknowledge the detailed acts of injustice towards the Palestinians in order for such principled acts to play a crucial political and psychological role.[38]

In July 2000, prior to his departure for the Camp David summit, Barak stipulated to the Israeli cabinet his four "red lines", the fourth being: "No Israeli recognition of legal or moral responsibility for creating the refugee problem."[39] This formulation is interesting in several aspects. First, it implies that there was an outstanding Palestinian demand for an Israeli declaration on the events of 1948 that stands apart from material or political requirements. Second, it does not explicitly

---

37 The Holocaust was the result of a systematic, premeditated plan for genocide. The creation of the Palestinian refugee problem was a result, among other factors, from the expulsion of Palestinians from their homes and refusal to allow them to return. It was a tragic and opportunistically accelerated unfolding of the logic of circumstances, not a genocidal campaign.

38 Lustick, "Negotiating Truth," pp. 120–121.

39 See www.mfa.gov.il/mfa/go.asp?MFAH0hli0.

rule out some kind of response to this demand, short of formally accepting "legal or moral responsibility." Third, it opens the door to formulas about what occurred in 1948 that would include shared Israeli responsibility, Israeli sorrow and compassion for the plight of Palestinian refugees, acknowledgment of mistakes made and false propaganda employed that increased the number of refugees and aggravated their emotional and psychological difficulties, and readiness on the part of Israel to contribute materially and politically to a comprehensive solution to the refugee question in all its parts.[40]

Such analysis of Barak's statement, accentuating the opening it gave to the Camp David negotiations despite the negative form it took and the sparse results it bore, is complemented by considering the speech that Barak had given before the Knesset on 4 October 1999, expressing "regret for the suffering caused for the Palestinian people."[41] It is also revealing to consider how another of the four red lines, "a united Jerusalem under Israeli sovereignty," could just weeks later be interpreted as consistent with Israeli proposals that envisioned an end to Israeli sovereignty claims over most of East-Jerusalem.[42]

Of interest as well is that when the Barak government actually moved toward the limit of its negotiating position in the late fall and early winter of 2000, the prime minister also shifted his "red line" with regard to the refugee question. In an address to Jewish groups in Chicago prior to the Taba negotiations, he listed five elements that any agreement would have to include. Number four was: "No right of return for Palestinian refugees into Israel proper."[43] Significantly, this time Barak omitted any mention of Israeli unwillingness to offer a statement about the suffering of Palestinians or Israel's contribution toward that suffering.[44] In a formal statement released by the Barak government on 21 January 2001, regarding its position at Taba, the prime minister declared that "Israel will never allow the right of Palestinian refugees

---

40 Lustick, "Negotiating Truth," p. 121.
41 See "What's New about the Israeli Position on the Palestinian Refugee Question: Summary and Comments," BADIL, 14 October 1999, at http://www.badil.org/Publications/Press/1999/press77–99.htm.
42 Lustick, "Negotiating Truth," pp. 121–122.
43 See www.mfa.gov.il/mfa/go.asp?MFAH0iaa0.
44 Lustick, "Negotiating Truth," p. 122.

to return inside the State of Israel," yet again did not list refusal to make a statement of responsibility for the refugee problem as part of the Israeli government's position.[45]

On the Palestinian side, traditional demands for the complete return of all refugees were advanced in response to initial bargaining positions by Barak regarding Israeli sovereignty over the Temple Mount and mere "administrative autonomy" arrangements for Palestinians in Arab neighbourhoods of expanded East Jerusalem. Yet at Taba, these strong demands were effectively, if not formally, withdrawn as Israeli positions loosened – reflecting Palestinian focus on the importance of formal Israeli acknowledgment of Palestinian suffering as a consequence of Israel's creation, on the crucial need for unlimited immigration into the Palestinian state, and on a symbolic opportunity for return of some 1948 refugees to territory inside pre-1967 Israel.[46]

We have seen in the third part of this research that in the joint statement released by the Israeli and Palestinian delegations at the end of the Taba negotiations, the refugee issue was included as one of the four crucial questions that had been addressed and with respect to which gaps still remained. Nevertheless, these gaps were said to have narrowed sufficiently to warrant the belief that "in a short period of time and given an intensive effort and the acknowledgement of the essential and urgent nature of reaching an agreement, it will be possible to bridge the differences remaining and attain a permanent settlement of peace."[47]

As discussed earlier, the results achieved at Taba were largely along the lines of Clinton's Parameters. Although Clinton had emphasized the need to compensate and resettle refugees and guarantee full rights to immigrate into the Palestinian state, he did not refer explicitly to any statement of responsibility, regret, or blame that Israel might make. Clinton argued that "the end of the conflict must manifest itself with concrete acts that demonstrate a new attitude and a new approach by

45   See www.us-israel.org/jsource/Peace/tabatalks.html, cited in ibid.
46   Rashid Khalidi, "Attainable Justice," *International Journal*, Vol. 53, No. 2, Spring 1998, pp. 233–252, cited at Lustick, "Negotiating Truth," p. 122.
47   See www.mideastweb.org/Taba.htm.

Palestinians and Israelis toward each other." He further emphasized the need to "find a truth we can share."[48]

Significant progress was made at Taba compared to any previous Israeli-Palestinian negotiations on principled aspects of the refugee issue. To get a contrast to previous negotiations, let us cut back to talks of the Multilateral Working Group on Refugees in Ottawa in May 1992. There, the head of the Palestinian delegation made a demand on Israelis for "moral recognition of the immense injustice inflicted upon our people 44 years ago."[49] One member of that delegation, Rashid Khalidi, published a more detailed statement of his view, at that time, of the specific kind of Israeli response which would be required to move to a full and final resolution of the refugee question. Khalidi emphasized as "essential" that "the existential hurt that was done to the majority of the Palestinian people be acknowledged by those who caused that hurt, or their successors in power." He stated that this was all the more important precisely because "there can be no fundamental redress of that grievance."[50] Khalidi went on to stress the re-education and socialization programs that would be needed in Israel, along with symbolic actions and an acceptance in principle of the Palestinian *right of return*. Only then, he argued, would truly generous reparations along with immigration opportunities into the future Palestinian state in the West Bank and Gaza be acceptable as the basis for a final settlement.[51]

At Taba, however, the Palestinian side demanded less than Khalidi's formulation had contained: just an Israeli acknowledgment of its "moral and legal responsibility" for the fate of the Palestinian refugees and its "responsibility for the resolution of the refugee problem."[52] Significantly, the Palestinians' formulation at Taba did not include a demand that Israel accept the *right of return*. Nor did it insist on an Israeli for-

48 See "Remarks by the President at Israel Policy Forum Gala," Waldorf-Astoria Hotel, New York, 7 January 2001, at www.brookings.edu/press/appendix/peace_process.htm.

49 Lustick, "Negotiating Truth," p. 122.

50 Rashid Khalidi, "The Palestinian Refugee Problem: A Possible Solution," *Palestine-Israel Journal*, Vol. 2, No. 4, Autumn 1995, p. 74.

51 Ibid., p. 76.

52 See the Palestinian proposal on Palestinian Refugees at Taba, 22 January 2001, at www.mideastweb.org/taba.htm.

mulation that explicitly placed "sole" or even "central" or "primary" responsibility for the fate of the Palestinians or for the solution of the refugee problem on Israel.[53]

We have seen in the third part of this research that Israel's position at Taba acknowledged, albeit indirectly and implicitly, that Israel was to some extent responsible and ready to contribute "its part" to the solution of the problem. The Israeli negotiators were willing to formulate a narrative of the events of 1948 that emphasized the direct and disastrous consequences for Palestinians of the war surrounding Israel's establishment, omitting any reference to Arab leaders' orders resulting in the departure of the refugees. Such formulation represents a change if compared, for example, with the Israeli position during the negotiations of the Multilateral Working Group on Refugees in 1992. There, in his opening remarks to that group, the head of the Israeli delegation, Shlomo Ben Ami, refused to acknowledge any responsibility by Israel for the exodus of the refugees. While alternating between blaming "the Arabs" for the problem or defining it as inevitable, Ben Ami used only superficial and passive-voice phrasing to suggest the possibility of a link between Israeli victory and Palestinian catastrophe; he showed no interest in the notion of a narrative which could be shared.[54]

Representative and influential Israeli voices, such as Professor Shlomo Avineri and Ambassador Aviv Shir-On, have gone even further and demanded from the Palestinians to take moral responsibility for not only having rejected the U.N.'s resolution calling for a Jewish state to be established, but also to have declared war on the young state.[55] In fact, Shir-On countered calls for an Israeli apology for having caused the Palestinian refugee problem with an Israeli call for a Palestinian apology for the attempt at destroying the nascent Israeli state and killing its inhabitants in 1948.[56] Indeed, analogous to Israel's rejection of acceptance of responsibility for the creation of the refugee problem, Palestinians refusal to recognize any Arab role in creating and sustaining the Palestinian refugee problem or the exceptional circumstances

---

53   Lustick, "Negotiating Truth," p. 125.
54   For a reprint of Ben Ami's speech, see ibid.
55   Shlomo Avineri, *Yediot Acharonot*, 16 May 2003; Aviv Shir-On, Israeli ambassador to Switzerland, interview with the author in Bern, 21 April 2005.
56   Ibid.

that kept the issue politically alive longer than any other refugee question after the Second World War.[57]

Yet despite the progress that has occurred in the Israeli-Palestinian negotiations on the issue, it is evident that even at Taba, important gaps remained between the positions of both parties. The Israeli side was not willing to explicitly acknowledge legal, moral, or historical responsibility for the fate of the refugees or to assume sole responsibility for the solution of the refugee problem. This refusal is consistent with long-standing fears in Israel that any such declaration would expose Israel to virtually unlimited property, rights of return, and compensation claims. Moreover, Israel chose to include reference to "all those parties ... responsible for" the refugee problem, thereby implying that the Arab states and perhaps the Palestinians themselves played a role. The Israeli proposal further included explicit reference to Israel's initial acceptance of the 1947 United Nations partition plan and to the mutuality of suffering which resulted from the – implicitly allocated – failure of the Arab side to accept it.[58]

Most important yet, in this back-and-forth we can identify the outlines of the kind of agreement eventually reached by the German and Israeli governments in 1951. Not only did the German government not accept responsibility (legal or moral), but it explicitly included claims that the "overwhelming majority of the German people abominated the crimes committed against the Jews" and that they "did not participate in them." Such relativizations (which might also easily be termed "apologetics"[59]), including the recollection of "many among the German people who showed their readiness to help their Jewish fellow citizens," were eventually accepted by the Jewish/Israeli side, even though most historians would argue that a more truthful account would not have been so generous in its memory of German public opinion and civic virtue during the Third Reich. What Adenauer did say was that what happened to the Jews was awful ("unspeakable"), that his government and the people of Germany were aware that it was awful, and that it had been done "in the name" of the German people. That it had been

---

57 See Barkan, "Considerations Toward Accepting Historical Responsibility," p. 101.
58 Lustick, "Negotiating Truth," pp. 125–126.
59 Lustick indeed refers to it that way. See ibid., p. 126.

done in the name of the German people is what, Adenauer declared, warranted the new Germany's commitment to a measure of indemnification. On the other hand, no claim was made of full expiation, restitution, or rights to Jewish forgiveness.[60]

A more recent example of two states managing to find a formulation to close a chapter of the past and open a new one for the future involves the Sudeten Germans, several millions of whom were expelled from Czechoslovakia in 1945–46. It was only in 1997 when Germans and the Czechs reached an agreement as how to relate to that issue which has been a bone of contention between the two nations since the end of the Second World War: in a joint declaration of Germany and the Czech Republic, Germany expressed regret for occupying Czech territory in 1938, and the Czech Republic expressed regret for expelling the Sudeten Germans.[61] As with Adenauer's speech, the formulation of the Czech-German declaration was rather shallow; nevertheless, its significance was that Germany would not pursue claims on behalf of the Sudeten Germans, neither at present nor in the future, and that Germany would support the Czech application for membership in the European Union.

In addition, during the negotiations preparing the ground for the joint declaration, a Czech-German historical commission tried to adjudicate the conflicting claims between the Germans who had maintained that more than a quarter of a million had died in the expulsions and the Czech number of fifteen thousand to thirty thousand, which included in the Czech narrative several thousands who committed suicide. The commission of historical research stated that the Czech version was closer to the truth. Yet in the spirit of compromise – and as a matter of accurate historical record – it emphasized that the precise number would never be known.[62]

60 Ibid.
61 See the "German-Czech Declaration on Mutual Relations and their Future Development of 21 January 1997" at www.mzv.cz/servis/soubor. asp?id=1873.
62 See Barkan, "Considerations Toward Accepting Historical Responsibility," p. 97.

Principled aspects, namely the issue of recognition, have also long played a major role in Israeli-Palestinian overall relations – or rather their non-relations, to be precise. For several decades, the Palestinians did not recognize the State of Israel, while Israel has long refused to recognize the Palestinians. The issue was eventually solved in an exchange of letters in September 1993 between Yasser Arafat and Yitzhak Rabin. Yet scrutinizing the text of the mutual recognition reveals just another case where meagre formulations were eventually sufficient to satisfy both parties' need regarding principled aspects: in that exchange of letters, Arafat stated only that the PLO "recognizes the right of the State of Israel to exist in peace and security" – a phrase that projects Israel's right to exist onto a purely abstract level.[63] Rabin, on his part, wrote back merely that Israel recognized "the PLO as the representative of the Palestinian people" – not that the Palestinian people had a right to anything, let alone an independent state.[64] Yet this exchange of letters nevertheless enabled the State of Israel and the PLO to launch formal negotiations.

Therefore, based on the negotiations over the German-Israeli reparations agreement and the Czech-German joint declaration, both successful via a much less than fully accurate embrace by the successor regime of what had actually occurred, and based on the progress so far in negotiations between Israelis and Palestinians, it is relatively easy to picture a workable package of arrangements and declarations to enable a mostly internationally funded compensation, resettlement, and return arrangement to be agreed upon. The formulas utilized would allocate a part of the responsibility for the refugee problem to a portion of Israeli actions and policies in 1948, thereby justifying a significant but certainly not majority role for the commitment of Israeli resources. Israeli acknowledgement of and expressions of regret for injustices committed – to be worded, for example, either "in connection with the establishment of the State," "as a consequence of the establishment of the State," or "in the name of the State of Israel or Zionism" – would

63 Yonatan Touval, "Hamas and Israel: A bogus demand for 'recognition'," *International Herald Tribune*, 14–15 October 2006.
64 Ibid.

not require Israelis to deny their own truths and could satisfy Palestinian principled needs.[65]

Two elements are likely to be key: first, the political imperatives of consolidating Palestinian statehood. If Palestinians are to receive a viable state, with unrestricted access to it for their refugees, Palestinian leaders will likely act just as did Ben Gurion and Sharet: eagerly searching for formulas to make massive packages of aid for that state and its newly arriving citizens politically acceptable. Second, an expectation that no denial by Palestinians of the truth of what befell them would be required to achieve their statehood.[66] In this respect, the fact that all Israeli school textbooks make use of the most recent historical research, including the New Historians' studies, is a positive development,[67] bearing parallels to the kind of treatment of its own past that has featured in German textbooks since the 1960s.[68] At this point, Palestinian textbooks are still largely based on the old Palestinian historiography,[69] yet this is a normal phenomenon, as any nation under

---

65   Lustick, "Negotiating Truth," pp. 126–127.

66   Ibid., p. 127.

67   In Israel, in contrast to previous textbooks, all current textbooks admit that in certain places and at certain times, the IDF did expel Palestinians. However, they emphasise – as does Benny Morris – that there was no Israeli master plan for expelling the Palestinians. See Elie Podeh, "The Right of Return versus the Law of Return: Contrasting Historical Narratives in Israeli and Palestinian Textbooks," in Ann Lesch and Ian Lustick (eds.), *Exile and Return: Predicaments of Palestinians and Jews* (Philadelphia: University of Pennsylvania Press, 2005), pp. 46–47.

68   Israelis and Palestinians are not the only nations who still need to find the proper formulation regarding how to refer to their troubled past, and who could therefore also benefit from the German-Israeli and Czech-German precedent: Also Japan and Korea, as well as Japan and China, have a long road of conciliation ahead of them. In a 2005 interview, South Korea's president Roh Moo Hyun demanded: "Japan needs to reveal the truth, to sincerely apologize and, if necessary, to pay an indemnity." He referred to the dark episode of Word War II, were Japan used Koreans for forced labour and prostitution. See *Der Spiegel*, 14 March 2005.

69   The narrative portrayed in Palestinian textbooks still fully adheres to the old Palestinian assertion that Israel's policy is solely responsible for the displacement of the Palestinians. See Podeh, "The Right of Return versus the Law of Return," pp. 48–52.

foreign occupation is not eager to critically examine its own past.[70] It would nevertheless become a factor of immeasurable importance in any future normalization of ties between Israelis and Palestinians if both – maybe in the framework of a commission composed of historians from both sides – could agree on a common version of their historical interaction.

The principled aspects analysed in this chapter have presented vital insight into facets often neglected in the search for political solutions to the Palestinian refugee question. However, in order to find a solution acceptable to both Israelis and Palestinians, practical aspects will necessarily have to be addressed as well. The following chapter, therefore, which shall conclude this research, will examine a number of proposals focusing on both *practical* as well as *principled* solutions to the Palestinian refugee problem; those proposals shall be termed "integrated solutions."

---

70 In this respect, two factors provide further insight. First, the current Palestinian textbooks – the first generation of educational textbooks – reflect the elite's attempt to mold a shared identity. It has been demonstrated that textbooks during this stage tend to display a more nationalistic attitude. In contrast, since the current Israeli textbooks constitute the third generation of textbooks since 1948, Israeli textbooks have gone through a process of at least partial de-mythologization. The first- and second-generation textbooks were replete with myths, inaccuracies, and biases toward Arabs. With regard to the refugee problem, they consistently denied any Israeli involvement in acts of expulsion. It was only in the mid-1990s, as a result of the peace process and the appearance of the new historiography, that Israelis were willing to confront their past more openly. Thus, current Palestinian textbooks should not be compared with current Israeli textbooks but with Israel's first-generation textbooks. Second, most of the Palestinian textbooks had been written during the second intifada. It is reasonable to assume that during such a violent period, textbooks would reflect a more hard-line approach than during a peaceful period. Ibid., p.51.

13 INTEGRATED SOLUTIONS

After having separately reviewed both practical and principled suggestions for a solution of the Palestinian refugee problem, we shall now turn our focus on proposals which synthesise both practical as well as principled aspects; such proposals shall be termed *integrated solutions*.

As in the case of practical solutions, also the integrated solutions shall be listed and arranged according to the implied number of refugees returning to the State of Israel, starting with the option that would allow a full return of refugees and concluding with the one that involves no single refugee returning to Israel. First, the essence of each of the integrated solutions will be presented. Second, the proposal will be analysed as to its implications for both Israelis and Palestinians, carefully scrutinizing the respective advantages and disadvantages it involves for each side. Finally, its relevance in practical terms as a concrete solution to the problem will be assessed.

As stated above, the beginning shall be the proposal which would allow a total refugee return to Israel: a bi-national state.

13.1 A Bi-national State

One way to solve the question of Palestinian refugee return, would be to form one single state between the Jordan river and the Mediterranean Sea, encompassing the territories of Israel, the West Bank and the Gaza Strip. This would also allow Israel to claim all of the Land of Israel, while the Palestinians could claim all of historic Palestine. In such constellation it would not matter whether refugees would be returning to Israel or to a Palestinian state, as those two would form one single political entity. A bi-national state would also allow a full recognition of the Palestinian *right of return*. Thus, the right would be recognized coupled with the option for an actual return of any refugee wishing to do so.[1]

---

1   See "The One-State versus the Two-State Debate"; Hani Al-Masri, "The Cantons-State and the Liquidation of the Refugee Issue"; Nassar Ibrahim,

13.1.1 The Essence of the Proposal

On 9 January 2004, Palestinian Prime Minster Ahmed Qurei (Abu Ala) declared that if no progress in negotiations with Israel was soon achieved, the Palestinians would seek a single, Arab-Jewish state rather than further pursue the two-state solution.[2] Even if only a tactical move meant to create a sense of urgency on the Israeli side, this statement highlighted that if negotiations for a two-state solution were to fail, a bi-national state might be the only alternative. Some scholars even claim that Israelis and Palestinians are already living in the reality of one state.[3]

Yet what exactly is meant by the idea of a bi-national state? On the technical level, the term "bi-national" refers to a country in which two and only two national cultures are afforded pride of place, with juridic-ally entrenched rights for control of shares of the state's resources, positions of authority, symbols etc. On the substantive level, however, it reflects mutual recognition of the two ethno-national collectivities' rightful claims to the land.[4] In an Arab-Jewish bi-national state, Jewish law might apply to matters of marriage, divorce, burial etc. among Jews, while Christian and Muslim law and practice would apply for Arabs. In such a state Arabic and Hebrew would both be national languages, either one or two national anthems would be sung (or none at all), stamps would honour equally both national cultures, land and other important resources would be allocated according to an agreed formula, and so forth. Such a state could go far toward satisfying the

---

"Problems with the Two-State Solution and the Dream of One Democratic State"; As'ad Ghanem, "The Binational State is a Desired Palestinian Project and Demand"; Mohammad Baraka, "Between the One-State and the Two-State Solution"; and Virginia Tilley, "A New Palestinian Political Season?" All these articles are available at Al-Majdal, Issue No.28, Winter 2005, at www.badil.org/al-majdal/2005/Winter/majdal28.pdf.

2   See The New York Times, 10 January 2004.

3   See, for example, Yosef Schwartz, „Zweistaatenlösung versus Einstaaten-realität," *Summary of the OeME-Herbsttagung in Bern*, 20 November 2004, pp.34–39. For an excellent analysis of the bi-national idea both in Israel and Palestine, see Tamar Hermann, "The bi-national idea in Israel/Palestine: past and present," *Nations and Nationalism*, Vol. 11, No.3, 2005, pp.381–401.

4   Hermann, "The bi-national idea in Israel/Palestine," p.382.

specific national, cultural, religious, and symbolic requirements of the two presently rival peoples.[5]

With regard to the Palestinian refugee question, the bi-national option is interesting in several aspects. First, one single state between the Jordan river and the Mediterranean Sea would signify that any Palestinian refugee wishing to return could do so, if the right of any Jew to immigrate to Israel was extended to equally apply for any Palestinian. Thus in the framework of a bi-national solution in which the Israeli and Palestinian populations would not be distinguished from each other territorially, all Palestinian refugees would, evidently, be permitted to return to unpopulated areas of the bi-national state. Second, there would be no more reason for Israel not to recognize the *right of return*, as demographic considerations would have no significance if both Israelis and Palestinians were to live in one single state. In fact, some claim that a bi-national state is the preferred or even only solution to the Palestinian refugee problem in general, and to the dispute over the *right of return* in particular.[6] One of the most unexpected proposals in this direction came recently from Libya: its leader Muammar Qaddafi advocated in

---

5   Ian Lustick, "The Cunning of History," *Boston Review*, December 2001/ January 2002, at www.bostonreview.net.

6   See, for example, former vice mayor of Jerusalem, Meron Benvenisti in "Heimatsuche im Geist des Judentums," *Neue Zürcher Zeitung*, 4 July 2005, p. 25; Ilan Pappe in his *A History of Modern Palestine: One Land, Two Peoples* (Cambridge, U.K.: University Press, 2004) pp. 267–268; Bassil Jaber, "Possible Solutions to the Refugee Question," (Hebrew) in Ephraim Yaar and Tami Hermann, *The Palestinian Refugees Issue and the Right of Return: Proceedings of a Symposium held on 29 December 2003* (Hebrew), (Tel Aviv: Tami Steinmetz Center, 2004), pp. 52–55; Marwan Bishara, "One state for two people," *International Herald Tribune*, 12 November 2003; Haim Hanegbi in an interview with *Haaretz* in the summer of 2003, as cited in Hermann, "The bi-national idea in Israel/Palestine," p. 387; Sara Ossitzky-Laser, "Preparing the Ground for a Binational/Federal State," (Hebrew) in Tamar Hermann and Ephraim Yaar (eds.), *Is the Israeli-Palestinian Conflict Solvable?* (Hebrew), (Tel Aviv: Tami Steinmetz Center, 2002), pp. 89–93; Ella Shohat, in an interview with *Tages Anzeiger*, 31 May 2000; Edward Said in an interview with *Die Weltwoche*, 25 March 1999; Azmi Bishara in an interview with the *Journal of Palestine Studies*, Vol. XXVI, No. 3, Spring 1997, p. 72.

his "White Book" the founding of "Isratine,"[7] a state which would also resolve the problem of Palestinian refugees and their return.[8]

Another proponent of a bi-national state elaborates his thoughts in the following manner:

> [T]he Palestinians in the territories and the Palestinians in Israel will form a single political unit within a binational state. There will be a Jewish political unit and a Palestinian-Arab political unit, which together will constitute a Jewish-Arab polity with two separate legislative chambers as well as a common parliament, (...) a binational state, a federal or confederal system comprising two ethno-national communities. Only in such a context will it be possible to resolve such problems as the refugees and the settlements. Settlements no longer will pose an insurmountable obstacle within the context of a single binational state: If the Israelis should choose to settle in the West Bank, then so be it; we [Palestinians], too, will have the right to set up residence in Jaffa, for instance.[9]

Thus, in the framework of a bi-national state, Israelis could be living all over the West Bank while Palestinians – refugees and non-refugees alike – could settle within Israel. A bi-national state would also allow Israel to fully recognize the Palestinian *right of return*. Yet what would be the implications of the bi-national proposal for Israelis and Palestinians? The following section will seek the answers.

---

7   The name "Isratine" is a combination of the first part of the word Israel with the last part of the word Palestine. There have also been suggestions to create a new flag modelled along the lines of a pastiche of the current Israeli flag and the Palestinian one to be pitched as the flag of that new state. See Lama Abu-Odeh, "The Case for Binationalism," *Boston Review*, December 2001/January 2002, at www.bostonreview.net.

8   See "Al Ghatafi Speaks," June 2006, at www.algathafi.org/medialeast/medialeast-en.htm.

9   Azmi Bishara in an interview with the *Journal of Palestine Studies*, Vol. XXVI, No. 3, Spring 1997, p. 73.

13.1.2 Analysis of the Proposal

Implications for the Israelis

As a matter of fact, Israel already is to a large extent, if not a bi-national state, certainly a multicultural one. With hundreds of thousands of recent immigrants from the former Soviet Union classified as non-Jews, and hundreds of thousands more foreign labourers from dozens of countries, it is no longer possible to think of the Israeli society – even leaving aside the West Bank which is effectually controlled by Israel – as divided between Jews and Arabs. Roughly speaking, the ethnic composition of the population living within Israel proper is 70 percent Jewish, 19 percent Arab, and 11 percent non-Jewish non-Arabs.[10] It is essential to note that Arab political parties, Arab votes, and the turnout of Arab voters have had a massive and sometimes decisive effect on the outcome of Israeli elections, and on the behaviour of several Israeli governments. Israel thus has already moved toward multinationalism.

Nevertheless, the idea of forming a bi-national state with the Palestinians is complete anathema for the vast majority of Israelis, who share a strong national consensus calling for the continued existence of an own state.[11] As to the tiny camp of Israelis favouring bi-nationalism, it can be divided into two subgroups. First there are those, mostly belonging to the radical, non-Zionist or anti-Zionist left, who favour bi-nationalism *per se*. Second are those who albeit would prefer a different scenario yet have concluded that the existing geopolitical and demographic realities dictate bi-nationalism.[12]

Until recently, bi-nationalism was not a significant – although a highly contested – option in the Israeli repertoire of possible solutions to Israeli-Palestinian conflict in general, and the refugee problem in particular. Thus, when in the summer of 2003 *Haaretz* published a

---

10 Lustick, "The Cunning of History."

11 The Israeli consensus against a bi-national state is best reflected by the fact that even Uri Avnery, a prominent figure on Israel's far left who has for decades advocated the idea of a Palestinian state alongside Israel, vehemently rejects the idea of a bi-national state. See Uri Avnery, "A Binational State? God Forbid!," *Journal of Palestine Studies*, Vol. XXVIII, No. 4, Summer 1999, pp. 55–60.

12 Hermann, "The bi-national idea in Israel/Palestine," p. 386–387.

lengthy interview with two public figures, Meron Benvenisti and and Haim Hanegbi, in which both expressed their support for a bi-national Israeli-Palestinian state, many within Israel were taken by surprise. The publication caused strong aftershocks, including many letters to the editor and opinion columns in the printed and electronic press. Most critique focused on the Jewish-Israelis losing a state of their own. Others reminded that nowhere in the world has a conflict between two national movements been resolved squeezing those two into the boiling pot of a bi-national state.[13]

Interestingly, there is also opposition to the idea of bi-nationalism on Israel's far left, the traditional support base for a two-state solution. These voices maintain that considering Israel's first world economy and the Palestinians' third world economy, the chances of real equality within a bi-national state are practically nil. Yet the question is idle, the argument goes, because nothing could motivate Israel to enter the adventure of bi-nationalism.[14]

Implications for the Palestinians

The collapse of the Oslo process and the repercussions of the second intifada, namely Israel's reoccupation of the Palestinian territories, signalled to a growing number of Palestinians, mostly intellectuals living in the diaspora, that an independent Palestinian state was unattainable and thus a bi-national state would be the solution most preferable and realistic for Palestinians.

Among Palestinian bi-nationalists, too, different subgroups can be identified. The first consists of people like the late Edward Said, who maintain that a bi-national state should not be seen as a short-term escape from the present dismal entanglement but as a long-term guiding principle, even if currently it is unpopular and viewed as unrealistic. The second subgroup regards a bi-national arrangement as merely the first step in creating a technically bi-national state with a Palestinian majority. A third group of Palestinian proponents regard

---

13 This statement was made by Shlomo Avineri, a prominent political scientist and former director-general of the Israeli foreign ministry. See Shlomo Avineri, "A History of Conflicts," Maariv Online, 19 September 2003 (Hebrew) in ibid., p. 389.

14 Ibid.

the bi-national rhetoric as a strategic means only. Well aware of the Jewish apprehension of a bi-national solution, they advocate using it as a tactic to advance a two-state arrangement. Many interpret a statement like Qurei's, mentioned earlier, along these lines. The common denominator of most Palestinian bi-nationalists is the espousal of the "one person, one vote" model. In practical terms, they demand a secular democracy with Arabs and Jews as equal citizens in the territory of mandated Palestine.[15]

Indeed, the bi-national solution offers a number of advantages for Palestinians. First of all, it would allow an all-encompassing return of Palestinian refugees, along with a formal recognition of the *right of return* by Israel. Yet compared to an own state in the West Bank and Gaza, the bi-national solution offers several additional, crucial benefits.

Almost forty years of occupation and the resulting political and economic incorporation of the Palestinian territories into Israel have rendered the Palestinian economy heavily dependent on Israel. Although two intifadas have sparked Palestinian attempts to disengage and separate from Israel, those attempts were more than offset by forms of structural dependency that ultimately proved to be stronger than political factors.[16] In other words, an independent Palestinian state would initially be equipped with an economy that is unable to sustain itself. Even the necessary investment of tremendous resources by the Palestinian state and the international community into building and developing Palestine's economy would not necessarily succeed. Naturally, it is impossible to predict whether in the end an independent and strong Palestinian economy would successfully be established or whether the Palestinian state would have to share the fate of numerous post-colonial countries of the third world. However, if a bi-national state was established, Israel's modern and developed economy could provide an important basis for that state's overall economy. In the words of a Palestinian scholar: "Palestinians would be like immigrants

---

15   Ibid., pp. 390–391.
16   Salim Tamari, "The Dubious Lure of Binationalism," *Journal of Palestinian Studies*, Vol. XXX, No. 1, Autumn 2000, p. 84.

to a wealthy metropole rather than nationals of a poor third-world country."[17]

Similarly, Palestinian refugees could also attach financial claims directly to the resources of the common state as national budget; to be distributed, after internal negotiations, among the state's national subjects, Palestinians and Israel alike.

In a bi-national state, Palestinians could not only benefit from Israel's developed economy, but also – although it might initially sound ironic – from the Israeli military. The integration into an already existing, efficient army would spare the Palestinians from having to develop defensive forces of their own – which in any event would be facing massive restrictions since Israel, if a two-state solution was realized, would most likely insist that the separate Palestinian state be demilitarised. Thus a bi-national state would not only solve the question of refugees – it could also turn Israelis and Palestinians from foes into military partners.

Yet the question arises whether the above discussed possible outcomes of a bi-national state, highlighting bi-nationalism's advantages for Palestinians, would outweigh the disadvantages involved for Palestinians. In fact, it appears rather probable that in a bi-national state, Israeli advantage in nearly all practical fields – economic, military, social – would be such that the Palestinians would be turned into an exploited underclass devoid of real power. A similar situation exists presently in Israel proper, with its Arab citizens living in circumstances visibly below those of Jewish-Israeli communities. Many parts of the administration and the economy are not accessible for Arabs, officially or unofficially.[18]

In addition, a bi-national state would make it considerably easier for Israelis to buy Arab land on the West Bank, control immigrations, and take further measures to safeguard their national "competitive edge". Some may argue that, over time, demographic facts in the bi-national state would alter this balance of power in favour of the Palestinians, who would immediately constitute close to fifty percent of the population. Since the state would be democratic, it would automatically follow that power and economic privilege would pass in due course into the hands

---

17 Lama Abu-Odeh, "The Case for Binationalism," *Boston Review*, December 2001/January 2002, at www.bostonreview.net.
18 See Uri Avnery, "A Binational State? God Forbid!," *Journal of Palestine Studies*, Vol. XXVIII, No. 4, Summer 1999, p. 58.

of the Palestinians. Although this might eventually be the case, the road to Palestinian superiority would hardly be a peaceful one, since most likely the transition of a previous minority taking over the rule as a majority and vice versa would be accompanied by violent struggle.[19]

13.1.3 The Proposal's Relevance

The only formula regarding a solution of the Palestinian refugee question that has ever attracted majorities on both sides is based on partition – division of the land into two closely related but politically separate sovereign states. Although the violent years of the second intifada have dramatically reduced the extent of expressed support for a two-state solution, it is reasonable to assume that significant majorities of Israelis and Palestinians are still willing to accept it in return for an adequate peace agreement.

Despite the differences of argumentation, most advocates of a bi-national solution acknowledge that this is not the most desirable option. Taking all aspects into account, the major question arises to what extent bi-nationalism is today a feasible political remedy for the question of Palestinian refugees (and the Israeli-Palestinian conflict in general). While for Israelis the issue of bi-nationalism is complete anathema, on the Palestinians side support for such idea is albeit broader, yet at present both the Israeli and the Palestinian political elites favour the formula calling for a two-state solution.[20]

Only a two-state solution holds out the prospect for both Israelis and Palestinians to think they may get all of what they absolutely need and much of what they strongly desire. What each side absolutely needs is access to a state apparatus that can regularize daily life with reasonable access to public resources for its members, international recognition of its rightful place in the family of nations, and the ability to foster immigration across its borders for nationals living abroad. Contrarily, the bi-national solution seeks to secure what is needed by abandoning what is strongly desired: Israelis and Palestinians are to share the land and immigration opportunities afforded by a single state ruling

---

19 Ibid., pp. 58–59.
20 Hermann, "The bi-national idea in Israel/Palestine," pp. 397–398.

the whole land, yet at the cost of having to perpetually encounter each other in micro and macro struggles to achieve a distribution of those resources. In fact, the ultimate strength of a two-state solution is that it uses what each side strongly wants – the desire to be rid of the other – to achieve the territory, resources, recognition and immigration opportunities each side needs.[21]

Bi-nationalism is an important idea and it deserves serious attention – yet not because it can replace the separate state idea as a target for diplomacy, but because a negotiated settlement may never be achieved; however, keeping in mind how bi-nationalism might arise as an unintended consequence of failed negotiations might make that failure less likely. In fact, if a bi-national state is to emerge, it will most likely result neither from Israeli nor Palestinian initiatives, but as a cumulative of the failure to achieve a two-state solution.[22]

Nevertheless, it is also worth remembering that a bi-national state in the whole country could be the first stage on the road to a separate Palestinian state.[23] That is what occurred in the United Kingdom: Ireland, unable to achieve independence from Britain, was annexed at the beginning of the 19th century. It took three quarters of a century for Irish Catholics to become fully enfranchised participants in the politics of the multinational United Kingdom of Great Britain and Ireland. The effective mobilization of those voters then laid the groundwork for the succession of most of Ireland in 1921 and the establishment of the Republic of Ireland.[24]

Yet the experience of the 20th century has shown that nation states, based on one ethnic majority, are by far the most fundamental and solid political construction in modern international relations, while multinational experiments often resulted in bloody civil-wars and the

---

21 Lustick, "The Cunning of History."

22 Ibid.

23 Yosef Schwartz also points to such solution: He suggest to turn the present *de facto* situation of Israel being a bi-national state (since it is so closely interwoven with the West Bank through settlements, roads, and military presence) into an actual, *de jure*, bi-national state, so that eventually Israelis and Palestinians can negotiate as equal partners the idea of two separate states. See his remarks in „Zweistaatenlösung versus Einstaatenrealität," *Summary of the OeME-Herbsttagung in Bern*, 20 November 2004, pp. 34–39.

24 Lustick, "The Cunning of History."

eventual political re-division along ethnic lines. Yugoslavia is probably the most striking example of inter-ethnic violence on the way to political independence, while the separation of Czechs and Slovaks was exceptional in the peaceful manner it occurred, but nevertheless proved the general rule that, in the current era, nations prefers to live in an own, nation state.

This is not only supported by examples from the Balkans and Central/Eastern Europe. See Canada: Two western communities divided by nothing but language, move perpetually at the brink of breakup. Half of the Quebecois want their own national state, and they might well achieve this in the foreseeable future. Take Belgium, where Flemings and Walloons have been living together for centuries, yet whose interaction has been most uneasy. Also in Scotland there is a strong movement for independence. The same goes for parts of Spain and Northern Ireland. Switzerland's "success story", on the other hand, is an anomaly, the result of a centuries-old process, the very opposite of an artificial creation imposed by an act of will; one will hardly find too many parallels between Switzerland and Israelis and Palestinians. In sum, it is utopian to believe that Israelis and Palestinians, two profoundly nationalistic peoples, could turn practically overnight from enemies into loving compatriots, able to live and function in one common society.[25]

Therefore, the bi-national solution does not have any practical relevance as to a realistic solution of the Palestinian refugee question; primarily because Israel would not accept such a proposal. Equally, it is also rather unlikely that a majority of Palestinians would support bi-nationalism. In addition, even if a bi-national state came to be established, it would be likely to collapse shortly afterwards. The solution to the Palestinian refugee question, thus, must be sought outside the realms of bi-nationalism.

---

25 Avnery, "A Binational State?," p. 58.

13.2   A Palestinian Compromise Solution

Joseph Alpher and Khalil Shikaki have taken the Palestinian maximalist demand of a full return of all Palestinian refugees coupled with an Israeli acknowledgment of full responsibility for the creation of the refugee problem and developed a modified version of it, which is to be more acceptable upon Israel and hence a more realistic option to solve the question of Palestinian refugees. They have termed their proposal a "Palestinian Compromise Solution."[26]

13.2.1 The Essence of the Proposal

Alpher and Shikaki's "Palestinian Compromise Solution" seeks to provide an acceptable and honourable resolution of the refugee issue while accommodating the realities on the ground, as well as Israel's demographic and security concerns. It does not envisage a massive return of Palestinian refugees into Israel, yet the individual moral right of Palestinian refugees to return to their homes and property *in the Palestinian state* would be fully acknowledged by Israel. In this sense, Israel would also accept the responsibility for creating the refugee problem. However, an actual *right of return* to Israel is a different matter; in fact, only the return of a limited number of refugees into Israel would be seen as feasible. This would reflect the changed situation of individual refugees and of the property that they had to abandon more than half a century ago, when the problem of the refugees was created. Individual refugees – having in fact resettled and made their homes elsewhere – would receive compensation. Most important, the number of refugees which would be allowed to return to Israel is to be determined in Israeli-Palestinian negotiations. In other words, Israel would not be "flooded" with refugees but would rather have a say in determining the number of refugees it was going to absorb.[27]

---

26   See Joseph Alpher and Khalil Shikaki, "The Palestinian Refugee Problem and the Right of Return," Weatherhead Center for International Affairs, Harvard University, May 1998, available at www.wcfia.harvard. edu/papers/98–07.pdf.

27   Ibid.

Those refugees not returning to Israel proper would be allowed to return to the Palestinian state if they so wished. The absorptive capacity of the Palestinian state – and not Israeli restrictions – would determine the number of those returning to the state. The Palestinians would in fact agree to a strategic trade-off: demanding a return to the 1967 borders so that they could absorb the largest possible number of refugees, in exchange for forgoing the full exercise of the *right of return*. Those refugees who would wish to remain in host countries may be resettled there if the host countries agree.[28]

Those refugees choosing not to return would receive individual compensation. Collective compensation would be paid to the Palestinian state and used for integration and absorption projects. Israel would carry the sole responsibility for finding and providing both forms of compensation, possibly under an international umbrella. The resettlement within host countries would probably require separate negotiations with them as well as the participation of international donors. Finally, to ensure the permanent nature of the agreement, refugee camps would be dismantled and UNRWA dissolved.[29]

13.2.2 Analysis of the Proposal

Implications for the Israelis

The Palestinian Compromise Solution takes Israel's core issue into account: it diminishes existential fears and demographic problems by removing the most threatening element in the Palestinian negotiating position – massive return into Israel.

Yet the proposal also includes several disadvantages for Israel. While the attribution of moral responsibility to the Arab side, rather than to itself, is central to the Israeli narrative, the proposal requires from Israel to at least implicitly acknowledge some actual guilt and moral responsibility on its own part; this could be perceived by Israel as a potential political threat and dangerous precedent. The provision allowing a limited number of refugees to return to Israel proper might also be regarded as a violation of Israel's sovereign control over its borders

---

28   Ibid.
29   Ibid.

and population, thereby establishing a precedent. Besides, Israel would not wish to pay both individual and collective compensation.[30]

In addition, Israel might also be reluctant towards the return of a large number of refugees to the Palestinian state, as that might lead to political instability there. Indeed, the economic and social burden on the Palestinian state might be very heavy due to its limited absorptive capacity and fragile economy; social and political disorder would also affect Israel negatively.

On the other hand, the proposal would altogether bring the refugee issue to an end, including the aspects which Israel wanted to bring to an end a long time ago: dismantling refugee camps and dissolving UNRWA, thereby removing the most prominent reminders of the existence of a Palestinian refugee problem. Coupled with the fact that there would be no massive refugee return to Israel and that the number of refugees who would actually return to Israel would be set up in mutual agreement, as well as the prospect of finally closing the file on Palestinian refugees provide a strong motivation for Israel to support such proposal.

Implications for the Palestinians

For Palestinians, the primary positive aspect of the proposal is that they could settle unlimited numbers of refugees within the sovereign Palestinian state. Yet the question arises whether it is not the natural right of every sovereign state to decide the number of people allowed to enter its territory. The most problematic aspect for Palestinians is that the proposal withholds from them what they require most, namely a full Israeli *recognition* of the *right of return;* instead, Israel would merely be required to recognize a right to return to the Palestinian state, thereby not satisfying Palestinian demands for an overall recognition of the right. In addition, most Palestinians would probably find it unsatisfactory that the Israeli recognition of responsibility for the creation of the refugee problem would not be formulated explicitly, but would supposedly be implied in Israel's recognition of the Palestinian right to return to the future Palestinian state.

Yet in the absence of absolute justice, the proposal does nevertheless grant a moral and political right to return to the Palestinian state

---

30   Ibid.

and also provides some form of realistic and reasonable justice while acknowledging realities on the ground. Palestinian refugees would benefit from the dismantling of refugee camps allowing them to move into permanent homes. In addition, it would provide a sense of finality at the psychological level.[31]

However, Palestinians might object that the return of only a limited number of refugees to Israel proper would not satisfy Palestinians' psychological and/or material needs, hence would lack the justice and finality it intends to provide. Without a full Israeli recognition of the Palestinian *right* to return and some explicit acknowledgment of responsibility, a majority of Palestinians is not likely to support this proposal.

13.2.3 The Proposal's Relevance

The Palestinian Compromise Solution adopts a right approach by separating some form of Israeli recognition of the *right of return* from its actual full implementation. By not envisaging a massive return and by awarding Israel a factual veto for refugee absorption, the proposal is compatible with most of Israel's demands and fears regarding the Palestinian refugee issue. Yet for Palestinians, it lacks the central components of a full Israeli recognition of the *right of return* and some explicit acknowledgment of responsibility on the part of Israel.

Furthermore, the proposal requires cooperation of host countries, particularly Jordan, Lebanon, and Syria, who may be asked to absorb a large number of refugees. While Jordan, which signed a peace treaty with Israel and has granted citizenship to its Palestinian refugees, might agree to cooperate, Lebanon and Syria might choose not to do so. In the case of Lebanon, it can be factually ruled out that it would agree to for a significant amount of Palestinian refugees to remain on its soil.

This proposal can only succeed on the condition that Israelis and Palestinians manage to agree on a certain number of refugees who are to return to Israeli territory. Yet the proposal does not offer any guidelines regarding how the parties are supposed to settle for a certain number of refugees; moreover, it does not have any provision for the case that

---

31   Ibid.

the two parties are not able to agree on a specific number. Therefore, in its present form, the Palestinian Compromise Solution cannot be expected to settle the question of Palestinian refugees.

13.3 An Israeli Compromise Solution

Joseph Alpher and Khalil Shikaki have not only developed a "Palestinian Compromise Solution" but also an "Israeli Compromise Solution,"[32] which equally intends to modify one side's – in this case Israel's – maximalist demands (no refugee return to Israel and no Israeli recognition of responsibility), with the goal of making it acceptable to the Palestinians.

13.3.1 The Essence of the Proposal

Israel is to acknowledge that, at least to some extent, it shares practical – yet not moral – responsibility, together with the other parties to the process that culminated in the 1948 war, for the plight and suffering of the refugees. That rectification of that plight by all parties is to be a central goal of the Arab-Israeli peace process. Israel further accepts the *right of return* to the Palestinian state, yet not to Israel proper. Israel "may" furthermore accept the repatriation of "tens of thousands" of Palestinian refugees on its territory as part of a family reunification program.[33]

Moreover, Israel would compensate refugees for lost property on a collective basis. The Arab countries concerned would create a similar mechanism for a collective compensation of Jewish refugees (based on the Arab states' acknowledgment of their obligations in this regard). Both programs would fall within the framework of the multilateral working group on refugees, yet without being linked operationally.

---

32   Joseph Alpher and Khalil Shikaki, "The Palestinian Refugee Problem and the Right of Return," Weatherhead Center for International Affairs, Harvard University, May 1998, available at www.wcfia.harvard.edu/papers/98–07.pdf.
33   Ibid.

Israel might also accept an international role in the actual negotiations over compensation.[34]

Israelis and Palestinians would need to reach an understanding regarding a harmonization of the inflow of refugees and Palestinian absorptive capabilities. Israel would drop any demand for direct physical control over the influx of refugees to the Palestinian state, not least in light of the expected difficulties to enforce such endeavour. On the other hand, the Palestinian state would commit itself to limit the flow of returnees according to its absorptive capabilities. That would provide Israel with a mechanism for reciprocity: if the pledge for a controlled inflow was blatantly violated, Israel could curtail some obligations of its own, such as financial compensation. Yet in order to prevent such a scenario, Israel would encourage and aid the expansion of Palestinian absorptive capabilities.[35]

A key component of the proposal would be an Israeli "statement of acknowledgment." While this would obviously be of major psychological-historical importance to Palestinians, it would simultaneously pose a great challenge to Israelis, whose historical narrative largely holds that the Arab side bears culpability and responsibility for the Palestinian refugee problem. The Israeli Compromise Solution suggests the following formulation:

1. Israel recognizes that the historical process culminating in the 1948 war generated a refugee problem that caused great suffering to the Palestinian people. As Israel, the Arab countries, and the Palestinians all participated in this historical process, all parties share, at least to some extent, the responsibility for the injustices of the past and for the plight of the Palestinians. Rectification of that plight by all the parties is a central goal of the Arab-Israeli peace process.
2. The Palestinians, having received financial compensation within the context of a settlement of Israeli and Palestinian refugee claims, consider this to satisfy their grievance and renounce any claim to exercise the *right of return* to the State of Israel.
3. Israel will continue its unilateral program of Palestinian family reunifications.

---

34 Ibid.
35 Ibid.

4. The Palestinian state will undertake, with Arab and international aid, the rehabilitation of the 1948 refugees, with the aim of resolving the refugee problem on Arab territory, as a condition for a stable Israeli-Palestinian peace.

5. The Arab host countries where Palestinian refugees reside recognize the right of those refugees to remain in the country, without forfeiting Palestinian citizenship.

6. This series of acts and understandings on the part of Israel and the Palestinian state are part and parcel of the overall Arab-Israeli peace process.[36]

Let us next examine the implications of this proposal on both Israelis and Palestinians.

13.3.2 Analysis of the Proposal

Implications for the Israelis

Obviously this solution offers several advantages to the Israeli side: it closes the file on the entire refugee question, puts an end to refugee status, and dissolves UNRWA. Most importantly, it poses no existential or demographic threat to Israel, from whose perspective the settlement is both final and consistent with its self-image. It is furthermore favourable for Israel that compensation funds will be paid out collectively only and that Jewish refugees from Arab countries will be compensated. The proposed involvement of the international community in the compensation issue suggests that Israel could more easily recruit funds for this undertaking and link it to international aid for the Palestinians.

On the other hand, unlike for the Palestinians, the proposed removal of operational linkage with the Arab States' compensation to Jewish refugees would be disadvantageous for Israel, as it would lose manoeuvring space that could have balanced the claims regarding Jewish and Palestinian refugees respectively. In addition, the statement of acknowledgment will certainly be met with rejection in parts of the Israeli public. Finally, accepting an international role in determining

---

36 Ibid.

the scope of compensation might invite intolerable pressures on Israel's financial capabilities.

However, the Israeli Compromise Solution would overall be a favourable solution for Israel, involving – if at all – not more than a tiny return of Palestinian refugees into Israel, and in addition to Israel being mostly exempt from having to accept historical responsibility.

Implications for the Palestinians

The proposal offers Palestinians the advantage that the inflow of refugees to the new state is solely dependent upon that state's own considerations, since the Israeli Compromise Solution operationally de-links the Jewish and Palestinian refugee issues, thereby denying the Arab states leverage over the Palestinian issue.

Yet the proposal also denies the Palestinians what is most crucial to them: an Israeli recognition of the *right of return*. A potential return to Israel proper is formulated in highly vague terms: Israel "may" accept an unnamed number of Palestinian refugees in the framework of family reunifications. The concept of Israel offering unilateral family reunification as the sole means of return to Israel proper would be unacceptable for Palestinians. They want the return of Palestinian refugees to be acknowledged as such, running under the title of *right of return* and not some by-pass formulation such as "family reunifications" or "humanitarian gesture." It is also objectionable for Palestinians to accept a linkage, however generalized, between compensation paid by Arab states to Jewish refugees and Israeli compensation to Palestinian refugees. Finally, Palestinians would probably see a disadvantage from the moral standpoint in the definition of Israeli compensation as collective rather than personal.[37]

Palestinians, thus, are not likely to accept the Israeli Compromise Solution in its present form.

13.3.3 The Proposal's Relevance

As discussed earlier, the inherent link of the Israeli Compromise Solution to the issue of Jewish refugees from Arab countries has become

---

37 Ibid.

obsolete, after Israelis and Palestinians agreed in Taba that this was not a subject of Palestinian concern, but rather a bilateral issue between Israel and the relevant Arab states.

While the proposal offers several concepts to Israel's advantage, it is overall much less favourable regarding Palestinian demands and needs. The proposal's key disadvantage for Palestinians is that Israel does not recognize the *right of return*. Many Palestinians would not consider an Israeli recognition that "the historical process culminating in the 1948 war ...caused great suffering" to be an achievement that justifies any significant concessions. This, on the other hand, might cause an Israeli leader to regard even such modest acknowledgment of Palestinian suffering as not being worth the risk, as any Israeli acknowledgment of guilt bears the risk of strong domestic opposition. Therefore, without a prospective Palestinian concession in return, Israel is not likely to risk internal frictions over the issue of responsibility and guilt.

Yet due to the above elaborated shortcomings regarding the Palestinian demands, most Palestinians would not accept the Israeli Compromise Solution; the decisive factor for Palestinian rejection would not be so much the fact that practically no refugees would be allowed to return to Israel but rather the lack of Israeli recognition of the *right of return* and of an unequivocal Israeli acknowledgment of responsibility. Therefore, also this proposal offers neither a complete nor a realistic solution to the Palestinian refugee question, but could at most serve a basis for further negotiations.

13.4 The Gush Shalom Proposal

In May 2001, the Israeli peace movement Gush Shalom published a proposal of its own to end the Israeli-Palestinian conflict.[38] While not reaching the extent of the Geneva Initiative, a fair portion of the Gush Shalom proposal is nevertheless dedicated to a proposed solution of the Palestinian refugee question.

---

38   See http://gush-shalom.org/archives/altpeace.html.

13.4.1   The Essence of the Proposal

Section 11 of the Gush Shalom peace proposal refers to the question of Palestinian refugees:

> Both parties agree that the human tragedy of the Palestinians must be resolved by a moral, just, practicable and agreed-upon solution that takes into consideration the character and essential needs of the two states.
>
> Israel acknowledges its share [sic] of responsibility for the creation of this tragedy during the course of the wars of 1948 and 1967. Both parties will establish a "truth commission" of historians – Israeli, Palestinian and international – that will examine in depth the precise causes that lead to the creation of the problem, and will issue an objective conclusive report within three years. This report will be incorporated into the school curriculum of both nations.
>
> Israel acknowledges the *principle* of the Right of Return, as a basic human right [emphasis added by the author].
>
> According to this right, each refugee will be given the choice between compensation and permanent settlement in another country, return to the State of Palestine, or return to Israeli territory, according to the following principles:
>
> (1) In order to heal the historical wound and as an act of justice, Israel will allow the return into its territory of an appropriate number of refugees, taking into consideration its national character and keeping a reasonable demographic balance. Both parties through negotiation will determine the number of refugees who will return as well as the criteria and priorities of the allocation of return permits. Returnees will be allowed back under a reasonable annual quota within a time-limit not exceeding 10 years.
>
> (2) A generous level of compensation will be determined for each refugee for property that remained in Israel, loss of opportunities, etc. The compensation will be paid by an international fund. Israel will contribute an appropriate portion to this fund, according to the assessment of the value of property remaining in Israel.
>
> (3) With the establishment of the State of Palestine, and according to its laws, each refugee who so desires will be accorded Palestinian citizenship, which will grant him/her the *right of return to the territory of the State of Palestine* [emphasis added by the author]. The international fund will enable the Palestinian state to absorb these refugees, as well as refugees currently residing in the West Bank and Gaza Strip, by providing suitable housing and employment opportunities.[39]

---

39   Ibid.

13.4.2 Analysis of the Proposal

Implications for the Israelis

The Gush Shalom proposal addresses several of Israel's key concerns. It starts by taking "into consideration the character and essential needs of the two states," an obvious reference to Israel's repeatedly expressed emphasis on having to preserve its Jewish character. This notion is spelled out unambiguously in the middle of the proposal, where a limited return of Palestinian refugees to Israel is advocated, "taking into consideration its national character and keeping a reasonable demographic balance." In other words, a two-state solution allowing Israel to retain its Jewish majority is envisaged.

Israel would need to envisage "its share of responsibility" for the creation of the Palestinian refugee problem, which is termed a tragedy. Such formulation stipulates that not all of the responsibility is to be found on Israel's side and that Israel would merely acknowledge its own part. Yet it might appear awkward to many Israelis having to concede an official formulation of responsibility – and thereby also acknowledging guilt – while the Palestinians are not required to do so; Israelis would object that it was the refusal of the Arab states to accept the U.N. partition plan and the subsequent declaration of war against Israel which laid the groundwork for the refugee problem. The precise allocation of guilt is to be undertaken by a commission of historians – an endeavour which might take forever, as no time limit is set.

A crucial point of the Gush Shalom proposal is the provision that "Israel acknowledges the principle of the Right of Return, as a basic human right." This formulation is interesting in several aspects. First, Israel would not *recognize* the *right of return* but merely *acknowledge* it; significantly, an acknowledgment is less binding and declaratory than an official recognition of the right. Second, although the *right of return* to be acknowledged by Israel is referred to as a "basic human right," it carefully avoided adding a specification like "to the State of Israel." Towards the end of the section on refugees, the proposal even explicitly refers to "the right of return to the territory of the State of Palestine." In other words, while "acknowledging" the *right of return* as "a basic human right," the proposal does not unequivocally include the return to Israeli territory to be part of this right. On the contrary, the limited applicability of that right is extensively elaborated.

In fact, Palestinian refugees returning to Israel are to be part of the proposed solution, yet not as an integral element of the *right of return*, but rather as a specific gesture "to heal the historical wound and as an act of justice." Return to Israel is not to be unlimited but merely to be granted to "an appropriate number of refugees," specifically after taking into consideration Israeli demographic concerns. Such "appropriate number" is as vague as the subsequently suggested "reasonable" annual quota of Palestinian refugees, which are to return to Israel within ten years. The concrete and binding number of refugees allowed to return to Israel is to be agreed upon in future Israeli-Palestinian negotiations. Thus, while the proposal suggests some refugee return to the State of Israel, that return is formulated highly unspecifically and would remain subject to Israeli-Palestinian negotiations – thereby granting Israel factual veto power.

Therefore, the proposal's overall essence is favourable for Israel, as the suggested solution prevents a potential massive inflow of Palestinian refugees by making the precise number of returnees conditional upon Israeli approval. Not only are Israeli demographic fears considered, but also the Jewish character of Israel is recognized. Setting a time limit "not exceeding ten years" after which no more refugee return would be possible safeguards Israel from return-claims beyond that date. Compensation to Palestinian refugees will not be paid by Israel alone, but by an international fund to which Israel "will contribute an appropriate portion" – again a formulation which does not bind Israel but rather leaves it room for generous interpretation. So does the provision calling upon Israel to acknowledge "its share of responsibility."

Implications for the Palestinians

The fact that Israel would have to acknowledge "its share of responsibility" implies that Palestinians, on their side, would have to accept some responsibility of their own. Most likely, Palestinians would be expected by Israel to acknowledge that the decision not to accept the U.N. resolution calling for a partition of mandated Palestine and subsequently going to war against their Jewish neighbours was erroneous. Yet such statement would run diametrically against the Palestinian self-perception and narrative, seeing itself as a mere victim with all of the responsibility being on Israel's side. However, it is also conceivable that the parties could agree that only Israel was to acknowledge some form of responsibility in order to satisfy Palestinian demands for such, while omitting any reference to the Palestinians' share of responsibility. Such scenario would be the one most advantageous for Palestinians.

Moreover, the fact that historical evidence for Israel's role in the refugee problem would be taught in Israeli schools would doubtlessly upgrade Palestinian support for the proposal. Yet most importantly, the Gush Shalom proposal offers Palestinians an Israeli acknowledgment of the principle of the *right of return* as a basic human right, in addition to the right for compensation and some refugee return – the three elements which form the Palestinian core demands. Obviously, as discussed above, the proposal is formulated in vague terms and leaves considerable room for interpretation. Nevertheless, Israel would be required to address issues of high importance for Palestinians; the final formulation – as seen in the previous chapter regarding German-Israeli negotiations after World War II – will in any event be the result of a compromise which, despite largely unsubstantial language, can prove to be satisfactory to both sides.

Thus Palestinians would receive an Israeli partial recognition of the *right of return*, yet only to a certain extent. Although some refugee return would be granted, it would not be unlimited. The total number and yearly quotas would have to be negotiated with Israel. Palestinians, therefore, would have to compromise both regarding a full recognition of the *right of return* as well as on the number of actual return. Nevertheless, of course, granted that all other final status issues find a mutually satisfactory solution, the Gush Shalom proposal does have the potential to largely fulfil Palestinian expectations and demands.

13.4.3 The Proposal's Relevance

A striking weakness of the Gush Shalom peace proposal lies in its vagueness: while it does provide some rough formula (a partial Israeli admission of responsibility along with a principled acknowledgment of the *right of return*), its details and extent still need to be agreed upon by the two parties. In other words, the success of the proposal is dependent upon Israelis and Palestinians being able to find a common denominator. Obviously, vague terminology can also be an advantage, namely to establish so-called "constructive ambiguity." This, however, did not work in the case of Oslo, where vague provisions and the postponement of difficult issues were central reasons for the process' overall failure. The question arises, thus, whether the idea of "constructive ambiguity" fits the dynamics and needs of Israeli-Palestinian negotiations, or whether only precise and unequivocal formulations stand the chance of providing a durable agreement.

Overall, the Gush Shalom proposal provides a good and largely creative basis for future Israeli-Palestinian negotiations. Yet it can only succeed on the condition that the two parties manage to find and agree upon a detailed formulation regarding the precise terms of implementation.

Not to be ignored is the fact that the Gush Shalom proposal is characterized by the same logical contradiction of terms as the Geneva Initiative: on the one hand, refugees are to be given the free choice whether or not they would like to return into Israeli territory. Yet, on the other hand, only a limited number of refugees would be allowed to exercise such choice. Thus again, there would be a collision between the refugees' free will and Israel's willingness (and capability) to absorb them. The following – and last – proposal is the only one existing to date which provides both partial Israeli recognition of the *right of return* and also proposes a form to implement it in a manner logically consistent with the rest of the proposal.

13.5 The Ayalon-Nusseibeh Proposal

On 27 July 2002, retired navy admiral and former head of Israel's internal security service, Ami Ayalon, and the Palestinian professor and president of Al-Quds University, Sari Nusseibeh, published a peace proposal consisting of six points – the fourth referring to the question of Palestinian refugees.[40] Although its suggestions are purely practical, the proposal was classified as an integrated solution because (unlike, for example, the Geneva Initiative) it does mention the *right of return*, which can be regarded as an implicit recognition of it, thereby also including a principled element.

---

40 See the Ayalon-Nusseibeh Statement of Principles at www.mifkad.org.il/en/principles.asp.

13.5.1 The Essence of the Proposal

The Ayalon-Nusseibeh proposal is short and concise, resting firmly on the principle of a two-state solution. Borders shall be agreed upon the basis of the 1967 lines. Jerusalem is to be an open city and the capital of two states, with the Arab neighbourhoods coming under Palestinian sovereignty and Jewish neighbourhoods under Israeli sovereignty. The Palestinian state is to be demilitarised, the international community guaranteeing its security and independence. Finally, after the implementation of the principles outlined in the Ayalon-Nusseibeh proposal, both parties would declare the end of the conflict.

With regard to the refugee question, the proposal's provision is blunt and unambiguous, and may therefore have greater appeal than a detailed plan:

> 4. Right of return: Recognizing the suffering and the plight of the Palestinian refugees, the international community, Israel, and the Palestinian State will initiate and contribute to an international fund to compensate them.
> – Palestinian refugees will return only to the State of Palestine; Jews will return only to the State of Israel.
> – The international community will offer to compensate toward bettering the lot of those refugees willing to remain in their present country of residence, or who wish to immigrate to third-party countries.

As opposed to the Geneva Initiative, the Ayalon-Nusseibeh proposal makes no reference to UNGAR 194.

13.5.2 Analysis of the Proposal

Implications for the Israelis

The Ayalon-Nusseibeh proposal sends an important message to the Israelis: Palestinians do not want to drown Israel in a sea of refugees. This is to counter Israeli fears that earlier Arab military plans to drive the Israelis into the sea might have been replaced by demographic means. The proposal rules out any refugee return to Israel and thereby neutralizes Israel's demographic fears.

Not only would Israel be exempt from having to absorb Palestinian refugees; the Ayalon-Nusseibeh proposal does not oblige Israel to acknowledge any responsibility for having created the refugee problem either. Israel, along with the international community and the

Palestinian state, would merely recognize "the suffering and the plight of the Palestinian refugees." These three actors are also to "initiate and contribute to an international fund" to compensate the Palestinian refugees. This is a vague formulation effectively placing little to no obligation on Israel's shoulders, since neither a financial amount nor a time period for the proposed payment is mentioned. The provision that "Jews will return only to the State of Israel" in itself is meaningless, since hardly any Jew ardently yearns to immigrate to a Palestinian state, and only comes as a symbolic counterweight to the proposal's core statement, namely that "Palestinian refugees will return only to the State of Palestine."

In short, the Ayalon-Nusseibeh proposal gives Israel what is desires most: an assurance that no Palestinian refugees will return to Israel, along with the absence of any admission of responsibility and guilt. It therefore does not come as a surprise that the proposal's suggested formula regarding refugees encounters solid acceptance among Israelis. Reasons for the low Israeli support of the overall Ayalon-Nusseibeh text are not to be found in its ideas regarding refugees, but rather in the intended Israeli withdrawal to 1967 borders and the factual division of Jerusalem.

Implications for the Palestinians

On the Palestinian side, the situation presents itself diametrically opposed to that in Israel: similar to the Geneva Initiative, a majority of Palestinians welcome the overall suggestions of the Ayalon-Nusseibeh text, yet reject its formula regarding refugees.

For Palestinians, the proposal presented by Ayalon and Nusseibeh is equivalent to a blanket waiver of the *right of return*. It is primarily for this reason that the proposal did not only receive very little support from Palestinians, but also Nusseibeh's reputation and his already limited support among Palestinians significantly dropped after the publication of the proposal.[41] However, although the Ayalon-Nusseibeh proposal

---

41 Galia Golan, "Plans for Israeli-Palestinian Peace: From Beirut to Geneva," *Middle East Policy*, Vol. XI, No. 1, Spring 2004, pp. 44–45.

has not attracted the masses of Palestinians, a surprising number of prominent Fatah leaders nevertheless stated their support.[42]

Nusseibeh countered Palestinian critics with the claim that only a Palestinian waiver of the *right of return* into Israel proper will lead to a solution of the conflict. He repeatedly charged the Palestinian political and intellectual leadership of being weak and not explaining the Palestinians what can realistically be attained.[43]

Maybe the proposal's most important impact was the resulting public debate among Palestinians regarding the *right of return*. Since the publication of the Ayalon-Nusseibeh text, discussions have taken place in Palestinian newspapers, inside political parties and in the refugee camps, even assuming the form of an exchange of communiqués between Fatah's youth organization (supporting the proposal) and another faction in Fatah (reiterating the traditional position of the Palestinian leadership).[44]

Obviously, the proposal's provision that no refugee at all would return to Israel signifies the complete opposite of the maximalist Palestinian demand that any refugee wishing to return needs to be given the choice of doing so. Yet Palestinian critique of the Ayalon-Nusseibeh proposal has not so much focused on the fact that the *right of return* was not going to be implemented to Israel, but rather that Israel does not have to clearly and unequivocally recognize that right in principle, and that Israel would not be required to offer an admission of responsibility or to express some form of apology. By reducing it to the mere phrase "Palestinian refugees will return only to the State of Palestine," the

---

42 Among them Col. Salah Jedid, a senior officer in the General Intelligence Service, Col. Ahmed Salhub, from the Preventive Security Forces in Hebron, and Hamadan Sa'ifan, a senior Fatah leader from the northern West Bank. Ami Makbul, who replaced Marwan Barghouti as head of Fatah's West Bank steering committee, is another key figure who has expressed support for the Ayalon-Nusseibeh document. Most of these leaders are unknown to Israel or to the West in general, but they have strong influence within Fatah institutions. See Arnon Regular, "Fatah Leaders Give their Backing to Nusseibeh and Ayalon's Plan for 'Two States for Two Peoples'," *Haaretz*, 19 March 2003.

43 See the interview with Nusseibeh in *NZZ am Sonntag*, 23 November 2003.

44 Sari Hanafi, "Opening the Debate on the Right of Return," *War Without Borders*, Middle East Report 222, Spring 2002, at www.prrn.org.

right of return is factually given up both practically *and* in principle. Thus while Palestinians realize that the *right of return* cannot possibly be fully implemented, they nevertheless want to have it acknowledged on a principled bases, along with some Israeli acknowledgment of responsibility. The Ayalon-Nusseibeh proposal, therefore, falls short of satisfying Palestinians both on a practical and on a principled level.

13.5.3   The Proposal's Relevance

Unlike the Geneva Initiative, the Ayalon-Nusseibeh proposal does not resile from mentioning the *right of return*; however, it does not explicitly recognize that right either. The term "right of return" appears solely as the title of the proposal's fourth point and is not further mentioned in the subsequent lines describing a mechanism for return. Nevertheless, the Ayalon-Nusseibeh text is logically consistent and does not fall into the pitfall of contradicting itself (see, e.g., the Geneva Initiative or the Gush Shalom proposal) by offering Palestinian refugees a free choice as to whether or not they would like to return to Israel, while simultaneously limiting the amount of possible refugee return to Israel and making it conditional upon Israel's sovereign discretion. The Ayalon-Nusseibeh proposal rests on the simple basis that in exchange for Israel's withdrawal to the 1967 borders it closes the file of 1948 by letting Palestinians refugees return "only to the State of Palestine."[45]

So far, support for the proposal has not been high on either the Israeli or the Palestinian side.[46] Nusseibeh was correct when he bluntly stated that as long as Palestinians insist on a full implementation of

---

45   Other prominent supporters of the idea of a *"right of return* only to the Palestinian state" are Henry Siegman (see, e.g., his "Sharon and the Future of Palestine," *The New York Review of Books*, Vol. 51, No. 19, 2 December 2004, at www.nybooks.com) and Zbigniew Brzezinski (see his open-ed "A grand U.S.-European Mideast strategy" *International Herald Tribune*, 26 October 2004); Khalil Shikaki (see his "The Principle Facets of the Refugee Problem," *Palestine-Israel Journal*, Vol. 9, No. 3, 2002, p. 93.

46   By July 2006, 254,391 Israelis and 161,000 Palestinians have signed the proposal. See www.mifkad.org.il. Israeli support for the Ayalon-Nusseibeh proposal increased after the publication of the Geneva Initiative and its provisions regarding prospective refugee return to Israel.

the *right of return*, there will not be a Palestinian state.[47] Palestinians will certainly have to compromise on their maximalist claim that all refugees be allowed to return to Israel; as discussed earlier, Palestinians are aware of the need to compromise and are willing to do so. Yet the low support the Ayalon-Nusseibeh proposal has generated among Palestinians demonstrates that Palestinians are not willing to compromise the *right of return* in the manner suggested by Ayalon and Nusseibeh. Palestinians are clearly bothered by the absence of an even symbolic Israeli recognition of the *right of return*, as well as by the absence of some form of Israeli apology and acknowledgment of responsibility.

The relatively low support from Israel's side for the proposal certainly does not lie in its provisions regarding refugees. In fact, the Ayalon-Nusseibeh proposal fully meets Israel's long defended stance regarding refugees: no return to Israel, no formal acknowledgment of the *right of return*, and no acknowledgment of historical responsibility. Also regarding compensation payments, Israel is not to contribute the bulk but can rather refer to the international community being responsible for that part. There are thus other elements of the Ayalon-Nusseibeh text, particularly Jerusalem and borders, which do not appeal to a significant number of Israelis.

Therefore, the Ayalon-Nusseibeh proposal in its present form is not an adequate formula to solve the question of Palestinian refugees as – while being extremely attractive for Israel – it is not acceptable for Palestinians. The proposal's concise formulation certainly well serves the principle of simplicity, yet in order to form the basis for a permanent Israeli-Palestinian agreement it would need to be further elaborated. It would also be commendable to introduce some form of a time table in order to make the later implementation more predictable and binding for both parties. Yet one positive aspect of the proposal is that it can certainly serve as a model for any successful Israeli-Palestinian agreement regarding refugees in that it is future-orientated and intends to draw a final line under the past.

***

---

47   See the interview with *Der Spiegel*, No. 3, 2002.

This fourth and final part has first analysed purely practical approaches, followed by purely principled approaches, and has concluded with integrated solutions combining both practical and principled elements. The analysis and evaluation of each proposal has demonstrated that those formulas relying only on practical elements are insufficient, since the Palestinians are unlikely to accept a solution which does not include some reference to the *right of return* and some Israeli position towards its role in the creation of the refugee problem. The principled proposals discussed do accept those issues left out by the practical approaches, yet without any practical provisions they do not suffice to represent a mutually accepted solution on the question of Palestinian refugees. Therefore, the approach of the integrated solutions is the only possible way to bring the refugee problem – and with it most likely the entire Israeli-Palestinian conflict – to an end.

The fourth part has examined five different existing integrated solutions and evaluated the advantages and disadvantages of each. While some good and precious ideas have been raised in the different proposals, each one was demonstrated to also have its shortcomings. The following chapter shall therefore have two goals: first, it shall present a summary of the preceding four parts. Second, based on those findings, an attempt shall be made to present a guideline for future Israeli-Palestinian negotiations – whenever they will resume – necessary for finding a successful formula to end the refugee question.

Conclusions

14.1 Summary

14.1.1 Historical Background

In order to understand the present dimensions of the Palestinian refugee question, one needs to trace its historical roots. The research therefore started with a review of the events which from 1947 to 1948, and to a smaller extent also in 1967, led to the creation of the Palestinian refugee problem. It was shown that the reasons for the exodus were multi-layered and complex. The course of events was divided into four stages, the first two roughly stretching from the U.N. partition plan in 1947 to the declaration of the State of Israel in May 1948 and the last two ending in July and November 1948, respectively.

The exodus was caused by a combination of civilian flight from a war zone, active expulsion by Jewish and later Israeli troops, orders from Arab officials and commanders to leave, and the lack of an efficient Palestinian leadership. Increasing economic problems and the collapse of law and order were coupled with a fear of Jewish attacks and atrocities. Together with the lack of help from the Arab world and the Arab Higher Committee, the overall situation resulted in a Palestinian feeling of impotence and abandonment. Such a situation on the ground enabled the final and decisive catalyst to flight in most places, namely either attacks by Jewish militias and the IDF, respectively, or Arab Palestinian fear of such attack being imminent.

In the period from 1947 to 1948 more than 700,000 Palestinians became refugees. Around two thirds of them remained within the territory of mandated Palestine, mainly in the West Bank and the Gaza Strip, while one third left for surrounding countries. Both the refugees and the host countries assumed the situation to be temporary; yet in the absence of a political solution the refugees were not able to return and the situation was further amplified in 1967, when another 300,000 Palestinians from the West Bank and Gaza fled (primarily to Jordan).

Unlike other refugees, the Palestinian refugees enjoy a special status. While most refugees worldwide are the concern of the UNHCR,

Palestinian refugees fall under UNRWA, which was established in 1949 by the U.N. General Assembly specifically to deal with the Palestinian problem. The term "Palestinian refugee" as used by UNRWA was never formally defined by the U.N., and the definition used in practice evolved independently of the UNHCR's 1951 definition of a refugee. It is striking that in the UNHCR's definition there is no mention of descendents and that refugee status ceases to apply to a person who has acquired a new nationality and enjoys the protection of the country of his new nationality. Thus, under such definition, the number of Palestinians qualifying for refugee status would be well below half a million; however, an Arab veto excluded the Palestinians from that definition. Instead, UNRWA has been applying an extremely broad definition of a Palestinian refugee, qualifying any persons who resided in Palestine between June 1946 and May 1948 and their descendents in the male line. Consequently, the number of Palestinian refugees is constantly increasing.

Besides, in order to heighten the pressure regarding a final arrangement on both Israel and the Arab host countries, the Palestinian refugees adopted the strategy of natural reproduction. As a result, the overall Palestinian population has massively grown, UNRWA counting around 4.2 million Palestinian refugees in its area of operation, i.e. West Bank, Gaza Strip, Jordan, Syria, and Lebanon, and the worldwide Palestinian population is estimated to number around eight millions.

Jordan presently counts the largest population of Palestinian refugees, reaching 1.7 millions. Palestinians form two thirds of Jordan's overall population and are generally endowed with the same rights as the country's other citizens. Fewer than one in eight Palestinian refugees in Jordan lives in a refugee camp, and most camps have effectively become urban neighbourhoods.

The second largest concentration of Palestinian refugees is found in the Gaza Strip, almost reaching one million, half of them living in refugee camps, as well as in the West Bank, numbering almost 700,000, with a quarter of them living in refugee camps. Those refugees are stateless and live in a combination of highly limited Palestinian autonomy and Israeli occupation. Their economic situation has radically deteriorated in the years following the outbreak of the second intifada in 2000.

Also, the Palestinian refugees in Syria, numbering close to 420,000 and a quarter of them living in refugee camps, are stateless. However, they have largely free access to the country's labour market and social services. Their situation is overall comparable to that of the rest of the Syrian population.

The situation is radically different in Lebanon which is in a constant struggle to harmonize its fragile sectarian balance; Palestinians are considered a disruptive element which need to be removed in the long run. Palestinians in Lebanon face numerous restrictions of employment, are not allowed to own real estate, and are limited in their freedom of movement. Accordingly, a lot of them are living in desolate conditions in overcrowded refugee camps. A great number have therefore left the country, and their actual number in Lebanon, contrary to UNRWA's official number of 400,000, amounts to probably less than 200,000.

14.1.2   The Legal Background of the *Right of Return*

One cannot address the issue of Palestinian refugees without facing the term *right of return*. Since the *right of return* is primarily a legal concept, the analysis of the Palestinian refugee question requires also an examination of the legal implications of the *right of return*. The existence of such right, however, is highly contested. While Israelis deny that there is an actual legal right for Palestinian refugees to return, Palestinians see such right to be an integral part of international law.

A discussion of the different views Israelis and Palestinians, respectively, have on the *right of return* has revealed two seemingly irreconcilable positions. On the one hand, for most Israelis the *right of return* means nothing less than four million refugees at Israel's doorstep; yet for reasons of demography and the Jewish identity of the state, a massive return of Palestinian refugees to Israel is out of the question for the vast majority of Israelis. While prior to the second intifada there seemed to be an Israeli readiness to accept a limited number of refugees, yet at present, after continuous years of violence, that readiness has completely disappeared.

For the Palestinians, on the other hand, the *right of return* has been their central claim on the refugee issue since 1948. While most Israelis reduce the refugee problem to a humanitarian matter, i.e. destitute people living in refugee camps which need to be resettled and provided permanent residence, Palestinians view the matter quite differently. They emphasize the political nature of the problem, as well as the need for principled recognition by Israel of its responsibility for the events of 1948 and the fate that consequently befell the Palestinians. The notion of "justice" is crucial to Palestinian claims; they put strong emphasis on getting recognition for having experienced a grave historical wrong-doing. Palestinians further stress the notion of "choice," referring to the personal choice each refugee needs to have as to whether he wants to return or not.

However, it is important to stress that the majority of Palestinians realize that Israel will not under any circumstances agree to an unlimited *right of return*. A demand for such, therefore, is unrealistic; some Palestinians call for a distinction between *attainable* as opposed to *absolute justice* to be made. In fact, most Palestinian alternatives to an unconditional *right of return* do insist that Israel recognizes the principle of the *right of return* and compensation, yet simultaneously offer a willingness to negotiate the specific modalities of return. In other words, while demanding an Israeli recognition is part of the Palestinian political agenda, flooding Israel with refugees is not.

Yet does a *right of return* legally exist? The question was traced by examining the two accepted sources of international law, namely an *international treaty* to which Israel is a party or a rule of *customary international law*.

Regarding an *international treaty*, supporters of the *right of return* cite the "Convention on the Elimination of All Forms of Racial Discrimination," Article 5–(d) (ii), stating "the right to leave any country, including one's own, and to return to one's country." They also refer to the 1966 "International Covenant on Civil and Political Rights," in which Article 12(4) states that "No one shall be arbitrarily deprived of the right to enter his own country." Supporters of the Israeli position have argued the definition of "one's own country" and claimed that only citizens can be considered to belong to that country. They also argued that the scope of the *right of return* was of crucial importance: while it might be granted to the individual it was not formulated to apply for masses of people. Supporters of the *right of return*, on the other hand, dispute that view and counter that a mass of people is nothing but an accumulation of individuals who all have the right to return to their place of origin.

As to *customary law*, supporters of the *right of return* claim that the Universal Declaration of Human Rights, which allows each person the return to his country, is a major source of customary rule. This is countered by the claim that the Universal Declaration has a doubtful character as a source of international law. The primary source of international law for supporters of the *right of return* to make their case remains UNGAR 194. Palestinians see it as a reflection of customary international law requiring repatriation for wartime displacement. Israel, on the other hand, based on the formulation of UNGAR 194 ("should"), refers to it as a mere request. In addition, Israel denies UNGAR 194 any binding character as it is passed by the U.N. General Assembly, while only the Security Council has the authority to pass binding resolutions. Finally, as the section on refugees is but a small part of UNGAR 194, its acceptance would also imply the adoption of the other stipulations, such as an internationalisation of Jerusalem – a demand neither Israelis nor Palestinians would easily support.

It is also essential to refer to state practice regarding refugee return. The late twentieth century has witnessed great efforts to allow refugee return; Bosnia and Herzegovina probably being the prime example. Also the practice of what was termed "ethnic cleansing" became internationally unacceptable after the Yugoslavian civil war in the 1990s. However, the situation was different at the beginning of the twentieth century, when forced resettlement and exchange of ethnically or religiously defined populations did serve as an accepted solution to ethnic conflicts and were considered a legal measure to promote peace and stability.

There were population exchanges involving Bulgaria, Greece, and Turkey in 1919, inspiring another large wave of refugees after the Greek-Turkish War in 1922. After the end of the Second World War, millions of Germans were transferred from Poland and Czechoslovakia. An additional policy of population transfer was adopted in 1947 to settle the dispute between Hindus and Muslims in British India, resulting in the mass relocation of millions. The same year saw the beginning of the Palestinian refugee problem.

State practice has changed since then. The mass transfer of populations that took place during the Turkish invasion of Cyprus in 1974 was condemned by the international community. So were the atrocities committed in the Yugoslavian civil war. Thus, while expulsions were deemed acceptable if not legal in the first half of the twentieth century, they are now rejected as illegal. The crucial question nowadays, therefore, relates to the appropriate reaction to the transfer.

There are two approaches: one dealing with immediate response, the other one focusing on late response to refugee problems. Regarding *immediate response*, the crucial precedent to support claims for a legal right to individual return can be found in the Dayton agreement of 1995 regarding Bosnia and Herzegovina, which states that all "refugees and displaced persons have the right freely to return to their homes of origin." This formulation was the resolution of the international community to undo the ethnic cleansing policy implemented in former Yugoslavia between 1991 and 1995. It is backed by an elaborate institutional apparatus that oversees the implementation of this policy. With the heavy involvement of this apparatus, refugees began a slow process of return to their homes.

This is still not the case in Cyprus, which serves as an example for a *late response*. Just as in the case of Palestinian refugees, there is one major difference between Cyprus and Bosnia-Herzegovina: time. While refugees in Bosnia were able to return in the immediate years following their displacement, the time frame of Cyprus' refugees stretches over more than thirty years, while in the case of the Palestinian refugees it is over more than half a century.

When U.N. Secretary General Kofi Annan in 2003 issued a plan, which was also endorsed by the Security Council, to solve the Cyprus conflict, he clearly stressed the need for taking into account that "the events in Cyprus happened 30 to 40 years ago," further acknowledging the "legitimate claims" of both the refugees and those who currently reside in their property. His compromise further envisioned a limited, rather than a full return and considered the demographic composition of Cyprus; no mention was made of a right to return. Although the plan was ultimately rejected by the Turkish side, it nevertheless reflects the U.N.'s reading of international law, namely that the lapse of time, as well as demography, are relevant considerations for negotiating governments, in addition to the premise that governments have the authority under international law to negotiate away individual rights in the context of a peace agreement.

Moreover, unlike in the case of Bosnia and Cyprus, the goal in the Israeli-Palestinian context is not to establish a heterogeneous society under the umbrella of one state, but rather to create two sovereign states for two peoples. On such grounds, the demand for an unconditional Palestinian *right of return* are put into perspective by the time lapse, the collision with rights of those living in the expellees' areas for more than fifty years, and the inherent contradiction to a two-state solution.

In sum, the examination of the legal aspects of the *right of return* demonstrated the difficulty of proving that such clear-cut right exists; on the other hand, one cannot refute international law granting some *right of return* to Palestinian refugees. A judge would be needed to decide such question, yet in international law there usually is no judge. Also the question of Palestinian refugees will not be decided in court, but in direct negotiations between the two parties. In other words, the debate over the *right of return* will be determined by politicians – not by lawyers. It is therefore essential to analyse the – although to date unsuccessful – political attempts undertaken so far to solve the question of Palestinian refugees.

14.1.3   Political Background

During the Cold War, there were no significant official Israeli-Palestinian negotiations and therefore the issue of Palestinian refugees was not addressed. The Oslo agreements signified a breakthrough, as for the first time official Israeli-Palestinian negotiations were held with the purpose of finding a peace settlement between the two peoples. The Oslo process classified the question of Palestinian refugees as a final status issue to be addressed only at the end of the process.

Before official negotiations on refugees began, two prominent representatives from the Israeli and Palestinian leadership, respectively, Abu Mazen and Beilin, worked out a proposal in 1995 that also offered a solution to the issue of Palestinian refugees. It included a mutual understanding to recognize each other's difficulties on the subject of the *right of return*, with neither side giving up its principled stand on the issue. Most of the item dealt with a compensation and rehabilitation mechanism, intended to ensure that in practice the *right of return* would be less attractive to the refugees than absorption either in their present home, or in a third country. While no refugee would return to Israeli territory, there would be no limitation on immigration to a Palestinian state. Yet due to the lack of support from several Israeli prime ministers and the chairman of the Palestinian Authority, the Beilin-Abu Mazen agreement was denied any success.

In 2000, the issue of refugees was fully addressed in official Israeli-Palestinian negotiations for the first time. After Israeli Prime Minister Barak's strategy of first reaching a separate peace agreement with Syria had failed, he decided to hammer out an agreement with the Palestinians. A secret preparatory meeting was held in Sweden in May 2000, yet a leak to the press ended these talks. The main showdown, however, was to follow in July, when the Israeli and the Palestinian leader gathered for a major summit in Camp David, with U.S. President Clinton acting as mediator.

The summit had come into being under rather unlucky circumstances. Although Barak had succeeded in persuading Clinton to support an Israeli-Palestinian high-level summit to solve all outstanding issues, the Palestinians had serious reservations, as they felt that the necessary groundwork needed for carrying out the ultimate round of negotiations to end the conflict had not yet been sufficiently laid out. Besides it was quite unrealistic to expect a century old conflict, which could not have been solved in the preceding seven years of Oslo, to be solved in the course of a fortnight. So it could not really come as a surprise that Camp David ended without producing the final agreement.

Yet at the beginning of the Camp David talks, there was still some hope. About one month before the summit, Arafat had signalled to Clinton willingness to compromise: "On the refugee issue, yes, there's Resolution 194, but we have to find a happy medium between the Israel's demographic worries and our own concerns."[1] On the first day of Camp David, Arafat opened by revealing to Clinton: "We want *the principle* of the right of return to be laid down, and afterward we can talk about the practical details of its implementation" [Emphasis added by the author]. This pragmatic approach was to counter American and Israeli fears that the Palestinians intended to flood Israel with a massive wave of Palestinian refugees. However, the only issue which the Palestinians were not ready to negotiate was some form of Israeli principled recognition of the *right of return*. This entailed, on the other hand, that the Palestinians would not agree to discuss practical solutions as long

---

1   Charles Enderlin, *Shattered Dreams: The Failure of the Peace Process in the Middle East, 1995–2002* (New York: Other Press, 2003), p. 164.

as the Israelis did not start by recognizing the principle of the *right of return* – the foundation for a vicious circle was laid.

Matters were further complicated by a deadlock on the issue of Jerusalem. In fact, the issue of Jerusalem took all other topics – foremost refugees – hostage and there would be no progress in any other field if the question of Jerusalem remained unsolved; which unfortunately it did. It is therefore wrong to state that Camp David failed over the issue of refugees; in fact, the issue of refugees could not be seriously addressed because of the deadlock over Jerusalem.

This meant in concrete terms that Israel at Camp David was neither willing to recognize the principle of the *right of return*, nor to accept any responsibility for having created the problem. The Israeli approach indeed did not derive from responsibility but was rather of a humanitarian nature, meaning that Israel was willing to further allow Palestinian family reunifications – as long as this occurred under the framework of a humanitarian Israeli gesture and not in any connection with the *right of return*. Israel further signalled readiness to participate in an international fund to compensate refugees, with Clinton assuring his support to raise the necessary financial means.

For Palestinians to accept the Israeli position would have signified a momentous compromise – a compromise they could not make: after the summit, several Palestinian negotiators disclosed they could not have afforded to make concessions on the refugee question before the other key issues – primarily Jerusalem – were resolved. In fact, there exist strong indications that Arafat had indeed been willing to accept a limited *right of return*, in all likelihood within the framework of "family reunification", so long as the Palestinians received recognition of that right and a viable state with Palestinian sovereignty over East Jerusalem and the Haram al-Sharif/Temple Mount. Yet far from offering Palestinians sovereignty over Haram al-Sharif/Temple Mount, Barak even insisted on Israeli sovereignty over the compound.

Despite its ending in failure, Camp David still offers two crucial lessons regarding the refugee issue. First, while Palestinians will not give up the demand for a principled recognition of the *right of return*, Israel will not agree to a massive return of refugees. Second, the core elements of a permanent settlement – refugees, Jerusalem, borders, and security – cannot be resolved in isolation, but rather in an overall package.

The failure of Camp David was soon followed by the outbreak of the second intifada. The rapidly rising blood toll made further negotiations increasingly difficult. Meanwhile, based on the experience of Camp David, Clinton presented in December 2000 what became known as the "Clinton Parameters." They were not the terms of a final deal, but guidelines for final accelerated negotiations which Clinton hoped could be concluded in the coming weeks; time pressure was at its height, as Clinton was to leave office in January 2001.

On the issue of refugees, the Clinton Parameters differed little from the ideas discussed at Camp David: the refugees would primarily return to the future Palestinian state. Refugees not moving there would have the right to choose between rehabilitation in their current places of residence, relocation to a third country, or return within the borders of Israel subject to that country's sovereign discretion. A new international mechanism would be set up to look after the rehabilitation of the refugees, to which Israel would contribute as part of its compensation to the refugees. Although reluctantly, both parties eventually accepted Clinton's parameters and agreed to continue peace negotiations.

The following – and to date last – round of official Israeli-Palestinian negotiations was held in January 2001 in the quiet seclusion of Taba. Despite the background of ever increasing violence and the pressure of impending Israeli elections which the present government was unlikely to survive, negotiations in Taba nevertheless became infinitely more productive than the preceding ones in Camp David. In fact, Israelis and Palestinians were never closer to an agreement on refugees than at Taba. Although the election victory of Ariel Sharon in Israel and the continued Palestinian intifada signified an end to any further Israeli-Palestinian negotiations – and along with it the Oslo process as a whole – a concrete outline of a possible solution to the refugee question had started to crystallize in Taba.

Accordingly, the Israeli delegation concluded in Taba that Israel would have to make three central contributions in order to enable an agreement on the question of refugees: first, a solemn declaration of sorrow regarding the Palestinian refugee problem, eventually coupled with an acceptance of some responsibility for its creation. Second, payment of reparations for property lost. Third, absorption of a proportion of the refugees. In addition, the Israeli delegates accepted the Palestinian objection that the issue of Jewish refugees from Arab countries was not an Israeli-Palestinian matter, but rather a bilateral one between Israel and the respective countries.

On the other side, the Palestinian delegates at Taba recognized that Israel could not agree to a full implementation of the *right of return*, since that would pose a demographic threat to the Jewish majority of the state. Consequently, a compromise started to develop, aiming primarily at the voluntary return of refugees into the future Palestinian state, with the alternative of full integration into their present host countries or absorption in a third country. Such mechanism was later elaborated to great detail in the Geneva Initiative – the unofficial continuation of Taba.

Yet while in Taba almost full agreement with respect to principles for resolving the Palestinian refugee problem was achieved, coupled with progress regarding formulation of a narrative which would by-pass a full Israeli recognition of the *right of return*, the Palestinians never indicated whether such formulation would substitute their claims for Israel to recognize the *right of return*.

Taba signified the end of official Israeli-Palestinian negotiations. Yet there were a number of private proposals and ideas regarding a solution of the Palestinian refugee question. They were listed and analysed in the fourth and last part of this research.

14.1.4 Proposals for Sustainable Solutions

The proposals were divided into three categories: practical, principled, and integrated. *Practical solutions* refer to ideas to end the refugees' existence as such, providing them with a permanent home via financial compensation and resettlement in either their present host countries or third countries. Formal questions such as whether to recognize the *right of return* or not were scrutinized in the chapter dealing with *principled solutions*. Finally, proposals synthesizing both practical and principled were examined in the chapter of *integrated solutions*.

Successful and durable solution to a refugee problem is a combination of three factors: voluntary repatriation, host country absorption, and third country resettlement, to be complemented by the right to claim restitution of property, and/or compensation for losses caused by the refugee-producing state. As the element of repatriation to Israel has been and continues to be the major stumbling block for an Israeli-

Palestinian agreement on refugees, this issue was deemed the most intractable one and special attention was devoted to it in this research. While an involvement of the international community will certainly help overcome issues like compensation, host country absorption, and third country resettlement, Israelis and Palestinians still need to find a formula which, on the one hand, satisfies the Palestinian demand regarding the *right of return,* and, on the other hand, does not contravene Israeli demographic concerns.

The attempt to find such a formula was initiated with the analysis of *practical solutions.* The first one was Abu Sitta's plan for a complete return of Palestinian refugees into Israel, which was deemed unrealistic as Israel could never agree to such endeavour.

The Citizenship/Residency Approach would also allow for a massive return of Palestinian refugees, yet their demographic impact on Israel would be softened by not granting them citizenship but mere residency. As a result they would not have any electoral power. Yet Israel would accept such approach only if the number of incoming refugees was somehow subject to its approval.

The 1948 Approach proposes to let only those Palestinians who were actually born in the territory of what became Israel to return. This would automatically reduce the number of refugees to return, plus since those people would mostly be well beyond child-bearing age, they would not pose any long-term demographic threat to Israel. Yet it is doubtful that Palestinians would accept such approach, especially if the returnees were not allowed to be accompanied by their families and children.

The most detailed proposal was provided by the Geneva Initiative. It suggested several options of return, Israel being one of them, provided that Israel gave its sovereign consent to each case of return. Yet Israel's sovereign right to deny entry into its territory would inevitably conflict with the refugees' apparent free choice for return. Coupled with the fact that the document does not mention the term *right of return* one single time made it unacceptable for most Palestinians; interestingly, also most Israeli critique of the Geneva Initiative focused on its provisions on refugees, fearing a disproportionate human influx.

An attempt to prevent a massive return of refugees to Israel was presented by the Internal Approach, which focuses on those refugees who became displaced within Israel. If allowed to return to their villages and places of origin, they would not in any way affect Israel's demographic composition as they already are living within Israel. The Internal Approach is not overly attractive to either Israel (it would have to reverse the strategies and policies applied towards the Arab minority since the establishment of the state) or the Palestinians (since only those already living in Israel – none of them residing in a refugee camp – would benefit from such approach). Yet the Internal Approach might be – at least partially – applied if negotiations were to reach a stage where a diplomatic compromise was needed.

Israel's Traditional Approach to the Palestinian refugee question was not to accept any *right of return* and consequently no refugee return into Israel. Accordingly, the refugee problem would have to be solved primarily by return to a Palestinian state, absorption in third countries, and the payment of compensation. Just as Abu Sitta's approach is unacceptable for Israelis, so is this formula unacceptable for Palestinians.

Finally, the last practical solution discussed was Agha and Malley's proposal for return into swapped areas. This idea is highly interesting as it would not only result in Israel being exempt from any refugee absorption, but in addition, Israel's overall Arab population would even decrease. The proposal's underlying idea is to settle Palestinian refugees in Arab populated areas within Israel, close to the border of the future Palestinian state, in order to subsequently transfer these areas along with their Arab inhabitants – Arab Israelis and returning Palestinian refugees alike – to the neighbouring Palestinian state. While it is already hard to imagine that the Palestinian Authority would accept such approach, it most definitely would not be tolerated by Israel's Arab citizens who could count on the support of Israel's legal system to prevent such transfer. While Agha's and Malley's eloquently formulated proposal represents an interesting intellectual exercise, it lacks any relevance to the situation on the ground.

The analysis of *principled solutions* began with Peled and Rouhana's Transitional Justice. Their approach singles out two major steps as being necessary for reconciliation: recognition and restitution. Recognition entails revealing the historical truth about the injustices committed and according the victims dignity and respect. Restitution is to be the primary form of according recognition to victims of historic injustice and would also represent some form of acknowledgment. The question of restitution automatically raises the issue of responsibility in that it requires identifying the actor responsible for the injustice; it further raises the question whether the present generation, or immigrants who arrive after the injustice had been committed, can be held accountable for the actions of their predecessors.

Applied to the *right of return*, Peled and Rouhana's Transitional Justice suggests separating the *right of return*, which is referred to as non-negotiable for the Palestinians, from the means and ways of realizing that right in practice. While the latter would have to be determined by Israeli-Palestinian negotiations which are not part of Transitional Justice, such negotiations would ideally be enabled by it. The logic goes that if Israel was to recognize the *right* to return, this would satisfy an essential Palestinian demand and would enable negotiations regarding the means of implementing the *right of return* in a way that would take Israeli concerns and interests into account.

Thus Peled and Rouhana's Transitional Justice takes the right approach of separating the recognition of the *right of return* from its actual implementation. In fact, an initial recognition of the right might be the vital precondition for talks regarding its implementation to begin at all. However, the fact that Transitional Justice does not involve any practical consequences reduces it to – at best – merely a platform on which an agreement on actual refugee return could be eventually worked out. In other words, in terms of solving the question of Palestinian refugees, Transitional Justice alone cannot be but the beginning, as in order to find a solution acceptable upon both Israelis and Palestinians, practical aspects need to be addressed as well.

The analysis of principled solutions proceeded with an attempt to draw conclusions from what is probably the most relevant historical precedent regarding two nations with a troubled past aiming to find a formulation allowing a better future: German-Israeli negotiations following World War II. It is important to stress that in no way was the Palestinian nakba equal to the Jewish holocaust. The parallel rather lies in the fact that before establishing formal diplomatic relations, Israel expected Germany to acknowledge its responsibility for the crimes committed, followed by some means of compensation. Although the following German declaration was actually unsubstantial in terms of the wording used, it was still sufficient to satisfy Israel's need for such principled recognition of responsibility, and the two nations started a process of normalization.

Accordingly, in the Israeli-Palestinian context, one could imagine a mutually accepted formula allocating a part of the responsibility for the refugee problem to a portion of Israeli actions and policies in 1948, thereby expressing a significant but certainly not major Israeli role. While giving the Palestinians some psychological recognition of their suffering, such formula would not require Israelis to deny their own truths. Two elements are likely to be key: first, the political imperative of enabling Palestinian statehood. Second, an expectation that no denial by Palestinians of the truth of what befell them would be required to achieve their statehood. If Palestinians are to receive a viable state, with unrestricted access to it for their refugees, Palestinian leaders will likely act just as Israeli politicians dealing with Germany after World War II did: eagerly searching for formulas to make massive packages of aid for that state and its newly arriving citizens politically acceptable. Yet such principled formulas will necessarily have to be accompanied by practical aspects as well.

This leads us to a number of *integrated solutions*, which include both practical and principled aspects. At the end of the range, allowing a full recognition of the *right of return* coupled with an unlimited refugee return, stands the option of a bi-national state. If Israel, West Bank and Gaza were to form one single state, demographic considerations would lose any relevance. However, as the determination to keep their own national state is one of the few national consensuses Israelis have, the option of a bi-national state is not realistic. Besides, recent history has shown that multinational states often prove to be highly instable.

A Palestinian compromise solution demanded the return of only a limited number of Palestinian refugees into Israel, while Israel would acknowledge the individual moral right of Palestinian refugees to return to the Palestinian state. The number of Palestinian refugees allowed to return to Israel would be determined in Israeli-Palestinian negotiations. It is doubtful that such a proposal would receive the support of a majority of Palestinians, as they would neither receive a full Israeli recognition of the *right of return* nor an explicit Israeli acknowledgment of responsibility for the creation of the refugee problem. The proposal's weakest part is that its success depends upon Israelis and Palestinians managing to agree on a certain number of refugees who are to return to Israeli territory, yet does not offer any guidelines regarding how the parties are supposed to settle for such a number. Moreover, it does not offer any provisions for the case that the two parties are not able to agree on a specific number of refugees.

Also an Israeli compromise solution was examined, a proposal modifying Israel's maximalist demand of no refugee return and no Israeli recognition of responsibility. Instead, Israel is to acknowledge some practical responsibility to the events culminating in the 1948 war and the plight of refugees. Israel would further accept a *right of return* to the Palestinian state, yet not to Israel proper; in contrast to the Palestinian compromise solution, however, Israel would deny any moral *right of return*. Instead, Israel might accept several "tens of thousands" of Palestinian refugees as part of a unilateral program of family reunifications – a concept rejected by Palestinians. Also an Israeli recognition that "the historical process culminating in the 1948 war …caused great suffering" would hardly be considered by Palestinians to be an achievement that justifies concessions.

While being overall consistent with earlier Israeli positions on refugees (such as presented in Taba), the Israeli compromise solution is problematic regarding Palestinian needs. At first glance, the suggested formulation of an Israeli admission of historical responsibility does not seem to fulfil Palestinian expectations; yet at the same time, the experience of German-Israeli negotiations has shown that also a limited acknowledgment of actual responsibility may suffice to fulfil the other side's needs in that respect. However, in Palestinian eyes, the lack of a full recognition of the *right of return* stands out as the primary disadvantage; it is rather unlikely that Palestinians would deem an Israeli recognition of the *right of return* to be sufficient even on a merely principled basis (i.e., without reference to any actual return) if that right was explicitly limited to apply merely to the Palestinian state.

According to another formula, the Gush Shalom proposal, Israel would indeed recognise the principle of the *right of return* to be a basic human right. Moreover, Israel would also acknowledge its share of responsibility for the Palestinian refugee problem. Some actual return of refugees is to follow, with the precise number of returnees to be determined by Israeli-Palestinian negotiations. The shortcoming of the Gush Shalom proposal lies in its vagueness: while it does provide some rough formula for a partial Israeli admission of responsibility along with a principled acknowledgment of the *right of return*, details and extent still need to be agreed upon by the two parties. In the case of Oslo, such attempt toward constructive ambiguity did not work.

Nevertheless, the Gush Shalom proposal overall provides a good and creative basis for future Israeli-Palestinian negotiations. However, it is characterized by the same logical contradiction as the Geneva Initiative, promising refugees free choice regarding their options for return, while granting Israel veto power regarding the entry to its territory.

The last formula discussed, the Ayalon-Nusseibeh proposal, suggests a partial Israeli recognition of the *right of return* and also proposes a form to implement it in a manner logically consistent with the rest of the proposal, namely to the Palestinian state only. While finding wider acceptance in Israel, Palestinian reactions to the proposal have shown a strong disapproval of such formula to solve the refugee question. The focus of Palestinian critique was not so much that Palestinian refugee return would only be exercised to the Palestinian state, totally excluding Israel, but rather that the *right of return* merely appears as the title of the relevant section, not offering any explicit Israeli recognition of that right. Thus while the Ayalon-Nusseibeh proposal's formula regarding refugees is perceived as highly attractive by most Israelis, the vast majority of Palestinians deems it unacceptable, which signifies that the proposal in its present form is not adequate to solve the Palestinian refugee question.

Hence what are the characteristics of a formula to solve the question of Palestinian refugees which indeed might be acceptable upon both Israelis and Palestinians? We have seen that solutions referring merely to practical aspects are either totally unacceptable for one party, or if the solution itself appears to be reasonable for both parties, it still lacks an agreed position regarding the *right of return* and historical responsibility. Such issues are addressed by principled solutions, which, however, only offer a key to an agreement if coupled with practical aspects. Integrated solutions, therefore, are characterised by the necessary and right approach of addressing both practical and principled aspects of the Palestinian refugee problem. It was demonstrated that the concept of a bi-national state and the Ayalon-Nusseibeh proposal lack relevance since the former is rejected by Israelis and the latter by Palestinians; consequently, a future solution is likely to be along the lines of the presented Israeli and Palestinian compromise solutions and/or the Gush Shalom proposal. Yet while they are heading in the right direction, an analysis of the three proposals has also revealed each one of them to have its shortcomings. It is therefore the goal of the following section to present the guidelines necessary for a successful Israeli-Palestinian agreement on Palestinian refugees.

14.2 Recommendations for Future Negotiations

Israeli-Palestinian negotiations regarding the refugee problem have often resembled a *dialogue des sourds*: Palestinians have insisted on a recognition of the *right of return*, while the Israelis have maintained that such recognition would equal the end of Israel's Jewish character. As a result, a fateful misunderstanding has been perpetuated: while a majority of Israelis think that peace with the Palestinians would necessarily entail the return of masses of refugees to Israel and is therefore impossible, the Palestinian leadership's minimal demand merely seeks some formal recognition of the *right of return*. Palestinians are not insisting on a return of millions of refugees to Israel, as they understand the impossibility of realizing such endeavour. In fact, it is in both Israelis' and Palestinians' interest to provide the Palestinian refugees with a choice-based approach which will offer them a variety of structured options, of incentives and disincentives, such that only a few will actually choose to return to Israel.[2]

The approach to getting the Palestinians to embrace a *"right of return to their homeland, the Palestinian state"* has proven to be unproductive. Therefore, future Israeli-Palestinian negotiations will have to find a way to accommodate a Palestinian *right of return* to Israel, while avoiding any actual return that threatens Israel's Jewish character. This will certainly be a complex and subtle task, yet claims that this would equal the impossible effort to square the circle are incorrect.

---

2   Jerome Segal has presented a lot of precious thoughts regarding the essence of finding a solution to the Palestinian refugee problem. See his "Right of Return Confusions," 13 January 2001, at www.prrn.org.

The following objectives were sought by the Palestinians:

1. That Israel would accept responsibility for the refugee problem
2. That Israel would recognize "in principle" a *right of return* for Palestinian refugees
3. That Israel would accept UNGAR 194
4. That returning to Israel would be one of the options available to refugees.

Each of these formulations can be interpreted in various ways, and accordingly could involve the return to Israel of only one thousand just as well as one million refugees. What is truly striking about the gaps in the negotiations between Israelis and Palestinians is that they are about conceptualisation rather than outcomes. The Israeli government was prepared, as an outcome, to allow a certain number of refugees to return, yet it insisted on them to be returning not by right, but as a matter of Israeli humanitarian policy.[3] A closer examination of the four Palestinian objectives will help finding a possible formula for solution.

1. *Responsibility:* A distinction needs to be made between overall responsibility for the creation of Palestinian refugees, and responsibility for specific acts that caused people to become refugees. With respect to the latter, there is no doubt that during the 1948 war there was more than one instance where Palestinians were forcibly expelled. As this is to some extent already part of Israel's high school curriculum, it might as well be acknowledged in the negotiations.

The question of overall responsibility for the refugee problem is quite a different matter. Here Israelis can reasonably maintain that there would be no refugee problem had the Arab world accepted the U.N. partition plan, if war had not been launched against the newly created Israel, or if there had not been broad Palestinian support for such efforts. Moreover, had Israel lost the 1948 war Palestine's entire Jewish population would have become refugees, provided they had survived at all.[4]

---

3   Ibid.
4   Aviv Shir-On, Israeli Ambassador to Switzerland, did not reject the option of some Israeli apology for its part in the creation of the Palestinian refugee problem; however, such apology would have to be in reciprocity with a

Besides, the issue of moral responsibility is disconnected from the *right of return*, as any such right is not conditional upon having been forcibly evacuated. Whether a refugee left a war zone out of fear or mere prudence does not affect the generally recognized right to return once the hostilities have ceased.[5]

2. *A Right of Return for Palestinian Refugees:* it is essential to distinguish between recognizing a right that pre-exists and consequently shapes the negotiations, as opposed to rights established as a result of the negotiations. With respect to the latter, both sides need to realize that the negotiations will result in the refugees having specific mutual agreement upon rights. The issue regarding a possible pre-existing *right of return* is a different matter.

The Palestinian position claims that all refugees (and their descendents) have the right to return to their former homes within present Israel. Yet in most cases these homes no longer exist or have been inhabited by Israelis for over half a century. While Palestinians have legitimate claims for compensation for their homes, pursuing actual return to houses that have become other people's homes is hardly worth pursuing. The question is rather whether they have a right to return to the areas from which they came, or perhaps more generally a right to live anywhere in Israel.

Regarding the issue of rights, let us consider an analogy: it makes sense to acknowledge to a group of people that each of them has a certain right, and at the same time insist that it is legitimate to regulate the implementation of that right. Let us, for example, suppose that a ferryboat has the capacity to carry two hundred people on its daily route. The company sells 1,000 annual passes giving the holders the right to use the boat whenever they please. As a rule, no more than 50 pass-holders show up on a given day. Yet one day all 1,000 pass-holders show up. Each of them has a right to use the ferry, yet it is quite appropriate to enforce the rule that says no more than 200 are allowed at a time. To insist on the legitimacy of rules for the collective exercise of individual rights does not imply any denial of the existence of those

Palestinian apology for having started the war in 1948. Interview with the author, Bern, 21 April 2005.

5   Segal, "Right of Return Confusions."

rights for each individual. Indeed, it is hard to imagine any rights of individuals which under some circumstances would not be subject to appropriate restriction.[6]

Applied to governments with the responsibility to protect a common good, one can speak of the legitimacy of rules of implementation. When considering the bearer of the rights, one speaks of limitations of the right itself. Thus, one might say: "Yes, you have a right to take the ferry, but that does not give you the right to board if it is already at full capacity. You have to wait even if it is a long time, even if it means missing your only opportunity. Of course, if you do not board, you get compensation."

Obviously there are no perfect analogies, but conceptualising the issue in the above described way, Israel could tell Palestinian refugees: "Yes, we recognize a right of return, yet it is not an absolute right. It is conditioned by our rights as well, our rights to sovereignty and self-determination. Because Israel has a right to determine that it wants to continue to exist as a Jewish state, we insist on a framework for regulating the exercise of rights of refugees to return." This would allow Israel to accept a *right of return* "in principle." Since both Israelis and Palestinians have eventually accepted the 1947 U.N. partition plan, calling for "two states, one Arab and one Jewish," one could imagine Israelis and Palestinians entering into a mutual exchange of rights-recognition: Israel would recognize a *right of return*, and Palestinians would recognize that Israel has the sovereign right to choose to retain its Jewish character, and thus to a right to regulate the implementation of the *right of return*. In the words of Khalil Shikaki, who sees this as a win-win situation: "Israel must recognize the right [to return] while the Palestinian state must shoulder the bulk of responsibility for its exercise."[7] However, retaining Israel's Jewish character should not be used as a hammer or excuse to deny Palestinian rights, but rather to structure a principled position with respect to how to approach and understand Palestinian rights.

---

6   Ibid.
7   See Khalil Shikaki, "The Right of Return," *Wall Street Journal*, 30 July 2003.

3. *UNGAR 194:* Official Israeli negotiators have refused to accede to Palestinian demands that they recognize UNGAR 194. For the Palestinians, acceptance of UNGAR 194 is fundamental to settling the refugee problem, as it gives them international legitimacy. There is no reason for Israel to be inflexible on the issue, as the resolution does not mention any rights; it only states that the refugees should be allowed to return to their homes. It neither affirms nor denies that this is a matter of right.

The main point regarding UNGAR 194 is that its scope is open to interpretation. For the purposes of negotiations, the key issue is that whatever is agreed upon by way of implementation of UNGAR 194 must be confirmed to be an adequate fulfilment of UNGAR 194. If such an "adequate fulfilment" clause is part of the agreement, it would be recommendable to affirm that the agreement was based on mutual acceptance of UNGAR 194.[8] Therefore, Israel should not treat any mention of UNGAR 194 as anathema.

4. *The Option of Returning:* The option of actual return to Israel has been a dominant theme in this research for it is a central issue. For Palestinian leaders, the key is meaningful choice. They need to be able to turn to the refugees, telling them that they do have an opportunity to return to Israel, but that they also have a variety of other attractive options. For Israelis, the key is a solution that poses no demographic threat to them. Numerous tools could be imagined to prevent Israel being overwhelmed by refugees, the following being just two examples:

a) *Establishing a Rate of Return.* Ideally, the Palestinian leadership would like to avoid any regulation to return to Israel, preferring to offer the refugees a menu of alternative options sufficiently attractive so as to avoid any need to restrict implementation. The desired outcome would be that the vast majority of the refugees would decide to accept compensation and resettlement elsewhere rather than Israel.

Israel obviously could not tolerate such a situation in which there are no guarantees that it will not be flooded with Palestinian refugees, and just as any other sovereign state, Israel would require some safeguard. Several of the proposals discussed in the fourth part have suggested

---

8   This was the approach taken in the Geneva Initiative.

that Israelis and Palestinians agree on a maximal number of Palestinian refugees returning to Israel. However, as discussed earlier, a factual quota runs contrary to the concept of free choice.

Alternatively, the parties might agree that the rate of returning refugees must be such as not to alter Israel's Jewish character. It could be agreed that Palestinian return be limited to a certain percentage of Israel's Jewish immigration. Thus, for instance, if in the previous year 50,000 Jews moved to Israel, then one fifth of that number – 10,000 – of Palestinian refugees would be allowed to return in the following year, thereby keeping the immigration pool to the same population ratio as found in Israel's overall population.

Establishing a regulated rate of return would mean that if more Palestinians seek to return than this number allows, they are transferred to a queue. The more who wish to return, the longer the queue and thus the longer the wait. This would signify that choosing the option of returning to Israel would become increasingly unattractive compared to resettlement elsewhere accompanied by immediate access to a generous financial package for assistance and compensation.[9]

b) *The 1948 Refugees*. As discussed earlier, only a minority of the Palestinian population desiring to return to Israel was born on its territory. In addition, most of the 1948 refugees are well past child-bearing age, and they therefore do not pose a long term demographic threat to Israel. Therefore, they should be given priority when granting return to Israel. Doing so would allow Israel to enable refugee return without significantly affecting its Jewish majority, and Palestinians would have achieved the return of any refugee who has actually ever been to the place he or she desires returning to.

In any event, these two tools, regulating the rate of return and giving priority to the 1948 refugees, would need to operate within the larger context of compensation coupled with resettlement alternatives outside Israel. In addition, an Israeli-Palestinian agreement on refugees is only feasible within the framework of an overall agreement, solving also the other crucial outstanding issues such as Jerusalem and borders. Factually renouncing the call for total refugee return would be a Palestinian concession, which would call for Israel to make a concession

---

9   Ibid.

of its own (most likely in the negotiations regarding Jerusalem). Given these circumstances, a rich menu of return-choice could be devised, accompanied by some regulatory structure to safeguard Israel's demographic needs.

From a political point of view, a choice-based approach has significant advantages. It would allow the Palestinian leadership to avoid charges by their own people of having abandoned the *right of return*, in addition to giving it the opportunity to deliver to the refugees a variety of attractive alternatives. Significantly, such a choice-based approach is also in Israel's interest. While other approaches might well achieve a verbal statement by the PLO affirming that the refugee claims have been satisfied, in order to truly end the conflict it will be necessary for millions of Palestinians refugees to actually feel that they themselves have made a decision about return, resettlement and compensation. Only then will the refugee issue be finally resolved, a necessary condition for a durable solution of the conflict.[10]

In general, it would also be advisable to alter the practice of excluding official representatives of the Palestinian refugees from negotiations on the issue. Instead of viewing them as an obstacle and a threat it would be far more beneficial to regard them as a productive force which should be actively included into future negotiations. This would effectively counter distrust and opposition among the Palestinian refugees. Besides, an agreement developed with the involvement of official representatives of Palestinian refugees and backed by them would doubtlessly gather the support of a majority of Palestinians. This would after all also be in Israel's interest.

In sum, of all permanent status issues, the refugee question most readily ignites passions and fears on both sides. For Israelis, any talk of the *right of return* raises fears of Israel's destruction through demographic means and, it follows, of the rejection of any viable two-state solution. For Palestinians, the experience of dispossession is central to national identity, and the call for return is at the root of the national movement. As mutual trust has disintegrated during the second intifada and the relationship between the two sides has descended into an escalating cycle of violence, the refugee question, with all it conjures up

---

10   Ibid.

for both peoples, has regained centre stage. Addressing the reciprocal interests and concerns is thus of primary importance.[11]

It would be wrong to regard the issue of Palestinian refugees as an obstacle to an eventual peace settlement. For Palestinians, the refugee question is fundamentally a national and political one, neither monopolised by the refugee community nor susceptible to resolution by satisfaction of their immediate material needs. Therefore, it would be a precarious mistake to believe that the refugee question can be addressed by merely dealing through practical steps with the refugee population per se. Indeed, any practical steps (e.g., some resettlement, improvement in camp conditions) viewed by Palestinians as a substitute for a political settlement, and without being complemented with principled aspects, would be thwarted by them.

The basic building blocks of a viable solution to the Palestinian refugee problem are the following: some form of acknowledgment of responsibility for the fate of the refugees by Israel; some mutually accepted formulation regarding the *right of return*, most likely a symbolic recognition of it by Israel; resolution of the refugee problem essentially through repatriation to a Palestinian state, resettlement in Arab host countries, in third countries, and a symbolic number returning to Israel; and a compensation for hardship and lost property.[12] The question of formulation is crucial. While in the event of an otherwise satisfactory agreement, Palestinians will be prepared to forgo massive return to Israel and will accept the return of a limited number of refugees, they will nevertheless reject the concepts of "family reunification" and "humanitarian measure," as well as the use of the term "symbolic return", since Palestinians regard such terminology as incompatible with a genuine recognition of the *right of return*. Regarding an assurance for Israel, it would be advisable to include a time frame regarding implementation and a clause that the agreement will represent the end of claims. On the Palestinian side, the challenge is to ensure that, once unveiled, such a solution triggers minimal opposition. For that purpose, the involvement of refugees in the process of developing a solution will be extremely helpful.

---

11 "Palestinian Refugees and the Politics of Peacemaking," *ICG Middle East Report*, No. 22, 5 February 2004, p. 23.
12 Ibid., p. 24.

The fate of the Geneva Initiative offers important lessons.[13] *First*, there is need for an inclusive process of public dialogue and the dissemination of relevant information on the Palestinian side. The collapse of the peace process, ongoing violence, absence of hope, and radicalisation of attitudes hardly represented favourable conditions for the unveiling of an initiative that sought to address the refugee problem more openly and bluntly than had been done in the past. Groups and individuals opposed to the initiative as a whole unsurprisingly seized on this aspect in an effort to de-legitimise both its sponsors and the concept itself and – again unsurprisingly – had some success.

Secondly, a viable overall solution is necessary. Palestinians who negotiated the Geneva Initiative were willing to go further than previously on the refugee question because they felt the package as a whole – particularly as related to the territorial issues and Jerusalem – was satisfactory.

Thirdly, there is the question of timing. On the Palestinian side, the Geneva Initiative mobilised strong and effective opposition on the refugee issue in part because it was not a concrete agreement ready to be implemented. Indeed, in present circumstances, its prospect for acceptance by the Israeli government seems remote at best. Under such conditions, it is far easier to mobilise opposition than support. This highlights the political risks Palestinians take in putting forward compromise ideas in a vacuum, without sufficient guarantees of a satisfactory comprehensive resolution. For this reason, some Palestinians who agree with the substance but dispute the process argue that by presenting a compromise on the refugee question in a political vacuum, the negotiators acted prematurely and exposed their efforts to widespread criticism that undermined a solution that would have been far more acceptable as part of an actual settlement.

Thus the question of Palestinian refugees cannot be solved without a general resolution of the Israeli-Palestinian conflict, and vice versa. In other words, there will be no Israeli-Palestinian peace agreement if the question of refugees remains unresolved, and the question of Palestinian refugees will not be resolved without the concrete prospect for an overall Israeli-Palestinian agreement. Various elements of the proposals presented and analysed in this research can serve as an inspiration to

---

13   See also ibid., pp. 24–25.

provide a compromise solution once Israeli-Palestinian negotiations are to resume. A solution to the Palestinian refugee question can only come as a result of such bilateral negotiations, during which the precise formulas and formulations need to be developed. However, one aspect must be as crisp and clear to future negotiators as it is to dispassionate outside observers as well as to many Israeli and Palestinian activists. An agreement on refugees can only find reciprocal support if it includes some recognition of the *right of return* while it excludes a massive return of refugees to Israel.

Finally, the most important element necessary for a successful agreement is the mutual will, combined with courage and respect, to achieve such compromise. This basic conclusion was lucidly illustrated in the summer of 2003, when a European student organization organised a week long encounter in Copenhagen between a number of Israeli and Palestinian students with various backgrounds and political views.[14] The participants only shared the readiness to attempt developing a solution to several aspects of the conflict. Regarding refugees, after fierce negotiations and debates, they succeeded in developing the following formula:

> Israel recognizes that all Palestinian refugees have the *right* to return to Israel. However, only an agreed amount will return to Israel. The amount will be agreed on by both governments. Only the Palestinian government will decide who is within this fixed amount. This fixed amount of Palestinian refugees will become Israeli residents with Palestinian citizenship. After a certain amount of years these residents can apply for citizenship.
>
> Israel should officially apologize for the suffering inflicted upon the Palestinian refugees. All refugees with lost property within the state of Israel will get compensation for the land or house they owned. The compensation can be financially [sic] or it could be a house in evacuated settlements. A regional committee dealing with the status of the Palestinian refugees in the Middle East will be established, but there will be no more claims on Israel.[15]

It is interesting to note that such agreement of sorts was reached in the middle of the intifada, and before the Geneva Initiative could provide

---

14 See the documentation of "The European Role in the Israeli-Palestinian Conflict: Perceptions and Future Possibilities," 4–10 August 2003, Copenhagen, at www.projects.aegee.org/pie/Conferences/kbh/docu_Copenhagen_conf_03.pdf, p. 12.

15 Ibid.

any inspiration.[16] So while it is true that the question of Palestinian refugees – not at least because of its strong emotional component – is the most difficult one to solve out of all Israeli-Palestinian issues, there is no reason why official negotiators should not be able to replicate what a group of students has managed to accomplish in a matter of days; a claim that is backed by the fact that Israelis and Palestinians were able to formulate a document such as the Beilin-Abu Mazen Draft. Therefore, it is inappropriate to put off overall Israeli-Palestinian negotiations by arguing that it is a forgone conclusion that the issue of refugees dooms any such talks to fail.[17] In the end, there remains the irrefutable basic fact that the sooner Israelis and Palestinians tackle the refugee issue in sincere negotiations, the sooner will a solution be found – both to the specific question of refugees as well as to the Israeli-Palestinian conflict as a whole. However, as to the prospect of a mutually acceptable two-state solution, time is of the essence.

---

16 In another Israeli-Palestinian encounter, held in December 2004 in Hol-land (www.dialogue-lab.org/wg/ipc/stk/Egmond04_Docu.pdf), during an informal discussion between an Arab and a Jewish participant, the following formula was developed: Each Palestinian refugee is to receive the right to visit his former house in Israel. At that occasion he could meet the present owner. The refugees would receive a document stating that they are the owners of the house, yet they are not entitled to sell it, and the present owners continue to live there.

17 Such view is quite common in Israel and was recently illustrated by Israel's ambassador to Switzerland, who explained that Israel could not accept the Arab League's 2002 peace proposal because of the – erroneous – assumption that the return of Palestinian refugees to Israel was an integral part of that plan. See the interview with Aviv Shir-On, „Leider haben wir es hier mit einer Déjà-vu-Situation zu tun," *Neue Zürcher Zeitung*, 14 July 2006, p. 7.

Bibliography

Primary Sources

Interviews

Akram, Susan, Professor for International Law at Boston University, Boston, 9 December 2003.

Al-Qaq, Anis, Representative of the Palestinian Authority in Switzerland, Bern, 14 April 2005.

Allan, Pierre, Professor of Political Science and Dean of the University of Geneva's Faculty of Social Sciences, insider to the Geneva Initiative, Basel, 24 May 2004.

Aviv Shir-On, Israeli Ambassador to Switzerland, Bern, 21 April 2005.

Brynen, Rex, Professor of Political Science at McGill University and leading expert on the political aspects of the Palestinian refugee question, Montreal, 3 December 2004.

Jaradat, Muhammad, co-founder of the Palestinian refugee organisation BADIL, Bethlehem, September 2004.

Lustick, Ian, Professor of Political Science at the University of Pennsylvania, Philadelphia, 3 November 2003.

Malley, Robert, former special assistant to President Clinton for Arab-Israeli Affairs, phone interview, 19 October 2004.

Nye, Joseph, Professor of International Relations at Harvard University, Zurich, 28 January 2003.

Peled, Yoav, Professor of Political Science at Tel Aviv University, Tel Aviv, 23 January 2005.

Peters, Joel, Professor at Ben Gurion University and former member of the Track II negotiations on refugees, Jerusalem, 25 January 2005.

Pitteloud, Jacques, Coordinator of Switzerland's intelligence agencies, Bern, 7 June 2004.

Shehata, Samer, Assistant Professor at Georgetown University, Washington D.C., 4 November 2003.

Siegman, Henry, Senior Fellow at the Council on Foreign Relations, New York, 31 October 2003.

Walzer, Michael, Professor at the School of Social Science, Princeton, 8 December 2003.

Documents, Declarations, Statements, etc.

Absentees' Property Law of 5710/1950, 14 March, 1950, in Fischbach, Michael, *Records of Dispossession: Palestinian Refugee Property and the Arab-Israeli Conflict*, New York: Columbia University Press, 2003, pp. 21–25.

Ayalon-Nusseibeh Statement of Principles, at www.mifkad.org.il/en/principles.asp.

Balfour Declaration, in Laqueur, Walter and Rubin, Barry, eds., *The Israeli-Arab Reader: A Documentary History of the Middle East Conflict*, New York: Penguin Books, 2001, p. 16.

Barak's Red Lines, July 2000, www.mfa.gov.il/mfa/go.asp?MFAH0hli0.

Beilin, Yossi, "Private Response on Palestinian Refugees," Taba, 23 January, 2001, at www.monde-diplomatique.fr/cahier/proche-orient/israelrefugees-en.

Beilin–Abu Mazen Draft Agreement, at www.mideastweb.org/beilinabu mazen1.htm.

Beilin–Eitan Agreement, at www.knesset.gov.il/process/docs/bei-eit_eng.htm.

Clinton Parameters, December 2000, in Laqueur, Walter and Rubin, Barry, eds., *The Israeli-Arab Reader: A Documentary History of the Middle East Conflict*, New York: Penguin Books, 2001, pp. 562–64.

Convention on the Reduction of Statelessness, Art. 10, 30 Aug., 1961, at http://193.194.138.190/html/menu3/b/o_reduce.htm.

Convention relating to the Status of Refugees, at www.unhchr.ch/html/menu3/b/o_c_ref.htm.

Declaration of Principles on Interim Self-Government Arrangements between Israel and the PLO, ["Oslo Agreement"] (September 1993), in Laqueur, Walter and Rubin, Barry, eds., *The Israeli-Arab Reader: A Documentary History of the Middle East Conflict*, New York: Penguin Books, 2001, pp. 413–422.

Discussion Draft, presented by the U.S. in Camp David on 13 July, at www.brookings.edu/press/appendix/peaceprocessappen_aa.htm.

Final Report of the United Nations Economic Survey Mission for the Middle East, published by the United Nations Conciliation Commission on 28 December 1949, at http://domino.un.org/unispal.nsf.

Framework Agreement on Permanent Status, (FAPS), 20 May 2000, at www.brookings.edu/press/appendix/peaceprocessappen_z.htm.

Framework for Peace in the Middle East Agreed at Camp David, in Lapidoth, Ruth and Hirsch, Moshe, eds., *The Arab-Israeli Conflict and its Resolution: Selected Documents*, Dordrecht: Martinus Nijhoff Publishers, 1992, pp. 196–198.

General Comment 27 of the Human Rights Committee, at http://hei.unige.ch/~clapham/hrdoc/docs/ccprgencom27.html.

General Framework Agreement for Peace in Bosnia Herzegovina, Dec. 14, 1995, at www.ohr.int/dpa/default.asp?content_id=380.

General Progress Report and Supplementary Report of the United Nations Conciliation Commission for Palestine, Covering the Period from 11 December

1949 to 23 October 1950 published by the U.N. Conciliation Commission on 23 October 1950, at http://domino.un.org/unispal.nsf.

Geneva Initiative, at www.geneva-accord.org.

Geography in Palestine [Palestinian textbook], sixth grade, 2001.

Geography of Palestine [Palestinian textbook], seventh grade, 2001.

German-Czech Declaration on Mutual Relations and their Future Development, 21 January 1997, at www.mzv.cz/servis/soubor.asp?id=1873.

Global IDP Database of the Norwegian Refugee Council, at www.reliefweb.int.

Gush-Shalom Peace Proposal, at http://gush-shalom.org/archives/altpeace.html.

Human Rights Watch, "Syria/Lebanon: An Alliance beyond the Law – Enforced Disappearances in Lebanon," May 1997, Vol. 9, No. 3, at www.prrn.org.

"Increased Palestinian Adherence to the Right of Return Following the Geneva Initiative," MEMRI, Special Dispatch No. 634, 26 December 2003.

Islamic Culture [Palestinian textbook], twelfth grade, 1998.

Islamic Education [Palestinian textbook], sixth grade, part 1, 2000.

Knesset Law on Nationality, 1952, at www.mfa.gov.il/MFA/MFA Archive/2000_2009/2001/8/Acquisition%20of%20Israeli%20Nationality.

Lapidoth, Ruth and Hirsch, Moshe eds., *The Arab-Israeli Conflict and its Resolution: Selected Documents*, Dordrecht: Martinus Nijhoff Publishers, 1992.

Laqueur, Walter and Rubin, Barry (eds.), *The Israeli-Arab Reader: A Documentary History of the Middle East Conflict*, New York: Penguin Books, 2001.

List of Israeli Reservations to the Roadmap, Israeli Government Press Office, 25 May 2003, at www.mideastweb.org/roadmapreservations.htm.

Moratinos Account of the 2001 Taba Talks, at www.mideastweb.org/moratinos.htm.

Nottebohm Case (Liechtenstein v. Guatemala), Second Phase, Judgement of 6 April 1955, at www.icj-cij.org/icjwww/idecisions/isummaries/ilgsummary550406.htm.

Our Beautiful Language [Palestinian textbook], seventh grade, part 1, 2001.

Palestinian Center for Policy and Survey Research's, "Refuges Polls in the West Bank/Gaza Strip, Jordan and Lebanon on Refugees' Preferences and Behavior in a Palestinian-Israeli Permanent Refugee Agreement," January-June 2003, at www.pcpsr.org/survey/polls/2003/refugeesjune03.html#findings.

Palestinian National Education [Palestinian textbook], second grade, 2001.

Palestinian National Education [Palestinian textbook], seventh grade, 2001.

Palestinian National Education [Palestinian textbook], sixth grade, 2000.

Palestinian National Education [Palestinian textbook], fifth grade, 1998.

Palestinian Position Paper on Refugees, Taba, 22 January, 2001, at http://monediplo.com/focus/mideast/a3276.

The Palestinian Society: Demographic Education [Palestinian textbook], eleventh grade, 2001.

Potsdam Conference Protocol, 2 August 1945, at www.yale.edu/lawweb/avalon/decade/decade17.htm.

President Bush's Letter to Ariel Sharon, April 2004, at www.bitterlemons.org/docs/bushletter.html.

Principles in Human Geography [Palestinian textbook], sixth grade, 2000.

PSR Press Release of the joint Palestinian-Israeli Public opinion poll, 16 December 2003, at www.prrn.org.

"Remarks and Questions from the Palestinian Negotiating Team Regarding the United States Proposal," i.e., the Palestinian response of 2 January 2001 to the Clinton Parameters, at www.nad-plo.org/eye/new15.html.

Report of the Director of the United Nations Relief and Works Agency for Palestine Refugees in the Near East, September 28, 1951, at http://domino. un.org/unispal.nsf.

Report of the U.N. Secretary-General on his mission of good services in Cyprus, 1 April 2003, at www.un.org/Docs/sc/sgrep03.html.

Report of the U.N. Secretary-General to the Security Council, S/24472, Annex, 21 August 1992.

Roadmap for Middle Eastern Peace, 30 April 2003, at www.mideastweb.org/quartetrm3.htm.

"The Taba Negotiations (January 2001)," *Journal of Palestine Studies*, Vol. XXXI, No. 3, Spring 2002, pp. 79–89.

U.N. General Assembly Resolution 55/153, 30 January 2001, *Nationality of Natural Persons in Relation to the Succession of States*, at www.unhcr.org/cgi-bin/texis/vtx/excom/opendoc.pdf?tbl=EXCOM&id= 42bc068d2.

U.N. General Assembly Resolution 3236 (1974), at http://domino.un.org/UNISPAL.NSF/9a798adbf322aff38525617b006d88d7/025974039acfb 171852560 de00548bbe?OpenDocument&Highlight=2,3236.

U.N. General Assembly Resolution 302 (IV) of 8 December 1949, at http://domino. un.org/unispal.nsf.

U.N. General Assembly Resolution 194, 11 December 1948, in Laqueur, Walter and Rubin, Barry, eds., *The Israeli-Arab Reader: A Documentary History of the Middle East Conflict*, New York: Penguin Books, 2001, pp. 83–86.

UNHCR Mission to Bosnia-Herzegovina, at www.unhcr.ba.

Universal Declaration of Human Rights, at www.un.org/Overview/rights.html.

Unofficial translation of a letter by Arafat, faxed to Clinton on 28 December 2000, at www.brookings.edu/press/appendix/peaceprocessappen_ac.htm.

U.N. Partition Resolution for Palestine, 29 November 1947, in Laqueur, Walter and Rubin, Barry (eds.), *The Israeli-Arab Reader: A Documentary History of the Middle East Conflict*, New York: Penguin Books, 2001, pp. 69–77.

UNRWA's Definition of a Refugee, at http://www.un.org/unrwa/refugees/whois. html. Note on the Applicability of Article 1D of the 1951 Convention relating to the Status of Refugees to Palestinian refugees, Decision taken by the UNHCR in 2002, at http://domino.un.org/unispal.nsf.

U.N. Security Council Resolution 1475 (2003), 14 April 2003, at http://daccessdds.un.org/doc/UNDOC/GEN/N03/323/10/PDF/N0332310.pdf?OpenElement.

U.N. Security Council Resolution regarding the Dayton Accord on 15 December 1995, at www.nato.int/ifor/un/u951215a.htm.

U.N. Security Council Resolution 744 (1992), 25 August 1992.

U.N. Security Council Resolution 242, 22 November 1967, Laqueur, Walter and Rubin, Barry (eds.), *The Israeli-Arab Reader: A Documentary History of the Middle East Conflict*, New York: Penguin Books, 2001, p. 116.

Memoirs, Speeches, etc.

Abed el-Shafi's opening statement in Madrid 1991, at http://mondediplo.com/focus/mideast/a2299.

Albright, Madeleine, *Madame Secretary: A Memoir*, New York: Miramax, 2003.

Arafat, Yasser, "The Palestinian Vision of Peace," *New York Times*, 3 February 2002, p. A15, at www.thejerusalemfund.org/carryover/pubs/20010314ftr.html.

Barak, Ehud, "The Myths Spread About Camp David Are Baseless," in Shamir, Shimon and Maddy-Weitzmann, Bruce, eds., *The Camp David Summit – What Went Wrong?*, Brighton: Sussex Academic Press, 2005, pp. 117–47.

Begin, Menachem, *The Revolt*, rev. ed., New York: Dell, 1977.

Beilin, Yossi, *The Path to Geneva: The Quest for a Permanent Agreement, 1996–2004*, New York: RDV Books, 2004.

Beilin, Yossi, *Manual for a Wounded Dove* (Hebrew), Tel Aviv: Miskal, 2001.

Beilin, Yossi, *Touching Peace* (Hebrew), Tel Aviv: Miskal, 1997.

Beilin, Yossi, "What really happened at Taba," *Haaretz*, 16 July 2002.

Ben Gurion, David, *War Diaries*, (Hebrew), 3 Vols., ed. G. Rivlin and E. Orren, Tel Aviv, 1982.

Ben-Ami, Shlomo, *Scars of War, Wounds of Peace: The Israeli-Arab Tragedy*, New York: Oxford University Press, 2006.

Ben-Ami, Shlomo, *A Front Without a Rearguard: A Voyage to the Boundaries of the Peace Process* (Hebrew), Tel Aviv: Miskal, 2004.

Bishara, Azmi, Interview with the *Journal of Palestine Studies*, Vol. XXVI, No. 3, Spring 1997, pp. 67–80.

Clinton, Bill, *My Life*, New York: Alfred A. Knopf, 2004.

Clinton's outline of his proposals in a public speech to the Israel Policy Forum, 7 January 2001, at www.brookings.edu/press/appendix/peace_process.htm.

Ginossar, Yossi, "Factors that Impeded the Negotiations," in Shamir, Shimon and Maddy-Weitzmann, Bruce, eds., *The Camp David Summit – What Went Wrong?*, Brighton: Sussex Academic Press, 2005, pp. 51–59.

Hanieh, Akram, "The Camp David Papers," *Journal of Palestine Studies*, Vol. XXX, No. 2, Winter 2001, pp. 75–97.

Herzl, Theodor, *Der Judenstaat: Versuch einer modernen Lösung der Judenfrage*, Zurich: Manesse-Verlag, 1988.

Herzl, Theodor, *Gesammelte zionistische Werke: in fünf Bänden*, Berlin: Jüdischer Verlag, 1934.

Hess, Moses, *Rom und Jerusalem: Die letzte Nationalitätenfrage, Briefe*, Vienna: Löwit, 1935.

Hirschfeld, Yair, *Oslo: A Formula for Peace: From Negotiations to Implementation* (Hebrew), Tel Aviv: Am Oved Publishers, 2000.

Indyk, Martin, "Sins of Omission, Sins of Commission," in Shamir, Shimon and Maddy-Weitzmann, Bruce, eds., *The Camp David Summit – What Went Wrong?*, Brighton: Sussex Academic Press, 2005, pp. 100–107.

Kellner, Leon, ed., *Theodor Herzels Zionistische Schriften*, Berlin-Charlottenburg: Jüdischer Verlag, 1905.

Klein, Menachem, *The Geneva Initiative: An Inside View* (Hebrew), Jersusalem: Carmel, 2006.

Klein, Menachem, "Track II Plans," in Shamir, Shimon and Maddy-Weitzmann, Bruce, eds., *The Camp David Summit – What Went Wrong?*, Brighton: Sussex Academic Press, 2005, pp. 178–185.

Lipkin-Shahak, Amnon, "The Roles of Barak, Arafat and Clinton," in Shamir, Shimon and Maddy-Weitzmann, Bruce, eds., *The Camp David Summit – What Went Wrong?*, Brighton: Sussex Academic Press, 2005, pp. 42–50.

Malley, Robert, "American Mistakes and Israeli Misconceptions," in Shamir, Shimon and Maddy-Weitzmann, Bruce, eds., *The Camp David Summit – What Went Wrong?*, Brighton: Sussex Academic Press, 2005, pp. 108–14.

Malley, Robert, "Former Peace Team Member Discusses U.S. Failures under Clinton Administration," 7 March 2001, Report from a Palestine Center briefing.

Malley, Robert and Agha, Hussein, "A Reply to Barak," *The New York Review of Books*, Vol. XLIX, No. 10, June 13, 2002, pp. 46–49.

Malley, Robert and Agha, Hussein, "Camp David: The Tragedy of Errors," *New York Review of Books*, Vol. XLVIII, No. 13, August 9, 2001, pp. 59–65.

Nusseibeh, Sari, Interview with *NZZ am Sonntag*, 23 November 2003.

Peres, Shimon (with Arye Naor), *The New Middle East*, New York: Henry Holt, 1993.

Pundak, Ron, "From Oslo to Taba: What Went Wrong?," *Survival*, Vol. 43, No. 3, Autumn 2001, pp. 31–45.

Ross, Dennis, *The Missing Peace: The Inside Story of the Fight for Middle East Peace*, New York: Farrar, Straus and Giroux, 2004.

Shamir, Shimon and Maddy-Weitzmann, "Past, Present and Future – A Political Debate," Roundtable Discussion between Yuli Tamir, Yuval Steinitz, Dan Meridor, Yossi Beilin, in Shamir, Shimon and Maddy-Weitzmann, Bruce, eds., *The Camp David Summit – What Went Wrong?*, Brighton: Sussex Academic Press, 2005, pp. 221–250.

Sher, Gilead, "Lessons from the Camp David Experience," in Shamir, Shimon and Maddy-Weitzmann, Bruce, eds., *The Camp David Summit – What Went Wrong?*, Brighton: Sussex Academic Press, 2005, pp. 60–67.

Sher, Gilead, *Just Beyond Reach: The Israeli-Palestinian Peace Negotiations, 1999–2001*, (Hebrew), Tel Aviv: Miskal, 2001.

Shir-On, Aviv, „Leider haben wir es hier mit einer Déjà-vu-Situation zu tun," Interview in the *Neue Zürcher Zeitung*, 14 July 2006, p. 7.

Tamari, Salim, "The Dubious Lure of Binationalism," *Journal of Palestinian Studies*, Vol. XXX, No. 1, Autumn 2000, pp. 83–87.

Yatom, Danny, "Background, Process and Failure," in Shamir, Shimon and Maddy-Weitzmann, Bruce, eds., *The Camp David Summit – What Went Wrong?*, Brighton: Sussex Academic Press, 2005, pp. 33–41.

Newspapers and Periodicals

Der Spiegel
Frankfurter Allgemeine Zeitung (FAZ)
Frankfurter Rundschau
The Guardian
Haaretz
International Herald Tribune (IHT)
The Jerusalem Post
The Jerusalem Times
Jerusalem Report
Maariv
Neue Zürcher Zeitung (NZZ)
The New York Times
NZZ am Sonntag
Tages Anzeiger
Washington Post
Yediot Achronot

Secondary Sources

Articles

Abu-Odeh, Lama, "The Case for Binationalism," *Boston Review*, December 2001/January 2002, at www.bostonreview.net.
Agha, Hussein and Malley, Robert, "The Last Negotiation: How to End the Middle East Peace Process," *Foreign Affairs*, Vol. 81, No. 3, May/June 2002, pp. 10–18.
Agterhuis, Sander, "The Right to Return and its Practical Application," p. 7, at www.prrn.org.
Akram, Susan, "Palestinian Refugees and their Legal Status: Rights, Politics, and Implications for a Just Solution," *Journal of Palestine Studies*, Vol. XXXI, No. 3, Spring 2002, pp. 36–51.
Akram, Susan, "Reinterpreting Palestinian Refugee Rights under International Law," in Aruri, Naseer, ed., *Palestinian Refugees: The Right of Return*, London: Pluto Press, 2001, pp. 165–194.

Akram, Susan and Rempel, Terry, "Temporary Protection as an Instrument for Implementing the Right of Return for Palestinian Refugees," *Boston University International Law Journal*, Vol. 22, No. 1, 2004, pp. 1–162.

Al-Awda, "Defend the Right of Return," 13 October 2003, at www.al-awda. org.

Al-Huda, Manar-al-Husayni, "Lebanon and the Peace Process: excerpts on refugees," at www.prrn.org.

Allison, Graham, "Conceptual Models and the Cuban Missile Crisis," *The American Political Science Review*, Vol. LXIII, No. 3, September 1969, pp. 689–718.

Al-Masri, Hani, "The Cantons-State and the Liquidation of the Refugee Issue," *Al-Majdal*, Issue No. 28, Winter 2005, at www.badil.org/al-majdal/2005/Winter/majdal28.pdf.

Al-Masri, Hani, "Palestinian and Arabic Media and the Issue of Refugees," at www.prrn.org.

Al-Mawed, Hamad Said, "The Palestinian Refugees in Syria: Their Past, Present and Future," 1999, at www.prrnorg.

Alpher, Joseph, "Concept Paper: the Palestinian refugee problem and the right of return," *Middle East Policy* (Refereed), Vol. 6, No. 3, 1 February 1999, p. 167 (1). (webposted)

Alpher, Joseph and Shikaki, Khalil, "The Palestinian Refugee Problem and the Right of Return," Weatherhead Center for International Affairs, Harvard University, May 1998, at www.wcfia.harvard.edu/papers/98– 07.pdf.

Alpher, Yossi, "Refugees forever?" 14 January 2002, at www.prn.org.

Aruri, Naseer, "The Marginalization of the Basic Rights of the Palestinian Refugees: Geopolitics Over International Law," *Nexus*, Vol. 8, 2003, pp. 61–76.

Avnery, Uri, "A Binational State? God Forbid!," *Journal of Palestine Studies*, Vol. XXVIII, No. 4, Summer 1999, pp. 55–60.

BADIL, "Peace Agreements and Refugees – Lessons Learned," *Occasional Bulletin 14*, December 2003, at www.badil.org/Publications/publications.htm.

BADIL, "What's New about the Israeli Position on the Palestinian Refugee Question: Summary and Comments," 14 October 1999, at http://www.badil. org/Publications/Press/1999/press77–99.htm.

Baraka, Mohammad, "Between the One-State and the Two-State Solution," *Al-Majdal*, Issue No. 28, Winter 2005, at www.badil.org/al-majdal/2005/Winter/majdal28.pdf.

Barkan, Elazar, "Considerations Toward Accepting Historical Responsibility," in Lesch, Ann and Lustick, Ian, eds., *Exile and Return: Predicaments of Palestinians and Jews*, Philadelphia: University of Philadelphia Press, 2005, pp. 85–105.

Baskin, Gershon, "Right of Return to Palestine," 25 May 2006, at www.amin. org/eng/uncat/2006/may/may25–1.html.

Benvenisti, Eyal, "The Right of Return in International Law: An Israeli Perspective," at www.prrn.org.

Benziman, Uzi, "Corridors of Power: The Genie of Geneva," *Haaretz*, 7 November 2003.

Bookmiller, Robert and Nakjavani Bookmiller, Kirsten, "Behind the Headlines: The Multilateral Middle East Talks," *Current History*, January 1996, pp. 33–37.

Brynen, Rex, "The 'Geneva Accord' and the Palestinian Refugee Issue," 29 February 2004, at www.prrn.org.

Brynen, Rex, "Much Ado about Nothing? The Refugee Working Group and the Perils of Multilateral Quasi- negotiation," *International Negotiations*, Nov. 1997, at www.prrn.org.

Brynen, Rex, "Palestinian Refugees and the Middle East Peace Process," at www.prrn.org.

Brynen, Rex, "The Roadmap and the Refugees," at www.prrn.org.

Brynen, Rex and Tansley, Jill, "The Refugee Working Group of the Middle East Multilateral Peace Negotiations," at www.prrn.org.

Brynen, Rex, Eileen Alma, Joel Peters, Roula el-Rifai and Jill Tansley, "The 'Ottawa Process': An Examination of Canada's Track Two Involvement in the Palestinian Refugee Issue," *IDRC Stocktaking II Conference on Palestinian Refugee Research*, Ottawa, 17–20 June 2003, at www.prrn.org.

Brzezinski, Zbigniew, "A grand U.S.-European Mideast strategy," *International Herald Tribune*, 26 October 2004.

Carnevale, Peter, "Psychological Barriers to Negotiations," in Shamir, Shimon and Maddy-Weitzmann, Bruce, eds., *The Camp David Summit – What Went Wrong?*, Brighton: Sussex Academic Press, 2005, pp. 210– 218.

Christison, Kathleen, "Splitting the Difference: The Palestinian-Israeli Policy of James Baker," *Journal of Palestine Studies*, Vol. XXIV, No. 1, Autumn 1994, pp. 39–50.

Cohen, Hillel, "Land, Memory, and Identity: The Palestinian Internal Refugees in Israel," *Refuge*, Vol. 21, No. 2, 2004, pp. 6–13.

Cohen, Hillel, "The Internal Refugees in the State of Israel: Israeli Citizens, Palestinian Refugees," *Palestine- Israel Journal*, Vol. 9, No. 2, 2002, pp. 43–51.

Cook, Jonathan, "Palestinians recall day of catastrophe," 3 May 2006, at http://english.aljazeera.net.

Dassa Kaye, Dalia, "Madrid's Forgotten Forum: The Middle East Multilaterals," *The Washington Quarterly*, Vol. 20, No. 1, Winter 1997, pp. 167–86.

Doraï, Mohamed Kamel, "Palestinian Emigration from Lebanon to Northern Europe: Refugees, Networks, and Transnational Practices," at www.prrn.org.

Drake, Laura, "The Future of Palestinian Refugees in Lebanon," in Ginat, Joseph and Perkins, Edward, eds., *The Palestinian Refugees: Old Problems – New Solutions*, Brighton: Sussex Academic Press, 2001, pp. 200–29.

El-Abed, Oroub, "Palestinians in Egypt," and "The invisible Palestinians of Egypt. Refugees face discrimination, poverty and no access to basic services," at www.prrn.org.

Eldar, Akiva, "How to Solve the Palestinian Refugee Problem," *Haaretz*, 29 May 2001.

Eldar, Akiva, "The Israeli Media and the Refugee Problem," at www.prrn.org.

Farah, Randa, "A Report on the Psychological Effects of Overcrowding in Refugee Camps in the West Bank and Gaza Strip," April 2000, at www.prrn.org.

Firro, Kais, "Palestinian Refugees in Lebanon since 1982," in Ginat, Joseph and Perkins, Edward, eds., *The Palestinian Refugees: Old Problems – New Solutions*, Brighton: Sussex Academic Press, 2001, pp. 193–199.

Fischbach, Michael, "Palestinian and Mizrahi Jewish Property Claims in Discourse and Diplomacy," in Lesch, Ann and Lustick, Ian, eds., *Exile and Return: Predicaments of Palestinians and Jews*, Philadelphia: University of Pennsylvania Press, 2005, pp. 207–224.

Fischbach, Michael, "The United Nations and Palestinian Refugee Property Compensation," *Journal of Palestine Studies*, Vol. XXXI, No. 2, Winter 2002, pp. 24–50.

Fried, Shelly, "The Refugee Issue at the Peace Conferences, 1949–2000," *Palestine-Israel Journal*, Vol. 9, No. 2, 2002, pp. 24–34.

Friedman, Adina, "Unraveling the Right of Return," at www.prrn.org.

Gelber, Yoav, "The Historical Background," in Ginat, Joseph and Perkins, Edward, eds., *The Palestinian Refugees: Old Problems – New Solutions*, Brighton: Sussex Academic Press, 2001, pp. 17–33.

Ghanem, As'ad, "The Binational State is a Desired Palestinian Project and Demand," *Al-Majdal*, Issue No. 28, Winter 2005, at www.badil.org/al-majdal/2005/Winter/majdal28.pdf.

Golan, Galia, "Plans for Israeli-Palestinian Peace: From Beirut to Geneva," *Middle East Policy*, Vol. XI, No. 1, Spring 2004, pp. 38–51.

Gordon, Evelyn, "Why not say yes to the 'right of return'," *The Jerusalem Post*, 25 May 2005.

Haddad, Mohanna, "Palestinian Refugees in Jordan and National Identity, 1948–1999," in Ginat, Joseph and Perkins, Edward, eds., *The Palestinian Refugees: Old Problems – New Solutions*, Brighton: Sussex Academic Press, 2001, pp. 150–168.

Haddad, Simon, "Palestinians in Lebanon: Towards Integration or Conflict?," webposted on 14 May 2000, at www.prrn.org.

Hanafi, Sari, "Opening the Debate on the Right of Return," *War Without Borders*, Middle East Report 222, Spring 2002, at www.prrn.org.

Hastings, Lynn, "Implementation of the Property Legislation in Bosnia Herzegovina," *Stanford Journal of International Law*, Vol. 37, 2001, pp. 221–254.

Hermann, Tamar, "The bi-national idea in Israel/Palestine: past and present," *Nations and Nationalism*, Vol. 11, No. 3, 2005, pp. 381–401.

Ibrahim, Nassar, "Problems with the Two-State Solution and the Dream of One Democratic State," *Al-Majdal*, Issue No. 28, Winter 2005, at www.badil.org/al-majdal/2005/Winter/majdal28.pdf.

ICG, "Palestinian Refugees and the Politics of Peacemaking," *ICG Middle East Report*, No. 22, 5 February 2004, pp. 1–25, at www.icg.org.

Jaber, Bassil, "Possible Solutions to the Refugee Question," (Hebrew) in Yaar, Ephraim and Hermann, Tamar, *The Palestinian Refugees Issue and the Right of Return: Proceedings of a Symposium held on 29 December 2003* (Hebrew), (Tel Aviv: Tami Steinmetz Center, 2004), pp. 52–55.

Jagerskiold, Stig, "The Freedom of Movement," in L. Henkin, ed., *The International Bill of Rights*, New York: Columbia University Press, 1981.

Keller, Adam, "A Comparison of three Drafts for an Israeli-Palestinian Peace Agreement," at http://gush-shalom.org/archives/compare_eng.html.

Khalidi, Rashid, "Attainable Justice: Elements of a Solution to the Palestinian Refugee Issue," *International Journal*, Vol. 53, No. 2, Spring 1998, pp. 223–252.

Khalidi, Rashid, "The Palestinian Refugee Problem: A Possible Solution," *Palestine-Israel Journal*, Vol. 2, No. 4, Autumn 1995, pp. 72–78.

Khalidi, Rashid, "Observations on the Right of Return," *Journal of Palestine Studies*, Vol. 21, No. 2, Winter 1992, pp. 29–40.

Khalidi, Walid, "Plan Dalet: Master Plan for the Conquest of Palestine," *Journal of Palestine Studies*, Vol. XVIII, No. 1, Autumn 1988, pp. 3–70.

Khawaja, Marwan and Tiltnes, Aage A., "On the Margins: Migration and living conditions of Palestinian camp refugees in Jordan," *Fafo-report 357*, Oslo, 2002, at www.prrn.org.

Klug, Tony, "The Infernal Scapegoat," *Palestine-Israel Journal*, Vol. VIII, No. 3, pp. 7–15.

Knowlton, Brian, "Bush Shifts Views on the West Bank," *International Herald Tribune*, 15th April 2004, p. 1.

Köhler, Wolfgang, „Balanceakt zwischen zwei Extremen," *Frankfurter Allgemeine Zeitung*, 27 March 2002, p. 2.

Koltermann, Ulrike, "Who really wants them? Palestinians in Lebanon fed up with being a bargaining chip," *The Jerusalem Times*, 27 June 1997.

Landau, David and Eldar, Akiva, "A Jewish state? 'Definitely'" in *Haaretz*, 18 June 2004.

Lapidoth, Ruth, "Do Palestinian Refugees Have a Right to Return to Israel?," at www.us-israel.org.

Lapidot, Ruth, "Legal Aspects of the Palestinian Refugee Question," at www.jcpa.org/jl/vp485.htm.

Lawand, Kathleen, "The Right to Return of Palestinians in International Law," in *International Journal of Refugee Law*, Vol. 8, No. 4, October 1996, pp. 532–568.

Lazaroff, Tovah, "Lieberman's land swap plan illegal," *The Jerusalem Post*, 26 March 2006.

Lee, Luke, "The Preventive Approach to the Refugee Problem," *Williamette Law Review*, Vol. 28, 1992.

Lustick, Ian, "Negotiating Truth: The Holocaust, *Lehavdil*, and al-Nakba," in Lesch, Ann and Lustick, Ian, eds., *Exile and Return: Predicaments of Palestinians and Jews*, Philadelphia: University of Philadelphia Press, 2005, pp. 106–130.

Lustick, Ian, "Through Blood and Fire Shall Peace Arise," *Tikkun*, May/June 2002.

Lustick, Ian, "The Cunning of History," *Boston Review*, December 2001/January 2002, at www.bostonreview.net.

Maoz, Moshe, "Traditional Positions and New Solutions," in Ginat, Joseph and Perkins, Edward (eds.), *The Palestinian Refugees: Old Problems – New Solutions*, Norman: University of Oklahoma Press, 2001, pp. 109–121.

Marshy, Mona, "Social and Psychological Effects of Overcrowding in Palestinian Refugee Camps in the West Bank and Gaza – Literature Review and Preliminary Assessment of the Problem," August 1999, at www.prrn.org.

Masalha, Nur, "The Historical Roots of the Palestinian Refugee Question," in Aruri, Naseer ed., *Palestinian Refugees: The Right of Return*, London: Pluto Press, 2001, pp. 43–45.

Mendes, Philip, "A Historical Controversy: The Causes of the Palestinian Refugee Problem," at www.prrn.org.

Moughrabi, Fouad, "The Politics of Palestinian Textbooks," *Journal of Palestine Studies*, Vol. 31, No. 1, Autumn 2001, pp. 5–19.

Palestine-Israel Journal, "Roundtable Discussion on the Right of Return: A Just Solution for the Palestinian Refugees," *Palestine-Israel Journal*, Vol. 9, No. 2, pp. 67–73.

Pedersen, Jon, Sara Randall and Marwan Khawaja, eds., "Growing Fast: The Palestinian Population in the West Bank and Gaza Strip," *Fafo-report*, No. 353, 2001, at www.prrn.org.

Peled, Yoav and Rouhana, Nadim, "Transitional Justice and the Right of Return of the Palestinian Refugees," *Theoretical Inquiries in Law*, Vol. 5, No. 2, July 2004, pp. 317–332.

Peteet, Julie, "From Refugees to Minority: Palestinians in Post-War Lebanon," *Middle East Report*, No. 200, July–September 1996, at www.prrn.org.

Podeh, Elie, "The Right of Return versus the Law of Return: Contrasting Historical Narratives in Israeli and Palestinian School Textbooks," in Ann Lesch and Ian Lustick, eds., *Exile and Return: Predicaments of Palestinians and Jews*, Philadelphia: University of Philadelphia Press, 2005, pp. 41–56.

Prettitore, Paul, "The Right to Housing and Property Restitution in Bosnia and Herzegovina: A Case Study," BADIL Resource Center for Palestinian Residency and Refugee Rights – Working Paper 1, 2003.

Quigley, John, "Repatriation of Displaced Palestinians as a Legal Right," *Nexus*, Vol. 8, 2003, at www.nexusjournal.org., pp. 17–29.

Quigley, John, "Displaced Palestinians and a Right of Return," *Harvard International Law Journal*, Vol. 39, No. 1, 1998, pp. 171–229.

Rabinowitz, Danny, "Return of the Native," *Haaretz*, 8 August 2003.

Regular, Arnon, "Fatah Leaders Give their Backing to Nusseibeh and Ayalon's Plan for 'Two States for Two Peoples'," *Haaretz*, 19 March 2003.

Rosand, Eric, "The Right to Return under International Law following Mass Dislocation: The Bosnia Precedent?," *Michigan Journal of International Law*, Vol. 19, 1998, pp. 1091–1139.

Rosenthal, Ruvik, „Die Euphorie in dem langen, heissen Sommer nach dem Juni-Krieg," *Frankfurter Rundschau*, 6 June 1997, p. 18.

Sabel, Robbie, "The Palestinian Refugees, International Law, and the Peace Process," *Refuge*, Vol. 21, No. 2, 2004, pp. 52–61.

Said, Edward, "Introduction: The Right of Return at Last," in Aruri, Naseer, ed., *Palestinian Refugees: The Right of Return*, London: Pluto Press, 2001, pp. 1–6.

Salem, Tanja, "Palestinian Refugees: How Can a Durable Solution Be Achieved?," Centre for European Policy Studies, Working Paper No. 6, July 2003, at www.prrn.org.

Sanders, Michael, "Solving the Israel-Palestine Conflict," 11 December 2001, at www.worldnetdaily.com.

Schechla, Joseph, "The Invisible People Come to Light: Israel's 'Internally Displaced' and the 'Unrecognized Villages'," *Journal of Palestine Studies*, Vol. XXXI, No. 1, Autumn 2001, pp. 20–31.

Schwartz, Yosef, „Zweistaatenlösung versus Einstaatenrealität," *Summary of the OeME-Herbsttagung in Bern*, 20 November 2004.

Segal, Jerome, "Right of Return Confusions," 13 January 2001, at www.prrn.org.

Shiblak, Abbas, Residency Status and Civil Rights of Palestinian Refugees in Arab Countries (Ramallah: Shaml, 2001) at www.shaml.org/publications/monos/mono1.htm#Residency Status: A Case of Uncertainty.

Shikaki, Khalil, "The Right of Return," *Wall Street Journal*, 30 July 2003.

Shikaki, Khalil, "The Principle Facets of the Refugee Problem," *Palestine-Israel Journal*, Vol. 9, No. 3, 2002, pp. 90–96.

Shlaim, Avi, "The Debate about 1948," *International Journal of Middle East Studies*, Vol. 27, 1995, pp. 287–304.

Siegel, Ellen, "After Nineteen Years: Sabra and Shatila Remembered," *Middle East Policy Council Journal*, Vol. VIII, No. 4, December 2001, at www.mepc.org/public_asp/journal_vol8/0112_siegel.asp.

Siegman, Henry, "Sharon and the Future of Palestine," *The New York Review of Books*, Vol. 51, No. 19, 2 December 2004, at www.nybooks.com.

Smith, Charles, "Book Review: The Truth about Camp David: The Untold Story about the Collapse of the Middle East Peace Process," *Middle East Policy Council Journal*, Vol. XII, No. 1, Spring 2005.

Sontag, Deborah, "Quest for Middle East Peace: How and Why it Failed," *New York Times*, 26 July 2001, reprinted in the *Journal of Palestine Studies*, Vol. XXXI, No. 1, Autumn 2001, pp. 75–85.

Susskind, Yifat, "Background Resource: The Crisis of Palestinian Refugees and the Right of Return," 2001, at www.prrn.org.

Tilley, Virginia, "A New Palestinian Political Season?," *Al-Majdal*, Issue No. 28, Winter 2005, at www.badil.org/al-majdal/2005/Winter/majdal28.pdf.

Tovy, Jacob, "Negotiating the Palestinian Refugees," *Middle East Quarterly*, Spring 2003, at www.meforum.org/article/543.

Ugland, Ole, ed., "Difficult Past, Uncertain Future: Living Conditions Among Palestinian Refugees in Camps and Gatherings in Lebanon," *Fafo* at www.prrn.org.

Zakay, Dan, Yechiel Klar and Keren Sharvit, "Jewish Israelis on the 'Right of Return': Growing Awareness of the Issue's Importance" in *Palestine-Israel Journal*, Vol. 9, No. 2, 2002, pp. 58–66.

Zell, Marc and Shnyder, Sonia "Palestinian Right of Return or Strategic Weapon?: A Historical, Legal and Moral-Political Analysis," *Nexus*, Vol. 8, 2003, at www.nexusjournal.org, pp. 77–136.

Zureik, Elia, "Palestinian Refugees and the Middle East Peace Process," at www.prrn.org.

Books

Abu-Sitta, Salman, *From Refugees to Citizens at Home: The End of the Palestinian-Israeli Conflict*, London: Palestine Land Society and Palestinian Return Centre, 2001.

Aruri, Naseer, ed., *Palestinian Refugees: The Right of Return*, London: Pluto Press, 2001.

Balabkins, Nicholas, *West German Reparations to Israel*, New Brunswick, N.J.: Rutgers University Press, 1971.

Bar-Siman-Tov, Yaacov, *Peace Policy as Domestic and as Foreign Policy: the Israeli Case*, Jerusalem: Hebrew University of Jerusalem, Leonard Davis Institute for International Relations, 1998.

Bowker, Robert, *Palestinian Refugees: Mythology, Identity, and the Search for Peace*, Boulder: Lynne Rienner Publishers, 2003.

Cohen, Herb, *Negotiate This!*, New York: Warner Books, 2003.

Enderlin, Charles, *Shattered Dreams: The Failure of the Peace Process in the Middle East, 1995–2002*, New York: Other Press, 2003.

Fischbach, Michael, *The Peace Process and Palestine Refugee Claims: Addressing Claims for Property Compensation*, Washington, D.C.: United States Institute of Peace Press, 2006.

Fischbach, Michael, *Records of Dispossession: Palestinian Refugee Property and the Arab-Israeli Conflict*, New York: Columbia University Press, 2003.

Flapan, Simha, *The Birth of Israel: Myths and Realities*, New York: Pantheon, 1987.

Gazit, Shlomo, *The Palestinian Refugee Problem*, Final Status Issues Study No. 2, Tel Aviv: Jaffee Center for Strategic Studies, 1995.

Gelber, Yoav, *Palestine 1948: War, Escape and the Emergence of the Palestinian Refugee Problem*, Brighton: Sussex Academic Press, 2001, 2006.

Ginat, Joseph and Perkins, Edward (eds.), *The Palestinian Refugees: Old Problems – New Solutions*, Norman: University of Oklahoma Press, 2001.

Heller, Mark, *A Palestinian State: The Implications for Israel*, Cambridge, MA: Harvard University Press, 1983.

Heller, Mark and Nusseibeh, Sari, *No Trumpets, No Drums: A Two-State Settlement of the Israeli-Palestinian Conflict*, New York: Hill and Wang, 1991.

Herf, Jeffrey, *Divided Memory: The Nazi Past in the two Germanys*, Cambridge, Mass.: Harvard University Press, 1997.

Khalaf, Issa, *Politics in Palestine: Arab Factionalism and Social Disintegration, 1939–1948*, Albany, N.Y.: State University of New York Press, 1991.

Khalidi, Rashid, "Toward a Solution," in Center for Policy Analysis on Palestine, *Palestine Refugees: Their Problem and Future*, Washington, DC: CPAP, 1994.

Khalidi, Rashid and Rabinovich, Itamar, *The Palestinian Right of Return: Two Views*, Occasional Paper No. 6, Cambridge, MA: American Academy of Arts and Sciences, October 1990.

Klieman, Aharon, *Compromising Palestine: A Guide to Final Status Negotiations*, New York: Columbia University Press, 2000.

Kurz, Rosemarie und Bürgi, Chudi, eds., *Thymian und Steine*, Basel: Lenos Verlag, 1995.

Laqueur, Walter and Rubin, Barry eds., *The Israeli-Arab Reader: A Documentary History of the Middle East Conflict*, New York: Penguin Books, 2001.

Lesch, Ann and Lustick, Ian, eds., *Exile and Return: Predicaments of Palestinians and Jews,* Philadelphia: University of Philadelphia Press, 2005.

Moore, John, ed., *The Arab-Israeli Conflict, vol I: Readings*, sponsored by the American Society of International Law, Princeton: Princeton University Press, 1974.

Morris, Benny, *The Birth of the Palestinian Refugee Problem Revisited*, New York: Cambridge University Press, 2004.

Morris, Benny, *Righteous Victims: A History of the Zionist-Arab Conflict, 1881–2001*, New York: Vintage Books, 2001.

Morris, Benny, *Israel's Border Wars: 1949–1956: Arab Infiltration, Israeli Retaliation, and the Countdown to the Suez War*, Oxford: Clarendon Press, 1993.

Morris, Benny, *The Birth of the Palestinian Refugee Problem, 1947–1949*, Cambridge: Cambridge University Press, 1988.

Neifeind, Harald, *Der Nahostkonflikt – historisch, politisch, literarisch,* Schwalbach: Wochenschau Verlag, 1999.

Nowak, Manfred, *UN Covenant on Civil and Political Rights: CCPR Commentary*, Kehl: NP Engel Publishers, 1993.

Pappe, Ilan, *A History of Modern Palestine: One Land, Two Peoples*, Cambridge: Cambridge University Press, 2004.

Peretz, Don, *Palestinians, Refugees, and the Middle East Peace Process*, Washington, DC: United States Institute of Peace Press, 1993.

Plascov, Avi, *The Palestinian Refugees in Jordan 1948–1957*, London: Frank Cass, 1981.

Quandt, William, *Peace Process: American Diplomacy and the Arab-Israeli Conflict since 1967*, Washington, DC: Brookings Institution, 2001.

Quigley, John, *The Case for Palestine: An International Law Perspective*, Duke, NC: Duke University Press, 2005.

Roumani, Maurice, The *Case of the Jews from Arab Countries: A Neglected Issue*, Tel Aviv: World Organization of Jews from Arab Countries, 1983.

Sagi, Nana, *German Reparations: A History of the Negotiations*, Jerusalem: Magnes, 1980.

Sayigh, Yezid, *Armed Struggle and the Search for State: The Palestinian National Movement, 1949–1993*, Oxford: Oxford University Press, 1997.

Schäfer, Barbara, ed., *Historikerstreit in Israel: Die „Neuen" Historiker zwischen Wissenschaft und Öffentlichkeit*, Frankfurt: Campus Verlag, 2000.

Segev, Tom, *The Seventh Million: The Israelis and the Holocaust*, New York: Hill and Wang, 1993.

Shamir, Shimon and Maddy-Weitzmann, Bruce, eds., *The Camp David Summit – What Went Wrong?*, Brighton: Sussex Academic Press, 2005.

Shlaim, Avi, *The Iron Wall: Israel and the Arab World*, New York: Norton & Company, 2000.

Stone, Julius, *Israel and Palestine, Assault on the Law of Nations*, Baltimore and London: The John Hopkins University Press, 1981.

Swisher, Clayton, *The Truth about Camp David: The Untold Story about the Collapse of the Middle East Peace Process*, New York: Nation Books, 2004.

Takkenberg, Lex, *The Status of Palestinian Refugees in International Law*, New York: Oxford University Press, 1998.

Yaar, Ephraim and Hermann, Tamar, *The Palestinian Refugees Issue and the Right of Return: Proceedings of a Symposium held on 29 December 2003* (Hebrew), Tel Aviv: Tami Steinmetz Center, 2004.

Zertal, Idith, *From Catastrophe to Power: Holocaust Survivors and the Emergence of Israel*, Berkeley: University of California Press, 1998.

Ron Robin / Bo Stråth (eds.)

Homelands

Poetic Power and the Politics of Space

Bruxelles, Bern, Berlin, Frankfurt am Main, New York, Oxford, Wien, 2003.
406 pp., 3 ill.
Multiple Europes. Vol. 23
General Editor: Bo Stråth
ISBN 978-90-5201-190-5 / US-ISBN 978-0-8204-6608-8 pb.
sFr. 59.– / €* 40.70 / €** 41.80 / € 38.– / £ 25.– / US-$ 45.95

* includes VAT – valid for Germany   ** includes VAT – valid for Austria

This book historically surveys the contested poetics of space and place associated with the term «homeland» in the Middle East, Balkans, Ireland, South Africa and Germany in the nineteenth and twentieth centuries. These cases of contested homeland discourses are contrasted with a case of non-contention in Sweden. The contributors do not narrate events preceding the conflicts in these divisive areas of the world, they offer and confront representations of homeland from multiple and, at times, unusual perspectives. Ambiguity and variety are one common denominator of this very uncommon collection. These scholarly representations of homeland are saturated with the contradictions of imagination and culture. They all contain a subtext concerning the role of the nation state and its relationships to multiple understandings of homeland in contemporary global cultures and politics. The different and sometimes incompatible opinions voiced here are bound by a common hope to affect the current discourse on nationalism, community, homeland and exile.

With contributions by: Ron Robin – Bo Stråth – Rema Hammami – Salim Tamari – Karma Nabulsi – Issam Nassar – Ilan Gur Ze'ev – Fania Oz-Salzberger – Maoz Azaryahu – Mark Levine – Ilan Pappe – Mariangela Veikou – Senadin Musabegović – Heidi Grunebaum – Yazir Henri – John D. Brewer – Rolf Petri – James Kaye.

The Editors: Ron Robin is Professor of History the University of Haifa. He is a graduate of the Hebrew University, Jerusalem and University of California, Berkeley. His most recent book is *The Making of the Cold War Enemy: Culture and Politics in the Military-Intellectual Complex.*

Bo Stråth is Professor of Contemporary History at the European University Institute, Florence. He has published widely on issues of modernity and democracy in Europe, in a historical and a comparative perspective.

PETER LANG
Bern · Berlin · Bruxelles · Frankfurt am Main · New York · Oxford · Wien

Dieter Mahncke / Alicia Ambos / Christopher Reynolds (eds.)

European Foreign Policy

From Rhetoric to Reality?
Second Printing

Bruxelles, Bern, Berlin, Frankfurt am Main, New York, Oxford, Wien,
2004, 2006. 381 pp., 3 tables, 6 graphs
College of Europe Studies. Vol. 1
General Editors: Dominik Hanf, Dieter Mahncke, Inge Govaere
and Jacques Pelkmans
ISBN 978-90-5201-247-6 / US-ISBN 978-0-8204-6627-9 / Art. No. 29247 pb.
sFr. 66.– / €* 45.50 / €** 46.80 / € 42.50 / £ 29.80 / US-$ 50.95

* includes VAT – valid for Germany   ** includes VAT – valid for Austria

There is agreement in political and academic circles that the European Union needs a common foreign and security policy (CFSP). The question is how to move from recognised necessity to practical implementation: from rhetoric to reality. Many efforts have been made, and indeed the creation of a European foreign policy is 'work in progress'. Bringing together a multinational team of both young researchers and established academics, this volume offers a comprehensive analysis of this process, uniquely combining the examination of the foundations, institutions, procedures and obstacles of EU-level foreign policy with an extensive range of case studies exploring European policy 'on the ground' in key areas such as the Balkans, Africa or the Middle East.

Of use and interest to students of European politics and the general reader alike, it breaks through the Euro-jargon to provide a clear, accessible and up-to-date account of this unprecedented system of international relations, with a particular focus placed on the questions of why EU member states participate in the CFSP and what impact it enables them to have in geopolitics.

With contributions by: Alicia Ambos – Dieter Mahncke – Christopher Reynolds – Wolfgang Wessels – Inge Govaere – Roberto Francia – Miguel Angel Medina Abellán – Peter van Ham – Armin Michael Mayer – Christine Stockhammer – Kathrin Ahlbrecht – Ines von Behr – Anja Fiedler – Radhia Oudjani – Alejandro Ribó Labastida.

The Editors: Dieter Mahncke is Alfried Krupp von Bohlen und Halbach Professor of European Foreign Policy and Security Studies and Director of the Department of Political and Administrative Studies at the College of Europe in Bruges.

Alicia Ambos is consultant at NATO's Political Affairs Division in Brussels.

Christopher Reynolds is a researcher in political science at the Technical University of Munich.

PETER LANG
Bern · Berlin · Bruxelles · Frankfurt am Main · New York · Oxford · Wien